ARTICULATORY
ACQUISITION
and BEHAVIOR

Harris Winitz

University of Missouri—
Kansas City

ARTICULATORY

ACQUISITION

and BEHAVIOR

PRENTICE-HALL, INC., *Englewood Cliffs, New Jersey*

Printed in the United States of America

ISBN: 0-13-049320-1

Library of Congress Catalog Card Number: 68-54387

10 9 8 7

PRENTICE-HALL INTERNATIONAL, INC., *London*
PRENTICE-HALL OF AUSTRALIA, PTY. LTD., *Sydney*
PRENTICE-HALL OF CANADA, LTD., *Toronto*
PRENTICE-HALL OF INDIA PRIVATE LIMITED, *New Delhi*
PRENTICE-HALL OF JAPAN, INC., *Tokyo*

to Shevie ←——————

Preface

This book is an attempt to bring articulation, as studied by the speech pathologist, within the mainstream of present-day psycholinguistic thought. The methods and models of descriptive linguistics, instrumental phonetics, and learning theory offer a promising new framework in which to understand articulatory behavior and to assess procedures for articulatory correction. My approach, however, has been directive, not comprehensive. Basic information from linguistics, the behavioral sciences (especially learning theory), and instrumental phonetics is, for the most part, introduced only when needed to underline certain issues of articulatory acquisition or behavior. In addition, articulatory behavior associated with organic or severe psychogenic involvement is not treated.

The book contains five chapters. Chapter 1 describes the vocal behavior of infants prior to the development of a language system. The child's sound productions are charted and their relation to other variables is reviewed. In addition, conditioning models are used to generate hypotheses about the origin and development of prelanguage utterances.

In Chapter 2 phonetic and phonemic mastery are first distinguished; next, the concept of distinctive features is presented; finally, those learning variables thought to play a role in phoneme development are surveyed. In the concluding sections of this chapter some preliminary evidence is given to support the point of view that articulatory errors are learned or, perhaps more correctly, represent the learning of a phoneme system that is at variance with the adult phoneme system.

Chapter 3 treats articulatory development along

traditional lines. Although it summarizes studies on the relation between articulation and a variety of somatic and mental variables, this chapter includes more detail than usual for a chapter of this type; my purpose is to describe for the student of articulation how subjects are selected, how data are collected and analyzed, and what measures or tests are used to arrive at the results. In the last pages of this chapter methodological approaches are discussed, and some suggestions are made regarding future research studies in articulatory development.

Chapter 4 is devoted to two topics: assessment of articulatory performance and articulation tests. In the first section a detailed account is drawn concerning the type of errors that may contribute to the unreliability of an articulation test. In the second section five types of articulation tests are discussed and evaluated.

Chapter 5 is devoted to articulatory programming. The term programming, as used in this chapter, refers to the systematic study and development of appropriate teaching procedures. A teaching machine that aids this process is described. Chapter 5, by exciting and stimulating young scientists in speech pathology to turn their research talents to the study of articulatory behavior as well as modification, may serve as a starting point for future research in articulatory programming.

This book has been used as a text in a graduate course in articulation at Western Reserve University. When used at the graduate level, it may be supplemented with outside readings drawn from the references included at the end of each chapter. In my own course I began with a review of the elementary principles of phonemics and learning theory, an unnecessary step if students have a basic knowledge of these areas. At the undergraduate course level, the instructor may need to begin with the usual introductory material and reserve this book for the latter half of the course.

I am indebted to many people for their contribution to this book. My professors at the University of Iowa, James Curtis, Frederic Darley, Orvis Irwin, Wendell Johnson, Boyd McCandless, Howard Meredith, Dorothy Sherman, and D. C. Spriestersbach, provided me with the basic foundations for understanding child development in general and child language in particular. A course from Eugene McDonald, at Pennsylvania State University, stimulated me to direct my full attention to the behavioral manipulation of articulatory responses. The concepts presented in this text have been derived from the writings of many behaviorists, linguists, speech pathologists, and speech scientists, whose papers are referenced in the bibliography of each chapter.

My colleagues at the Bureau of Child Research and the Department of Speech, University of Kansas (1959–1963), assisted me in synthesizing much of contemporary behavioral theory. They also provided generously of their time to help plan and execute some of the experiments reported in this book. These colleagues are Fred Girardeau, Neil Goetzinger, Frances Horowitz, James Neelley, Gerald Siegel (now of the University of Minnesota), and Joseph Spradlin. Gerald Siegel and Joseph Spradlin, in addition to Eric Sander, University of Kentucky, and Martin Young, Illinois State University, edited various portions of this text and contributed countless good suggestions, almost all of which were incorporated into the final manuscript.

I am indebted to Betty Bellerose for her assistance in locating and preparing materials for Chapter 3. She and Linda Preisler collaborated with me in many of the experiments included in this text.

Many of my students at Western Reserve University evaluated critically the manuscript and offered excellent ideas for the revision. Among these were Darrell Cook, John Crocker, S.J., Judith Duchan, Cornelius Koustaal, Joseph Millin, Lawrence Turton, and Elizabeth Wiig.

I acknowledge with gratitude the support of David Ruhe, M.D., who, under the auspices of the Kellogg Foundation, provided the services of Wesley Heisey, an electronic engineer. Mr. Heisey designed and built the teaching machine described in Chapter 5 and also contributed his skill in many other services essential to the execution of experiments described in this text. Many of the research projects reported here were supported by funds from the United States Public Health Service under the auspices of the National Institute of Mental Health (MH–3987, MH–05397, and MH–08631), National Institute of Neurological Diseases and Blindness (1T1–NB–5437), and the National Institute of Child Health and Human Development (HD–00962 and HD–01657).

The libraries of the University of Kansas and Western Reserve University, and Linda Hall Library of Science and Technology, on the campus of the University of Missouri—Kansas City, were gracious and efficient in procuring the needed references. Allie Ballenger, Joan Makowski, and Sharon Shorney nobly deciphered and typed my endless scribbles and revisions. I could not have done without their services.

Lastly I wish to thank R. L. Schiefelbusch, Director of the Bureau of Child Research, University of Kansas, and Paul H. Ptacek, Chairman of the Program in Speech Pathology, Western Reserve University, for their encouragement in this project and their skill in freeing me from many tasks peripheral to teaching.

H. W.

Contents

4/ARTICULATORY TESTING AND PREDICTION 237

5/ARTICULATORY PROGRAMMING 275

ARTICULATORY
ACQUISITION
and BEHAVIOR

1

To both laymen and students of child behavior the utterances of children seem to fall into two discrete stages: vocalizations that have no apparent wordlike meaning and vocalizations that are the words of a language. The infant's birth cry marks the beginning of a stage generally thought to continue until the child utters his first words, at which time the child, in addition to celebrating his first birthday, finds himself tottering between a language and a non-language world. Many of his vocalizations still resemble those of the past year, but now he has added wordlike vocalizations that are understood and responded to by his parents. He has entered the second stage of his vocal career—the linguistic or language stage—because the utterance units he now uses are functional units of the community language. Although he has uttered most of the sounds before, they have not been used as units of a language system.

At this point we are confronted with a need to define the term "language." Perhaps one of the best definitions is that given by Carroll (1953, p. 10): "A language is a structured system of arbitrary vocal sounds and sequences of sounds which is used, or can be used, in interpersonal communication by an aggregation of human beings, and which rather exhaustively catalogs the things, events, and processes in the human environment." One of the key phrases in this definition is "structured system," for every language is composed of a set of rules which need

1

to be learned by both the speaker and the listener. For example, the following sequence of words makes no sense in English: *House the large is green there*. If we rearrange the words, we can produce several English sentences, such as: *There is a large green house* or *Is a large green house there* or *A large green house is there*. If the intonation patterns of the sentences as they might be spoken by native Americans are disregarded, we can see that the order of the words seems to determine the "sense" of the three sentences. The order in which we utter the words of our language, then, will be determined by the rules of word order (syntax) for a particular type of utterance (question, command, etc.). Similarly, the way we use the sounds of our language will be determined by the rules of sound usage, which belong to the language subsystem known as *phonology*.

Definition of a Phoneme

Phonology as a branch of linguistics involves the study of phonemes and the rules for phoneme sequences. Phonemes are often thought to be speech sounds like [i] or [t]. The phoneme, however, has quite a different meaning in linguistics; it is defined as a unit of a spoken language that signals semantic distinctiveness. For example, examine the following five words: *Ted, bed, red, led, fed*. As speakers of English we are able to respond to these five words as distinct semantic entities simply because we have learned that the five initial consonants, /t/, /b/, /r/, /l/, and /f/, are "different." Speakers may vary the pronunciation of these consonants, but if each pronunciation remains within an acceptable range of variation for each of the five phonemes, the meaning of each of the five words will remain unchanged. We may, for instance, not aspirate or release the /t/ in /bet/ without changing the "meaning" of *bet*—i.e., [bet], [betʰ] and [bet⁻] are still considered to be the same word. The sounds [t], [tʰ], and [t⁻] are different productions, to be sure, but in English they do not contribute to a difference in word meaning.[1]

The phoneme is not a new concept to students of articulation, but one that is often not well stressed. The distinction between a phonemic unit and a phonetic unit is a valuable one, and in the pages ahead it will often be made use of. By convention, slash marks (/ /) will refer to phonemes and brackets ([ ]) to phones or phonetic units. The concept of a phoneme is well described in several linguistic textbooks (Gleason, 1961, or Hockett, 1958, for example).

Essentially an abstraction, the phoneme comprises a group or category

[1] Classical phonemics does not guarantee perceptual outcomes. (Indeed it was not developed for this purpose.) For example, the lax and unaspirated [p] in [spɪl] when [s] is spliced away is heard as /bɪl/ rather than /pɪl/, although it is an allophonic variant of /p/ (Lotz and others, 1960).

of phonetic responses or phones; the phones are elements of the phoneme which do not characterize differences in word meaning. The set of phones that describes a particular phoneme for a particular language is obtained through intensive linguistic analysis. The pronunciation of words by native speakers who serve as informants is phonetically transcribed. Phones that contrast—make a difference in word meaning—are then identified.

Vowel and consonantal charts of English usually introduce us to the phonetic sounds of English. Although these charts describe the phonetic production (manner and place of articulation) of the English sounds, their primary purpose is to list the vowel and consonantal phonemes of English. These are the "sounds" of English that contrast.

When phonetic variations are grouped together they are called allophones of a phoneme. Thus, in English we know that /k/ and /t/ contrast. The allophones of the /k/ and /t/ phonemes are variations of the /k/ and /t/ sounds, respectively, which do not contrast. Examples of allophones for /k/ are [kʰ] (aspiration), [k] (no aspiration), and [k˙] (unreleased). For /t/, similar variants (allophones) can be found. The /l/ phoneme, as another example, has several allophones, such as [l], [l̥] (voiceless), and [ɫ] (called the dark [l], usually found in word-final position).

Linguists make use of two rules of allophonic variation, *complementary distribution* and *free variation*. Complementary distribution can best be introduced by an example. In English the /k/ is aspirated in the initial position but is not aspirated in initial /s/ blends—e.g., /kʰɪl/ and /skɪl/. The two [k]'s are mutually exclusive—where one allophone occurs the other does not. This is referred to as complementary distribution. Tabulation of those phones in complementary distribution is a procedure used by linguists to identify variants of phonemes. Phones that are not in complementary distribution (that is, they are mutually substitutable) are said to be in free variation. Examples in English are [v] and [vf] (unvoicing of v in final position) and [p] and [pˡ] (lateral release before /l/). These two principles are used by a linguist when analyzing the phonemic structure of a language. He knows, for example, that phones in complementary distribution do not contrast. He also knows that the phones in free variation may contrast. An additional criterion used by linguists to establish classes of phones is that of articulatory similarity. This criterion by and large is an arbitrary one (Gleason, 1961, p. 265).

We have now laid the groundwork for a definition of the phoneme: "A *phoneme* is a class of sounds which (1) are phonetically similar and (2) show certain characteristic patterns of distribution [free variation or complementary distribution] in the language or dialect under consideration."[2]

[2] From *An Introduction to Descriptive Linguistics*, Revised, by H. A. Gleason, Jr., copyright © 1955, 1961 by Holt, Rinehart and Winston, Inc. All rights reserved.

For purposes of clarification, assume an isolated culture whose language has only the following three words:

[ri] or [ji]   for *eat*
[il]   for *sleep*
[ru]   for *be merry*

These utterances occur repeatedly and, when pronounced by an interviewer, are understood by the natives. Other utterances serve no purpose in that they are totally ignored.

For these four utterances, three consonants, [r], [j], and [l], and two vowels, [i] and [u], are identified. Note that [r] and [j] are in free variation in that "eat" can be uttered with an initial [r] or [j]. Also, [l] and [r] are in complementary distribution in that [r] occurs in the initial word position and [l] in the final word position. The obvious contrast is that of the /i/-/u/, in that free variation of the /i/ and /u/ would cause confusion between the words "eat" and "be merry." The vowel and consonant charts are as follows:

VOWEL CHART   CONSONANT CHART

Front Back   Alveopalatal
/i/   /u/   /r/

Although there are a total of five phones, the language contains only three phonemes, /i/, /u/, and /r/. The phonemes of this language do not correspond to the same three phonemes of English. For example, the /r/ phoneme of this language includes an [l] and a [j] allophone while the English /r/ phoneme does not have these allophones. Lastly, it should be noted that our choice of phonemic symbols is arbitrary.

Phonetic and Phonemic Symbols

In most cases the phonetic symbols used in this text are those of the International Phonetic Alphabet (IPA). When non-English phones are used or when uncommon variants of English phonemes are used, they will be explained in the text where the symbol first appears.

As mentioned, slash marks will be used to symbolize phonemes. The symbols within these slash marks will not always be consistent with the symbols used by American linguists. This has been done so that speech pathologists familiar with phonemic theory but unfamiliar with the symbols of the American linguists will not be faced with an unnecessary encumbrance.

The term "sound," as used in this text, is synonymous with the term "phone." The author will use (phonemic) slash marks, however, to identify certain sounds, as in the phrase "the production of the /s/ sound." This phrase simply means the production of those sounds belonging to the /s/ phoneme.

Prelanguage Utterances

Throughout the ages the infant's early utterances have been the subject of continued curiosity. Even Charles Darwin expressed more than a passing fancy for this subject when, in 1877, he published an article on the "mental development" of an infant and devoted a large portion of his article to infant vocalizations. Since and before that time additional accounts of early vocal utterances have been published. The most comprehensive attack on this subject was made by Orvis C. Irwin about two decades ago. Irwin's findings corroborate, for the most part, many of the early biographical studies, and since his study involved many infants, the ensuing discussion of infant vocal behavior will be restricted to his investigation. First, the findings of Irwin's studies are presented, and second, some of the criticisms directed toward his methodology and experimental procedures are reviewed.

Before looking in detail at Irwin's study, let us examine the reasons for interest in infant vocalizations and clarify some of the terms used to discuss infant vocal behavior. Generally, the most frequent justification put forward for studying infant vocal behavior involves the correlation between prelanguage and language utterances. Speech pathologists and students of language behavior often assume that infant vocalizations in some way prepare, determine, or establish the basis for language utterances. Absence of infant vocalizations, therefore "may signify" language retardation. A second but related reason for studying infant vocalizations concerns the prediction of later childhood behavior. A paucity of infant vocalizations may be one of the defining factors of intellectual, social, or language delay. To establish what is normal in prelanguage vocal behavior is thus important.

In the main, prelanguage utterances refer to vocalizations prior to the child's first words. Most children begin to utter their first words at about one year of age[3] (Darley and Winitz, 1961). As one might expect, language utterances—usually identified as jargon or babbling—continue to occur long after the child has acquired a fairly complex language system. Even at 30 months, the terminal age in Irwin's investigation, many of the utterances of his subjects were not identifiable as words.

[3] The identification of the child's early words is a difficult procedure (see Darley and Winitz, 1961).

Before proceeding further, let us define clearly certain key terms. The term *prelanguage* refers to utterances (e.g., phones) prior to their use as linguistic units (e.g., phonemes or words). Because prelanguage utterances do not point to any specific referent or convey meaning to another person, the term *vocal utterances* or *stimuli* describes such undirected voicings of the child. Utterance units, however, that evoke responses from other individuals, usually the child's parents, are referred to as *verbal utterances or stimuli*. In the early stages of language learning the child may utter one-word phrases, such as [mik] for "give me some milk." This utterance signals "meaning" to a listener, and, in this sense, the utterance is defined as verbal. That is, the stimulus [mik] has a *functionally* equivalent referent, as the child, after forming these sounds, is likely to be offered milk. In some cases the vocalization may not bear any phonetic resemblance to the English equivalent, but if it is understood by the parent—that is, serves as a stimulus to him in discriminating among several referents—it is considered to be an early language response. Admittedly, the boundary, as discussed later, is not clear and distinct between language and prelanguage utterances. These operational definitions, however, should cause no difficulty because they are used simply to distinguish, in a very broad sense, language from prelanguage utterances.

In summary, then, utterances that have a functional but not necessarily a phonetic equivalent are defined as verbal utterances. In the early stages of language acquisition, verbal utterances are difficult to identify, but within a short period of time (by at least two years of age) they can be identified with little difficulty. On the other hand, utterances that serve no functional use in the usual sense are called vocal utterances. Nevertheless, as shown later, it is possible to condition these responses.

The term *babbling* is used sometimes to describe infant utterances in two ways: (*a*) as a stage in language development and (*b*) as a general term for prelanguage vocalization. Berry and Eisenson (1956, p. 19), for example, state: "At about six or seven weeks of age the infant begins to show by his reactions that he is aware of the sounds he is making. He indicates definitely that he enjoys producing sounds, and that he produces sounds when he is enjoying himself." Myklebust (1957, p. 356) defines babbling as "the pleasurable use of vocalization by the child in the preverbal period. As this definition implies, neither the very early use of reflexive vocalization nor utilitarian vocalization (vocalization such as the infant uses for calling attention to himself) by the infant is included." In this discussion no distinction will be made between the terms babbling, prelanguage utterances, and infant vocal utterances. The term babbling as used in this text will thus not be restricted to one period or to one type of prelanguage utterance, but simply will refer to a vocal response that may be conditioned.

Research of Orvis C. Irwin

Method

Irwin and his associates (Irwin, 1941, 1942, 1945, 1946, 1947a, 1947b, 1947c, 1947d, 1947e, 1948a, 1948b, 1948c, 1948d, 1951; Irwin and Chen, 1945, 1946a, 1946b; Chen and Irwin, 1946; Winitz and Irwin, 1958a, 1958b) studied the speech sound utterances of 95 white infants during the first two and one-half years of life. For 35 subjects data were available for most of the ages studied. The infants, from homes in Iowa City, Iowa, were considered to be physically normal, and had a median birth weight of seven and one-half pounds. With few exceptions the children came from monolingual environments. The socioeconomic status of the group was described by Irwin and Chen (1946b, p. 431) as follows: "These infants were from middle class homes, the parents being professional, business, clerical, and some laboring people." The infants were divided approximately equally with respect to sex and family constellation. "Only children" were defined as having no older siblings, while "infants with siblings" signified the presence of an older sibling; the age interval between the child and his sibling was not considered. As the study progressed, some of the families moved away, so that fewer subjects were available at the older age levels.

The data were collected in the following manner: the spontaneous, unstimulated speech sounds of the infants were transcribed on paper in the abbreviated International Phonetic Alphabet as modified by Irwin from Fairbanks' description (1940). Fairbanks lists 15 simple vowels (1940, p. 21), 25 consonants (1940, p. xi), and 5 diphthongs (1940, p. 30). These phonemes will be given when we discuss the results of Irwin's study (pp. 13–14). Irwin grouped the sounds of two vowel pairs, [ə]-[ʌ] and [a]-[ɑ], making two vowels instead of four, and excluded the two vowels [ɝ] and [ɒ], presumably because the latter two vowels do not occur in the repertoire of infant vocalizations. Two consonants, which do not occur in standard English, were added: [x] and [ç]. The glottal stop [ʔ] was also included. Lip-smacking sounds and clicking sounds were omitted in the transcriptions.

Irwin thus had at his disposal 28 consonants, 11 vowels, and 5 diphthongs. Diphthongs were recorded by Irwin, but for the results to be discussed, only the individual sounds of the diphthongs are reported.

The sounds were recorded within "breath units," and the standard sample or record consisted of the sounds made by an infant on 30 breaths, not necessarily consecutive. A "breath" consisted of those exhalations that contained noncrying vocalizations. Each "record" or transcription of 30 breaths took approximately 30 minutes to collect. The foregoing procedures were developed after it was found that agreement among observers for arbitrary time samples was low; they provided for high agreement among the several examiners in this study (Irwin, 1945). With the exceptions of the "reliability" sessions, only one examiner was present at each session.

All the data were collected during the afternoon after the child had his noon meal. No attempt was made to control the infant's position during the making of a record, although almost all were sitting or held in an upright position. Usually one parent, the mother, was present. The data were grouped and reported in 15 two-month intervals or age levels, beginning with months 1 and 2 (age level 1) and ending with months 29 and 30 (age level 15). About two records were made for each child for each age level.

Throughout the investigations the transcribed speech sounds were referred to as phonemes.[4] Carroll (1961) and Lehiste (1960) have pointed out that this term is not consistent with formal linguistic terminology, since infants' sounds are not used to signal meaning within a linguistic code or language. In the second year of life, vocalizations interpreted as words began to increase. However, no analysis of the phonemic system of individual subjects or groups of subjects was made. Thus the term *phoneme* is still inappropriate when applied to the transcription of sounds that occurred in the words of these subjects. The term *phone,* however, is not correct because the sounds were, for the most part, transcribed within the English phonemic system.

The transcription procedure used by Irwin and his colleagues was determined, for the most part, by the fact that they were trained primarily as English-speaking recorders. As recorders they did not usually make distinctions between allophones of English phonemes (e.g., [k] and [kʰ] were transcribed as /k/), although [s] and [z] were transcribed as separate phones. The [k] and [kʰ] phones are allophones of the phoneme /k/ in English but are phonemic in Hindi (Gleason, 1961, p. 260). The [s] and [z] phones are allophones of the phoneme /s/ in Spanish (Brown, 1956, p. 254) but are phonemic in English. In addition, Irwin's procedures may have led to some inconsistencies. For example, phones such as [l̥] (unvoiced [l]) and [l̥ʰ] (breathy voiceless [l] or in some cases a full fricative, often called a "lateral lisp") may have been transcribed as [l] or [θ] or [s], etc.

Findings

PHONEME TYPE AND FREQUENCY. Irwin presented his findings in several different ways. We shall discuss first the measures of phoneme type and

---

[4] In this book our references will always be to segmental ("sound") phonemes (e.g., /s/, /t/, /ʃ/) rather than to suprasegmental ("intonation") phonemes. Suprasegmental phonemes are those of pitch, stress, and juncture.

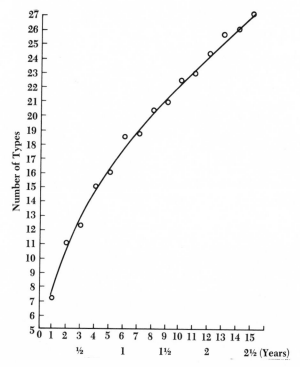

[Figure 1.1] The graph for phoneme type from the first two months of life to two and one-half years. SOURCE: Irwin and Chen, 1946a, Figure 2, p. 190.

phoneme frequency. Phoneme type refers to the number of different phonemes in the record of a given child; phoneme frequency refers to the number of phonemes, regardless of the number of types, in the record of a given child.

The function for phoneme type is graphed in Figure 1.1. Here it may be observed that the average child utters approximately 7 phonemes at age level 1 (months 1 and 2) and 27 phonemes at age level 15 (months 29 and 30).[5] Figure 1.1 shows that the number of phoneme types increases with age.

[5] Linguists, who influenced or were influenced by the Trager-Smith (1962) system, generally agree that English, as spoken in this country, contains 24 consonant phonemes (Hockett, 1958, p. 60; Gleason, 1961, p. 50). Hockett (1958, p. 60) lists 7 simple vowels, and Gleason (1961, p. 50) lists 9 simple vowels; Hockett (1958, p. 60) also lists 7 diphthongs. As was stated, Irwin had used 28 consonant categories and 11 vowel categories. According to present-day linguistic thought Irwin's transcription procedure added 1 additional consonantal phoneme and from 2 to 4 vowels. Thus, at this time, it might be more correct to say that the child utters 22 to 24 phonemes rather than 27 phonemes by age level 15. We need to

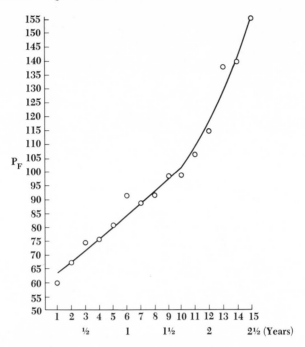

[Figure 1.2] The graph for phoneme frequency from the first two months of life to two and one-half years.
SOURCE: Irwin, 1947a, Figure 1, p. 433.

The function for phoneme frequency is presented in Figure 1.2. It may be noted from this graph that the average number of phonemes in 30 exhalations is approximately 62 at age level 1 and 156 at age level 15. These data, however, need to be interpreted with some caution, since infant exhalations increase with age. Although we would expect an increase in phoneme utterances with increasing age, when measured for a standard time interval, utterances derived from the exhalation phase of the breath cycle confound duration of sampling unit or time with age. That is, the exhalation phase of breathing for the human infant increases with age as his breathing cycle more closely approximates that of the adult, and thus the chances for increased vocalization also increase.

remember, however, that the former two numbers (22 and 24) do not take into account the fact that the simple vowel /i/ (high central vowel) was excluded and some simple vowels like /i/ and /ɪ/ (correctly written as [i] and [ɪ] do not have independent phonemic status, i.e., [i] and [ɪ] are allophones of /i/. (The contrast between "beat" and "bit" involves the pure vowel [ɪ] versus the diphthong [ɪi].) Also, 3 of the consonants were non-English consonants, but they occurred at such low frequencies that they probably did not greatly influence the average figure.

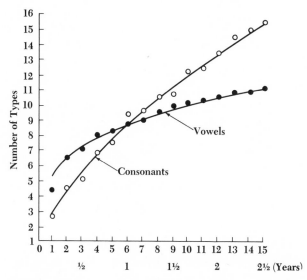

[Figure 1.3] The graph for vowel and consonant types from the first two months of life to two and one-half years.
SOURCE: Chen and Irwin, 1946.

VOWEL AND CONSONANT TYPE. In Figure 1.3 the curves for vowel and consonant types are presented. In this graph vowel types are shown to be more frequent than consonant types in the speech of infants prior to the first year of life. After one year of age the infant utters more consonant than vowel types. Since the infant is gradually learning to approximate the number of vowels and consonants in adult speech (see below), this finding for the last year and a half is expected.

VOWEL AND CONSONANT FREQUENCY. The curves for vowel and consonant frequency are presented in Figures 1.4 and 1.5, respectively. Note in Figure 1.4 that vowel frequency increases only slightly in the first two years of life. In the first 2 months 49 vowels occur; in months 23 and 24 about 60 vowels occur; between months 23 and 24, and 25 and 26 the change appears to be abrupt. The function for consonantal frequency shows a continuous increase from months 1 and 2 to months 29 and 30.

VOWEL PROFILES. The frequency of each vowel for all subjects at selected age levels is presented in Figure 1.6. In this analysis Irwin did not combine the [ʌ] and [ə] vowels. Here it may be noted that the newborn infant utters mainly three vowels, /ɪ/, /ɛ/, and /ʌ/.[6] By two and a

---

[6] Although Irwin symbolized the infant sounds with brackets, [ ], we shall use slashes, / /, to indicate that by and large phonemic transcription rather than phonetic transcription was used.

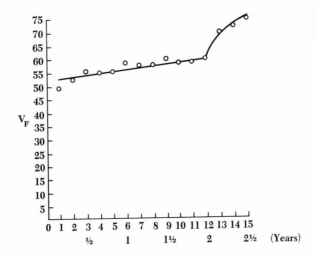

[Figure 1.4] The graph for vowel frequency from the first two months of life to two and one-half years.
SOURCE: Irwin and Chen, 1946a.

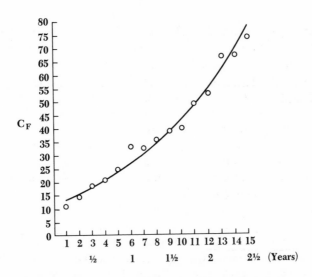

[Figure 1.5] The graph for consonant frequency from the first two months of life to two and one-half years.
SOURCE: Irwin and Chen, 1946a.

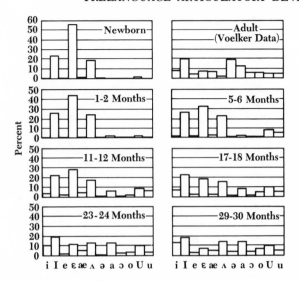

[Figure 1.6] Vowel profiles depicting proportional values of vowels at selected age levels.
SOURCE: Irwin, 1948b.

half years of age the vowel profiles approximate the adult vowel profiles. The adult data, gathered by Voelker (1934), represent the frequency of English phonemes transcribed from 5946 radio announcements. A total of 660,594 sounds were originally recorded.

The proportion of front, middle, and back vowels for each age level is shown in Figure 1.7. As grouped by Irwin, the front vowels were /i/, /ɪ/, /e/, /ɛ/, and /æ/; the middle vowels were /ʌ/, /ə/, and /ɑ/; and the back vowels were /ɔ/, /o/, /ʊ/, and /u/. In Figure 1.7 it may be seen that front vowels gradually decline in frequency. Back vowels increase in frequency while the middle vowels, in general, maintain their proportions with age.

CONSONANT PROFILES. The profiles for consonantal development are presented in Figure 1.8. Only four consonants, /k/, /g/, /h/, and /ʔ/, occur in the first 2 months of life. By 5 and 6 months the /b/, /m/, /w/, /d/, /n/, and /r/ also appear. By 29 and 30 months the profile approximates the adult profile reported by Voelker. It may be noted that the two English phonemes /tʃ/ and /dʒ/ are not acquired by two and a half years of age.

The consonants were also studied with regard to place and manner of articulation. For place of articulation the sounds were grouped as follows: labial, /p/, /b/, /m/ and /hw/; labiodental, /f/ and /v/; linguodental or simply dental, /θ/ and /ð/; postdental, /t/, /d/, /n/, /s/, /z/, /ʃ/, /ʒ/, /l/, /r/ and /j/; velar, /ŋ/, /k/, /g/, and glottal, /h/ and /ʔ/.

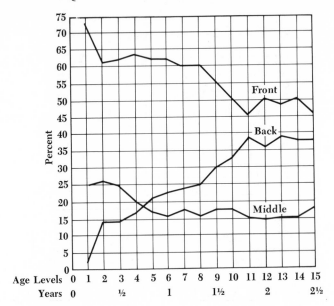

[Figure 1.7] Proportion of infant vowel categories as a function of age.
SOURCE: Irwin, 1948b.

The development of these six sets of sounds is presented in Figure 1.9. It appears from this graph that glottals occur with great frequency in the early months but decline with age. Postdentals, labials, and labiodentals all increase with age. Velars and dentals remain essentially constant with age. The early predominance of velar and glottal production is undoubtedly related to the infant's reflexive responses, such as chewing, sucking, and swallowing. The infant between the third and fourth age levels (six to nine months), however, develops a variety of sounds. Learning conditions, to be discussed shortly, may play a role during this period in the development of such diversity in sound productions.

In Figure 1.10 consonants were grouped by manner of production as follows: nasals, /m/, /n/, and /ŋ/; stop-plosives, /p/, /b/, /t/, /d/, /k/, /g/, and /ʔ/; semivowels, /r/ and /l/; fricatives, /f/, /v/, /θ/, /ð/, /s/, /z/, /ʃ/, /ʒ/, and /h/; and glides, /hw/, /w/, and /j/. In the early months the infant's repertory consists primarily of three stops, /ʔ/, /k/, and /g/, and one fricative, /h/. This fact is reflected in the high position of the plosive and fricative curves in the early months of life. At about four months, the glides, nasals, and semivowels appear. With age, utterances belonging to the nasal, glide, and semivowel categories increase; and with the decline in use of the /h/ fricative, the proportion of these three consonant categories increases.

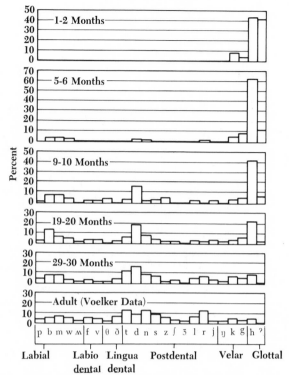

[Figure 1.8] Consonant profiles depicting proportional values of consonants at selected age levels. SOURCE: Irwin, 1947d.

A similar interpretation about learning conditions may be made from Figure 1.10 as well as from Figure 1.9. That is, all groups but the fricatives increase in frequency between six and nine months. At first, the stops decline from their early height, but then begin to increase at about nine months of age, suggesting that between six and nine months an infant's vocalizations may well reflect his exposure to the surrounding environment, presumably the verbal environment.

That environmental forces are at work by at least six months of age is additionally supported by Weir's (1966) observation that Chinese infants show tonal variations over individual vowels, as is typical of their language, at six months, but that Russian and American infants do not.

MATURATION AND LEARNING. From these data several hypotheses about the developmental order of the sounds can be made: one may involve the neurological and muscular prerequisites for sound development; a second, the language environment of the infant. Although a certain level of neuro-muscular development is undoubtedly essential for the learning of articu-

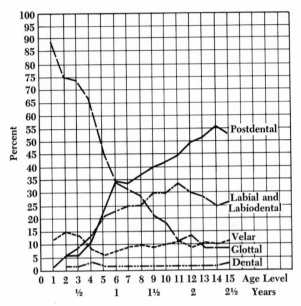

[Figure 1.9] Proportions of infant consonants by place of articulation as a function of age.
SOURCE: Irwin, 1947d.

lation skills (McCarthy, 1952), no evidence is available at present to indicate when the neuromuscular development is completed for any given speech sound. The developmental sequence undoubtedly reflects both cortical and neuromuscular maturation (see Lenneberg's [1967] exhaustive, well-done volume on the biology of language) as well as exposure to language stimulation and to environmental contingencies.

Perhaps one way to disentangle environment from maturation is to compare the babbling of children from diverse language backgrounds. We should recognize, however, that the terms "maturation" and "learning" have many interpretations when applied to the developing organism. Maturation usually implies biological determiners which may operate in at least three not completely independent ways: (a) as prerequisite to sound production learning (the readiness principle); (b) as the underlying (cortical or peripheral) correlate of sound production and sound production learning, and (c) as a preprogrammed neurological unit whose parts are in partial or complete working order and which is set into motion by language stimulation or results from a series of complex biological and environmental interactions. Acknowledging the obvious fact that babbling cannot take place without biological prerequisites and that babbling like all human behavior has biological correlates, it is still no easy matter by cross-language comparisons to determine when

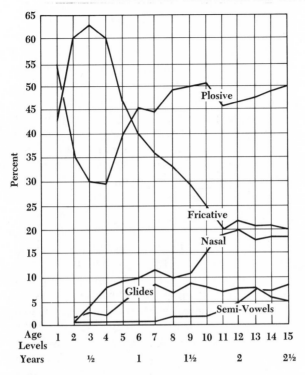

[Figure 1.10] Proportions of infant consonants by manner of articulation as a function of age.
SOURCE: Irwin, 1947e.

environmental factors, because of the complexities mentioned in item *c* above, begin to operate. For example, infants may be unable to hear differences between certain phonetic features yet the mechanisms which permit learning to take place may be operative. Possibly the language signals of all young infants regardless of their language environment are roughly constant because the auditory mechanism heavily distorts all incoming speech stimuli. Another possibility is that environmental factors antedate the development of certain articulatory features (frication as opposed to stopping, for example) or feature complexes (certain phone or syllable types). If this is so it would give the impression that speech sound development is almost entirely of biological origin, because the acquisition of phonetic features, regardless of the unit in which they appear, would be ordered among languages. It is easy to see, then, that during the first year of life the development of sound types may be ordered from language to language, but this observation would not necessarily imply that environmental factors are not operating or that they are minimal. It would only imply that the mechanisms of sound production—not the behavior of sound production—is solely determined by biological growth constants.

The above discussion suggests a number of interesting experiments. One, posed as a question, is as follows: Would one find differences in the vocal output of young infants of about three months of age who had been systematically exposed to different portions of the speech spectrum or to varying percentages of speech sounds? Later we will discuss several investigations of infant vocal conditioning, but we will see that as yet there have been no studies which systematically alter the sound or speech environment of the young infant, as this is no easy experimental task. Nor is there any information on the developing ability of infants to distinguish between phonetic features or whether these vary as a function of the complex (phone) in which they are embedded.

It is still possible, however, that with carefully designed studies naturalistic settings may reveal the point in time at which environmental factors begin to exert their influence. Correlations between infant and adult phone types, holding articulatory features constant, may be one general approach. If, for example, the rounding (or nasalization) of vowels is more general in one language than in another, a corresponding difference might appear in the babbling of infants sometime after the onset of rounding. The features under study might not be full or complete movements, but only rudimentary patterns, as suggested by Bullowa and others (1964). Also acoustic and physiological measurements might supplement distinctive feature comparisons.

Costly as it may be, investigators studying infant vocalizations should exercise all precautions to assure reliability of measurement. No doubt phoneticians reflect their own phonemic experience; this suggests that the development of a specialized and appropriate recording system might be the first experimental concern. When transcriptions are begun, it would be desirable if the recorders were phoneticians from varying language backgrounds.

Because of the methodological problems mentioned above comparisons between the babbling of children in English speaking and non-English speaking environments, from the few available sources, are all but impossible. However, there is one investigation, that of Nakazima (1962), which minimizes many of the possible sources of error mentioned above. Nakazima (1962) compared the vocal output of several Japanese and American infants whose families at the time of the investigation were residing in Japan. Unavoidable and difficult to control was the influence of the Japanese language on the American children, since all the American families employed Japanese maids. Nakazima does not indicate the average amount of time the maids spent with the American infants. He does say, however, that by one year of age the American children were learning Japanese.

Despite the fact that the results of Nakazima's (1962) study can be questioned, and that quantitative comparisons between his study and that of Irwin's are difficult, certain similarities emerge. Since Nakazima found no obvious differences between the Japanese and American children of his study, subsequent remarks pertain to his subjects as a group. Similarities seem to be apparent as soon as non-crying vocalizations are recorded. Both Irwin and Nakazima report that [ə] and [ə]-like sounds, front vowels and back consonants are frequent in the first two months of life. Stops, such as [p], [b] and [d], according to Irwin, are relatively frequent in the third, fourth, fifth and sixth months, and, according to Nakazima are dominant in the sixth to eighth month interval. Nakazima found [j] to be frequent during the second, third and fourth months, and while Irwin found a few instances of [j] during the third and fourth months it was not until the fifth and sixth months before the relative frequency of this sound was greater than 1%. Front fricatives, such as [s], [f], [ʃ] and [θ], and their voiced counterparts appear late in the records of Irwin and Nakazima, but their time of onset is considerably different—almost all appearing with considerable regularity by one year, according to Irwin, and not yet available or very infrequent before one year, according to Nakazima. One striking difference between the two studies pertains to the [ɸ] sound (voiceless bilabial fricative), common in Japanese and rare in English. It is very frequent in the utterances of the infants residing in Japan, beginning with the six month of life, and totally absent, according to Irwin (1947d, 1947e), and unmentioned by Lewis (1951). Nor does Leopold (1947), a linguist skilled in German phonology, and, therefore, very much aware of the occurrence of [ɸ] in German, report the appearance of this sound in the babbling of his child, although he notes the occurrence of [β] (voiced bilabial fricative) at nine months. Leopold's daughter was later exposed to both German and English and began speaking both languages, but she heard primarily, in the early months of life, the speech of her mother, who did not speak German at that time.

Another interesting way to determine the early effects of environmental factors on babbling was suggested by Lenneberg and others (1965). Their study was motivated by the premise that infant cooing responses are "not contingent upon specific, acoustic stimuli," but rather are a consequence of a biologically determined maturational schedule. They further propose that cooing and crying noises are the "primordium" of man's instinct to talk, and, therefore, will occur regardless of the linguistic atmosphere into which the child is placed. (Philosophical opposition to babbling as an early sign of man's peculiarly distinctive faculty of language might be mustered by those who claim that primates other than man babble. However, one taking this point of view would doubtless acknowledge that the babbling of animals is not contingent upon hearing speech or a function of conditioning.) Lenneberg and his associates recognize that vocalizations may occur or vary as a result of sensory stimulation or conditions of reinforcement, but they insist that babbling is a genetic trait of man and, therefore, its onset is not related to environmental or social forces.

To test their hypothesis Lenneberg and others (1965) compared the vocalizations of infants of hearing and deaf parents, from about two weeks to three months of age. The frequency of vocalizations was found to be similar for the infants of both groups; response types were not reported. Overall frequency, measured in time units, would not reflect, necessarily, consonantal or vowel type or even consonantal or vowel frequency. Thus, the measures used in this study may have obscured important differences between the children with hearing parents and those with deaf parents.

Unfortunately the procedures of this very creative study were contaminated by the presence of a voice-operated relay in the bedrooms of the children of deaf parents. It had been installed to call attention to the needs of the children and was operative during the entire time of this study. When actuated the relay flashed a light which signalled to the deaf parent that the child was crying or vocalizing. The light was clearly visible to the children, in some instances flashing in their faces. The light may have served as an elicitor for or a reinforcer of vocalizations.

No doubt babbling is tied to maturational prerequisites, but a considerable amount of additional research needs to be done before the complete story is told. However, with the above considerations in mind we shall return to Irwin's investigation and examine the influence of social and family factors on infant vocalizations.

VARIABLES RELATED TO INFANT VOCALIZATIONS. *Occupational Status.* Phoneme frequency and phoneme type were studied also with regard to family occupational status (Irwin, 1948c, 1948d). Families of the infants under study were categorized as either laboring or nonlaboring (i.e., professional, business, and clerical). The Minnesota Occupational Scale was used as the criterion scale.

In Figure 1.11 the curves for phoneme type are presented. Differences in sound production between children from the two occupational groups were significant at the latter age levels. But the curves do not begin to diverge until age level 4 (seven and eight months), before which time occupational status does not seem to be an important variable.

In Figure 1.12 the curves for phoneme frequency are presented. Again occupational status is significant at the later age levels, and the curves do not begin to diverge until age level 4. From the phoneme type and phoneme frequency curves for the two occupational groups, it appears that by the seventh and eighth months variables associated with occupational status are affecting infant vocal productions. Thus, at least by

occupat status
later
Sig. at
age levels.

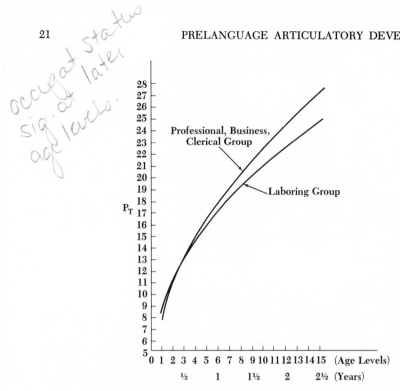

[Figure 1.11] Phoneme type curves for laboring and nonlaboring groups.
SOURCE: Irwin, 1948c.

eight months of age infant vocal responses reflect the child's exposure to his surrounding environment.

Sex and Family Constellation. Comparisons between sexes and comparisons between only children and children with siblings for phoneme type and frequency were also made (Irwin, 1946b, 1947a, 1948a). The differences were found to be nonsignificant.

Intelligence. The relationship between intelligence and speech sound measures was studied for the subjects of the original study as well as for a later group of subjects. Irwin and Chen (1945) studied the relation between two infant sound measures and two intelligence measures, IQ and MA. Intelligence was measured by the Kuhlmann Intelligence Test. The speech measures were referred to as the differential number index and the differential percentage index. Both were derived by comparing each child's phoneme type and percentage of phoneme type scores, respectively, with the average adult scores for these measures. Difference scores for each subject were obtained.

Subjects, ranging in age from 1 to 24 months, for whom Kuhlmann

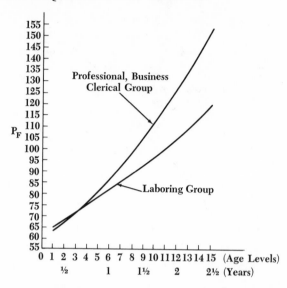

[Figure 1.12] Phoneme frequency curves for laboring and nonlaboring groups.
SOURCE: Irwin, 1948d.

scores were available, were divided into four groups of subjects. The
age interval for each group was 6 months. The number of subjects in
each group ranged from 18 to 32. The correlations computed for each
subgroup separately ranged from .18 to .56 for MA and —.25 to .46 for
IQ. Only 1 of 16 correlations was significant.

In a second study, Spiker and Irwin (1949) correlated Kuhlmann
Intelligence Test scores with infant vocal measurements for 48 subjects
selected from age levels 1 to 14. When scores for a subject were available at more than one age level, they were included; thus 117 "subjects"
were tested. By a statistical procedure, the effect of age was held constant. The correlations with IQ were as follows: phoneme type, .27
(p = .01); phoneme frequency, .08; consonant type, .16; consonant
frequency, .11; vowel type, .44 (p = .01); and vowel frequency, .24
(p = .01).

In a third study (Harms and Spiker, 1959) the testing procedures were
refined, and a moderate relation between IQ measures and phoneme type
and phoneme frequency, respectively, were obtained. Twenty subjects
(ten males and ten females) were included in each of four age-interval
groups. The chronological age range for all subjects in each of the groups
was no greater than two months. The four age groups were: (1) 16 to
18 months, (2) 20 to 22 months, (3) 24 to 26 months, and (4) 28 to 30
months.

Subjects were tested on two occasions. The interval of testing ranged from 36 hours to 7 days, and for the great majority of the children the interval was 2, 3, and 4 days. On each of these two occasions Kuhlmann and Cattell scores were obtained, and 60 breath samples were recorded. Intelligence test scores for each intelligence test were averaged for the two occasions.

Correlations between intelligence test scores and speech scores were made within the separate age levels. Phoneme type and phoneme frequency scores were based on all 120 breath samples. The correlations ranged from —.02 to .71. In most instances the correlations for Groups 2, 3, and 4 were significant. Correlations were also averaged for the last three age groups; correlations of .63 were obtained between phoneme type and both intelligence tests, and correlations of .46 and .41 were obtained between phoneme frequency and the Kuhlmann and Cattell tests, respectively. All of the above four correlations are significant.

Catalano and McCarthy (1954) have made the first attempt to correlate infant vocal measures with later intelligence scores. The intelligence scores were derived from the Stanford-Binet, Form L, Intelligence Test. The subjects originally ranged from 6 to 18 months of age. They were tested approximately 32 months later. At that time the subjects ranged in age from 36 to 54 months.

The subjects were 23 infants, still available for testing, from a sample of 100 institutionalized infants. The IQ's ranged from 55 to 104. For several vocal measures the correlations ranged from .04 to .45. This latter coefficient, the only significant correlation, was obtained for consonant type. In summary, intelligence and infant speech scores are moderately related, but thus far the evidence indicates that infant vocal measures cannot be used as reliable predictors of later intellectual performance.

The use of infant vocal measures as a predictor of intelligence is tempered by the findings of Winitz and Irwin (1958a). These investigators, using correlational procedures, determined the extent to which the infant maintains his rank in the group from early to late age levels. With data available from the original study, correlations were computed between odd-numbered age levels 1, 3, 5, 7, 9, 11, 13, and 15 for phoneme type and phoneme frequency. The low correlations obtained suggest these vocal measures are probably too unstable from one age level to another to serve, in general, as reliable predictors of later performance of any kind.

Speech Environment. Infant vocal production has been related to conditions of speech stimulation and deprivation. Brodbeck and Irwin (1946) compared orphanage infants of age levels 1 (months one and two), 2 (months three and four), and 3 (months five and six) with nonorphanage infants of the same age. The nonorphanage or family infants had served as subjects in the longitudinal study reported above. The number of orphanage infants ranged from 26 to 35, and the number of normal infants ranged from 62 to 80 at the three age levels.

The orphanage infants received excellent care of their physical needs but received little personal attention. The measures used were phoneme type and frequency, consonant type and frequency, and vowel type and frequency. The means for the orphanage children fell consistently below those for the family children; however, none of the differences was statistically significant.

In a later study Irwin (1960) examined the effect of speech stimulation on infant vocal production. The mothers of the 24 experimental subjects were instructed to read to their infants about 15 to 20 minutes per day from illustrated storybooks for children. Storybooks were provided by the experimenter, and frequent consultations were held with the parents to assure that the reading program was carried out. The reading program began when the child was 13 months and was continued until he was 30 months.

Though a control group was not selected at this time, the performance of the experimental subjects was compared with that of a comparable sample of low socioeconomic children (N = 10) drawn from the original study. Phoneme frequency was selected by Irwin as the criterion measure. The experimental group performed significantly better than the control group at all but the first two age levels, months 13 and 14, and 15 and 16.

Although this study seems to indicate that systematic speech stimulation improves vocal output (phoneme frequency), data for the control subjects, it should be noted, were obtained at least 15 years before the experimental subjects were tested. Since child-rearing practices change, the differences between the control and experimental subjects might conceivably reflect other familial factors besides speech stimulation. In any event, the relation between speech stimulation in infancy and later vocal behavior is an intriguing area of investigation and warrants further research.

Lynip's Hypothesis

In a monograph published in 1951, Lynip challenged the basic premise of Irwin's procedure. He stated (p. 227) as follows: "Before adequate study can be given the pre-speech utterances of infants, two conditions must exist: (a) the gathering of data must be devoid of such handicaps as the fallibilities of the human ear and of the use of phonetic systems, (b) these data must be analyzed in an objective manner."

In an attempt to satisfy these conditions, Lynip tape-recorded the vocal utterances of one infant from birth to 56 weeks of age. Using a sound spectograph the energy distributions of the speech spectra were examined. (Lynip) concluded (pp. 246, 248) as follows:

[handwritten margin notes: Child's Vowel Sound Not Comparable To adult]

. . . This infant . . . did not produce a single vowel or consonant sound that was comparable to adult vowels and consonants until about the end of her first year and . . . even at that time the sound was only approximately the equivalent of an adult sound. This study and this method show that any vowel utterance may better be expressed in units of measurement more precise than the generalized forms of phonetic symbols. Because evidence herein submitted shows that one or many syllables of this infant's pre-speech utterances are essentially incomparable to adult sounds, it follows that any record that represents such sounds as adult speech may be therein unreliable. Such inaccuracy of representation was inevitable as long as reliance was put on auditory senses. . . .

The import of this research on the general field of literature is . . . to show the necessity and possibility for by-passing any use of phonetic symbols and any complete dependence on the hearing sense for analyzing pre-language utterances.

Before we accept Lynip's strong suggestion that a phonetic analysis is invalid, two major instrumental considerations need to be examined. They are: (1) the findings to date which illustrate the complexity and ambiguity which results from "absolute" measurements of the physical dimensions of vowels, and (2) an acoustic analysis as a supplement to phonetic analyses. We will ignore, for the moment, two other considerations—namely, narrow versus broad transcription and fallibilities of the spectrograph.

Considerable investigation has been devoted to the identification of the significant acoustic features of English sounds (Bogert and Peterson, 1957, pp. 144–171). Vowels, for example, are distinguished by their varying frequency regions of energy concentration, called formants. Usually only the first two or three formants of vowel spectra are used. The distinction among vowels is not, however, always clear (Curtis, 1954). In many cases vowels uttered by homogeneous subjects (of the same sex and age) and perceived as different have similar, in some instances identical, formants. On the other hand, vowels perceived as the same will show quite different formant relationships. For heterogeneous speakers the formant differences of the same vowels are often great. Thus, if one is to identify a vowel from the visual spectrogram, the age and sex of the subject must be known.

The physical differences between adult and infant vowels are greater than the differences between adults and children. In a preliminary analysis this fact was verified by Winitz (1960), who obtained frequency estimates of the first two formants for a small number of infant vowels. The non-word vocalizations of five infants, from 9 to 15 months, were tape-recorded. Ten judges trained in English phonetics transcribed the vowels into the symbols of the IPA as listed by Fairbanks (1940). The transcription was thus essentially phonemic. Of 67 vowels, 31 were agreed upon by seven or more judges as to the vowel uttered. The lack of agreement for 36 vowels may indicate that the infants' attempts to learn the central tendencies of adult vowels are currently off target. Thus, English-speaking adults would encounter difficulty when asked to place these sounds within adult categories.

Two-dimensional plottings (formant one versus formant two) of the 31 agreed upon vowels revealed that relationship among the several vowels, [i], [ɪ], [ɛ], [æ], [ɑ], [ʊ], and [u], was similar to that found for adults. Like the vowels of children, however, the resonant frequencies of the infants were higher than those of adults.

Possibly, the relative difference between formants may be a consideration in vowel perception. Fischer-Jørgensen (1962, p. 123) states as follows:

> It has for a long time been generally assumed that the decisive thing was the absolute frequency position of the formants, not the relations between formants. This seems to be true in the case of a single speaker, and roughly speaking, it is also true of a homogeneous group, e.g., a group of male speakers or of female speakers, but if the vowels of men, women, and children are compared, it turns out that the whole vowel pattern is shifted to higher frequencies for children. To a certain extent, then, the relations between formants seem to be decisive.

Peterson (1961, p. 24), who has done extensive work on vowel perception, has commented, "Neither a fixed formant frequency nor a formant frequency ratio hypothesis is adequate to explain vowel perception fully." He has suggested many additional areas for future research, among them fundamental frequency, resonator band-width, stimulus amplitude and duration, and phonetic environments.

In view of the results of the study by Winitz and of the problems pertaining to vowel identification cited above, it seems somewhat unreasonable to conclude, as Lynip has done, that because infant spectrograms do not "look" like adult spectrograms, the perceptual identification (phonetic transcription) of infant sounds cannot be done with a fair degree of reliability.

The second primary consideration involves acoustical information as supplemental to phonetic identification. For example, a spectrographic analysis (Peterson and Coxe, 1953) of the acoustical traces of [eɪ] revealed that [ɛɪ] and [ɛe] best describe this diphthong. If we ignore for the moment the fact that most American linguists transcribe phonemically the vowel and off-glide in question as /eɪ/ (usually written as /ey/) whose "allophones" may be [ɛɪ], [ɛi], [ɛe], etc., and accept the fact that [ɛɪ] is correct by convention, then this study by Peterson and Coxe clearly indicates that an acoustical analysis can supplement or clarify phonetic identification.

No one would seriously question this general approach, one which is presently common in instrumental phonetics laboratories.[7] Thus we would not in the case of Lynip's research suggest that his acoustical findings are irrelevant, only that they need to be considered within the boundaries of present knowledge (e.g., vowel formants of heterogeneous versus homogeneous speakers) and as one of several descriptions of sounds.

Two additional points, previously mentioned, now need to be considered. First, the use of narrow versus broad transcription as a means to reduce the acoustic variance of vowels. A study by Fairbanks and Grubb (1961) is relevant here. They demonstrated that when individual vowels are first identified and then preferred samples of an identified vowel are agreed upon, acoustical differentiation is very clear (formant one versus formant two). Clearly, highly trained listeners, individuals competent in the science of narrow transcription, can minimize perceptual variance often introduced into acoustical studies of speech sounds.

Winitz (1960), for example, introduced perceptual variance into his study because he did not ask his recorders to distinguish between phonetic and phonemic transcription. Lehiste (1960) has suggested that broad phonemic categorization might be difficult because the infant's prelanguage utterances are not uttered within a learned (phonemic) interval. She speculates as follows:

> I would expect the sounds of infants in a prelinguistic stage to form a fairly continuous pattern, without differentiation of ranges representing the different phonemes. The differentiation probably does not take place until the random vocalizations have been organized into a code—in other words, until the infant begins to associate meaning with sounds.

Second, the fallibilities of the spectrograph or any other acoustical measuring device need to be considered. It is very possible, of course, that substantial agreement about the phonetic product, when all precautions as outlined are taken, can occur in light of conflicting acoustical evidence.

---

[7] Ladefoged (1964) in his monograph on West African languages dramatically punctuates this viewpoint. His use of instrumental procedures (spectrographs, x-ray-films, photographs, pressure and flow recordings, etc.) supplemented and in some cases clarified the nature of certain seemingly similar articulatory production of Africans.

In such situations it is possible that the electronic equipment or the methods for processing the data are not sufficiently precise.

In summary, several problem areas are involved, which to some extent are measurement problems but in the broader sense are theoretical or operational. If the aim of an investigation is to assess the predictive utility of sound frequency (phoneme frequency), for example, investigators who wish to predict intellectual skills from vocal utterances need not be concerned with the fact that the sounds are not English sounds. On the other hand, if sound type (phoneme type or distinctive feature type) is the criterion measure, then the transcription method, "phonemic" or "phonetic," may have a decided influence on the results. Furthermore, relations among acoustic, perceptual, and physiological measurements of infant sounds are a legitimate area of investigation. It seems important to know how sounds made by infants are perceived and how these perceptions relate to certain acoustic signals and laryngeal and articulatory movements. (In a monograph edited by Lind, 1965, acoustic and physiological measurements were correlated with the cries of the newborn infant, a procedure which should prove generally to be valuable in infant vocal research.) At the same time, the investigator should be aware of problems encountered previously by investigators in this area. Lynip's criticism of Irwin's work is thus essentially irrelevant in that it fails to specify the conditions under which phonetic transcription is invalid.

Implications of Irwin's Research

The consonantal and vowel profiles obtained by Irwin and his colleagues might well have been altered if different transcription measures were used, but his findings probably give a fairly good picture of the development of infant prelanguage utterances within the first year and a half. How to assess clearly the value of Irwin's research is another question. The most important query might be: Do infant sound utterances have relevance for language learning? Carroll (1961, p. 337), who is familiar with Irwin's findings, suggests:

> The particular sound-types uttered by the babbling child have little relevance for later learning, for the types appear in more or less random sequences which bear little relation to the sequence observed after true language learning starts. In fact, after babbling stops (usually before the end of the first year) the child may appear to have temporarily lost the ability to produce certain sounds.

On the other hand, Carroll (1961, p. 337) suggests that infant vocalizations are important because they make it "possible for the infant to learn, through appropriate reinforcement, the instrumental communicative character of vocal sounds." This is a legitimate premise, and in the next few pages it will be examined in relation to some of the basic concepts of learning theory.

Definition of Learning Terms

Reinforcement

A reinforcer is defined as an event that accompanies or follows a response and increases the likelihood of the response occurring on subsequent occasions. Reinforcement is thus a set of events which increases the probability of responses, whereas nonreinforcers are a set of events that do not have this property.

This definition is essentially the one given by Spence and labeled by him as the *empirical law of effect*. As Spence (1956, p. 33) states, "It does not imply, it should be noted, any theory as to how the effects operate to bring about the change in response probability."

Reinforcers may belong to one of four subsets. According to Spence (1956, pp. 33–34) they are:

> (1) *Primary appetitional reinforcers.* Included in this group are environmental objects (e.g., food, water) which, by virtue of maintenance schedules controlled by the experimenter, evoke consummatory responses in the subject. (2) *Secondary appetitional reinforcers,* stimulus cues which in the past experience of the organism have regularly accompanied the consumption of such needed objects as outlined above. Examples are the sight and odor of food as distinguished from food in the mouth. The sight of a water dispenser is another instance. (3) *Primary aversive reinforcers,* environmentally manipulated changes involving the cessation or reduction in intensity of an existing noxious stimulation (e.g., electric shock). And (4) *secondary aversive reinforcers,* the cessation or reduction in intensity of acting stimulus cues that in the past experience of the subject have regularly accompanied a noxious stimulus. Each of these types of events may be identified as a *reinforcing event,* a *reinforcer,* or a *reward.*

Motivation

Drive or motivation refers, in general, to those experimental conditions which, when imposed upon the organism, facilitate learning. The energizing conditions may be the hours of food deprivation or the intensity of a shock. For example, when food pellets are used as reinforcers and are placed at the end of a runway, rats under 24 hours of food deprivation will more quickly learn to traverse the runway than rats under 5 hours of food deprivation. Similarly, human adults will learn a multitude of tasks more rapidly when they are placed under a high, as opposed to a low, motivational state. (This statement is qualified later.) Social deprivation is one example. Subjects who have been deprived of social interchange, especially those subjects who have been deprived of social interaction for some time, will tend to participate in more tasks and acquire these tasks more quickly than subjects not so deprived. Subjects who are placed in isolation chambers and whose general health is maintained (sensory deprivation), to give an extreme example, are usually quite active and learn well when they are released. In summary, then, response activity, especially when applied to a learning situation, can be heightened when a deprivational or noxious state has been imposed upon the organism. As we will see later, these external conditions usually facilitate the acquisition of a new response or heighten the activity of an old response.

Incentives refer to those objects or events that possess reinforcing properties. _Incentive motivation_ refers to the motivational property of reinforcers. For example, if two groups of rats are placed under equivalent deprivational states but receive different magnitudes of the incentive (for instance, one pellet of food versus two pellets of food) for an equal number of trials, learning (acquisition) will be accelerated for the group receiving the larger incentive.[8]

Extinction

Extinction refers to the decay or nonoccurrence of a learned response that is no longer reinforced. In some cases the responses of adults may be extinguished (unlearned) because they are not continued. We are consistent with our definition of extinction, however, if we use the term to mean participation in an act which is itself no longer reinforcing as well as to mean the nonreceipt of an incentive following the performance of a task.[9]

Partial Reinforcement

Greater resistance to extinction for tasks acquired under partial reinforcement schedules than under continuous (100 percent) reinforcement

---

[8] Since our discussion involves an introduction to learning concepts and methods for the student of articulatory behavior, no distinction is made between performance and learning and between rate of learning and final level of learning (asymptotic performance).

[9] Actually one can argue that the loss of the skill to drive a car, for example, is the result of the fact that a person no longer needed to drive, i.e., it was nonreinforcing. Our objective here is simply to define and describe learning phenomena, not to engage in discussions found in learning texts.

is one of the more stable laws of psychology. In the partial reinforcement paradigms subjects are not reinforced for all correct responses; only a designated percentage of the responses is reinforced. The percentage of reinforcements used in various studies has ranged from 0 (no reinforcement) to 100 percent (continuous reinforcement), with percentages in the neighborhood of 50 percent yielding the greatest resistance to extinction (Lewis, 1960).

Learning Paradigms

Subjects when presented with a stimulus will often respond "reflexively." Thus, if an electric shock or a loud noise is administered to an individual, he may jump. This stimulus is referred to as the unconditioned stimulus (US), and the response as the unconditioned response (UR). If a tone is repeatedly paired with the shock or the loud noise and precedes the US by a short interval of time, the tone itself will soon evoke the jumping response. This stimulus is the conditioned stimulus (CS), and the response is the conditioned response (CR). Since the US described above is aversive or noxious, this conditioning paradigm is called *classical aversive conditioning.*

In *classical reward conditioning* the US is a nonnoxious stimulus. For example, if food (US) is presented to a hungry animal it will salivate (UR). A bell (CS), which is repeatedly paired with the US and which precedes the US by a short interval of time, will eventually elicit the salivation. The salivatory response elicited by the CS is called a conditioned response (CR).

Conditioning that does not involve an innate reflex is referred to as *instrumental conditioning.* Here the subject is presented with a stimulus, such as a light. If he makes a response, finger pointing or bar pressing, for example, he will be given a reinforcer (food, money, or other reward). The CS is the light and the CR is the finger pointing or the bar pressing. The reinforcer obtained by the nonreflexive action (CR) has been programmed to occur when the conditioned stimulus (CS) is presented. In operant conditioning the experimenter usually selects a response that occurs frequently in the behavior of the organism. When the reinforcers are appetitional, as in the case just described, the paradigm is referred to as *instrumental reward conditioning,* and when they involve the termination or averting of a noxious stimulus, the paradigm is called *instrumental aversive conditioning.* For example, a rat contained within a box with a metal floor that can be electrified and an exit from which he can escape soon learns to run from the box when the floor is electrified. The floor itself, or a bell that is repeatedly paired to precede the shock, will eventually evoke the CR (running response). The term *operant conditioning* .

usually applies to the first kind of instrumental conditioning—namely, instrumental reward conditioning.

The instrumental conditioning paradigms described make use of the *discrete trial* method. Here the presentation of the stimulus, as arranged by the experimenter, determines the initiation of the trial. The trial interval is defined as being from the presentation of the stimulus to the occurrence of the response, or when a certain predetermined time interval has elapsed.

Besides the discrete trial method there are two additional variants of instrumental reward conditioning that are important to know for later considerations. The first is the *free-operant* method and the second is the *controlled-operant* method (Spiker, 1960). In the *free-operant* paradigm a child might be placed in a bare room in which a lever, mounted on one wall, extends into the room. When the child presses the lever, a reinforcer is presented. The reinforcer might be a small piece of candy ejected automatically into the room through a chute near the lever, or presentation of a colorful cartoon on one of the walls, etc.

In the *controlled-operant* paradigm the subject is also confined in a room. A light stimulus is presented for a period of time during which the subject's responses (lever pressings, for example) will be reinforced. This light stimulus is sometimes referred to as a *discriminative stimulus* or a *positive stimulus* (S^D). During the absence of light, the subject's responses are *not* reinforced. This absence of a stimulus or the presentation of a second stimulus which does not lead to reinforcement is symbolized by S^Δ and is often called the *negative stimulus*.

Evidence for a Vocal Operant

Continuing evidence from the psychological literature indicates that verbal and vocal responses are capable of being conditioned (Krasner, 1958; Salzinger, 1959). The findings of several studies employing birds (Ginsburg, 1960; Lane, 1961), dogs (Salzinger and Waller, 1962), cats (Molliver, 1963), and human infants (Rheingold and others, 1959; Weisberg, 1963; Todd and Palmer, 1968) have indicated that vocal responses prominent in the repertoire of these organisms may be conditioned.

Let us discuss first some of the studies that have employed birds, a particularly vocal animal, as subjects. Ginsburg (1960), using nine shell parakeets about four to five weeks of age, and seeds as incentives, found that the vocalizations (chirps) increased under continuous and partial reinforcement and under discriminative stimulus control (light onset). Lane (1961), using a type of chickenfeed, chick-starter crumbles, as incentives, studied the vocal behavior of four-month-old Bantam chicks. The rate of emission of the chicks' vocalizations depended upon the frequency of reinforcement per number of trials, known technically as the schedule of reinforcement. In addition, it was found that (a) vocal responses decreased in frequency when the incentive was withheld (extinction) and that (b) discrimination reversal occurred when light onset became the negative stimulus and light offset became the positive stimulus. Grosslight and others (1962) supported the major findings of Ginsburg and Lane (continuous reinforcement and discriminative stimulus control) with Mynah birds.

Rheingold and others (1959) conducted the first investigation of vocal conditioning in human infants. The infants, who had a median age of three months, were studied on six consecutive days. Three periods, each nine minutes in duration, constituted the experimental sessions for each day. For all six days vocal responses were recorded live by an observer. Days 1 and 2 provided a control base line in that vocalizations were not reinforced. On days 3 and 4 vocalizations were followed by three social rewards administered by the experimenter. "They were a broad smile, three 'tsk' sounds, and a light touch applied to the infant's abdomen with thumb and fingers of the hand opposed" (Rheingold and others, 1959, p. 68). Their results indicate that vocal responses increased in frequency from days 1 and 2 to days 3 and 4, and then decreased in frequency (extinction) on days 5 and 6 to the level of responding found on days 1 and 2.

The increased vocalizations obtained by Rheingold's group may not have been a function of one or more of the rewards used in this study. The utterance of *tsk* and the light touch to the abdomen may have functioned as UCS's. That is, the "social" rewards may have elicited unconditioned vocal responses just as food placed in an animal's mouth will elicit an unconditioned salivatory response in the dog. In addition, the rewards may also have functioned as discriminative stimuli (S^D's). That is, if vocalizations were learned in response to a smiling and responding adult, then the rewards used by the experimenter in this study simply provided an appropriate stimulus setting for additional vocalizations. Their data seem to show, although not conclusively, that this latter situation may not have been the case, since an adult was present during the base line evaluation and during extinction. However, the adult was not responding—smiling or vocalizing.

Weisberg (1963), by using appropriate control groups, was able to disentangle the effects of social reinforcement on vocalizations from other stimulus conditions. He employed six groups of infants, all three months of age. These groups were (a) no experimenter present, (b) experimenter present, facing child with a blank expression, (c) noncontingent social stimulation (social rewards, rubbing of chin, smile and *yeah* sound, were administered on a prearranged schedule), (d) noncontingent nonsocial stimulation (a door chime was administered on a prearranged schedule), experimenter facing child with a blank expression, (e) contingent social stimulation (the above social rewards were administered following each infant's vocalization), and (f) contingent nonsocial stimulation (the chime was sounded after each infant's vocalization, experimenter facing child with a blank expression).

A base line method of control for conditioning and extinction, similar to that employed by Rheingold and others was used. The interval of testing was over an eight-day period. The results indicate that vocal responses were increased in the contingent social reinforcement group but not in any of the other groups. Weisberg suggests that the reason the nonsocial stimulus failed to act as a reinforcer when it followed infant vocalizations (contingent nonsocial reinforcement group) was because it occurred in the presence of an unresponding adult. No control group was employed to test this hypothesis.

Will the presence of an experimenter increase the acquisition rate of infant vocalizations when the reinforcers are phrases uttered by a female voice? This was the question asked by Todd and Palmer (1968). Using procedures similar to those of Rheingold and others and Weisberg, Todd and Palmer compared the vocalizations of two groups of infants about three months in age, distinguished only by the presence of an adult, expressionless, but in full view of the experimental subjects. During the conditioning phase of the experiment vocal responses actuated a relay system which resulted in the playing of five seconds of tape-recorded speech—a female voice saying the phrases "hello baby, pretty baby, and nice baby." The experiment took place during a six-day interval, two days for each test phase—baseline, conditioning and extinction. Vocalizations were found to increase significantly from the baseline phase to the conditioning phase for the two groups of infants, but vocal emissions were considerably greater when the experimenter was present. Weisberg's finding that the sound of a door chime did not increase vocalizations seems not to be a function of the presence or absence of an adult, but rather that auditory stimuli must be social to be reinforcing. However, this remark should be regarded as tentative, pending the outcome of further research.

In summary, then, the above three studies suggest that (a) vocalizations may be increased as early as three months by the application of conditioning procedures; (b) social responses, such as smiles and vocalizations, are effective reinforcers; and (c) the mere presence of an unresponding adult will not increase vocalizations. Mowrer's theoretical position (see section immediately below) as well as the usual discrimination learning paradigm would suggest that infant vocalizations will increase when a human face is present. Actually Weisberg found that the operant vocal level was decreased, although not significantly, for the subjects who did not see a human face. In addition, Todd and Palmer found that prerecorded verbalizations increased vocalizations when an experimenter was present. Possibly the presence of a human face serves to increase vocalizations, but the effect may not be strong at three months of age. As yet no study which yields information relative to the conditioning of specific sounds or sound groups has been conducted.

It was noted in the discussion of Irwin's findings on the relation between socioeconomic class and the indices of infant vocal behavior that differences between family occupational groups for nonorphanage children were not evident until about seven or eight months. After that time the curves began to diverge. Yet, from the findings of the three studies reported directly above on infant vocal conditioning, we know that the vocal behavior of infants of three months can be conditioned. Vocal conditioning thus seems to occur very early in the life of the infant, even though increased vocal responses do not occur until several months later.

Mowrer's Autism Theory of Vocal Acquisition

Although many interpretations of infant babbling have been presented, the original and creative work of Mowrer (1952, 1958, 1960) is significant. He has referred to his theory of infant babbling as the autism theory. Mowrer has presented evidence from his research with talking birds to support his theoretical position. Briefly, Mowrer's theory is as follows: (a) the organism must first "identify" with the trainer, (b) the trainer's voice becomes a stimulus which signifies the presentation of primary reinforcement, (c) the sound of the trainer's voice takes on secondary reinforcing properties for the bird,[10] (d) the solitary bird produces vocalizations because they are rewarding (reminiscent of primary reinforcement), and (e) if the trainer is present, the bird will often vocalize because the trainer provides an immediate stimulus for primary reinforcement.

To support this notion of autistic sound production, Mowrer has introduced an intervening motivational variable identified as hope. Hope, an acquired drive, implies, when aroused, imminent occurrence of a desired event or presentation of a promise. Presentation of an incentive (food, for example) provides "relief" for the organism. When an organism subsequently, by itself, produces sounds, it thus simulates conditions (invokes hope) under which primary reinforcement was obtained. In this way the vocal responses of the environment (e.g., trainer's sounds) are learned and are eventually used as instrumental acts. Many of Mowrer's concepts are implicit in the following discussion.

[10] Secondary reinforcement as applied to infant vocalizations will be described in detail later (pp. 39–42).

Acquisition of Early Vocal Behavior by the Human Infant

We know that the vocalizations of the human infant in the first two months of life are largely cries and reflexive sounds—i.e., vocalizations associated with eating, sucking, swallowing, etc. By at least six months of age the infant begins to vocalize a diversity of sounds. In an attempt to understand the infant's vocal sound development within a framework of learning, I shall present three periods of infant vocal production and offer some tentative hypotheses about these three periods. Though these periods may be considered sequential, they overlap to some extent.

The first stage comprises the period of time when the infant first begins to vocalize. In this period prelanguage utterances are described as anticipatory goal responses. During the second period, the infant's vocalizations are responses that occur when he is apparently satiated. The repetitive and continuous vocalizations are usually observed by the sixth month. The third period involves infant utterances that serve as verbal stimuli—"words" to the ear of an adult. This period usually begins after the child's first birthday.

Period I: Fractional Anticipatory Goal Response

Mowrer's hope concept may possibly be translated into an expectancy mechanism described by Spence (1956, pp. 134–135) as the fractional anticipatory goal response (r_g). Spence has used the fractional anticipatory goal response as a construct to aid in theorizing about instrumental conditioning. The concept, as its name seems to imply, refers to fractional components of the goal response which occur prior to the goal response and which determine or make possible the learning of an instrumental response; the instrumental response must be learned, of course, for it leads to the achievement of the goal response. The goal response, symbolized by R_g, in the case of instrumental reward conditioning, is defined as the appetitional feeding response—i.e., the behavioral response of eating or drinking that follows the instrumental (conditioned) response. For example, a rat may be trained to run down an alley if he is rewarded with food pellets. The act of eating the food pellets is the goal response, and the running is the learned instrumental response. The conditions are similar when instrumental aversive conditioning is used. For example, a young child by pressing a lever when he hears a pure tone avoids an impending shock that would produce a painful reaction; avoidance of the shock is the goal response and the lever pressing is the learned instrumental act.

In instrumental conditioning the reinforcement contingencies are usually arranged so that a subject needs to learn a chain of responses before he achieves the response that is to be reinforced. In alley running, for example, the rat must enter the goal box at the end of the alley before he is reinforced, but in learning to do so he must learn to run down the alley. The fractional anticipatory response, denoted r_g, has been used to help explain the chain of learned responses that ultimately lead to a strengthening of the conditioned response. In our example, learning to run down the alley rapidly and without side excursions presumably occurs because the rat anticipates the goal response of eating and, therefore, makes anticipatory responses that are similar to, but only fractional components of, the actual eating responses. At first, fractional anticipatory responses, such as salivation, sucking, and swallowing with the absence of food in the mouth, are elicited in the alley by stimuli that directly precede the goal box—e.g., the color, texture, or shape of the alley. As trials continue, stimuli that are farther removed spatially from the goal box elicit portions of the goal response presumably by the process of stimulus generalization (see Chapter 2, pp. 102–105). The r_g's are also assumed to elicit internal interoceptive cues, s_g's. In the case of hunger, for example, an s_g would be any one of a number of afferent stimulations which accompany this deprivation state. The s_g in turn becomes conditioned to the instrumental response. The r_g's are linked by stimuli from the alley and from interoceptors.

Initially, then, the stimulus cues of the alley directly preceding the goal box elicit consummatory responses, r_g's, which in turn evoke interoceptive cues, s_g's, which in turn elicit a running response which brings the animal to the goal box. Hence, the symbolization r_g-s_g. As trials continue, another point in the alley near the previous point elicits r_g's, by the process of stimulus generalization, which in turn elicit s_g's, which in turn elicit a running response which brings the animal to the first stimulus point in the alley. The chain is repeated again and the animal arrives in the goal box. In time the animal learns to run efficiently from the start box to the goal box, and presumably each locomotor response is linked by an intervening r_g-s_g chain.

A quote from Spence (1956, pp. 134–135) will help to make this concept clear:

> . . . stimulus cues in the goal box and from the alley just preceding the goal box become conditioned to the goal response, R_g. Through generalization the stimulus cues at earlier points in the runway are also assumed to acquire the capacity to elicit R_g, or at least noncompetitional components of R_g that can occur without the actual presence of the food (e.g. salivating and chewing movements). As a result this fractional conditioned response, which we shall designate as r_g, moves forward to the beginning of the instrumental sequence. Furthermore, the interoceptive stimulus cue (s_g) produced by

> this response also becomes a part of the stimulus com-
> plex in the alley and thus should become conditioned
> to the instrumental locomotor responses.

Elsewhere Spence (1956, p. 51) states: "The interoceptive stimulus cues (s_g) produced by this classically conditioned response in turn are assumed to become conditioned to the instrumental running response and thus become a determiner of it."

Within the framework of the theoretical model provided by Spence, K is regarded as an intervening variable representing, quantitatively, "the motivational property of the conditioned r_g-s_g mechanism and which is defined in terms of the experimental variables that determine the vigor of the latter" (Spence, 1956, p. 135). Furthermore, the habit strength (that is, the strength of this learned response, however defined) of this classically conditioned mechanism is presumed to be a function of several variables, such as (a) number of conditioning trials given in the goal box, (b) similarity of cues between the goal box and any point in the alley way including internal proprioceptive cues from the running response that may be distinctive, and (c) the vigor of the unconditioned consummatory response to the goal object as determined, for example, by the sweetness or hardness of the goal object.

We shall now employ the r_g-s_g concept to try to explain conditions under which the early vocalizations of human infants occur. Our basic assumption is that the human infant's chewing and sucking responses which are a function of mastication become conditioned to a sequence of stimulus events that occur in the feeding situation. Prominent in the feeding situation are such stimulus elements as (a) the food, (b) the individual administering the food, (c) the sensory changes that accompany the feeding such as variations in light intensity, and (d) the vocalizations of the individual administering the food. Within the framework of the r_g-s_g mechanism it is assumed that chewing, salivating, etc., and therefore vocalizations become conditioned to the sequence of events that lead to feeding.

With these considerations in mind the following hypotheses are illustrative of those which can be generated by the principle of fractional anticipatory goal response:

1. In the early months of life (perhaps the second or third month) vocalizations will occur more frequently prior to feeding than at other times and will resemble eating responses. This is because cues of the feeding sequence are assumed to acquire the capacity to elicit components of R_g or r_g. Irwin (1947d) found that velars and glottals, sounds that are phonetically similar to those heard in mastication and deglutition, comprised approximately 90 percent of all sounds uttered in the first four months of life. The phonetic evidence is not entirely convincing, however,

since the frequency of the /h/ sound constituted between 44 percent and 50 percent of all sounds uttered during this interval. The /h/ sound would be associated with a vigorous exhalation rather than with deglutition or mastication. However, "lip-smacking sounds" and "clicking sounds," commonly heard in mastication and deglutition, were omitted in the transcriptions (Winitz and Irwin, 1958a) and if recorded would no doubt have increased the number of sounds related to deglutition and mastication.

2. At first, vocalizations will be made to events that are closely antecedent to the feeding situation, but later they will be made to events that are further displaced from the feeding situation. This hypothesis follows from the r_g-s_g concept and would appear to need no further elaboration.

3. The duration of vocalizations, prior to feeding, will be proportional to the length of the feeding period. This follows from research reported elsewhere (Kimble, 1961, pp. 170–173) as well as Spence's (1956) consideration of this variable. Research in this area has generally indicated that quantitative variation of the incentive (size and number of pellets, for example) affects asymptotic performance, but not rate of approach to asymptote. When consummatory time in the goal box is kept constant, however, performance differences are not apparent. According to Spence (1956, p. 140), "One interpretation of these findings would be that the same magnitude of r_g was conditioned under the different reward conditions but that more conditioning of it occurred, i.e., a greater habit strength was developed, in the case of the subjects that were in the goal box for a longer period." Thus, differential infant feeding periods should produce differences in the habit strength of the r_g mechanism—i.e., infants who are fed over a longer period of time should tend to vocalize (chew and suck) earlier in the sequence of events that lead to feeding.[11] Interestingly enough one can say that infants will babble, if the chewing and lip-smacking sounds leading to feeding may be considered babbling, even though they may never have heard the voice of the individual administering the food—for reasons somewhat different than those suggested by Lenneberg and others (1965).

Period II: Vocalizations as Secondary Reinforcers

Secondary reinforcement as it has been studied in the free-operant or controlled operant situation may be a useful model for the study and explanation of early infant babbling. There are numerous ways to test the effect of secondary reinforcement; however, we shall describe those paradigms that have been most frequently employed in research studies

---

[11] If alley runways could be soundproofed and the chewing, sucking, and swallowing, etc., responses could be recorded, quantitative measurement of the r_g responses with animals might be made. Hence a more detailed account of this mechanism might be made.

(Girardeau, 1961). In all test situations primary and secondary reinforcement is given under primary motivating conditions—that is, the animal is under a basic deprivation state. In the following discussion we shall consider paradigms in which the deprivation states are the same for primary and secondary reinforcement. Secondary reinforcement is tested by observing the strength of the learned response when the conditioned stimulus is present and when it is absent. No food or primary reinforcement is given to the subject during this period of time. Greater response strength in the presence of the conditioned stimulus indicates secondary reinforcement. This phenomenon has been demonstrated in a number of experiments (see Kimble, 1961, pp. 167–202).

PARADIGM I. (Free operant with release lever present.) Rats are confined within a box in which a release lever or bar extends from one of the sides. Below the lever is a chute with a small cup. In depressing the bar, a clicking sound results and a food pellet falls into the cup.

After this response is highly learned, subjects are assigned to one of two groups. For group A, every depression of the bar continues to produce the clicking sound, but no food drops into the cup. For group B, every depression of the bar produces no clicking sound and results in no food. Subjects are confined individually in the box and the same release bar is used throughout the experiment. A significantly greater frequency of bar presses for group A suggests that the clicking sound has reinforcing properties—i.e., it becomes a secondary reinforcer.

PARADIGM II. (Controlled operant with release lever not present.) The subjects are again confined within a box but one in which no release lever is present. In this case the subject is taught to discriminate between two continuous stimuli, each presented separately for a predetermined time interval: S^D, discrimination stimulus—a response made in the presence of this stimulus is reinforced; and S^Δ, negative stimulus—a response made in the presence of this stimulus is not reinforced. For example, S^D might be light, S^Δ darkness, and food the reinforcer during the S^D interval. A subject's responses involve locomoting to the food cup and eating. Secondary reinforcement effects are tested by dividing the subjects into two groups and making the same release lever available. For one group of subjects the S^D occurs for a short interval of time when the bar is pressed, and for the other group the S^D does not occur when the bar is pressed. No primary reinforcement is given to subjects in either group.

PARADIGM III. (Controlled operant with release lever present.) Here the clicking sound remains on for a certain time interval. When the subject, as in Paradigm I, presses the bar a food pellet is delivered. When the sound is not on, depression of the bar results in no food. The subject is reinforced for pressing the bar as long as the clicking sound (S^D) is on.

Secondary reinforcement is tested by providing the experimental subjects with either the same lever or a different kind of release mechanism, which may be a chain. A second release mechanism precludes almost entirely secondary reinforcement effects resulting from characteristic tactile and kinesthetic cues of the first release mechanism. Movement of the same or a different release triggers the sound onset. No sound occurs for the control group. And again no primary reinforcement is offered either group.

VARIABLES RELATED TO SECONDARY REINFORCEMENT. Two aspects of the secondary reinforcement phenomenon have come under considerable discussion and research. These concern the following related factors: (a) the timing of the neutral stimulus, a stimulus not previously associated with the responses under study, when it is initially paired with the primary reinforcer and (b) the reinforcing versus the cue properties of the neutral stimulus.

It was originally suggested by Keller and Schoenfeld (1950, pp. 239–240) that a stimulus must first be established as a discriminative stimulus before it can become a secondary reinforcer. This point has been discussed by Myers (1958) and Kelleher and Gollub (1962). Although some disagreement about this point still exists, the majority of research studies suggests that a stimulus has considerably greater eliciting strength when it precedes a primary reinforcer than when it occurs simultaneously with a reinforcer. There seems to be no point in reviewing the details of these experiments here.

The second point has been made by Wyckoff and associates (1952, 1958). They first noted that in many instances tests of secondary reinforcement have yielded either no effects at all or effects that just barely reach statistical significance regardless of the paradigm which was employed. Secondary reinforcement effects might be explained more parsimoniously in terms of cue effects, for a stimulus that is assumed to be a secondary reinforcer may merely evoke or facilitate a response rather than reinforce a response, as would be the case in the extinction phase of any discrimination experiment. Wyckoff and others (1958, p. 103) state:

> Cue properties are indicated when we observe a tendency for some response to occur *following* the onset of a stimulus, while reinforcing properties are indicated by an increase (or sometimes maintenance of a high level) in the strength of some response which *precedes* the onset of the stimulus.
>
> ... training was followed by a test during which lever-pressing produced a buzz but no water. During this test, secondary reinforcement might operate to increase the number of lever responses. However, the buzzer might also increase the number of lever responses through its action as a cue. When the buzzer sounded, S could be expected to run vigorously to the water dipper. This energetic activity would tend to keep S awake and in a more active state, which in turn would increase the probability of additional lever responses.

Using procedures similar to those defined as Paradigm II, the subsequent research of Wykoff and others (1958) seemed to support the above stated contention. During the test phase an equal number of bar presses was made whether or not the S^D, in this case a buzzer, was contingent on a bar press. These findings are certainly not encouraging for theories of language development which are built on the foundation of secondary reinforcement effects.

However, a study by Sidowski and others (1965), using children as subjects, seems to have disentangled the potential affects of these two variables. Their procedure was a variation of Paradigm III. During conditioning the children in both the cue and secondary reinforcement groups observed a stimulus, in this case a light, but the temporal sequence of the light for the two groups was different. The apparatus consisted of a lever, an illuminated dome that contained pennies, and a device that automatically dispensed pennies into a cup when the lever was pulled down. For the subjects in the "cue" group, the light remained on until the lever was pulled down; for the subjects in the secondary reinforcement group, the light appeared just prior to the dispensation of the penny and remained illuminated until the penny appeared in the cup. Thus the stimulus was observed during each conditioning trial for both groups of subjects, but for the "cue" group the light indicated the beginning of the conditioning trial and for the "secondary reinforcement" group the light indicated that the penny was to be dispensed—i.e., the light stimulus was an S^D. Although both groups, when tested during extinction, did better than the control group (a group that received no light following lever pressings), the secondary reinforcement group extinguished less slowly than the cue group. This finding suggests the operation of a secondary reinforcement effect as distinguished from a cue effect for those studies which have employed stimulus conditions which clearly indicate the presentation of the reinforcer.

Research by Zimmerman (1957) also suggests that a variant of Paradigm II may provide a situation in which secondary reinforcements effects may be very powerful. He provided evidence for strong secondary reinforcement effects with a "two stage" partial reinforcement procedure. In his study Paradigm II was employed with the following two changes: (a) the neutral stimulus was established as an S^D with partial reinforcement, and (b) the new response was partially reinforced with the secondary reinforcer (formerly the neutral stimulus). Under these conditions he found that the secondary reinforcement effects were intense and long lasting.

PARADIGMS AS MODELS FOR INFANT VOCAL BEHAVIOR. We can now see the relation between these paradigms and infant vocal behavior. The rat that performs the lever-pressing act continuously and repetitively to actuate the onset of an S^D (now a secondary reinforcer)—e.g., a clicking sound—may be likened to the infant who babbles. The infant vocalizes continuously and repetitively without any apparent primary reinforcer. This analogy will be extended further, but first we must consider the reinforcing properties of neutral stimuli when primary drives are minimal.

Kimble summarized the research in this area and found the evidence to be inconsistent (Kimble, 1961, p. 189). That is, there is conflicting evidence as to whether or not secondary reinforcement effects can be produced in satiated animals. For the human infant, however, a large number of stimuli may act as secondary reinforcers when primary drives are minimal or not present. We know that social reinforcers such as a smile and other "approval mannerisms" act as reinforcers for children and adults. Such social stimuli are reinforcing to the normal child and adult, although the strength of these social reinforcers in affecting behavior may vary from time to time. So far as we presently know, social stimuli may acquire considerable reinforcing strength in the early months of life.

Stevenson (1962) has suggested a sensory stimulation mechanism as an energizer of human behavior when primary drives are low in strength. He states:

> For normal children, increased age is accompanied by the development of an increasing need for sensory stimulation. This need is assumed to produce a primary drive of "stimulus hunger" which can be reduced by changes in the organism's sensory input. Other primary drives are assumed to restrict the opportunity for expression of stimulus hunger by increasing the organism's total stimulation to such a degree that further sensory stimulation is no longer reinforcing. Thus, we are concerned only with behavior which occurs when other drives have low strength. It is assumed that all but the most primitive forms of cognitive behavior are related to this need for sensory stimulation, rather than to needs of a more primary nature, such as hunger, thirst, and so forth.[12]

As already indicated, infant vocal responses can be conditioned with some types of social reinforcers (Rheingold and others, 1959; Weisberg, 1963; Todd and Palmer, 1968). It seems important, then, to know more about those events that have reinforcing properties for infant vocal responses.

Infant biographers, as noted previously, say that children who are no older than six months often vocalize repeatedly, and apparently for pleasure, when they are alone and their basic drives satisfied. Any or a

---

[12] Stevenson, H. W. "Piaget, behavior theory, and intelligence," in Kessen and Kuhlman, Thought in the young child. Monographs of the Society for Research in Child Development, 1962, 27 (Serial no. 83), 120. Copyright © 1962 by the Society for Research in Child Development, Inc. All rights reserved.

combination of the three paradigms previously presented may possibly be used as models to study or explain infant vocal learning during this developmental period. For example, by using features of Paradigms II and III with a two-stage partial reinforcement procedure, infant vocal learning in this period may be interpreted to occur as follows:

The mother's vocalizations precede and accompany the administration of food (primary reinforcement). In most instances the child will turn his head (instrumental response) in order to obtain the food. Sometimes, however, the mother will vocalize and the child will turn his head, but no food will be given (partial reinforcement). In time the mother's vocalizations follow other infant acts, such as looking at the parent, controlled body movement, and smiles. However, the mother will not always vocalize when the child responds.

Because an infant's vocalizations resemble his mother's vocalizations, they "acquire" secondary reinforcing properties, and since the vocalizations of mother and child are similar, the reinforcing properties of the mother's vocalizations transfer to the child's vocalizations. Maternal vocalizations, of course, occur almost continuously prior to and during the care of an infant. Quite understandably, the infant's own vocalizations may thereby acquire secondary reinforcing properties. In addition, the mother's vocalizations continue to be paired with the administration of food as well as with other primary reinforcing acts, thereby preventing extinction of the child's vocalizations.

In this second period of infant vocal behavior, infant vocalizations soon come to resemble adult English words in their phonetic, syllabic, loudness, and stress characteristics. A study by Bergum (1960) is relevant here. His findings suggest the presence of a linear gradient of stimulus generalization in tests of secondary reinforcement. The rats in his study more often selected goal boxes that were similar in color to the goal box in which primary reinforcement was given. Results of this kind would appear to be in agreement with Mowrer's (1952, p. 264) following statement: "When the bird itself happens to make somewhat similar sounds, it is now secondarily rewarded for having done so and tries to perfect these sounds so as to make them match as exactly as possible the original sounds. . . ."

As yet there is really no explanation for vocal drift (see Brown, 1958, pp. 198–202)—the seemingly graduate approximation of infant sounds toward those of the community language. What is the reason for phonemic drifting? Differential reinforcement, as it is usually conceived, does not seem to be a likely explanatory candidate. For parents reinforce strings of phonemes and not individual phonemes in a string. It would be of interest to know whether infants who are reinforced for a range of responses would drift toward the conditioned (discriminative) stimulus. A number of interesting experiments could be designed to test this hypothesis.

It may very well be that babbling represents something very different from what we have suggested above. Possibly babbling shows drifting because syntactic comprehension (and, of course, phonemic discrimination) of a very primitive sort has begun.

Another consideration is the articulation unit of the babbling response. In what way is articulation in the babbling stage similar to articulation of words? Although the syllables which the infant babbles may appear on the surface to be structurally similar to those uttered after words are acquired, basic articulatory arrangements may be absent, for example, timing factors and coarticulation of adjacent phonemes. Superficially the "articulatory units" show similarities between the prelinguistic and language stages. For example, Irwin's (1951) graphing of consonantal position reveals that by six months of age consonants occur in the initial, medial, and final positions of syllables; and Winitz' (1961) analysis of reduplication shows that syllables of all varieties are common in infancy. Although many of the articulatory errors of young children can be described (but not explained) under the rubric of assimilation (see Chapter 2, pp. 120–121), possibly articulatory considerations are as critical to understanding the dynamics of vocal drift as phonemic and syntactic considerations are.

Whatever may be the infant's sound-matching mechanism, he soon learns to imitate many of the sounds he hears, often in response to a parent's vocalization (see Miller and Dollard, 1941). The learning of imitative responses as instrumental acts has been discussed at length by Miller and Dollard (1941), who describe the conditions under which they occur. These mechanisms may apply to infant vocalizations but they need to be reinterpreted in light of the fact that infant responses during this period occur presumably because of their secondary reinforcing properties. The responses have not been learned as imitations which have led to the attainment of a goal object.

Let us reconsider suggestions made by some speech pathologists that prelanguage utterances, because they "enable" or "prepare" the child for later language learning, are critical for speech development. First, specific sounds and sound units need to be acquired in the prelanguage stage in order for them to be available as units in words. Second, vocalizations need to be learned as instrumental acts (responses that increase when reinforced) in order for a child to learn the instrumental communicative character of language, to borrow a phrase from Carroll (1961). Third, a diversity of prelanguage utterances need to be acquired before parents can reinforce utterances that appear to be approximations of English words. These three considerations are, of course, intertwined, but they seem to point to the fact that a child needs to respond to a situation with a vocalization that "resembles" an English word before it is interpreted by a parent as a word signifying a referent. When it is so interpreted, the parent will reinforce the vocalization, and thus a verbal operant will be acquired. Parents, however, possess different standards of word acceptability, and so the pattern of reinforcement varies from child to child.

Period III: Verbal Stimuli

Usually by the end of the first year of life (McCurry and Irwin, 1953; Winitz and Irwin, 1958b) several of the infant's utterances will be discriminated by the parent as an approximation of a particular word. He will reinforce these utterances, and in doing so the child will gradually refine his approximations until they match the adult English form. This shaping process is described by Skinner (1957, pp. 29–30) as follows:

> The parent sets up a repertoire of responses in the child by reinforcing many instances of a response. Obviously a response must appear at least once before it is strengthened by reinforcement. It does not follow, however, that all the complex forms of adult behavior are in the child's unconditioned vocal repertoire. . . . In teaching the young child to talk, the formal specifications upon which reinforcement is contingent are at first greatly relaxed. Any response which vaguely resembles the standard behavior of the community is reinforced. When these begin to appear frequently, a closer approximation is insisted upon. In this manner very complex verbal forms may be reached.

The research of McCurry and Irwin (1953) indicates that the child's early words are "word approximations" that become more like the adult forms with age. They considered a *word approximation* to be uttered when at least one phonetic element of the adult English word is present, and a *standard word* to be uttered when the phonetic elements are the same as those listed by Kenyon and Knott (1953). Again, these authors are apparently referring to phonemic rather than to phonetic elements.

McCurry and Irwin (1953) have tested the reliability of observers in assigning word meaning to the vocal responses of infants 19 to 22 months of age. They found observer agreement to be 91 percent, indicating that two observers demonstrated substantial agreement in identifying the referent of the child's verbalizations. One would like to know the criteria, if any, by which McCurry and Irwin distinguished phonetic patterns that they interpreted as attempts to pronounce standard words.

With the utterance of vocal units that serve as "words" for parents, the language behavior of the infant passes from the vocal to the verbal stage. Although it would be interesting to speculate about the complexities whereby a child learns a language—its words, morphemes, syntax—such an undertaking lies beyond the scope of this book. This is not to say that articulatory responses are learned outside the constraints of a natural language's grammar. Quite the contrary, the conversion of terminal grammatical strings to spoken English no doubt requires knowledge of higher order linguistic rules which, psychologically speaking, may need to be acquired before the phonetic rules can be learned.[13]

Linguists who strongly affirm the principles of generative grammar view the phonological and syntactical components of a language as interrelated systems (Chomsky, 1965; and Postal, 1968). The input to the phonology is the surface syntactic structure. The phonetic representation is the output of the phonological component. For purposes of discussion we can think of the surface structure of a sentence as simply a superficial grammatical description such as is usually obtained in a parsing exercise.

Surface structures show a history of development, a derivation, which assigns an unambiguous grammatical description to a sentence, and which pairs phonetic signals with semantic interpretations. Thus recent developments in linguistic theory suggest that the phonetic shape of a sentence is a function of both syntactic and phonological considerations. We assume, then, that the acquisition of articulatory responses involves grammatical considerations, which—for obvious reasons—will not be developed here.

An equally important consideration is that of the perception and conversely the production of the speech unit in the acquisition process. In 1954 Curtis in an article entitled "The case for dynamic analysis in acoustic phonetics" reemphasized forcefully an implicit consideration in the quantization of speech. He stated, "Researchers have sought to describe what have sometimes been called the 'invariant characteristics' of speech sounds which it is assumed would exist under all conditions of speaking . . . it has been further assumed that suitable acoustical analysis would be adequate to specify its significant acoustical characteristics" (Curtis, 1954, pp. 147–148). Fourteen years later with many significant publications in acoustic and physiological phonetics behind him Curtis notes that "neither acoustic phonetics research nor physiological phonetics research has so far succeeded very well in identifying invariant sets of acoustical or physiological characteristics which show neat one-to-one correspondence to the phonemes which we discriminate with relative ease (Curtis, 1968)."

One need only turn to any one of a number of investigations for this fact to become apparent. The interesting finding by Lisker and Abramson (1967), for example, shows the complexity in assigning, without reservation, the voiced-unvoicing opposition as an invariant physical signal in the

---

[13] The author is aware of the general criticisms that can be directed toward his proposals, and to a large extent is in sympathy with them. My characterization of phoneme learning is weak in many respects: it views phoneme learning (*a*) without reference to syntax and (*b*) without reference to the problems inherent in what is now referred to as "taxonomic phonemics" (which was characterized, though inadequately, on pp. 2 to 4).

perception of speech, since voice onset time is often obscured between /ptk/ and /bdg/ in running speech.

Acoustical phoneticians have advanced interesting hypotheses about the lack of an invariant relationship between the phoneme and its acoustic and physiological correlates (Liberman et al., 1967; Linbloom, 1963; Ohman, 1966; Kozhevnikov and Chistovich, 1965; and Stevens and House, 1963, to name a few). They have posited both peripheral causation, a smearing of the target phonetic values, and higher-order neurological causation, a unit sometimes called the syllable which governs a train of phonemes.

In summary, then, the emergence of the verbal period represents a host of considerations: behavioral contingencies, syntactical and phonological relationships, and the basic units including their operation of speech perception and production. More will be known about the development of speech and language as scientists increase their understanding of these basic processes.

SUMMARY

In this chapter the early development of infant vocal utterances was described. We concentrated heavily on the research findings of Orvis C. Irwin. Measures such as phoneme type and frequency, consonant type and frequency, and vowel type and frequency were included in this description. The relationships among these sound measures and several other variables (intelligence, occupational status, sibling status, etc.) were discussed. Some errors may have been introduced into these studies because the infant's utterances were encoded phonemically rather than phonetically.

Several learning terms and paradigms were introduced: reinforcement, motivation, incentive, extinction, partial reinforcement, and classical and instrumental conditioning. These terms were utilized in a summarization of studies on the conditioning of infant vocalizations of animals and humans. Also, Mowrer's autism theory of vocal production was summarized. Within Mowrer's framework and within the framework of learning theory, a theoretical outline for the study of infant vocal acquisition was presented. Three stages of infant vocalizations were outlined: (a) fractional anticipatory goal response, (b) secondary reinforcement, and (c) verbal stimuli.

Bergum, B. O. Gradients of generalization in secondary reinforcement. *Journal of Experimental Psychology*, 1960, *59*, 47–53.

Berry, M. F., and Eisenson, J. *Speech disorders, principles and practices of therapy*. New York: Appleton-Century-Crofts, 1956.

Bogert, B. P., and Peterson, G. E. The acoustics of speech. In L. E. Travis (Ed.), *Handbook of speech pathology*. New York: Appleton-Century-Crofts, 1957.

Brodbeck, A., and Irwin, O. C. The speech behavior of infants without families. *Child Development*, 1946, *17*, 145–156.

Brown, R. *Words and things*. Glencoe, Ill.: The Free Press, 1958.

Brown, R. W. Language and categories. Appendix in Bruner, J. S., Goodnow, J., and Austin, G. A. *A study of thinking*. New York: Wiley, 1956.

Bullowa, M., Jones, L. G., and Bever, T. G, The development from vocal to verbal behavior in children. In Bellugi and Brown (Ed.), *The acquisition of language. Monographs of the Society for Research in Child Development*, 1964, *29* (Serial no. 92), 101–107.

Carroll, J. B. *The study of language*. Cambridge: Harvard University Press, 1953.

Carroll, J. B. Language development in children. In Saporta, S. (Ed.) and Bastian, J. R. (Assist. Ed.), *Psycholinguistics, a book of readings*. New York: Holt, Rinehart and Winston, 1961.

Catalano, F. L., and McCarthy, D. Infant speech as a possible predictor of later intelligence. *Journal of Psychology*, 1954, *38*, 203–209.

Chen, H. P., and Irwin, O. C. Infant speech: Vowel and consonant types. *Journal of Speech Disorders*, 1946, *11*, 27–29.

Chomsky, N. *Aspects of the theory of syntax*. Cambridge: M. I. T., 1965.

Curtis, J. F. Systematic research in experimental phonetics: 3. The case for dynamic analysis in acoustic phonetics. *Journal of Speech and Hearing Disorders*, 1954, *19*, 147–157.

Curtis, J. F., Segmenting the stream of speech. Lincolnland Conference on Dialectology, Charleston, Ill., April, 1968.

Darley, F. L., and Winitz, H. Age of first word: Review of research. *Journal of Speech and Hearing Disorders*, 1961, *26*, 271–290.

Darwin, C. Biographical sketch of an infant. *Mind*, 1877, *7*, 291–294.

Fairbanks, G. *Voice and articulation drillbook*. New York: Harper & Row, 1940.

Fairbanks, G., and Grubb, P. A psychophysical investi-

REFERENCES

gation of vowel formants. *Journal of Speech and Hearing Research*, 1961, *4*, 203–219.

Fischer-Jørgensen, E. What can the new techniques of acoustic phonetics contribute to linguistics? In Saporta, S. (Ed.) & Bastian, J. R. (Assist. Ed.), *Psycholinguistics, a book of readings*. New York: Holt, Rinehart and Winston, 1962.

Ginsburg, N. Conditioned vocalization in the budgerigar. *Journal of Comparative Physiological Psychology*, 1960, *53*, 183–186.

Girardeau, F. Personal communication. 1961.

Gleason, H. A. *An introduction to descriptive linguistics*, Revised. New York: Holt, Rinehart and Winston, 1961.

Grosslight, J. H., Harrison, P. C., and Weiser, C. M. Reinforcement control of vocal responses in the Mynah bird (Growla Religiosa). *Psychological Record*, 1962, *12*, 193–201.

Halle, M. Phonology in generative grammar. In Fodor, J. A., and Katz, J. J. (Eds.), *The structure of language*. Englewood Cliffs, N.J.: Prentice-Hall, 1964.

Harms, I. E., and Spiker, C. C. Factors associated with the performance of young children on intelligence scales and tests of speech development. *Journal of Genetic Psychology*, 1959, *94*, 3–22.

Hockett, C. F. *A course in modern linguistics*. New York: Macmillan, 1958.

Irwin, O. C. The profile as a visual devise for indicating central tendencies in speech data. *Child Development*, 1941, *12*, 111–120.

Irwin, O. C. Developmental status of speech sounds of 10 feeble-minded children. *Child Development*, 1942, *13*, 29–39.

Irwin, O. C. Reliability of infant speech sound data. *Journal of Speech Disorders*, 1945, *10*, 227–235.

Irwin, O. C. Infant speech: Equations for consonant-vowel ratios. *Journal of Speech Disorders*, 1946, *11*, 177–180.

Irwin, O. C. Development of speech during infancy: Curve of phonemic frequencies. *Journal of Experimental Psychology*, 1947, *37*, 187–193. (a)

Irwin, O. C. Infant speech: The problem of variability. *Journal of Speech Disorders*, 1947, *12*, 173–176. (b)

Irwin, O. C. Infant speech: Variability and the problem of diagnosis. *Journal of Speech Disorders*, 1947, *12*, 287–289. (c)

Irwin, O. C. Infant speech: Consonantal sounds according to place of articulation. *Journal of Speech Disorders*, 1947, *12*, 397–401. (d)

Irwin, O. C. Infant speech: Consonant sounds according to manner of articulation. *Journal of Speech Disorders*, 1947, *12*, 402–404. (e)

Irwin, O. C. Infant speech: Speech sound development
of sibling and only infants. *Journal of Experimental
Psychology,* 1948, *38,* 600–602. (a)

Irwin, O. C. Infant speech: Development of vowel
sounds. *Journal of Speech and Hearing Disorders,*
1948, *13,* 31–34. (b)

Irwin, O. C. Infant speech: The effect of family occupational status and of age on use of sound types.
Journal of Speech and Hearing Disorders, 1948, *13,*
224–226. (c)

Irwin, O. C. Infant speech: The effect of family occupational status and of age on sound frequency.
Journal of Speech and Hearing Disorders, 1948, *13,*
320–323. (d)

Irwin, O. C. Infant speech: Consonantal position.
Journal of Speech and Hearing Disorders, 1951, *16,*
159–161.

Irwin, O. C. Infant speech: Effect of systematic reading
of stories. *Journal of Speech and Hearing Research,*
1960, *3,* 187–190.

Irwin, O. C., and Chen, H. P. Infant speech sounds and
intelligence. *Journal of Speech Disorders,* 1945, *10,*
293–296.

Irwin, O. C., and Chen, H. P. Infant speech: Vowel and
consonant frequency. *Journal of Speech Disorders,*
1946, *11,* 123–125. (a)

Irwin, O. C., and Chen, H. P. Development of speech
during infancy: Curve of phonemic types. *Journal
of Experimental Psychology,* 1946, *36,* 431–436. (b)

Kelleher, R. T., and Gollub, L. R. A review of positive
conditioned reinforcement. *Journal of Experimental
Analysis of Behavior,* 1962, Supplement to *5,* 543–
597.

Keller, F. S., and Schoenfeld, W. N. *A systematic text
in the science of behavior.* New York: Appleton-
Century-Crofts, 1950.

Kenyon, J. S., and Knott, T. A. *A pronouncing dictionary
of American English.* Springfield, Massachusetts:
G&C Merriam, 1953.

Kimble, G. A. *Hilgard and Marquis' conditioning and
learning,* 2nd ed. New York: Appleton-Century-
Crofts, 1961.

Kozhevnikov, V., and Chistovich, L. Speech: Articulation and perception. English translation from Russian.
Washington, D. C.: U. S. Department of Commerce,
1965.

Krasner, L. Studies of the conditioning of verbal behavior. *Psychological Bulletin,* 1958, *55,* 148–170.

Ladefoged, P. *A phonetic study of West African languages.* London: Cambridge University Press, 1964.

Lane, H. Operant control of vocalizing in the chicken.
Journal of Experimental Analysis of Behavior, 1961,
4, 171–177.

Lehiste, Ilse. *Personal communication.* 1960.

Lenneberg, E. H. *Biological Foundations of Language.* New York: Wiley, 1967.

Lenneberg, E. H., Rebelsky, F. G., and Nichols, I. A. The vocalizations of infants born to deaf and to hearing parents. *Vita Human,* 1965, *8,* 23–37.

Leopold, W. F. *Speech development of a bilingual child.* Vol. 2, Evanston, Ill.: Northwestern University Press, 1947.

Lewis, D. J. Partial reinforcement: A selective review of the literature since 1950. *Psychological Bulletin,* 1960, *57,* 1–28.

Lewis, M. M. *Infant speech: A study of the beginnings of language.* New York: Humanities Press, 1951.

Liberman, A. M., Cooper, F. S., Shankweiler, D. P., and Studdert-Kennedy, M. Perception of the speech code. *Psychological Review,* 1967, *74,* 431–461.

Linbloom, B. Spectrographic study of vowel reduction. *Journal of the Acoustical Society of America,* 1963, *35,* 1773–1781.

Lind, J. (Ed.). Newborn infant cry. *Acta Paediatrica Scandinavica,* 1965, Supplement *163.*

Lisker, L., and Abramson, A. S. Some effects of context on voice onset time in English stops. *Language and Speech,* 1967, *10,* 1–28.

Lotz, J., Abramson, A. S., Gerstman, L. J., Ingemann, F., and Nemser, W. J. The perception of English stops by speakers of English, Spanish, Hungarian, and Thai: A tape cutting experiment. *Language and Speech,* 1960, *3,* 71–77.

Lynip, A. The use of magnetic devices in the collection and analysis of the preverbal utterances of an infant. *Genetic Psychology Monographs,* 1951, *44,* 221–262.

McCarthy, D. Organismic interpretation of infant vocalizations. *Child Development,* 1952, *23,* 273–280.

McCurry, W. H., and Irwin, O. C. A study of word approximations in the spontaneous speech of infants. *Journal of Speech and Hearing Disorders,* 1953, *18,* 133–139.

Miller, N. E., and Dollard, J. *Social learning and imitation.* New Haven: Yale University Press, 1941.

Molliver, M. E. Operant control of vocal behavior in the cat. *Journal of Experimental Analysis of Behavior,* 1963, *6,* 197–202.

Mowrer, O. H. Speech development in the young child: 1. The autism theory of speech development and some clinical applications. *Journal of Speech and Hearing Disorders,* 1952, *17,* 263–268.

Mowrer, O. H. Hearing and speaking: An analysis of language learning. *Journal of Speech and Hearing Disorders,* 1958, *23,* 143–152.

Mowrer, O. H. *Learning Theory and Behavior.* New York: Wiley, 1960.

Myers, J. L. Secondary reinforcements: A review of recent experimentation. *Psychological Bulletin*, 1958, *55*, 284–301.

Myklebust, H. R. Babbling and echolalia in language theory. *Journal of Speech and Hearing Disorders*, 1957, *22*, 356–360.

Nakazima, S. A comparative study of the speech development of Japanese and American English in childhood (1)—a comparison of the developments of voices at the prelinguistic period. *Studia Phonologica*, 1962, *2*, 27–46.

Öhman, S. E. G. Coarticulation in VCV utterances: Spectrographic measurements. *Journal of the Acoustical Society of America*, 1966, *39*, 151–168.

Peterson, G. E. Parameters of vowel quality. *Journal of Speech and Hearing Research*, 1961, *4*, 10–29.

Peterson, G. E., and Coxe, M. S. The vowels [e] and [o] in American speech. *Quarterly Journal of Speech*, 1953, *39*, 33–41.

Postal, P. M. *Aspects of phonological theory*. New York: Harper & Row, 1968.

Rheingold, H. L., Gewirtz, J. L., and Ross, H. W. Social conditioning of vocalizations in the infant. *Journal of Comparative Physiology Psychology*, 1959, *52*, 68–73.

Salzinger, K. Experimental manipulation of verbal behavior: A review. *Journal of Genetic Psychology*, 1959, *61*, 65–94.

Salzinger, K., and Waller, M. B. The operant control of vocalization in the dog. *Journal of Experimental Analysis of Behavior*, 1962, *5*, 383–389.

Sidowski, J. B., Kass, W., Wilson, H. Cue and secondary reinforcement effects with children. *Journal of Experimental Psychology*, 1965, *69*, 340–342.

Skinner, B. F. *Verbal Behavior*. New York: Appleton-Century-Crofts, 1957.

Spence, K. W. *Behavior Theory and Conditioning*. New Haven: Yale University Press, 1956.

Spiker, C. C. Research methods in children's learning. Chapter 9 in P. H. Mussen (Ed.), *Handbook of Research Methods in Child Development*. New York: Wiley, 1960.

Spiker, C. C. and Irwin, O. C. The relationship between IQ and indices of infant speech sound development. *Journal of Speech and Hearing Disorders*, 1949, *14*, 335–343.

Stevens, K. N., and House, A. S. Perturbations of vowel articulations by consonantal context: an acoustical study. *Journal of Speech and Hearing Research*, 1963, *6*, 111–128.

Stevenson, H. W. Piaget, behavior theory, and intelligence. Chapter 7 in Kessen, W., and Kuhlman, C. (Eds.) Thought in the Young Child, *Monographs of* the *Society for Research in Child Development*, 1962, *27* (Serial no. 83).

Todd, G. A., and Palmer, B. Social reinforcement of infant babbling. *Child Development*, 1968, *39*, 591–596.

Trager, G. L., and Smith, H. L. *An outline of English structure, studies in linguistics, occasional papers 3*, Washington: American Council of Learned Societies, 1957.

Voelker, C. H. Phonetic distribution in formal American pronunciation. *Journal of the Acoustical Society of America*, 1934, *5*, 242–246.

Weir, R. H. Some questions on the child's learning of phonology. In Smith, F., and Miller, G.A. (Eds.) *The genesis of language*. Cambridge: MIT Press, 1966.

Weisberg, P. Social and nonsocial conditioning of infant vocalizations. *Child Development*, 1963, *34*, 377–388.

Winitz, H. Spectrographic study of infant vowels. *Journal of Genetic Psychology*, 1960, *96*, 171–181.

Winitz, H. Repetitions in the vocalizations and speech of children in the first two years of life. *Journal of Speech and Hearing Disorders Monograph Supplement 7*, 1961, 55–62.

Winitz, H., and Irwin, O. C. Infant speech: Consistency with age. *Journal of Speech and Hearing Research*, 1958, *1*, 245–249. (a)

Winitz, H., and Irwin, O. C. Syllabic and phonetic structure of infants' early words. *Journal of Speech and Hearing Research*, 1958, *1*, 250–256. (b)

Wyckoff, L. B. The role of observing responses in discrimination learning, Part I. *Psychological Review*, 1952, *59*, 431–442.

Wyckoff, L. B. Toward a quantitative theory of secondary reinforcement. *Psychological Review*, 1959, *66*, 68–78.

Wyckoff, L. B., Sidowski, J., and Chambliss, D. J. An experimental study of the relationship between secondary reinforcing and cue effects of a stimulus. *Journal of Comparative Physiological Psychology*, 1958, *51*, 103–109.

Zimmerman, D. W. Durable secondary reinforcement: Method and theory. *Psychological Review*, 1957, *64*, 373–383.

2

PHONETIC
AND
PHONEMIC
DEVELOPMENT

One concept in speech pathology that has remained unchallenged over the years involves the chronological development of speech sounds. We are traditionally taught that the competency to "produce correctly" each of the English sounds is acquired at a certain age level. The phrase "produce correctly" refers to the ability to make specific articulatory or phonetic movements in ways acceptable to a linguistic community. When viewed in this way, speech sound development involves a time-dependent mastery of motor responses. When mastery is not achieved by a certain age level, causal interpretations are often made to explain the absence of describable motor responses. At this time I shall not try to pinpoint or define the reasons why children do not achieve or produce certain sounds at a given age level. I simply wish here to clarify the meaning of an appropriate production.

The chronological development of speech sounds, then, has been interpreted to mean the developmental acquisition of the speech sounds of the language. However, something quite different, or at least more complex, seems to be taking place: the learning of a language with all its rules or subsystems of rules. One subsystem that is being acquired is that of phonology—that is, the learning of the contrastive elements of the community language. This is an entirely different concept from that of phonetic production learning.

Learning a system of phonemes first requires, to

be sure, ability to produce phonetic features (voicing, nasality, etc.) of the phonemes. As far as we can now ascertain, however, the phonetic productions are, for the most part, already in the child's speech repertoire at the time he starts to learn the phoneme system of English. (See pages 11–14, Chap. 1 for a more detailed discussion.)

Before describing the learning of a phoneme system, I will summarize the chronological development of speech sounds as well as the order of frequently misarticulated sounds. And before attempting to do either, I shall comment on procedures used in making phonetic transcriptions.

Note on Transcription

The studies to be reviewed have, for the most part, used a broad transcription procedure. In only a few instances has a distinction been made among the several allophones of the tested phonemes. For example, for the /r/ phoneme particular attention has been paid to the [ɝ], [r], and [ɚ] allophones. In many instances, however, phonetic variations are not recorded. For example, [kʰ] and [k] variations of the /k/ phoneme and the [l] and [ɫ] (the "dark" [l], a lateral made with dorsovelar coarticulation which usually occurs in the final position of a syllable in English) variations of the /l/ phoneme are usually not "marked" on test protocols.

Often, individual phonemes are examined in a variety of contexts—e.g., blends and singles tested in several word positions. Mastery of the phoneme is defined as the correct production of a preselected proportion of the total number tested, although interpretations of these data, as mentioned, usually involve phonetic inferences. As we will see shortly, this procedure is not the way a linguist establishes the phonemes of a language.

When phonetic variations are not considered, two possible sources of error may result: (a) articulation tests may sample different allophones of a phoneme as a function of the chance selection of words[1] and the position of the sound in a word[1] and (b) the child's alterations (complementary distribution or free variation) do not always correspond to those of the adult, so that some disagreement among examiners may result unless scoring procedures are made uniform prior to testing. With regard to this latter point, it is conceivable that one investigator may judge, for example, a child's aspiration of the [k] in the /sk/ phoneme cluster, as produced in [skʰeɪt], incorrect while another investigator may score it as correct; a retracted [s̩] in *soup* might be scored as correct by one examiner and as incorrect by another, even though both examiners

---

[1] A detailed discussion of articulation test variability is given in Chapter 4.

would probably score [ṣ] as correct if evaluated in the word *purse* ([pɝ·ṣ]).

Voegelin and Adams (1934, p. 108) were first to comment about this problem.

> Phonetic transcription is so flexible that more than the significant sounds may be recorded if desired. Some initial experimentation was carried out in this respect in recording the speech of children. It was found that the variation within a phoneme is greater for children than for standard adult speech. For example, where an adult will always pronounce an initial plosive (*p*, *t*, or *k*) aspirated, that is with a slight puff of air after the consonant proper has been said, children sometimes do this, sometimes pronounce these plosives unaspirated, and in a few amusing cases, even glottalize the plosive, that is the release of the closure made by the tongue is accompanied by a synchronous opening of the glottis. Such glottalized plosives do not occur in normal English speech but are characteristic of many American Indian languages. However, so long as children would pronounce *t*, for example, without voicing it, it was counted as correct. The analysis does not take into account variations within the phoneme, such as lack of aspiration, glottalization, retroflex formation, and relative forward and backward position. On the other hand, when the child's articulation of *t* was voiced, for example, and therefore was confused with the phoneme *d*, then this fact was entered into our analytic record. (The chief exception to this is our consideration of the glottal stop which is not phonemic in English but extraordinarily conspicuous in the speech of children.) In short, our treatment is phonemic, and variations within the phoneme which children make are so slight that they would probably not even be observed by parents and teachers in general.

Since items in articulation tests do not always include the same allophones of each of the phonemes tested, and since rules for the assessment of phonetic alterations are not always clearly agreed on, specific differences in the findings of comparable studies can occur. These errors of transcription and test construction may not be very serious in judging phoneme mastery if (*a*) correct production of the allophones of a phoneme is learned at the same or nearly the same age level, and/or (*b*) high interobserver reliability is demonstrated with regard to the phonetic differences that are to be included or ignored. Examiners trained to ignore certain differences such as aspiration may, moreover, agree among themselves, yet these subtle agreements may not be conveyed to examiners trained at other schools. Variability among investigations may thus increase.

Descriptive Studies

In this section a review of the findings of several developmental and clinical studies is made. "Developmental" here refers to studies in which the children were unselected with regard to articulatory errors; "clinical" refers to the study of subjects (children and adults) judged to be defective in articulation.

Developmental Studies

Three major studies on the development of speech sounds of American English-speaking children have been made. These investigations were conducted by Wellman and others (1931), by Poole (1934), later under the married name of Davis (1938), and most recently by Templin (1957). The discussion will include the findings for consonants only because vowels, for the most part, are mastered early and are generally found not to be defective.

TESTING PROCEDURES. Using pictorial stimuli and questions, Wellman and others (1931) elicited 133 speech sounds from 204 children at the Iowa Child Welfare Preschool. In this investigation a given age group included children whose birthdate fell within six months on either side of the investigated chronological age. The children ranged in age from two to six years and had a mean Stanford-Binet IQ of 115. The children were probably drawn from higher socioeconomic levels.

Poole (1934) studied the ability of 140 preschool children to articulate 23 consonants as tested in 62 items. Single-word responses were elicited by means of objects, pictures, and questions. Poole, selecting children between 2.5 and 8.5 years, defined a given age group as including children whose birthdate fell within six months on either side of the investigated chronological age.

Templin (1957) investigated the articulatory responses of 240 male and 240 female singletons, 30 of each sex at each of eight discrete age levels from three to eight years. She elicited 176 sound elements from each child in utterances that were either spontaneous (triggered by pictorial stimuli) or repeated. In the investigations by Wellman and others and in those by Templin, articulatory test items included, in addition to the unit consonants of English, consonant clusters, vowels, and diphthongs.

RESULTS. The findings for the three studies are presented in Table 2.1. In this table the earliest age is indicated at which a given percent of the children under test articulated correctly each consonant sound. In the Wellman and others and Templin investigations 75 percent of the children had to articulate a sound correctly before it was considered to be mastered. In the Poole study the performance criterion was more stringent; all of

[Table 2.1] Comparison of the Ages at Which Subjects Correctly Produced Specific Consonant Sounds in the Templin, the Wellman, and the Poole Studies*

Age Correctly Produced

Sound	TEMPLIN (1957)	WELLMAN AND OTHERS (1931)	POOLE (1934)
m	3	3	3.5
n	3	3	4.5
ŋ	3	—[a]	4.5
p	3	4	3.5
f	3	3	5.5
h	3	3	3.5
w	3	3	3.5
j	3.5	4	4.5
k	4	4	4.5
b	4	3	3.5
d	4	5	4.5
g	4	4	4.5
r	4	5	7.5
s	4.5	5	7.5[b]
ʃ	4.5	—[c]	6.5
tʃ	4.5	5	—[c]
t	6	5	4.5
θ	6	—[a]	7.5[b]
v	6	5	6.5[b]
l	6	4	6.5
ð	7	—[c]	6.5
z	7	5	7.5[b]
ʒ	7	—[c]	6.5
dʒ	7	6	—[c]
hw	—[a]	—[a]	7.5

* In the Wellman and others, and Templin studies a sound was considered mastered if it was articulated correctly by 75 percent of the subjects. The criterion of correct production was 100 percent in the Poole study.

[a] Sound was tested but was not produced correctly by 75 percent of the subjects at the oldest age tested. In the Wellman data the "hw" reached the percentage criterion at 5 but not at 6 years, the medial "ŋ" reached it at 3, and the initial and medial "θ" and "ð" at 5 years.

[b] Poole (Davis, 1938), in a study of 20,000 preschool and school-age children reports the following shifts: "s" and "z" appear at 5.5 years, then disappear and return later at 7.5 years or above; "θ" appears at 6.5 years and "v" at 5.5 years.

[c] Sound not tested or not reported.

SOURCE: Templin, M. C. Certain language skills in children, their development and interrelationships. *Institute of Child Welfare, Monograph Series*, No. 26, 54. Minneapolis: University of Minnesota Press, 1957.

the children had to articulate a sound correctly before it was considered to be learned. In each investigation the phoneme was considered to be mastered if the unit sound was correctly uttered in all of the word positions tested.

Referring to Table 2.1 again, we may observe that the Templin findings are listed in chronological order and are used as a base of reference for the other two studies. Despite the fact that two different percentage criteria were used, the three studies agree to a significant degree in the age placement of the sounds. Templin (1957, p. 54) reported, "There is complete agreement in the age placement on five of the seventeen sounds reported in all three investigations, a spread of one year on six sounds, and a spread of two or more on six sounds." We may note from Table 2.1 that the six phonemes for which there was, according to Templin, the greatest discrepancy were /f/, /r/, /s/, /t/, /l/, and /z/. (I would also add the /ʃ/ phoneme to this list.) An interesting observation (as we shall see) is that many of the foregoing seven sounds are among those most frequently misarticulated by children. At the present time we are unable to tell why this is true.

The findings of the three studies suggest that "phoneme" development is correlated with age in that (a) some sounds are mastered earlier than others and (b) most sounds are produced correctly by eight years of age. No data yet indicate, however, that this sequence is an orderly one—i.e., mastery in producing any given sound invariably precedes and follows mastery in producing every other sound.

Examination of Templin's findings (see Table 2.1, column 2) suggests that stops (with the exception of /t/) are mastered at an early age. The continuants (with the exception of /f/ and /h/) are mastered relatively late. The voicing feature often separates cognates by two or more years. Note in particular that /f/ is mastered at three and /v/ at six, /d/ at four and /t/ at six, /ʃ/ at four and a half and /ʒ/ at seven, and /tʃ/ at four and a half and /dʒ/ at seven. There is also considerable age variability among the glides. However, the findings indicate that development of phonetic features (point and manner of articulation) and age bear no systematic relation to each other. It is true that in general, when all sounds are considered, certain features are used more appropriately than others by a greater proportion of the children at the early age levels.[2] For ex-

---

[2] The term *appropriate usage* is used here and elsewhere to mean correct production of a phonetic feature in a feature complex (phoneme or phone) when the feature complex is defined as a correct production, i.e., the fricative feature produced in [s] would be regarded as appropriately used whereas the fricative feature in a lateral lisp would be regarded as inappropriately used. Thus, 100 percent appropriate usage of the fricative feature means correct production of all English fricative sounds. A child, for example, who substitutes [θ] for [s], [s] for [ʃ], and so on would not, according to Templin's (1957) and Menyuk's (1968) analyses, be regarded as having mastered frication even if further analysis shows that the fricative feature is contrastive.

ample, nasals and stops show a greater frequency of appropriate usage at an early age than fricatives and glides (Templin, 1957 and Menyuk, 1968). Although phonetic features are not bound by age restrictions, certain complexes of features (the respective phones or phonemes of the community language) are. A theory about appropriate usage which would argue for greater difficulty in the additivity of features would be a theory about phonemic acquisition or the articulation of phonetic complexes not feature acquisition. A description of phonemic acquisition will be given shortly.

There is an additional argument, presented in Menyuk's (1968) article, that would favor a maturational interpretation. It is the argument about language universals applied to phonetic acquisition. The concepts and principles of linguistic universals, which are touched on later in this chapter, cannot be developed here in any detail. It is sufficient for the purposes of the following discussion to think of linguistic universals as those items and rules that are the basic elements of the many natural languages.

Menyuk proposed that a universal ordering of phonetic units is possible and, to prove this thesis, she compared the development of certain distinctive features for American and Japanese children. Although the children studied spoke different languages, she found remarkable similarities in the order of development for several distinctive features: nasal, grave, voice, diffuse, continuant, and strident. (These features are explained below.) Both groups of children developed these features in the order given above.

There are a number of reasons why the author cannot accept Menyuk's findings as valid: a) Although the analysis for the Japanese children included only the ages one to three, the findings for the American children (which were based on Wellman's 1931 study [personal communique]) began at the age of two years and six months. b) The English analysis was based on appropriate usage in words, the Japanese on correct production in syllables. Thus response acquisition and response association were confounded. (See p. 304.) (These first two limitations were cited by Menyuk.) c) The age level differences show that the Japanese children mastered all features at three years, or at about the time the American children first began to show some progress. d) The interpretation of Wellman's data by Menyuk is open to question. Wellman reports sound mastery by word position and this is not completely taken into account by Menyuk. The sound element [-ŋ] is not mastered by five years, the terminal point of Menyuk's analysis, and [-m], [-n], and [-ŋ-] are not mastered until three years, yet 75 percent of the nasals (The figure should probably be 66 percent or two of three nasals.) are reported as correctly uttered by two years and six months. e) Menyuk used only six features, e.g., voicing was used but not unvoicing. Bipolarity, as a concept, does not imply equivalent development of binary phonetic values, when used simply to describe phonetic usage. f) Finally, the problem of analysis and comparison among languages, when the measure is appropriate usage and not phonemic contrasting or the abstract ordering of phonological rules, is a sticky one. For example, features may correlate differently for different languages. I do not mean to imply that distinctive feature principles have no use in the formal analysis of natural languages. My concern is for their validity in the analysis of phonetic development when biological interpretations are made.

Comparative data on language acquisition are critically needed. But, if we are to make statements about the biological bases of speech sound development, some formal criteria must be developed that are inherently meaningful. Most likely these will include statements about the physiological mechanism as a supplement to behavioral observations. Otherwise we may find ourselves trying to explain confusing bits of data such as the fricatives appearing late in two different languages although specific sounds or phonemes may be unordered (giving, for example, [s] early in one language and late in another).

Further, phonetic development in words should be distinguished from phonetic development prior to word learning. The former may, in part, have a physiological basis, the latter a physiological basis only in the sense that it supplements, clarifies or perhaps helps to explain, in part, an abstract phonological rule when maturation is sufficient.

Thus a valid inference from the data presented by Wellman and others, Poole, and Templin is that maturation of one or more physiological processes is not of great significance in determining the age-by-age development of consonants after age level three in the sense that maturation determines occurrence of phonetic features or in many instances the occurrence of appropriate usage of phonetic features.

A maturational theory that stresses sequence of stages also appears invalid when applied to phonetic development in words. In motor development the child often proceeds through an orderly sequence of acts, each learned act following a previously learned act. Presumably earlier acts are requisites for later acts, and each act must await maturation of certain physiological and neurological processes. We know that the child turns over before he sits up, sits up before he crawls, crawls before he walks. Although early motor acts have not been established as essential for late motor acts, the developmental sequence is fairly orderly. No comparable sequence of orderly development is apparent for phonemes. Examination of Appendix Four of Templin's study (1957, pp. 162–165) reveals that sounds that are not mastered until seven years are, nevertheless, uttered by a good proportion of the children at age three.[3] For example, the phonemes /ð/, /z/, /ʒ/, and /dʒ/ are not mastered by 75 percent of

---

[3] James McLean suggested to the author that there is considerable individual variation in phoneme mastery.

Templin's subjects until seven years of age. All of these sounds, however, occur with some frequency at age three: the lowest percentage of correct utterances is 13.7 percent for /-ʒ-/, and the highest percentage of correct utterances is 55.2 percent for /dʒ-/.

It may seem that we are not being entirely consistent in our approach in that we first report the apparent orderliness of phoneme development as observed by several investigators but then counter that this development, because it is not sequential, is not orderly. From one point of view, phoneme development may be viewed as orderly if one simply defines mastery as the age at which the correct production of all variants of a phoneme in all word positions and contexts is achieved. On the other hand, orderliness may imply that some sounds are acquired earlier than others or, more stringently, that certain phonemes (sounds) must be learned before other phonemes can be learned. The latter seems not to be the case.

The concept of sequential phoneme development is often utilized in clinical work. Thus, a sound error is not viewed as defective if 75 percent of the subjects of a normal population also make the same error. It should be clear that this criterion of phoneme development is nothing more than a statement of average performance by age. It in no way implies that the sequence of development will be the same for all children; it simply establishes criteria, based on normative data, for judging performance at given age levels. If it is used as a sequential developmental test, it may not predict those children who will later need articulatory correction; and if it is used as the sole determinant of sound selection in articulatory correction, it gives little if any specific information about articulatory teaching procedures. More will be said about the use of a developmental articulatory test in Chapter 4.

Clinical Studies

TESTING PROCEDURES. Three investigators, Hall (1938), Roe and Milisen (1942), and Sayler (1949), have systematically identified frequently misarticulated sounds. Hall (1938) studied the frequency of misarticulated sounds for defectively speaking children and adults. The children were initially identified by teachers and ranged in age from 7 years 2 months to 13 years 5 months. The adults were 83 first-year college students who were selected by use of a speech rating scale from a large number of freshmen. The details of this procedure are described in Chapter 3 (pp. 179–180). The articulatory responses were tested in each word position and sentences were used to elicit the responses.

Roe and Milisen (1942) examined the speech sound status of 1989 children in grades one through six from the public schools of nine Indiana cities. Twenty-five consonants and consonant blends were elicited in a total of 66 word positions. Sayler (1949) extended the work of Roe and

Milisen. She tested 1998 pupils in grades seven through twelve selected from six cities in Idaho. The sounds previously studied by Roe and Milisen were elicited in 56 sentences.

RESULTS. The findings for these studies are presented in Table 2.2. In this table the ten sounds most frequently in error are indicated. In some cases the data were analyzed with regard to the percentage of subjects who missed each sound, and in other cases the data were analyzed with regard to the total percentage of errors for each sound. When the combined findings of the studies listed in Table 2.2 are compared with the

[Table 2.2] The Ten Most Frequently Misarticulated Consonants as Reported in Several Studies*

Hall (children) (1939)		Hall (adults) (1939)		Roe & Milisen (Grade I) (1942)		Roe and Milisen (Grade VI) (1942)	
SOUND	% OF S's	SOUND	% OF S's	SOUND	% OF S's	SOUND	% OF S's
s	90.5	s	83.1	dʒ	91.2	z	84.5
z	47.6	z	75.9	z	88.1	dʒ	70.7
ʃ	47.6	dʒ	48.2	d	70.1	d	68.8
tʃ	42.9	ʃ	37.3	g	69.1	t	55.6
dʒ	33.3	tʃ	34.9	θ	68.8	hw	44.7
ʒ	28.6	hw	28.9	ð	57.3	θ	45.1
hw	23.8	ʒ	10.8	v	53.0	ð	41.4
θ	23.8	ð	10.8	s	48.9	g	39.7
r	19.0	ŋ	9.6	t	45.7	v	38.4
ð	9.5	θ	7.2	b	26.0	s	32.8

Roe and Milisen (grades I–VI) (1942)		Roe and Milisen (all grades and excluding voiced or voiceless errors) (1942)		Sayler (all grades) (1949)		Sayler (all grades and excluding voiced or voiceless errors) (1949)	
SOUND	% OF ERROR	SOUND	% OF ERROR	SOUND	% OF ERROR	SOUND	% OF ERROR
z	45.8	θ	30.3	hw	29.6	z	17.4
hw	40.0	s	19.7	z	28.9	v	9.3
θ	30.3	t	14.0	ð	19.6	tʃ	9.3
dʒ	30.2	ð	13.2	v	12.6	ŋ	9.2
d	25.0	z	12.4	tʃ	9.3	ð	9.0
s	19.9	dʒ	7.2	ŋ	9.2	hw	7.1
g	18.5	tʃ	6.4	f	3.1	f	3.1
ð	16.5	r	5.9	g	2.8	s	2.7
v	16.0	v	5.6	s	2.7	θ	2.6
t	14.0	k	4.7	θ	2.6	g	2.4

* The percentage of subjects making errors or the percentage of errors on each sound is given. The sound was considered in error if it was misarticulated in any word position tested.

art. altered

findings obtained by Templin (column 2 of Table 2.1) there appears to be some "agreement" between the acquisition of phonemes acquired late (four years and beyond) and the most frequently defective phonemes—namely, /s/, /z/, /θ/, /ð/, /ʃ/, /ʒ/, /tʃ/, /dʒ/, /v/, /r/, and [hw]. The phonetic feature most common to these sounds is, in general, frication or continuation. This feature, however, is for the most part not lost in the error sound; the variation is one of place of articulation not necessarily absence of frication, e.g., for /s/ one hears /θ/, /ʃ/, or [ḷʰ]; for /ʃ/ the frequent errors are /tʃ/ /s/ and [ḷʰ]; and for /θ/ the child usually substitutes /t/, /f/ and /s/. It can be seen that in the majority of cases the place of articulation is altered, but in a few instances frication is absent as shown by the frequent /t/ for /θ/ for the examples above (Van Riper and Irwin, 1958). In many of my own observations the /t/ substitution for /θ/ is a highly aspirated /t/, having fricative qualities. Other phonemes acquired late, such as /l/, /b/, /d/, /g/, /t/, and /k/, are not frequently found defective. When the results of Roe and Milisen (all errors—grades I through VI, column 5 of Table 2.2) are compared with Templin's, all of the most frequently defective sounds are shown as not mastered until four years. Three sounds, /d/, /s/, and /g/, are mastered by four and a half years, and seven sounds, /z/, [hw], /θ/, /dʒ/, /ð/, /v/, /t/, are not mastered until six years or beyond. Thus there seems to be a relationship between the late-appearing sounds and the most frequently defective sounds; however, the relationship is a qualified one in that frequently defective sounds are late-appearing sounds, but not all late-appearing sounds are frequently defective.

This, then, concludes our discussion on the descriptive studies of speech sound development. Their results are generally interpreted to mean that distinctive speech sound productions develop at successive age levels. In the following section a different point of view is presented. Speech sound development data, as we have already argued, do not give evidence to support hypotheses about *orderly* sequences of speech sound development if this is interpreted to mean that some sound productions are acquired before other sound productions.

Phoneme Acquisition

Phonemic acquisition involves the learning of the phoneme system of the community language—the functional units of the language that signal semantic distinctiveness. It also involves the learning of the acceptable phoneme sequences of the language (e.g., in English /sk/ is an acceptable initial word blend while /zk/ is not, and /ŋ/ occurs only in medial and final word positions). As Carroll (1964, pp. 13–14) succinctly states, "phonemes are the building blocks out of which meaningful or grammatically functional forms are composed; furthermore, they provide the critical basis for differentiating among these forms."

As English-speaking adults we have learned to distinguish between those sounds that are "different" and those sounds that are the "same." We learned these distinctions as children. This learning process was, of course, a gradual one. By this statement we mean simply that prior to the learning of the phoneme system of our language the child possesses an approximation of the adult phoneme system; that is, his phoneme system, though similar, does not correspond in a one-to-one fashion with the adult phoneme system.

Simplified Example

We think that an example of a child's phoneme system will be helpful here. Let us assume that a two-year-old child has learned the following six words:

1. [da] and [pa] for *dog*
2. [sa] for *there*
3. [æ t] for *up*
4. [fa] for *father*
5. [æ z] and [æ s] for *open*
6. [ta] for *cat*

From this record it is apparent that there are two vocoids[4] ([a] and [æ]) and six nonvocoids ([d], [p], [t], [s], [f], and [z]). The vocoids are in complementary distribution; that is, [æ] is in the initial position and [a] is in the final position. Two pairs of nonvocoids are in free variation: [d] and [p], and [z] and [s]. The initial sound contrasts are [d] or [p], [s], [f] and [t]; and the final sound contrasts are [s] or [z] and [t]. The two phones in complementary distribution are assigned to the same phoneme according to the rule of phonetic similarity. Thus the child may be said to have five phonemes, and these may be arbitrarily designated as /d/, /z/, /f/, /t/, and /a/.

PHONEMES	ALLOPHONES OF EACH PHONEME
/d/	[d] and [p]
/s/	[s] and [z]
/f/	[f]
/t/	[t]
/a/	[a] and [æ]

---

[4] Vocoids refer to vowel-like (syllabic) sounds and nonvocoids refer to consonant-like sounds. These two terms are generally restricted to phones. The terms vowels and consonants are, technically speaking, restricted to phonemes.

This imaginary child will acquire additional words, assuming that he is continually exposed to English and that he is normal in all other ways. This means that the phoneme contrasts just described will change, eventually conforming with the phoneme system of English. Thus the eight sounds listed above will be redistributed to form eight different classes or phonemes. In addition, new phonemes will be added.

Phoneme system learning is indeed a complex and involved process. Not very much is known about how it takes place. Later we will present some hypotheses and also consider ways to approach the study of this process. However, before proceeding it seems advantageous to discuss some of the descriptive research on child phoneme systems.

First, an account of the learned contrast between two sounds will help toward an understanding of this process. Gleason (1961, pp. 258–260), a famous linguist, tells how his daughter learned the /t/-/k/ contrast:

> My daughter rather early learned to distinguish between labial and non-labial stops. Later she learned to distinguish between voiced and voiceless stops. However, the contrast between /t/ and /k/ was established much later. There was a long period when enough other phonemic contrasts were in use to make her speech intelligible, at least to her parents, but when /t/ and /k/ were not distinguished, the latter occurred, as did various intermediate varieties. Thus *cake* was usually something which impressed adults as /téyt/, but occasionally as /kéyt/ or /téyk/ or even /kéyk/. These several pronunciations sounded different to adults, but apparently were all alike to her. That is, from her own point of view there was one voiceless non-labial stop /T/ which might be pronounced /TéyT/. Of course, *take, Kate* and *Tate* (all of which were in her vocabulary) were pronounced alike, that is, with the same range of variation, and hence all were confused. After some time she discovered the distinction and with increasing precision sorted out the four pronunciations and assigned each to its proper usage. When this had become as regular and consistent as it is in adult speech (we all make occasional slips!), her old phoneme /T/ had given way to /t/ and /k/. She had progressed one more step in acquiring the adult phonemic pattern of English.

Studies of the Normal Child

Several studies of the phoneme system of young English-speaking children have been made.[5] A study by Albright and Albright (1958), for

---

[5] Leopold (1947, 1961); Velten (1943); Albright and Albright (1956, 1958); and Weir (1962). See Jakobson (1941), for a review of studies on non-English-speaking children.

example, describes the consonant and vowel phoneme systems of a one-year-old child, as shown below.

CONSONANTS

	Labial	Apical	Velar	Glottal
Stop	b	d	g	?
Fricative				h
Nasal	m	n		

VOWELS

I	U
ə	
ɛ	ɑ

Phonetic transcription of the child's speech revealed a total of 41 phones, 27 vocoids, and 14 nonvocoids. Albright and Albright (1958, p. 260) stress manner rather than place when they talk about the child's consonantal system:

> This sound system may be described as one based mainly upon stop-continuant and oral-nasal contrasts. The voiced-voiceless contrast of conventional English did not seem to be established. There was a good deal of variation of [p] with [b] and of [t] with [d] in the child's speech, however, indicating that the voiced-voiceless contrast was probably developing.

It is not an easy task to establish the phonemic status of children's sounds. First, the linguist cannot easily ask his young informant whether or not two words (minimal pairs, for example) are the same or different. The child will not readily respond to questions like "How do you say this?" "Is this different from that?" "Do I say it like you now?" (See Gleason, 1961, Chapters 17 and 18.) The linguist simply has to rely upon "recurring utterance units" and, in some cases, responses to pictures. Parents and older siblings may be useful as "translators" (Albright and Albright, 1958).

Second, since the phoneme systems of young children are constantly changing, the sound alterations are extensive and complicated, as evidenced by the glide alterations of a 26-month-old child:

> The sound [w] alternated with [l] initially in utterances, [l] was replaced by zero [φ] following [ʊ] and [ɔ], and [l] was replaced by [o] following [ɛ] and [t]. The sound [ɫ] was an alternate of [l] before back vowels and after back consonants. The sound [w] alternated with [r] before [ɪ] and in clusters of a stop

plus [r]. . . . The sound [w] replaced [r] in combinations
of a vowel plus [r] before [aɪ]. In sequences of [av] plus
[r] followed by a vowel, [r] was replaced by [ə]. Zero
[ɸ] was an alternate of [r] in clusters of a stop plus [r],
and of [r] plus a stop: . . . Syllabic [ɝ] was replaced by
[ʊ́] before a stop: . . . The sounds [o] and [ʊ] replaced
[w] in clusters of a consonant plus [w]. Otherwise [w]
had no alternants and thus showed less alternation than
[l] and [r]. Also, [j] had no alternants (Albright and
Albright, 1958, pp. 259–260).

Studies of the Articulatory
Defective Child

The phoneme systems of young children who show articulatory defects
can also be described by the preceding methods. A description of a
child's phonological patterning may provide a systematic basis for understanding and modifying his articulatory errors. Before elaborating this last
statement, let us illustrate the relation between phonemic patterning and
articulatory errors. Assume we have administered an articulation test to a
young child and have found that the /s/ and /ʃ/ sounds are defective.
Our record indicates that /θ/ and /f/ are frequent substitutions for these
two sounds, while the [ɸ] (voiceless bilabial fricative) often replaces
/θ/. A phonological analysis reveals the situation depicted below, where
we may observe that the child has one phoneme where adult English
demands four.

PHONEMES	ALLOPHONES
/s-θ-ʃ-f/	[s], [θ], [ʃ], [f]
/ɸ/	[ɸ]

PHONETIC VARIATIONS

(a) Initial position: English [s] and [ʃ] →* [θ] and
English [f] → [ɸ]
(b) Medial position: English [f] → [ɸ], and English
[θ], [s], and [ʃ] in free variation
(c) Final position: English [s] and [ʃ] → [f], and
English [f] → [ɸ]

* means "replaced by" or "rewritten as"

The child has failed to partition the /s/, /θ/, /f/, and /ʃ/ phonemes; and
in addition, the [ɸ] sound (voiceless bilabial fricative) has phonemic
status in that it contrasts with /s-θ-f-ʃ/ and with the child's other phonemes. Articulatory training might then proceed along different lines than

those suggested by the usual articulation test, namely (1) the sound errors would be viewed as belonging to a phoneme system, (2) all current contrasts would be evaluated and related to the contrasts of English.

A phoneme with allophones [s], [θ], [f], and [ʃ] suggests that place of articulation has not been partitioned for the voiceless fricatives. Since partitioning has taken place for the voiced fricatives, and since the voiceless-voiced opposition has been learned for other sound types, the features representing place of articulation would be selected for initial training. Discrimination and generalization procedures described in Chapter 5 (pp. 276–285, pp. 288–292) would be employed. Initially the two sounds which show the maximum distinctive feature difference would be selected for discrimination, in this case the /f/-/ʃ/ contrast.

The next task would be to assess the distribution of /ɸ/. Occasionally [ɸ] is substituted for [f] in English (e.g., [hʌmɸrɪ]), but in no instances does it contrast with [f]. When contrastive pairs for our hypothetical example are determined, discrimination training would be given. It would be expected that many of the substitution errors would be corrected with minimal emphasis on production training (see pp. 276–279, Chapter 5).

In one instance the phonemic system of an articulatory defective child has been studied. Haas (1963), an English linguist, was asked to analyze the phonemic system of a six-and-one-half-year-old boy considered to be defective in articulation. The child was found to have seven consonantal phonemes. These phonemes and the allophones of each of the phonemes (in some cases a phoneme has only one allophone) are as follows:[6]

/p/	[p]
/d/	[d̥] (voiceless or devoiced [d]), [d], [b] [t]
/ʔ/	[ʔ]
/ʃ/	[θ], [ʃ], [s], [z̧] (voiceless [z])
/w/	[w], [ɫ^w] (labialized [ɫ])
/m/	[m]
/n/	[n]

The correspondence between the sound system of this child, designated K.C., and the sound system of an adult was also made by Haas. Following is a partial list of this analysis (Haas, 1963, pp. 243–244):

> 1. . . . there seems to be a one-to-one correspondence between K.C.'s [p] and the English /p/. The only exception is alternation with the glottal stop in some positions. The latter may correspond to any English plosive, to /h/, and even to /f/.

[6] We have arbitrarily assigned symbols to each of the seven phonemes, since this was not done by Haas.

2. The . . . lingual plosive [t] or [d̥] seems to correspond to English plosives other than /p/, i.e., to /b, d,
t, g, k/, . . . , also to /f/ . . . Sometimes we hear [b]
but this appears to vary freely with [d, d̥] . . .

3. The . . . sibilant corresponds to English voiceless
lingual fricatives: /θ, s, ʃ, ʒ̥/. It varies in pronunciation
freely between these four, sometimes sounds like a
combination of them. Of the voiced fricatives /ð, z,
ʒ/, there are not enough examples. English /ð/ may
well correspond to . . . [d̥] or [t] . . . , English /z/
to [z̥] . . .

Haas suggests that correction of this child's "articulation errors" may
best be achieved by observing the correspondence between the child's
phoneme system and the phoneme system of English. Those phonological
distinctions that, according to the child's present phoneme system, can be
acquired with least difficulty would be the place to start. Haas (1963,
pp. 244–245) recommends the following program:

> . . . the most important tasks would seem to be (a) to
> extend the range of distinctive articulatory positions (at
> first among the voiceless consonants with which he is
> familiar), (b) to introduce him to nonlingual fricatives
> as distinct from plosives, (c) to introduce the voiced-
> voiceless distinction.

In some cases articulatory errors may affect systematically those grammatical forms present in the child's language, or conversely, the child's
formation of grammatical structures may result in articulatory errors. This
problem has been given some preliminary attention by Applegate (1961).

Before giving an account of Applegate's findings, we must first define
the terms *morpheme, morph,* and *allomorph.* A morpheme is a minimum
unit of meaning or a minimum unit of grammatical significance in the
utterance of a language. These minimum units generally consist of short
sequences of phonemes, sometimes they consist of just one phoneme. For
example, the word *boys* consists of two morphemes, *boy* and *s.* The word
/bɔɪ/ means a class of individuals of the male sex, presumably young in
age. The /z/, which is not spoken alone in English, is not a word, yet it
does signal meaning. The meaning of /z/ is that it denotes plurality. We
know of two other common phonemes or sequences of phonemes that
indicate plurality. They are, of course, /s/ and /əz/. Thus, the plural
morpheme has three common morphs: /-z -s -əz/. The plural morpheme
may be transcribed as {-Z}; that is, {-Z} is a base form for /-z -s -əz/, just
as /k/ is a base form for [kʰ] and [k]. The {-Z} morpheme describes a
set of elements called *morphs.* Since the three morphs described belong to
the {-Z} morpheme, they are *allomorphs* of the morpheme {-Z}.

These three plural morphs are phonologically conditioned. This statement simply means that we can describe the distribution of these three morphs, or that these three morphs are predictable. The distributional facts are as follows: /-s/ occurs only after /p/, /t/, /k/, /f/, and /θ/, e.g., *cats, cups*; /-əz/ occurs only after /s/, /z/, /ʃ/, /ʒ/, /tʃ/, and /dʒ/, e.g., *bushes, buzzes*; and /-z/ occurs after all other consonants and vowels, e.g., *boys, girls*.

Morphology, then, is the subsystem of language which describes the morphemes, the allomorphs of each morpheme, and how each is distributed. From our brief description of the plural morpheme we do not expect the reader to have an understanding of morphology. However, the following list of English morphemes may help to give the reader a "feeling" for English morphology:

(*a*) the progressive morpheme {-ing}, as in bring*ing* and bak*ing*

(*b*) the past tense morpheme {-D₁}, as in rubb*ed* and bak*ed*

(*c*) the agenitive morpheme {-er}, added to nouns, as in pay*er* and outfield*er*

Now let us assume that we have examined the morphemic structure of a young, articulatory defective child and found that the distribution of the plural allomorphs is identical with that of the adult speaker with the exception that /-θ/ replaces /-s/ after /p/, /t/, /k/, and /f/, and no sound follows the /θ/ phoneme. The use of the /-z/ and the /-əz/, however, conforms to adult English usage. In all other phonological instances the /s/ is pronounced correctly. Descriptions such as these, then, would permit differentiation between an articulatory or phonetic problem, on the one hand, and a morphemic problem, on the other. Any description of the phonological conditioning of morphemes, whatever its accuracy, does not, however, mean that "phonetic context" causes, restricts, or sets the conditions for the permissible phoneme sequences. To stress this point, I will cite Gleason (1961, pp. 61–62):

> Any phenomenon is said to be *conditioned* if it occurs whenever certain definable conditions occur. This is not identical with saying that it is caused by these conditions. All that is implied is that they occur together in some way, so that one can be predicted from the other. . . .
>
> In the Blue Ridge Mountains of Virginia /-ɪz/ is used not only after /s z š ž č ǰ/ but also after /sp st sk/. Thus *wasps, posts,* and *tasks* are pronounced /wáspɪz/, /pówstɪz/, and /tǽskɪz/, not /wásps/, /pówsts/, and /tǽsks/ as in most dialects.[7] In both dialects the form

---

[7] Note: /ɪz/ ≃ /əz/; /š/ = /ʃ/; /ž/ = /ʒ/; /č/ = /tʃ/; /ǰ/ = /dʒ/ and /ow/ = /ou/.

> is phonologically conditioned; in both the selection is completely automatic and quite regular. They are merely different, and each seems entirely natural to the speakers.

It is possible, as we shall see, that phonetic responses may be affected by preceding or succeeding phones, but this problem does not concern us now.

I shall now give the findings of Applegate's study (1961). That study contains an analysis of the speech sound "errors" of two brothers, four and five years of age, in which the sound "errors" were studied as deviant morphological patterns. In particular Applegate noted that the verb suffixes (allomorphs) of the present tense (third person singular) and past tense had among their alternates the following phonetic forms [-t], [-d], and [-id]. For example, the present tense (third person singular) and past tense of "walk" was [wakt]. As might be suspected, fricatives were absent in the children's speech: /s/ was replaced by /t/, and /z/ was replaced by /d/. In some cases, however, the past tense was distinguished from the present tense (third person singular) by the inclusion of two allomorphs having the phonetic forms of [-ʔ] and [-iʔ]. For example, [dəd] (the third person singular for "do") became [diʔ], and [takt] (the third person singular for "talk") became [takiʔ]. All other present tense forms corresponded to those of standard American English. Stops ([p], [t], and [d], for example) were replaced by the glottal stop in the medial or final positions in words when the initial stop in (adult) English was the same as the medial or final stop. Because of the children's morphology, however, this substitution did not occur for words that had successive [t] or [d] stops. Thus the final [t] in [takt] for *talks* was not substituted by [ʔ] because the final [t] is a replacive for [s], the standard form, in the children's already acquired morphological system. However, the allomorph [-iʔ] would replace [t] in "talked" because in (adult) English this word has an initial [t] and a final [t]. Applegate therefore concludes that "articulation errors" may be described in terms of the relation between morphological structure of English (the dialect) and the morphological structure of the children's language (the subdialect), keeping in mind that "the children's speech does not represent a random attempt to imitate the language of the adult community. Instead, it is clearly an autonomous system with well-developed rules" (Applegate, 1961, p. 193).

In summary, then, it may be possible to describe children's articulatory errors as self-contained phonemic systems that are at variance with the adult phonemic system. The rules of children's systems have been learned or, perhaps better yet, invented. Their self-contained systems will no doubt have morphological forms (plurals or past tense forms, for example) that differ from the adult morphological forms. The phoneme systems of young children, although self-contained, are, of course, influenced by the adult phoneme system and perhaps by the adult morphemic system as well.

Their phonemic patterns show some correspondence, although are not always easily ascertainable, to the adult system. At any particular point in time, children's phonemic systems are self-contained systems derived from attempts to learn the rules of the adult system.

Although this presentation relies heavily on phonemic theory prevailing at the time this book was initiated, it should be mentioned that significant changes in phonological theory (See Halle, 1964a and Postal, 1968, for example.) have occurred in the past decade and that these will soon be presented by Halle and Chomsky in a forthcoming book, emphasizing once again in the phonological realm the burdens placed on psychologists now grappling with the psychological aspects of the syntactical components of a generative grammar. Both the preceding discussions and those which follow view phoneme system learning from the classical framework and are due the criticisms of this framework.

At this time it seems appropriate to reflect again on the descriptive studies of Poole, Wellman and others, and Templin. In these studies each phoneme was tested more than once, usually in several word positions and in several different words. Although the testing was certainly not so detailed and complete as that which would be done by a linguist, the criteria of correct production, either 75 percent or 100 percent, give us at the present time the best estimate of an age-by-age account of the development of the phoneme systems of young, English-speaking, American children. For example, if a phoneme is "produced correctly" by 75 percent of the children at age three, we can be fairly certain that the use of this phoneme closely corresponds to adult phonemic usage. The allophones and their distributions cannot, of course, be easily gleaned from their data.

There is little doubt that the growing correspondence, beyond the age of three, between the child's sound system and that of the adult can be described in phonemic terms. Yet it is difficult to imagine that at this late date phonemic learning is the primary process at work. Because children of three years of age show considerable sophistication in their use of syntactic structures (see Templin, 1947 and Menyuk, 1964, for example) and since it is reasonable to assume that syntactic development rests heavily on the acquisition of phonemic differences, it seems clear that the bulk of phonemic learning, at least on the perceptual side, is acquired prior to or not very much later than three years of age.

After age three the production of sound units may be influenced by a number of factors: (1) morphological development, (2) sound acquisition in words, and (3) mastery and refinement of certain motor units.

In 1958 Berko reported the findings of her study on the development of English morphology, a study now considered among the classics. Of interest here is the fact that in some instances morphological constraints determined the rate of acquisition of certain phonetic forms, as illustrated by the finding that preschool children used /-əz/ more appropriately in possessive than in plural contexts. Now although one can undoubtedly show that in certain instances the development of correct articulatory units rests heavily on morphemic development, as Applegate's (1961) and Berko's (1960) investigations suggest, it seems clear that the developmental or descriptive studies of sound acquisition do not reflect this fact, simply because the articulatory test protocols include primarily words free of morphemic constraints (free morphemes or stems which can appear as single words). For example, test words like *peas* and *aging*, used to evaluate the final [z] and [ŋ], are rare in Templin's articulation test protocol.

Not to be discounted, however, is the possibility that abstract principles of morphology (or as it is now called generative phonology, systematic phonology or simply phonology) govern much more than is presumed in the above discussion (Chomsky, 1964). For example, Stevens and Halle (1967) cite the example of a young child who uttered the word *sing* as /sɪŋg/ rather than /sɪŋ/ in an environment free of the former pronunciation. Apparently the addition of /g/ after /ŋ/ in the word *sing* is a generalized instance of an English phonological rule: nasals assimilate (see pp. 120–121 of this chapter) the place of articulation of the following stop. Using the symbol N to denote a very deep nasal structure, a characterization of this rule is as follows. The abstract -Ng becomes phonetically [ŋg] except in word final position where [g] is deleted. Thus, the pronunciation of /sɪŋg/ for *sing* is an instance in which this young learner of English applied the first rule—point of articulation of nasals preceding a stop—but failed to apply the second rule—deletion of final [g] after nasals in word final position.

However, irrespective of the phonological system used to describe phonetic differences between child and adult, the fact remains that phonetic variations cannot always be explained simply as deviations from the rules of the community language for children beyond three years of age because of the range of variability found for individual sounds when phonological conditions are kept constant (see the studies cited in the section immediately below as well as those which pertain to reliability of measurement found in chapter 4, pp. 238–247). In some instances, of course, phonological rules might be developed which are applicable to a particular child and which result in a consistent description of certain articulatory deviations. The above remarks should not be interpreted to mean, as we shall see below, that a clearly marked correspondence between the phonology of adult and child is not useful for articulatory retraining. Rather it is especially useful when extremely deviant phoneme systems are found for children beyond the preschool age. All that is suggested here is that the mastery of phonological structures, with the possible exception of certain abstract forms, takes place by three or four years of age. If our frame of reference is syntactic development, it is a fact that children of this age understand and use fairly complex sentence types. Also if a new phonological form is to be mastered beyond three to four years of age; the chances are the particular phonetic units which are governed by the new rule, are available.

If the above remarks are somewhat correct, then it may be concluded that the developmental studies reflect the motor side of the articulatory learning process, the acquisition of phonetic units and sequences in words, which has been termed appropriate usage above. This is the period of time during which the young child refines his articulatory productions. Although I will later refer to articulatory defectiveness as the incorrect learning of the phoneme system of the language, it will become clear that all that is implied is that a system which is deviant from the phoneme system of•the community language has been learned. The processes which account for this deviancy will also be discussed. At that time two conceptual models which may be extremely productive will not be mentioned, namely paradigms which relate to the interference and retention of speech responses and to the basic motor units of speech production; the former has been reserved for chapter five since it is relevant for articulatory retraining, the latter will not be considered at all since it is a new development in experimental phonetics (see pp. 47–48, Chapter 1), one which is not very well understood at this time. However, a complete accounting of the acquisition of articulatory units in words will not be forthcoming until more is known about the underlying motor commands of speech production.

In summary, then, the acquisition of sounds from about three to eight years of age reflects, for the most part, a process which relates most directly to the integration of phonetic units in words. At the beginning of this period of development the average child possesses most of the phonetic units which are to be integrated, as well as a perceptual understanding of the phonological and morphological systems of his language. The articulatory developmental process is, therefore, considered to involve some not very well understood behavioral and physiological mechanisms, whose origins no doubt antedate the age of three. Two conceptual models which may prove to be useful here involve the interference and retention of sound responses and the motor commands of speech. In addition when articulatory productions are considered defective, the deviations may be expressed as a phoneme system which is at variance with the adult system, that is a system which failed to converge with the norm of the community because of factors suggested below. In the case of divergent phoneme systems, sound integration in words has no doubt taken place, but the integrative units are nonacceptable, or using classical terminology the productions are defective.

Inconsistencies of Misarticulations

In 1951 Spriestersbach and Curtis reported that correct productions of the /r/ and /s/ phonemes occurred more frequently in consonantal blends than in singles. This study, as far as we know, was the first one conducted by speech pathologists on the alternations of defective articulatory productions. No doubt inconsistencies of misarticulations, as they have now come to be known, were recognized by many practicing clinicians. In fact, prior to this study, students of speech pathology were often taught by their instructors that one purpose of a diagnostic articulatory examination should be to test for instances in which the defective sounds are produced correctly. The purpose, as we know, is to teach generalization of the correct response to those instances where the response is uttered incorrectly. The study by Spriestersbach and Curtis was simply an attempt to describe systematically those instances of correct articulatory productions for children who were regarded as having the /s/ and /r/ sounds in error. They concluded that the inconsistent errors may be accounted for on a lawful basis, perhaps with regard to phonetic contexts. The term *phonetic context*, as it has been used in these studies, refers to all of the positions in which one or more allophones of a phoneme occur— e.g., in blends; in prevocalic, postvocalic, and intervocalic positions; in the initial, medial, and final position in words. Inconsistency of misarticulations has been reported also by Wellman and others (1931), Roe and Milisen (1942), Sayler (1949), Perkins (1952), Curtis and Hardy (1959), Siegel and others (1963), and Winitz (1963).

House (1961) has taken issue with the procedures employed in such studies. He selected an investigation by Curtis and Hardy (1959) in which alternations of the /r/ phoneme were studied for a group of children initially selected as having errors of the /r/ phoneme. House (1961, p. 195) stated:

> . . . this experiment is not a revelation about the articulatory effects of phonetic environment, since these effects have been described and discussed rather well in the linguistic literature. Similarly, it casts no new light on problems of phonemic classification, etc., since it does not utilize appropriate techniques to grapple with such subjects.

Curtis and Hardy (1961, pp. 198–199) replied:

> . . . the point which we tried to make, *viz.*, that the articulatory behavior of children varies systematically with respect to these subclassifications of /r/, both with respect to frequency of correct articulations and the

> nature of errors that occur, has not been previously de-
> veloped. Moreover, it could not be developed without
> data of the kind obtained in our study.
> . . . Granted that linguists have long made distinctions
> between a number of allophones of /r/, it still had not
> been demonstrated that these were distinctions which
> make a difference in evaluating the articulatory behavior
> of children, or planning a corrective program to correct
> articulatory errors.

House is, of course, arguing that articulatory errors should be analyzed by the methods of structural linguistics, some of which have already been mentioned. Possibly, a phonological approach would give a more comprehensive analysis of children's articulatory errors than would the approach used by Spriestersbach and Curtis and by Curtis and Hardy. However, this is not to say that the findings of these researchers are not useful. Indeed, they are, because they give a description of those instances where allophones of the /r/ and /s/ phonemes are correctly uttered for a group of children considered to have utterance defects of these sounds. Assuming their findings to be general, they have broad implications for articulatory retraining.

One final point should be made here. It pertains to the observation by Spriestersbach and Curtis and by Curtis and Hardy that the articulatory production of the /r/ and /s/ allophones are facilitated in some phonetic contexts. This should simply be read as a statement of phonological conditioning. This statement in no way suggests why the correct production of the /r/ and /s/ allophones should be facilitated in some phonetic contexts and not in others.

Finally we should mention that it is possible, but not very likely, that the Iowa findings were the result of a perceptual error—i.e., that /r/ and /s/ tend to be heard correctly in blends more often than in singles because the blend is heard as a unit sound.

Some Hypotheses and Data
About Phonemic Acquisition

In the previous section some of the preliminary findings on the phoneme systems of children were discussed. It was mentioned that the phoneme systems of children are only an approximation of the adult phoneme system. No attempt was made, however, to guess at the progressive shape of these approximations, and most importantly I did not hint at what the first stage might be. Some hypotheses and research along these lines have been made, and I shall now present this material. However, before doing so, it is essential to introduce the concept of distinctive features.

Distinctive Features

In the advanced study of grammar (universal) feature specifications are sought at both the grammatical and phonological "level." The phonological component, as conceived by Halle (1964a, 1964b) and others, makes use of a finite set of phonetic features, called distinctive features. All of us have been trained to know the distinctive features of English phonemes. Sometimes we use the terms "place of articulation" and "manner of articulation" instead of "distinctive features." For example, the /z/ phoneme is regarded as voiced, nonnasal, apico-alveolar fricative. All four features are combined to describe the form of the /z/ sound. By changing a single feature, we form other sounds—e.g., by changing voiced to voiceless the /z/ becomes an /s/, by changing frication to plosion the /z/ becomes a /d/. As another example let us consider the English vowels /ɛ/ and /ɔ/ (Francis, 1958, p. 97). The /ɛ/ of most dialects of English is a mid-front, lax, short, unround vowel. The vowel /ɔ/ is a mid-back, lax, long, round vowel. Only the first two features of these two vowels, mid and front, and mid and back, within the set of English vowels are "distinctive." Yet each of these two vowels is described by five phonetic features, three of which are different and two of which are the same. When vowels and consonants are considered jointly the "vocalic" feature is "distinctive."

One might, therefore, distinguish between "phonetic" and "distinctive" features for a particular natural language, distinctive features being those phonetic features that are also contrastive features. Or one can say that certain (universal) distinctive features are not utilized as minimal elements in the phonological oppositions of a language. In any event when we refer to distinctive features we are referring to the elements of a feature complex, without regard to sequence, and not to phonemes or phones.

A clear and systematic definition of distinctive features is provided by Berko and Brown (1960, pp. 525–526):

> The "distinctive features" of an individual phoneme would be those aspects of the process of articulation and their acoustic consequences that serve to contrast one phoneme with others. In English speech the phoneme /b/ is always a stop (i.e., it is produced by an abrupt explosion of air), and in this respect it contrasts with a phoneme such as /v/, which is a fricative (i.e., it is produced by means of a constricted, continuous stream of air). The /b/ phoneme is also voiced, and in this respect, it contrasts with /p/. Jakobson, Fant, and Halle (1952) have proposed that any phoneme may be described as a bundle of concurrent distinctive features. They have given us a list of these features (about a

[Table 2.3] The Distinctive Features of 29 English Phonemes*

	VOCALIC/ NONVOCALIC	CONSONANTAL/ NONCONSONANTAL	COMPACT/ DIFFUSE	GRAVE/ ACUTE	FLAT/ PLAIN	NASAL/ ORAL	TENSE/ LAX	CONTINUANT/ INTERRUPTED	STRIDENT/ MELLOW
o	+	−	+	+	+				
a	+	−	+	+	−				
ɜ	+	−	+	−					
ʌ	+	−	−	+	+				
e	+	−	−	+	−				
ɪ	+	−	−	−					
l	+	+	−						
r	+	+	+						
ŋ	−	+	+			+			
ʃ	−	+	+			−	+	+	+
tʃ	−	+	+			−	+	−	−
k	−	+	+			−	+	−	
ʒ	−	+	+			−	−	+	+
dʒ	−	+	+			−	−	−	−
g	−	+	+			−	−	−	
m	−	+	−	+		+			

f	−	+	−	+	−	+	+	+
p	−	+	−	+	−	+	−	−
v	−	+	−	+	−	−	+	+
b	−	+	−	+	−	−	−	−
n	−	+	−	−	+	−	−	−
s	−	+	−	−	−	+	+	+
θ	−	+	−	−	−	+	+	−
t	−	+	−	−	−	+	−	−
z	−	+	−	−	−	−	+	+
ð	−	+	−	−	−	−	+	−
d	−	+	−	−	−	−	−	−
h	−	−	−	−	−	+	+	−
#[a]	−	−	−	−	−	−	−	−

* The features are presented as binary contrasts, "+" indicating presence of the first feature and "−" indicating presence of the second feature (from Jakobson and others, 1952, and Contreras, 1961).

[a] as in *hill* versus *ill* or *tall* versus *all*

SOURCE: Jakobson, R., Fant, G. M., and Halle, M. *Preliminaries to speech analysis*. Acoustics Laboratory, Massachusetts Institute of Technology, Tech. Rep. No. 13, 1952. Reprinted by permission of the M. I. T. Press, Cambridge, Massachusetts.

di' feat=
artic +
acoustic
terms

dozen) that is presumably adequate for the specification of the phonemes of all languages. Each feature is characterized in both articulatory and acoustic terms, and, perhaps because the authors are impressed with the binary computer as an analogue to human nervous processes, each is conceived as operating on a two-alternative basis. This distinctive feature analysis, which is completely general, makes it possible to compare the phonemic system of one language with the systems of other languages. It is also extremely economical.

Distinctive Feature System of
Jakobson, Fant, and Halle[8]

A distinctive feature analysis for 28 English phonemes (Jakobson, Fant, and Halle, 1952) is presented in Table 2.3. It may be noted from Table 2.3 that there are nine binary contrasts. For each of these binary contrasts the plus mark indicates the presence of the first distinctive feature and the minus sign indicates the presence of the second distinctive feature. For example, looking at the first binary contrast (vocalic/nonvocalic) we note that /ɑ/ is marked "+" and /s/ is marked "−". Therefore, /ɑ/ has the vocalic feature and /s/ has the nonvocalic feature.

The zero phoneme, designated /#/, refers to the absence of a phoneme. Jakobson, Fant, and Halle report that the zero phoneme contrasts in English in the initial prevocalic position. Examples of minimal pairs are *hill* and *ill*, and *hue* and *you*.

The distinctive features are defined as follows:

1. Vocalic/nonvocalic:
   acoustically—presence (versus absence) of a sharply defined formant structure;
   genetically—primary or only excitation at the glottis together with a free passage through the vocal tract.

2. Consonantal/nonconsonantal:
   acoustically—low (versus high) total energy;
   genetically—presence (versus absence) of an obstruction in the vocal tract.

3. Compact/diffuse:
   acoustically—higher (versus lower) concentration of energy in a relatively narrow, central region of the spectrum, accompanied by an increase (versus decrease) of the total amount of energy and its spread in time;
   genetically—forward-flanged (versus backward-flanged). The difference lies in the relation between the shape and volume of the resonance chamber in

[8] See M. Halle's "On the Basis of Phonology" edt. by Fodor and Katz (1964a) for further revision of the distinctive feature representation of English phonemes. Included in this revision is substitution of voiced/voiceless for lax/tense.

front of the narrowest stricture and behind this stricture. The resonator of the forward-flanged phonemes (wide vowels, and velar and palatal, including post-alveolar, consonants) has a shape of a horn, whereas the backward-flanged phonemes (narrow vowels, and labial and dental, including alveolar, consonants) have a cavity that approximates a Helmholtz resonator.

4. Grave/acute:

acoustically—concentration of energy in the lower (versus upper) frequencies of the spectrum;

genetically—peripheral (versus medial). Peripheral phonemes (velar and labial) have an ampler and less compartmented resonator than the corresponding medial phonemes (palatal and dental).

5. Flat/plain:

acoustically—flat phonemes are opposed to the corresponding plain ones by a downward shift or weakening of some of their upper frequency components;

genetically—the former (narrowed slit) phonemes, in contradistinction to the latter (wider slit) phonemes, are produced with a decreased back or front orifice of the mouth resonator, and concomitant velarization expanding the mouth resonator.

6. Nasal/oral (nasalized/nonnasalized):

acoustically—spreading the available energy over wider (versus narrower) frequency regions by a reduction in the intensity of certain (primarily the first) formants and introduction of additional (nasal) formants;

genetically—mouth resonator supplemented by the nose cavity versus the exclusion of the nasal resonator.

7. Tense/lax:

acoustically—more (versus less) sharply defined resonance regions in the spectrum, accompanied by an increase (versus decrease) of the total amount of energy and its spread in time;

genetically—greater (versus smaller) deformation of the vocal tract away from its rest position. The role of muscular strain, affecting the tongue, the walls of the vocal tract and the glottis, requires further investigation.

8. Interrupted/continuant:

acoustically—silence (at least in the frequency range above the vocal cord vibration) followed and/or preceded by a spread of energy over a wide frequency region (either as burst or as a rapid transition of vowel formants) (versus absence of abrupt transition between sound and "silence");

genetically—rapid turning on or off of source either through a rapid closure and/or opening of the vocal tract that distinguishes plosives from constrictives or through one or more taps that differentiate the discontinuous liquids like a flap or trill /r/ from continuant liquids like the lateral /l/.

9. Strident/mellow:
acoustically—higher intensity noise versus lower intensity noise;
genetically—rough-edged (versus smooth-edged). Supplementary obstruction creating edge effects (. . .) at the point of articulation distinguishes the production of the rough-edged phonemes from the less complex impediment in their smooth-edged counterparts (Jakobson and Halle, 1957, pp. 233-235).

We need to emphasize again that the development of the above set of distinctive features is motivated primarily by two considerations: (1) universality—a set of features applicable to all the languages of the world, and (2) economy (Other terms that might be appropriate here are naturalness and simplicity.)—a set of features which describes linguistic reality (linguistic competence). The above considerations, Jakobson and his colleagues believe, are best served by bipolar features.

We have stressed above as well as below the principle of universal feature specification and so we shall not discuss it here. However, the second consideration, economy, will be explained by the following example. In English the three front voiceless consonants /p/, /f/, and /t/ are distinguished, according to traditional practices, in the following way: (1) /p/-/f/, stop (interrupted) versus continuant and bilabial versus labio-dental; (2) /p/-/t/, bilabial versus apico-alveolar; and (3) /t/-/f/, apico-alveolar versus labio-dental and interrupted versus continuant. The differences multiply as more sound oppositions are considered. Note that for these three sounds a total of "five" different features (stop, continuant, labio-dental, bilabial and apico-alveolar) are used, whereas in the Jakobsonian system (see Table 2.3) a total of four features are used (grave, acute, continuant, and interrupted). But note also that the traditional procedure allows cross-contrasts to occur; labial is opposed to labio-dental, as well as to apico-alveolar. By employing more general categories the Jakobsonian approach avoids cross contrasts, resulting in a set of binary features which has general application.

Using the distinctive feature analysis of Jakobson, Fant, and Halle (1952), Saporta (1955) has tabulated a matrix of differences for 19 English consonants. This matrix of differences is presented in Table 2.4.

Saporta used Table 2.3, with some slight modifications to determine each degree of difference. For example, in Table 2.3 we note that /f/ and /θ/ differ on the following dimensions: grave and acute, and strident and mellow. Since the distinction of strident and mellow is minus in /θ/ and irrelevant in /f/, it is considered a "semi-contrast." The degree of difference is calculated as one. For the grave and acute dimension /f/ is a plus and /θ/ is a minus; the degree of difference is calculated as two, resulting in a total of three degrees of difference.

[Table 2.4] Units of Difference for 19 Consonants
Based on Table 2.3*

	m	p	b	f	v	θ	ð	n	t	d	s	z	ʃ	ʒ	tʃ	dʒ	ŋ	k	g
m	—
p	4	—
b	4	2	—
f	4	2	4	—
v	4	4	2	2	—
θ	7	5	7	3	5	—
ð	7	7	5	5	3	2	—
n	2	6	6	6	6	5	5	—
t	7	3	5	5	7	2	4	5	—
d	7	5	3	7	5	4	2	5	2	—
s	7	5	7	3	5	2	4	5	4	6	—
z	7	7	5	5	3	4	2	5	6	4	2	—
ʃ	8	6	8	4	6	5	7	8	7	9	3	5	—
ʒ	8	8	6	6	4	7	5	8	9	7	5	3	2	—
tʃ	8	4	6	6	8	7	9	8	5	7	5	7	2	4	—
dʒ	8	6	4	8	6	9	7	8	7	5	7	5	4	2	2	—
ŋ	3	7	7	7	7	8	8	3	8	8	8	8	5	5	5	5	—
k	8	4	6	6	8	5	7	8	3	5	7	9	4	6	2	4	5	—
g	8	6	4	8	6	7	5	8	5	3	9	7	6	4	4	2	5	2	—

* Because Saporta made some slight modifications of the values given in Table 2.3, the unit differences vary occasionally from those indicated in Table 2.3.

SOURCE: Saporta, S. Frequency of consonant clusters. *Language*, 1955, *31*, 27.

Another way to describe degrees of difference between phonemes is a system devised by Miller and Nicely (1955) which, unlike the system of Jakobson and others, is motivated only by the contrasts of English. The following features were considered: voicing, nasality, affrication, duration, and place of articulation. Strictly speaking the duration feature is not a distinctive phonetic feature in English. However, for the moment we will ignore this fact. A digital notation was used to classify 16 consonants according to these five distinctive features. The classification scheme is summarized in Table 2.5.

In Table 2.5 we may note that consonants are either voiced (1) or unvoiced (0); nasal (1) or nonnasal (0); affricated (1) or nonaffricated

[Table 2.5] Consonant Classification Developed
by Miller and Nicely (1955)

Consonant	Voicing	Nasality	Affrication	Duration	Place
p	0	0	0	0	0
t	0	0	0	0	1
k	0	0	0	0	2
f	0	0	1	0	0
θ	0	0	1	0	1
s	0	0	1	1	1
ʃ	0	0	1	1	2
b	1	0	0	0	0
d	1	0	0	0	1
g	1	0	0	0	2
v	1	0	1	0	0
ð	1	0	1	0	1
z	1	0	1	1	1
ʒ	1	0	1	1	2
m	1	1	0	0	0
n	1	1	0	0	1

Source: Miller, G. A., and Nicely, P. E. An analysis of perceptual confusions among some English consonants. *Journal of the Acoustical Society of America,* 1955, 27, 347.

(0); "long" (1) or "short" (0) in duration. In addition, the place of major constriction in the mouth is described as either front (0), middle (1), or back (2).[9]

Limitations of the Distinctive Feature Approach

Like the phoneme, however defined, a distinctive feature is an abstraction which is proving to be extremely useful in linguistic research (Halle, 1964b). As a concept it has undergone definitional changes as a result of recent developments in phonological theory (see Postal, 1968).

Acoustical and physiological phoneticians generally agree that the conceptual framework of distinctive feature systems, in addition to being provocative, serves as a guiding principle in the theoretical development of speech perception and production models, although they may reject certain details of the several distinctive feature systems which have been proposed. Further they recognize that speech perception and production involves considerations—such as timing factors and coarticulation effects

[9] The student interested in empirical descriptions of distinctive features can find many significant publications of very recent origin to whet his appetite. (See, for example, Ladefoged, 1967).

—which are not specified in distinctive feature models. Thus, it is not surprising to hear Fant (1962a), in a later publication, remark that the system he helped to develop may have application for phonological theory, but it is not precise enough to grapple with problems of phonetic theory and speech sound recognition. He comments as follows:

> The limitations of the preliminary study of Jakobson, Fant and Halle are that the formulations are made for the benefit of linguistic theory rather than for engineering or phonetic applications. Statements of the acoustic correlates to distinctive features have been condensed to an extent where they retain merely a generalized abstraction insufficient as a basis for the quantitative operations needed for practical applications. It should also be remembered that most of the features are relational in character and thus imply comparisons rather than absolute identifications. The absolute references vary with the speaker, his dialect, the context, the stress-pattern, etc., according to normalization principles which have not been fully investigated (Fant, 1962a, p. 405).

Fant then proposes a system that is not dependent upon the beginning and termination of the phoneme boundaries. He divides the spectrum of a speech utterance into "sound segments" that are not only smaller than phonemes but often extend from one phoneme to another. According to Fant (1962a, pp. 11–12):

> ... A sound segment is of the dimension of a speech sound or smaller and there may occur several successive sound segments within the time interval of the speech wave traditionally assigned to the phoneme. The number of successive sound segments within an utterance is, therefore, generally larger than the number of successive phonemes ...
>
> When sound segments are decomposed into bundles of simultaneous sound features it is often seen that a single sound feature carrying a minimal distinction may extend over all sound segments of importance for a phoneme, including sound segments which essentially belong to adjacent phonemes.

Fant's "distinctive feature" approach is determined by his major interest, computer recognition of a speech wave. He wishes to build a computer that will translate a speech wave into the spoken phonemes of a language. Preliminary research in this area has begun and is described in detail elsewhere (Fant, 1962a, and 1962b).

Curtis (1963), like Fant, has voiced similar reservations about the present distinctive feature schemes. With regard to Jakobson, Fant, and

Halle's system, he questions whether the relationships between the features and their acoustic, physiological and perceptual correlates are clear enough to permit operational definitions for the purposes of experimental study, observation and quantitative description. Curtis also wonders whether phoneme contrasting is a compound decision-making process which can be viewed as the summation of a number of binary-valued decisions and, as far as the present systems are concerned, whether subjects can reliably discriminate all of the binary features individually when all other binary features are held constant.

It should also be pointed out that two pairs of phonemes whose sums of distinctive feature differences are the same may not be equally discriminative; that is, the sum of binary contrasts for two different pairs of consonants may be three, for example, yet for one pair the threshold of audibility may be lower (Gemelli and Black, 1957). Absolute as well as relative differences need to be taken into account if a distinctive feature analysis is applied to discrimination learning. The sequence and order of the phonemes also need to be considered (see Leopold, 1947)—phoneme contrasting may be learned in the initial position but not in the final position, etc.

Although there is need for additional research in this general area, the implications of the distinctive feature approach for the study of articulatory acquisition and programming are enormous. We shall continue to use the concept of "distinctive features" in this text.

Jakobson and Halle Schemata for the Development of Phoneme Contrasts

Berko and Brown (1960, p. 528) comment that:

> Jakobson (1941) has been far in advance of all others, both linguists and psychologists, in distinguishing the learning of phonemic contrasts from simple babbling. This author believes that phonological development, viewed as the progressive differentiation of the phonemes of the community language, reveals universal human regularities. In his 1941 work he describes the sequence in which phonemic contrasts seem to emerge in any language, and in 1956 with Halle he sets forth such a sequence in terms of their "distinctive features" analysis of the phoneme. Jakobson and Halle (1956) believe that the child begins in a "labial stage" in which his only utterance is /pa/. This involves the consonant-vowel contrast.

This first contrast, one of vowel/consonant opposition, involves a physiological or sequential (syntagmatic) contrast between two sounds of the same syllable. According to Jakobson and Halle (1956, pp. 38–40) a labial sound, denoted /p/ and a central or back vowel, denoted /a/ constitute the primordial contrast. They state as follows:

> In this phase speakers are capable only of one type of utterance, which is usually transcribed as /pa/. From the articulatory point of view the two constituents of this utterance represent polar configurations of the vocal tract: in /p/ the tract is closed at its very end while in /a/ it is opened as widely as possible at the front and narrowed toward the back, thus assuming the horn-shape of a megaphone (Jakobson and Halle, 1956, p. 37).

This first contrast is conceived of as a motor contrast or a syllable unit rather than as a minimal pair contrast. An outline of subsequent phonemic distinctions has been proposed by Jakobson and Halle (1956, p. 41). The sequence is assumed to be an orderly one in that "the greatest possible phonemic distinctions are made first, with smaller differentiations following later" (Berko and Brown, 1960, p. 528). Distinctions are defined in terms of the degrees of distinctive feature difference between phonemes or groups of phonemes. Phoneme sequence learning, as proposed by these two eminent linguists, is essentially a discrimination hypothesis in that physical stimuli that are most distinctive are learned first and discriminations involving finer and finer differences are subsequently learned. This hypothesis, as will be seen in Chapter 5, is a valid one, but it is probably not complete in that other variables described below are also involved in phoneme system learning.

It should be mentioned that the details of Jakobson's (1941) original formulations, which are very much in evidence in Jakobson's and Halle's (1956) schema for the development of phoneme contrasts, were derived from two major observations about phonemic distinctions in a great number of natural languages: (1) the frequency with which a contrast occurs—for example, the nasal-oral consonantal opposition occurs in all languages with the exception of a few American Indian tongues (Jakobson and Halle, 1956)—and (2) the dependent relation of contrasts—for example, back consonants do not occur unless front consonants are present, but front consonants can occur without the presence of back consonants, giving, in the case of the nasals, no languages where /ŋ/ appears without the presence of a front nasal (Jakobson, 1941). With his extraordinary knowledge of the many languages of the world, Jakobson examined the growth of phoneme contrasts for children from diverse linguistic backgrounds. Using acoustic and physiological information to supplement his analysis, Jakobson derived a conceptual outline of phonemic development that seemed to explain cross-language differences.

Prior to the publication of Jakobson's theoretical outline of phonemic growth, investigators had noted that the range of differences among children from dissimilar linguistic communities was so great that the development of general or universal laws of phonemic acquisition was precluded. However, with Jakobson's suggestion that phonemic (distinctive) features rather than phonemes are the underlying elements at work, chaos seemed to give way to order.

Let's see how this process is presumed to operate. Consider the following consonantal matrix:

	BILABIAL	LABIO-DENTAL
Nasal	L_1	L_2
Continuant	L_2	L_1
Stop	L_1	L_2

where L_1 and L_2 are two different natural languages.

Note that in the above matrix that nasals, stops and continuants as well as bilabial and labio-dental placement are common to L_1 and L_2. Assume now that the oral-nasal distinction is the first consonantal contrast to take place. The primordial consonant phoneme divides into a nasal and an oral phoneme as shown below.

For language L_1 the contrast involves a bilabial-nasal versus an oral-continuant-stop. For language L_2 the oral-nasal contrast involves a labio-dental-nasal versus an oral-continuant-stop. Yet, although the sound patterns (phonemes) are different, the contrast—in this case oral-nasal—is constant, resulting in a universal pattern of development.

Employing all distinctive features of the consonantal matrix indicated above would give the following phonemes for L_1 and L_2.

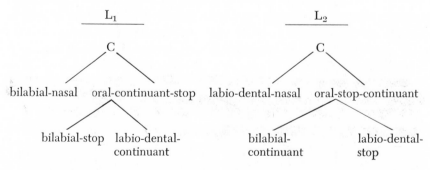

We should note again that universal regularity, as illustrated in the two examples given directly above, refers to the development of dis-

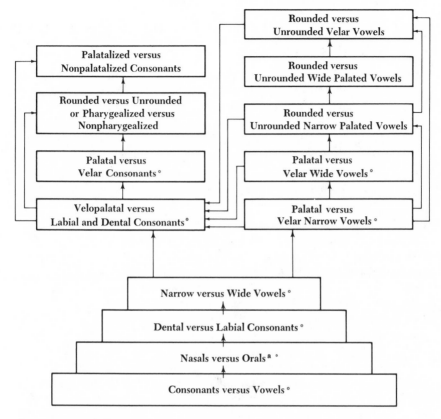

° Oppositions most applicable to English.

ª A consonant contrast: the oral-nasal vowel contrast appears much later, although not indicated above.

[Figure 2.1] Pictorial representation of Jakobson and Halle's model for the development of phoneme contrasts. Some contrasts are prerequisites for other contrasts. These prerequisites are indicated by an arrow. For example the fourth contrast, Narrow versus Wide Vowels, cannot occur until the first three contrasts are learned. After the Narrow versus Wide Vowel contrast is learned, one of two contrasts is learned: either Velopalatal versus Labial and Dental or Palatal versus Velar Narrow Vowels. From here on the reader can trace the phoneme splits that can occur, using the arrows to direct himself and remembering that not all contrasts occur in every language.

SOURCE: Adapted from Jakobson and Halle, 1956.

tinctive features and not to phonemes. The process is governed by the operation of distinctive features; the phonemes are outcomes of this process.

Let us refer to Figure 2.1 where the successive differentiations proposed by Jakobson and Halle are given. This schema has been developed to apply to differentiations that would be learned in most of the languages of the world. Hence, the reason Berko and Brown used the phrase "universal human regularities." The successive stages are clearly marked by arrows. Note in particular that all of the stages are not directly subsequent to each other (for example, the velopalatal versus labial and dental consonant contrast may directly follow the palatal versus velar narrow vowel contrast). Also, those distinctions that seem most applicable to English are marked with an asterisk.

In Table 2.6 the differentiation process is outlined for the major English vowels and most of the English consonants. We have used the distinctive feature classification proposed by Jakobson, Fant, and Halle (see Table 2.3, pp. 80–81), using the feature specifications for /r/ and /l/ by Contreras (1961), and the schema just discussed in arriving at the chain of events presented in Table 2.6. It should be considered to be nothing more than a characterization of the phonemic fractionization process.

Referring to Table 2.6 we note that the consonantal vowel split occurs first. Although the first split may involve a contrast between /p/ and /a/, the split continues until all consonants contrast with all vowels. Thus, the child may be said to have two phonemes, a vowel phoneme denoted /V/, and a consonantal phoneme denoted /C/. The allophones of the /V/ phoneme include all of the vowels uttered by the child, and the allophones of the /C/ phoneme include all of the consonants uttered by the child. The allophones of each phoneme may include phones not found in English. Second, we note that the consonantal versus nonconsonantal split occurs, permitting the /l/ to contrast with the vowels. Since the consonants already contrast with the vowels, the consonantal versus nonconsonantal split spreads to the consonants as well. Thus, the child now has four phonemes, /V/, /C/, /h/, and /l/; the [l] is no longer an allophone of the /V/ phoneme, but an allophone of /l/, and the [h] is no longer an allophone of the /C/ phoneme but an allophone of /h/. As the child learns to distinguish each successive pair of distinctive features, a chain reaction is set off; this is somewhat analogous to the mitotic division of a zygote. The process of cleavage divides the single-celled zygote first into two cells and then into four cells. The process of phonemic cleavage divides simple babbling into two phonemes and then into three, and so on. The two processes, however, are different in that once a distinctive contrast is learned, it is continually introduced into successive phonemic cleavages. The end result of this fractionation process is a phoneme system that conforms with the English phoneme system.

[Table 2.6] Pictorial Representation of the Hypothesized Stages of Phoneme Contrast Development in English Based on Table 2.3 and Figure 2.1 (adapted from Jakobson and Halle, 1956)

Process	Results (phonemes)

1. Non-vocalic versus Vocalic

   /C/ — /V/
   (all consonants but [r] and [l]) — (all vowels and [r] and [l])

   C — V

2. Consonantal versus Nonconsonantal

   /l/   /V/   /h/
   [l]
   [r]

   l — h — C — V

3. Nasal versus Non-nasal or Nasal Consonants (NC) versus Oral Consonants (OC)

   /NC/   /OC/
   [n]   [d]
   [m]   [t]
   [ŋ]   [b]
         [p]
         (etc.)

   NC — OC — l — h — V

4. Dental versus Labial Consonants or Acute Consonants (AC) versus Grave Consonants (GC)[a]

   /AC/   /GC/
   [t]   [p]
   [d]   [b]
   [s]   [f]
   [z]   [v]
   /N/   /m/
   [n]   [m]
   [ŋ]   (grave)
   (acute)

   AC — GC — N — m — l — h — V

5. Narrow Vowels versus Wide Vowels[b] or Diffuse Vowels (DV) versus Compact Vowels (CV)

   /DV/   /CV/
   [ʊ]   [o]
   [ə]   [a]
   [ɪ]   [ɛ]

   DV — CV — above consonants

6. Narrow Vowels (Diffuse): Palatal Vowels versus Velar Vowels[c]

   /ʊ/   /ə/   /ɪ/
   grave (velar)   grave (velar)   acute
   and flat   and plain   (palatal)

   ʊ — ə — ɪ — CV — above consonants

[Table 2.6 (Continued)] Pictorial Representation of
the Hypothesized Stages of Phoneme Contrast
Development in English Based on Table 2.3
and Figure 2.1 (adapted from Jakobson
and Halle, 1956)

Process	Results (phonemes)

7. Wide Vowels (Compact): Palatal versus Velar

/o/	/ɑ/	/ɛ/	
grave (velar)	grave (velar)	acute	o — ɑ — ɛ — ʊ — ə —
and flat	and plain	(palatal)	ɪ — above consonants

8. Velopalatal versus Labial and Dental Con-
   sonants or Compact Consonants (CC) versus
   Diffuse Consonants, Grave Diffuse Consonants
   (GDC) and Acute Diffuse Consonants (ADC)

/CC/	/GDC/	
[ʃ]	[f]	
[tʃ]	[v]	
[ʒ]	[p]	
[dʒ]	[b]	
[k]	/ADC/	
[g]	[s]	
	[z]	
	[d]	
	[t]	
	[θ]	
	[ð]	
/r/[d]	/l/[d]	CC — GDC — ADC —
/ŋ/	/n/	r — ŋ — n — m — l —
(compact)	(diffuse)	h — above vowels

9. Palatal versus Velar Consonants or Interrupted
   Consonants (IC) versus Continuant Consonants (Ct C); Tense Consonants (TC) versus Lax Consonants (LC), and Mellow Consonants versus Strident Consonants

(a) interrupted   continuant

/CIC/	/C Ct C/	
[k]	[ʃ]	
[g]	[ʒ]	
[tʃ]	/GD Ct C/	
[dʒ]	[f]	
/GDIC/	[v]	
[p]	/AD Ct C/	CIC — GDIC — ADIC
[b]	[s]	— C Ct C — GD Ct C
/ADIC/	[z]	— AD Ct C — r — ŋ
[t]	[θ]	—n — m — l — h —
[d]	[ð]	above vowels

[Table 2.6 (Continued)] Pictorial Representation of
the Hypothesized Stages of Phoneme Contrast
Development in English Based on Table 2.3
and Figure 2.1 (adapted from Jakobson
and Halle, 1956)

Process		Results (phonemes)
(*b*) tense	lax	
/CITC/	/CILC/	
[k]	[g]	
[tʃ]	[dʒ]	
/p/	/b/	
/t/	/d/	CITC — p — t — f — ʃ
/f/	/v/	— AD Ct TC — CILC
/ʃ/	/ʒ/	— b — d — v — ʒ —
/AD Ct TC/	/AD Ct LC/	AD Ct LC — r — ŋ —
[s]	[z]	n — m — l — h —
[θ]	[ð]	above vowels
(*c*) strident	mellow	tʃ — dʒ — s — θ — k —
/tʃ/	/k/	g — z — ð — p — t —
/dʒ/	/g/	f — ʃ — b — d — v —
/s/	/z/	ʒ — r — n — ŋ — m —
/θ/	/ð/	l — h — o — a — ɛ —
		ʊ — ə — ɪ

ᵃ The dental versus labial contrast and all subsequent contrasts pertain only to oral
phonemes. The use of "semi-contrasts" results in sounds which have no phonemic
assignment. "Semi-contrasts" are not used in Halle's (1964b) reformulation causing
no problem in future characterizations of this process.
ᵇ Narrow Vowels = high front, high back and mid central
Wide Vowels = low front, low back and low central
ᶜ Palatal Vowels = front
Velar Vowels = central and back
ᵈ According to Jakobson (1941) the liquids develop later than is suggested here.
SOURCE: Jakobson, R., and Halle, M. *Fundamentals of language.* The Hague: Mouton
& Co., 1956, 41.

Berko and Brown (1960, pp. 528–529), however, are quick to comment
that the sequence outlined by Jakobson and Halle is indeed speculative.
They state as follows:

> Jakobson and Halle are familiar with the interna-
> tional literature on speech acquisition and, presumably,
> derive their conclusions from this literature. However,
> the Jakobson and Halle report does not set down the
> detailed empirical support for the various generaliza-
> tions that are made and does not give any explicit at-
> tention to methodological considerations. Necessarily,
> therefore, we must regard their generalizations as hy-
> potheses rather than facts that have been established to
> the satisfaction of the reader.

Nonetheless, a great deal of research can be generated from the Jakobson and Halle proposal. First, it would be interesting to determine whether a sequence such as theirs, or one similar to theirs, actually does take place. Second, the details of phonemic fission need to be studied. What are the conditions under which cleavage takes place? How long? What "errors" occur during this interval? Third, as new vocabulary items are introduced to the child, are words that make use of already existing contrasts more accurately produced than words that contain contrasts not yet learned? Fourth, what is the relation between discrimination (passive) of the distinctive features and the production use of the features? (More will be said about this topic a little later.) Fifth, does the assignment and continuous reassignment of phones to phonemes suggest that the progressive development of phonemes reflects only, in part, or not at all physical distinctions among phonetic features? Finally, what are the developmental variables that contribute to phonemic system learning? What are the age levels, for example, at which certain phonemic splits occur?

There is some recent evidence that seems to support an orderly sequence of distinctive feature discriminations, somewhat in line with the Jakobson and Halle schema. The study was conducted by Shvarchkin, a Russian investigator; and it is reported by Ervin and Miller (1963, p. 111) as follows:

> . . . He taught children between 11 and 22 months Russian words differing only in one phoneme at a time. He presented his results as a series of phonemic features that distinguish groups or classes of phonemes. The phonemic features are learned in a given order. By the end of the second year the children could distinguish all the phonemes of Russian.
>
> Vowel distinctions are learned first. The order of acquisition for the remaining features is: (a) vowels vs. consonants; (b) sonorants vs. articulated obstruants; (c) plain vs. palatalized consonants; (d) nasals vs. liquids; (e) sonorants vs. unarticulated obstruants; (f) labials vs. linguals (i.e., nonlabials); (g) stops vs. fricatives; (h) front vs. back linguals; (i) voiceless vs. voiced consonants; (j) blade vs. groove sibilants; (k) liquids vs. /t/.

Psychological Mechanisms of Phoneme System Learning

When a child is learning the phoneme system of a language he has the simultaneous task of distinctive feature selection and distinctive feature assignment. Faced with an array of acoustic features he needs to learn to make those discriminations that enable him to acquire the phoneme contrasts of his language. It is a sorting process whereby the distinctive phonetic features are distinguished from the non-distinctive phonetic features. Initially the selection process involves the discrimination of those features that are maximally different, but eventually the child learns all of the necessary (distinctive) differences among acoustic features. At the time the child is learning to distinguish features he is also learning to group features together. That is, the child is learning to ignore differences between features that at first may appear to be distinctive; each non-distinctive feature is then assigned to a certain category of features (phoneme bin).

This selection and assignment process involves several psychological mechanism, which will now be discussed. My primary intention is simply to suggest the psychological mechanisms that seem to be involved; the research conducted to date does not permit a complete psychological description of phoneme system learning.

DISCRIMINATION. The primordial discrimination, according to Jakobson and Halle, involves the consonant/vowel contrast. This category includes the production of /pa/ as well as /pa/ versus /a/, and /pa/ versus /ap/. Jakobson and Halle consider this first contrast syntagmatic rather than paradigmatic. In any event, the child soon learns the subsequent contrasts of consonantal versus nonconsonantal, nasal versus nonnasal, grave versus acute, etc.

The learned differentiation of the grave/acute contrast, for example, probably follows the general pattern of other learned discriminations. In the typical two-stimuli situation the subject is reinforced for approaching or responding to one stimulus, the positive stimulus, and is not reinforced for approaching or responding to a second stimulus, the negative stimulus. The strength of the approach and withdrawal responses are gradually increased until the subject is able to discriminate between the two stimuli with almost perfect accuracy. How is this done?

The grave and acute features occur simultaneously with most of the other features. The child must learn to ignore the other features while attending to the grave and acute features, which he can capably discriminate. He is reinforced for doing so. For example, the young child may be reinforced, perhaps with a smile, by looking toward milk when he hears his mother utter *milk*. He is not reinforced by looking toward milk when his mother utters *doll*. (All, if not most, of the early discriminations will probably not involve minimal pairs.) Eventually the child will be able to discriminate, for example, the labial and labio-dental sounds from the apico-dental and the apico-alveolar sounds, as evidenced by an appropriate response; thus, the grave/acute contrast will have become distinctive for him.

In applying discrimination theory to phonemic sequence learning one can make the assumption that the features are continuous; that is, there is a degree of gravity and acuteness, for example, and that some features occur with certain features more frequently than with others.

These models, the first by Spence and the second by Estes, are presented so that the student may become briefly familiar with two not necessarily distinct approaches to the study of discrimination theory. These models are essentially nonrelational in that they present operations and suppositions as to how stimuli become conditioned to appropriate responses, and how responses transfer (transposition) to related stimulus dimensions. A relational theory would consider discrimination and transposition to involve "conceptual" differences among stimuli—e.g., short versus long, and light versus dark. This latter learning situation may arise when language labels are used (see chapter 3, pp. 189–198). Application of these models to phoneme learning is implicit in this discussion.

Spence Model. A theory of discrimination proposed by Spence might be utilized to describe phoneme discrimination learning. Spence suggests that we consider two stimuli, denoted A and B, differing on the same physical dimension, for instance, size, and an arbitrarily selected response. In this instance the subject is trained, by the process of conditioning, to respond to stimulus A and not to respond to stimulus B. It is assumed that a generalization gradient develops about each of the two stimuli, which describes the tendency to respond in the case of stimulus A and not to respond in the case of stimulus B. The algebraic summation of these two tendencies, excitatory and inhibitory, is the effective response strength (the probability that a response will occur) for stimuli of any size within the originally designated interval.

The model as summarized by Spence (1942 pp. 259–260) follows. (In this summary the term "excitatory strength" roughly corresponds to "response strength"):

> Briefly, the theory proposes that discrimination learning is a cumulative process or building up of the excitatory tendency or association between the positive stimulus cue and the response of approaching it as the result of successive reinforcement, as compared with the excitatory tendency of the negative stimulus to evoke the response of approaching it, which received only nonreinforcement. This differential training continues, theoretically, until the difference between the excitatory strengths of the two stimulus cues is sufficiently great to overshadow always any differences in excitatory strength that may exist between other aspects of the stimulus situations which happen to be allied in their response-evoking action with one or the other of the cue stimuli on a particular trial, *e.g.*, the two food boxes or food alleys, which may be allied on one trial with one of the cue aspects and on the next with the other.

In extending the theory of differential response to two members of a stimulus series, certain further assumptions were made. A somewhat modified formulation of the essential characteristics of the hypothesis is presented with the aid of [Figure 2.2]. For purposes of exposition, the experimental situation is assumed to be a size discrimination, the subject being required to learn to go to a stimulus square 160 sq. cm. in area to obtain food, and not to a square of 100 sq. cm. It is postulated:

(a) That, as the result of training or reinforcement, the positive cue aspect (square 160) acquires a super-threshold excitatory tendency (E) to the response of approaching it of the amount represented by the solid line at that point.

(b) That there is a generalization of this excitatory tendency to other members of the size series, and that this generalization follows a gradient such as that represented by the upper curved line.

(c) That with failure of reinforcement of response to the negative cue aspect (stimulus 100), experimental extinction will take place and a negative or inhibitory tendency (I) will be developed to the amount indicated by the broken line at the point on the abscissa marked 100 sq. cm.

(d) That there is a generalization of this inhibitory tendency to other members of the size series according to the gradient shown by the lower curved line.

(e) That the effective excitatory strength of the size cue at any point in the series is the algebraic summation of these positive (excitatory) and negative (inhibitory) tendencies. This value is indicated by the magnitude of the distance between the upper and lower generalization curves.

(f) That the remaining attributes or dimensions of the

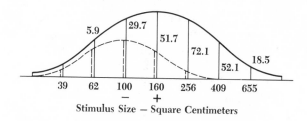

Stimulus Size — Square Centimeters

[Figure 2.2] Diagrammatic representation of the relations between the hypothetical generalization curves, positive and negative, after training on the stimulus combination 160 (+) and 100 (−).
SOURCE: Spence, 1942, Figure 1, p. 259.

> two stimulus figures being identical, their excitatory
> and inhibitory tendencies will cancel each other and
> hence need not be considered in determining the differ-
> ential excitatory strengths of the stimulus pair (*e.g.*,
> square 160 and square 100).

With this model one might theorize that phoneme discrimination learning, at least in the early stages of acquisition, involves excitatory and
inhibitory phonemic gradients. Assuming that these gradients can be
specified, using some system of distinctive features, one might predict
response tendencies to stimuli (phonetic variations) which are intermediate
to the conditioned stimuli. As we shall discover later, this condition cannot
apply to adults who have learned a natural language, since their responses
are categorically discrete. That is to say, stimuli either belong to phoneme
A or to phoneme B; the gradients do not seem to overlap (see Chapter 3,
pp. 195–196).

Estes Model. A promising approach to the study of discrimination behavior, as well as other behaviorial situations, is the growing field of
"statistical" learning theory. Learning theorists who take this approach
have developed mathematically precise formulations of their problems.
The model (Estes, 1959) in its simplest form assumes that the subject
will sample one or more elements of a stimulus (in some cases from a
pattern of stimuli) on each reinforced trial. The probability of a response
at any time is equal to the proportion of elements in the stimulus that are
connected to it. The sampling parameter, θ, is the average proportion of
stimulus elements sampled per trial from a stimulus set for a given
stimulus situation (a slope constant). Response probability, p_n, might be
characterized for a given learning situation as follows:

$$p_n = 1 - (1 - \theta)^{n-1}; \text{ if } 0 < \theta \leqslant 1$$

where n refers to the number of reinforced trials. We can see from this
equation that $(1 - \theta)$ (the probability that a stimulus element will remain
unconnected) decreases as the number of reinforced trials increases.

Estes and others have made a substantial contribution to discrimination
learning theory, but the theories are too elegant and esoteric to be presented here. We have introduced it simply to interest others in studying phoneme discrimination within the boundaries of a mathematically
sophisticated theory.

Further Considerations in Discrimination Learning. Spence's discrimination theory emphasizes that the excitatory strength will be strongest at
the point in the stimulus continuum where the positive stimulus occurs.
That is, the child, when he is able to discriminate all of the English
phonemes, has merely learned to respond differentially to the central
stimulus points of the phonemes. Ultimately he does learn to discriminate

between sets of stimuli, but he has not learned these as relational contrasting sets but rather in the way the psychological theories seem to suggest. (We will qualify this last statement later in this chapter when we discuss classification learning and again in Chapter 3 when we discuss discrimination learning.)

One additional point should be made at this time. The discrimination paradigm that most appropriately applies to phoneme contrast learning is known as successive discrimination. In this situation the subject hears only one of several possible stimuli at a time but learns to make a differential response to each of the two or more test stimuli when presented separately. This paradigm seems to describe the discrimination of phonemes best. It is an extension of the discrimination models that were previously presented, in that the subject hears only one stimulus on each occasion and makes a different response for each of two distinctive stimuli. The paradigm that most appropriately describes Spence's discrimination situation is called simultaneous discrimination. The subject sees both stimuli on each occasion but is reinforced for responding to only one of the two stimuli. For example, if the positive stimulus is to the left of the subject and the negative stimulus is to his right, the subject is reinforced for turning or going to the left side. When the positive stimulus is placed to the right of the subject and the negative stimulus to the left, the subject is reinforced for responding to the right spatial position.

When only one of the two visual stimuli is presented on a single trial, the paradigm is called successive discrimination. The usual situation calls for two identical stimulus elements, two white or black squares of the same size, for example, having distinct spatial properties. The reinforcement contingencies can be arranged so that when the black squares are presented, a left response is rewarded, and when the white squares are presented, a right response is rewarded. When auditory stimuli are used, only successive discriminations are possible. One of two stimuli is presented to both ears, and the subject is instructed to press one bar when he hears one stimulus and the other bar when he hears the other stimulus. The bars are spatially positioned, one to the left and one to the right, and the subject soon learns that he is reinforced for pressing the "correct" bar in the presence of the "correct" stimulus. The situation can, of course, call for only one bar which is to be pressed when one stimulus is heard and not to be pressed when the other stimulus is heard. We have used the two-bar arrangement.[10]

In phonemic discrimination learning the responses are not distinctive for all occasions, but they probably are on certain occasions. Thus, turning

---

[10] See Spiker (1963) for a theoretical discussion of successive and simultaneous discrimination and for references comparing and contrasting these two discrimination paradigms.

to the left when *mama* is uttered and to the right when *papa* is uttered can constitute distinctive responses for an occasion.

One final point should be made. Prior to the learning of phoneme contrasts, the early discriminations (or responses) probably involve distinctions of meaningful forms. The child, before he learns to utter words, apparently learns to discriminate many complex language forms, complex being defined as moderately long sequences of phonemes. These language forms, such as *mama, baby, dog,* are usually not minimal or subminimal pairs. These forms, therefore, have few elements in common; that is, they should be easily discriminated. As each form is repeatedly presented to the child, the stimulus elements (phonemes) of the form become conditioned to a "distinct" response. At some later time a new form is presented to the child and the stimulus elements are sampled; the sequence of elements (phonemes) are different but the elements are probably familiar to the child. He is at this time able to determine, by some generalization process, whether this sequence of elements is a previously learned one. When the form differs from other forms by one phoneme, as in minimal pairs, the form may be discriminated by virtue of the fact that (*a*) all of the phonemes have been discriminated previously, and (*b*) no such form has been learned previously.

STIMULUS GENERALIZATION. Another psychological mechanism that is involved in phoneme system learning is that of stimulus generalization. Stimulus generalization has been defined as a psychological process in which stimuli, similar to the conditioned stimuli, will elicit the conditioned response. Response strength (response criterion, such as the number or the percentage of responses) has been found to be inversely related to the difference between the *training* and *test stimuli*. We shall now explain the last two terms by reference to a study by Guttman and Kalish (1956).

These investigators trained 24 pigeons to peck at a light of a certain wavelength. When the pigeons pecked in the presence of this light (training stimulus or S^D), they were rewarded automatically with food. When the light was turned off (S^Δ) and the pigeons pecked, food was not delivered. After considerable training the pigeons learned to peck when the training stimulus was on and not to peck when the training stimulus was off.

As a test of stimulus generalization, subsequent to the S^D training, the pigeons were presented with a series of lights all of different wavelengths. They differed from the training stimulus from 10 to 70 mμ. These latter stimuli are called test stimuli. When the test stimuli were presented, reinforcement was not given for the pecking response.

The findings for the generalization test are presented in Figure 2.3. Response strength is greatest for the CS and decreases as the difference between the CS and the test stimulus increases. Thus, the number of pecking responses is greatest when the test stimulus resembles the train-

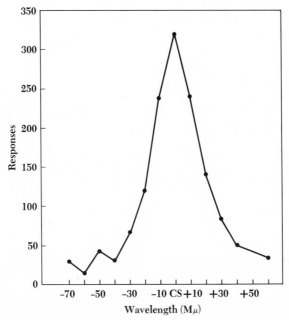

[Figure 2.3] Mean stimulus generalization gradient for pigeons trained to peck at a certain wavelength and tested at wavelengths that varied from 10 to 70 Mμ.
SOURCE: Guttman and Kalish, 1956, Figure 3, p. 83.

ing stimulus; it continually decreases as the test stimuli less and less resemble the training stimulus.

No doubt the process of stimulus generalization is involved in phoneme contrast learning. The child not only learns to discriminate features but must also learn to group together (generalize) certain features. This classing together of features will presumably occur if the features are "similar" and if the subject is reinforced for making the same response (either a motor or verbal response) to two physically distinct stimuli.

An experiment was conducted by Winitz and Bellerose (1963a) in order to determine whether stimulus generalization can be demonstrated with phonemes. It seems appropriate to discuss this experiment now, although the investigation was originally conducted to shed some light on the development of articulatory errors.

In that investigation children from the first and second grades were pretrained on the stimulus /ʃɜt/ for 10 trials. That is, they heard the stimulus /ʃɜt/ and uttered /ʃɜt/ for 10 successive trials. On the eleventh trial one of four stimuli were presented. They were: /tʃɜt/, /sɜt/, /θɜt/, and /tɜt/. The initial consonant of the test stimulus was scaled

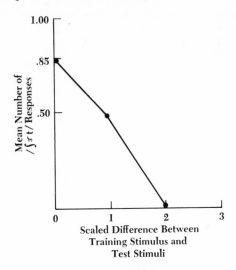

[Figure 2.4] Stimulus generalization gradient for the response /ʃɜt/. The initial consonant of each test stimulus was scaled according to five articulatory features, as described by Miller and Nicely (1955); the difference in scaled values between the training stimulus and each test stimulus is presented. The test stimulus were /tʃɜt/, /sɜt/, /θɜt/, and /tɜt/, and appear as 0, 1, 2, and 3.
SOURCE: Winitz and Bellerose, 1963a.

using the distinctive feature analysis of Miller and Nicely (1955) (/tʃ/, a phoneme not included by Miller and Nicely, was rated as having a difference of 0). The generalization gradient is presented in Figure 2.4. Here we can see that generalization does occur, that it can be obtained with stimuli that are currently distinctive, and that the strength of the generalization is, for the most part, inversely related to the distinctive difference between the training phoneme and the test phoneme.

In this study the authors also wished to determine whether the generalizations would continue if reinforced. Subjects who uttered /ʃɜt/ when they heard /sɜt/ on the eleventh trial were assigned to one of two groups. To both groups the stimulus /sɜt/ was presented for five more trials (trials 11 through 16). One group, labeled Group A, was reinforced on trials 11, 12, 13, 14, and 15 for uttering /ʃɜt/, and the second group, labeled Group B, was reinforced for uttering /sɜt/ on trials 11, 12, 13, 14, and 15. For Group A, reinforcement was withheld when /sɜt/ was uttered; and for Group B, reinforcement was withheld when /ʃɜt/ was uttered.

The findings are presented in Figure 2.5. It may be noticed that subjects

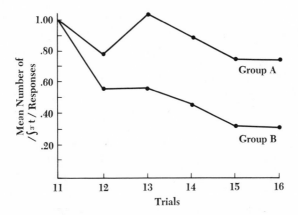

[Figure 2.5] Mean number of /ʃɝt/ responses for Group A (reinforcement of /ʃɝt/ and Group B (reinforcement of /sɝt/) on Trials 11 through 16 for those subjects (N = 9) in Group A and Group B) who uttered /ʃɝt/ on Trial 11. On Trials 1 through 10 the stimulus was /ʃɝt/ and on Trials 11 through 16 the stimulus was /sɝt/ for both groups.
SOURCE: Winitz and Bellerose, 1963a.

in Group A continued to utter, for the most part, the incorrect response. Subjects in Group B gradually learned to extinguish the incorrect response. Also, we may note from Figure 2.5 that subjects in Group B would have needed several additional trials before they eliminated their "articulation errors."

Generalization is an essential ingredient in the process of phoneme system learning, but it may in some cases account for the incorrect development of phoneme classes. Thus, if the experiment described above is a valid model of early articulation development, it would seem to suggest the following. As the child is confronted with the necessity to learn the correct allophone of a phoneme in an English word, he may at first select from his repertoire of sounds a sound that is phonetically similar. Sometimes the sound will be a phonemic substitution (allophone of another phoneme), and sometimes it will be a phone that does not occur in English. The sound will usually be one that the child has used in the past—that is, one that has considerable habit strength. (This latter point will be mentioned again when we discuss the findings of Lewis, 1951, later in this chapter.) If the generalization is reinforced, the child will learn an incorrect articulatory response.

CLASSIFICATION LEARNING. The two psychological mechanisms, discrimination and generalization, are brought to fruition in what is known as concept learning. Concept learning as defined by Hunt (1962, p. 6) is a "term which applies to any situation in which a subject learns to make an identifying response to members of a set of not completely identical stimuli." The term is applicable to phoneme system learning which, as we now recognize, involves primarily the learning of about 45 sets (phonemes). In the strictest sense, phoneme system learning does not qualify as a concept learning task. Hunt maintains that for a classification task to qualify, the subject must, among other things, "be able to instruct a human to apply the classification rule" (Hunt, 1962, p. 7). Since adults untrained in linguistic analysis are generally unable to give the phonological rules of their language, it seems best at this time to refer to phoneme system learning as classification learning rather than concept learning.

In order that classification learning may be understood, we shall carefully distinguish betwen *identification learning* and *classification learning*. Let us assume that we have cut four different-sized boxes from a sheet of white paper. Let us also assume that we have made up a list of four consonant-vowel-consonant syllables and arbitrarily assigned one syllable to one box. The complete list of paired items might look like the following list:

Stimulus	Response
□	tul
▭	mib
▭	vil
▭	dak

Now let us suppose that we presented the above paired items individually on a screen. A box would be presented first followed in two seconds by the correct syllable. This training would continue until the subject was able to utter the appropriate syllable when he saw each of the individually presented stimulus boxes. The presentation order of the pairs would, of course, be randomized. This type of learning is defined as *paired-associate learning* and it falls under the category of identification learning. Identification learning, then, involves the learning of a one-to-one association between individually presented stimuli and arbitrarily selected responses.

Now suppose we select a new group of subjects and teach them to associate the syllable *tul* with the first two boxes above and the syllable *mib* with the second two boxes above. Here we are asking the subject to learn to associate two stimuli with one verbal response. The subject learns to class not completely identical stimuli together, to which one identifying response is made. This type of learning, which is known as *classification learning*, seems to be the learning paradigm that most appropriately describes phoneme system learning.

An experiment by Shepard and Chang (1963) contributes to our thinking about phonetic groupings. In this experiment one verbal response was associated with four red colors and another verbal response was associated with four other red colors. The red colors were all of the same red hue but varied in brightness and saturation. Six different classifications were learned. These classifications are indicated in Figure 2.6. The eight stimuli, for all six classifications, are represented as points in a color space. The ordinate is brightness and the abscissa is saturation. The closer the distances between two points, the less the perceived similarity between the two colors. The stimuli colored black were to be associated with one response, and the stimuli colored white were to be associated with another response.

In Figures 2.6A and 2.6B we note that the black and white circles cluster in one region. According to stimulus generalization theory it should be easier to classify the black and white points when they cluster in a region than when they intermingle. This assumption was confirmed; classification A was the easiest to learn while classifications E and F were the hardest to learn. The mean number of errors for each stimulus in each classification was also determined. For example, the errors for the uppermost point in F were almost ten times as great for the same point in A.

If the black points are thought of as allophones of one phoneme and the white points as allophones of another phoneme, then phoneme system learning would be related, in part, to the overlapping or intermingling of the phonetic features of the two phonemes. When the phonetic features of two phonemes overlap greatly, phonemic contrast learning should be very difficult.

It also might be useful to think of Figure 2.6 as an acoustic space map, the points representing phonemes in an acoustic space. The acoustic space map would specify the similarities and differences between phonemes. Peters (1963b) has conducted some very original work along these lines. Normal and articulatory defective five- and six-year-old children rated the similarity of 13 consonants. For the rating session, pairs of con-

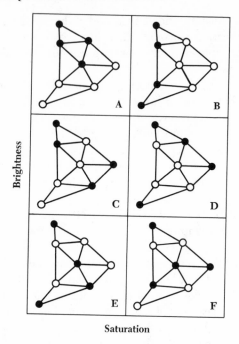

[Figure 2.6] Six orthogonal classifications of eight red colors. In the experiment described in the text the black circles were always associated with one verbal response, and the white circles were always associated with another verbal response.

Source: Shepard and Chang, 1963, Figure 3, p. 83.

sonants were combined with the vocoid [ʌ], for example [pʌ]-[kʌ], and the subjects were instructed to rate the similarity of the pairs. The ratings were converted (Torgerson, 1958, pp. 247–297) into a two-dimensional acoustic space, utilizing three factors, manner (Factor I) and place of articulation (Factor II), and voicing (Factor III).

Peters found that in general only three dimensions were necessary to account for interconsonantal distances. The acoustic spaces for normal-speaking children and articulatory defective children are given in Figure 2.7. Manner of articulation is represented on the first dimension, and place of articulation and/or voicing is shown on the second dimension. In a second study (Peters, 1963a) the acoustic space maps of adults were studied.

Peters (1963a) makes the following comparisons between the articulatory defective children and the normal-speaking children and adults:

In comparing the three groups, adults, children with normal speech, and children with articulation difficulties, there seemed to be differences in the levels of organization. The adults presented the most advanced structures, while the structures for the children with articulation difficulties showed the least organization. The distortion of the structures for the articulation-problem children took the form of random scattering and intermixing of the consonant groups in the space. There seemed to be one very important difference between the structures of the articulation group and those of the adults and normal-speaking children. This difference was the failure of manner to appear on Factor I for the children with articulation problems. Manner of articulation was always located on the first dimension for adults and children with normal speech. This seemed to be the most important articulatory feature of the consonants relative to perception. Voicing and place of articulation information was secondary, and the data did not indicate which was more important perceptually. The articulation-problem children showed general agreement among themselves on Factors II and III, but differed from each other, from the children with normal speech, and from adults on Factor I. The very feature that was most important in defining the auditory spaces of the normal-speaking children and the adults seemed to be least important in the perceptual spaces of the articulation group.

In the future, acoustic space maps may be utilized to set up programs of discrimination and articulation instruction. "Acoustic spaces" of subjects might be scanned by a computer in order to select the appropriate learning program for each subject.

MOTIVATION. Motivation or drive was defined earlier. Motivational variables are important both in the learning of a new task and in the replacing of an old task by a new one. Drive, as hypothesized by Spence, is presumed to multiply with existing habit (response) strength $(H \times D)$. In a number of articles Spence and his colleagues (Spence, 1956) have shown that learning occurs more rapidly under conditions of high drive than under conditions of low drive. In one investigation (Spence, 1956, pp. 226–229) paired-associate learning was studied as a function of two levels of anxiety. Anxiety was presumed to be an index of drive; it was measured by the Taylor Manifest Anxiety Scale (Taylor, 1953). Both high-drive and low-drive adults learned a set of paired associates. The results are shown in Figure 2.8. Here it may be observed that subjects who score high on the anxiety test demonstrate superior learning.

However, under some conditions high drive impairs the learning of new responses. In order to demonstrate this situation, Spence (1956, pp. 230–233) employed high-association and low-association word lists. In high-

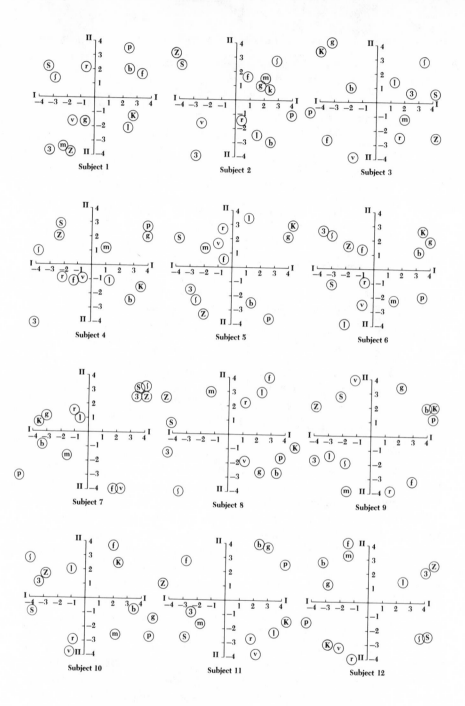

[Figure 2.7] Individual plots for twelve children with normal speech (Subjects 1 through 12) and twelve children with articulation problems (Sub-

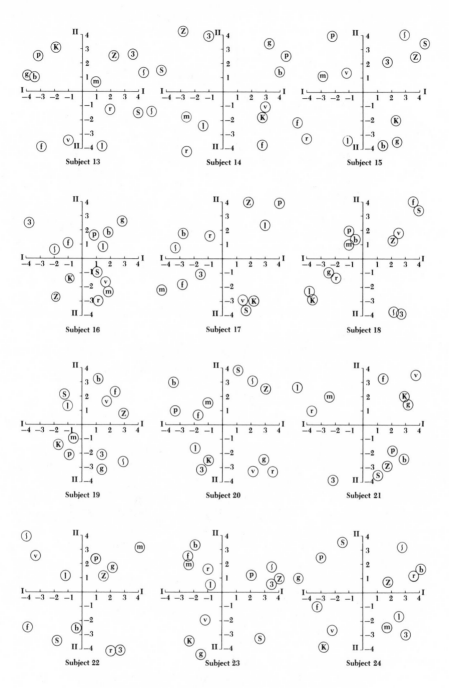

jects 13 through 24) with respect to the location of the consonants in two-dimensional Euclidean space.

SOURCE: Peters, 1963b.

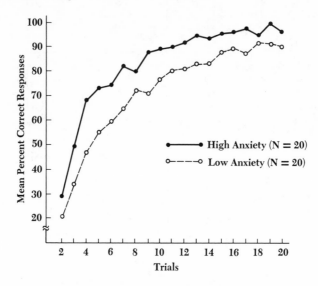

[Figure 2.8] Paired-associate learning as a function of anxiety under conditions of minimal interword pair competition and low initial stimulus-response strength.
SOURCE: Spence, 1956.

association word lists the association strength between paired words is high; in low-association word lists the associative strength between paired words is low. For example, if an individual is asked to respond to the stimulus word *boy* he will probably say *girl*. Thus, if a word list contains high-associative pairs, like *boy* and *girl*, learning will ordinarily be facilitated. In addition, associations like *boy-girl* will have considerably more potential for being elicited for high-drive subjects than for low-drive subjects, i.e., H × D.

However, if a low-associative word like *table* is paired with *boy*, then the response word *girl* will interfere with the acquisition of the pair of words *boy-table*. That is, when a low-associative response word is paired with stimulus words that have previously been shown to elicit certain words with considerable regularity (high association) the subject, as he learns this new pair, will find that the high-associative response words will compete initially with acquisition of the low-associative response pairs.

In order to explore paired-associate learning as a function of anxiety under conditions of high interword pair competition, Spence (1956, pp. 230–233) selected 12 paired adjectives. For four of these pairs the associative connections were very strong, and for the remaining eight pairs the associations were weak. For each of the four stimulus words paired with

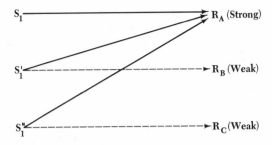

[**Figure 2.9**] Diagram showing how interword pair competition may be manipulated experimentally. $S_1 \rightarrow R_A$ is a stimulus-response tendency with high initial associative strength; $S_1' \rightarrow R_B$ and S_1'' and R_C are stimulus-response tendencies with low initial associative strengths. Further, S_1, S_1', and S_1'' are synonymous, so that strong associative tendencies exist also between R_A and S_1' and S_1'' (represented by unbroken arrow shafts).
SOURCE: Spence, 1956.

response words of high associative strength two synonymous stimulus words were selected that also had high associative strength with the response word. These synonyms were paired with response words of weak association. A diagram illustrating this arrangement is presented in Figure 2.9. The broken arrow shafts for the synonymous words, S_1' and S_1'' indicate the experimental pairing of these words. The unbroken arrow shafts indicate that the initial response strength of S_1' and S_1'' to R_A is high. Thus the learning of $S_1' \longrightarrow R_B$ and $S_1'' \longrightarrow R_C$ involves a strong competing response, R_A. This competitional response will be stronger for high-drive than for low-drive subjects, and thus the performance of high-drive subjects should be below that of low-drive subjects. The relative performance of the high- and low-drive subjects should be the same for the high (strong) associative pairs except in the early stages of learning. In the first few trials high drive should facilitate the weak-associative pairs ($S_1' \longrightarrow B$ and $S_1'' \longrightarrow C$). However, as learning progresses, S_1 will tend to evoke R_B and R_C. This generalization will occur because S_1' and S_1'' are highly synonymous with S_1.

The results of this study are given in Figure 2.10. It can be observed from this graph that the performance of high-drive subjects is inferior to that of the low-drive subjects for both high-association and low-association word pairs, and that the initial performance of the high-drive subjects is superior to that of the low-drive subjects for high-association pairs.

These findings on motivation might be applied to the study of articulatory learning. Let us assume that for a particular child the /w/ is consistently substituted for /r/. High anxiety (continuous correction by a parent, for example) should increase the likelihood that the error sound will be retained. For example, the associative strength of /w/ (incorrectly

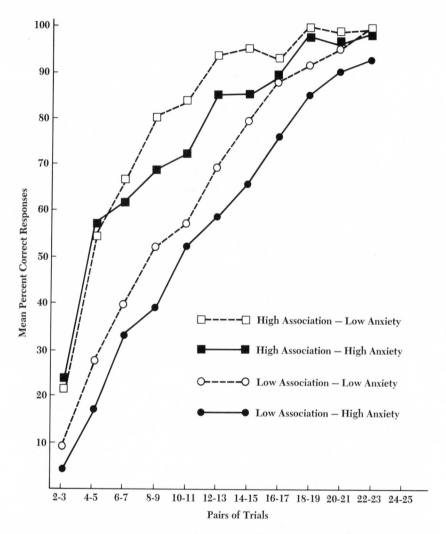

[Figure 2.10] Paired-associate learning as a function of anxiety under conditions of high interword pair competition. Word pairs of both high and low association value were interspersed within the same training list but were analyzed separately.
SOURCE: Spence, 1956.

used for /r/) in *rabbit* should be increased under conditions that induce high drive. This situation would be avoided in speech correction classes. Here the /r/ sound would first be taught in environments (such as nonsense syllables) in which competitional responses are minimal. In these environments high drive would facilitate the acquisition of /r/. Although this example does not parallel exactly the research of Spence previously described, the general principle of drive multiplication seems particularly applicable to articulatory learning.

FREQUENCY. The definition of reinforcement given earlier states that responses will increase in frequency if they are followed by reinforcing events. In the case of one selected response it follows that, other things being equal, the more frequently the response is reinforced the more likely it is going to occur. When two or more responses are involved, the same situation holds, providing that they are noncompeting responses and that the opportunity for reinforcement is the same. The many phonemes of English are not, however, equally frequent; thus, some phonemes will have a greater opportunity for reinforcement than will others.

In order to examine whether a relation exists between frequency and phoneme acquisition, we correlated the frequency of correct consonant productions in the initial and final positions in words with the frequency of these sounds as they occur in the English language. The frequency of correct responses was obtained from data provided in Appendix IV of the Templin (1957) study, collected from 60 three-year-old children. The frequency data were obtained from a study by French and others (1930), who studied 80,000 English words from approximately 19,500 telephone conversations.[11] For 22 initial consonants and 21 final consonants, the rank order correlations were .63 ($p \leqslant .01$) and .52 ($p \leqslant .05$), respectively. These findings suggest that the frequency of sounds as they occur in a language is an important variable in articulatory acquisition. Frequency of occurrence functions as a variable in two ways: (1) more frequent occurring sounds are discriminated more often; (2) more frequent occurring sounds are uttered, or attempted, more frequently. The correlations might have been higher than reported if information about frequency of sound occurrences for parents of children were known. However, this variable can easily be tested in controlled experimental conditions.

Another way to look at frequency is by examining the frequency of phonemic contrasts in minimal pairs. Denes (1963) has tabulated the frequency of phonemes in minimal pairs and of all phonemes found

[11] Jordan (1960) has computed rank order correlations between pairs of results for three frequency of occurrence studies (French and others, 1930; Travis, 1931; Voelker, 1934). For these computations word position frequencies (initial, medial, and final) for each sound were combined. The correlations reached or exceeded .94. Correlations of this magnitude indicate that there is high agreement among the three studies. Since the French study reported frequency of occurrence of sounds in the initial and final positions, it was selected for our correlations.

in two "Phonetic Readers," *English Conversations* by Scott (1942) and *Phonetic Readings in English* by Jones (1959). The "Phonetic Readers" contain speech material used to teach English to foreign students. All of the material in the texts is given in phonetic transcription, and the dialect is that of southern England.

Of interest here are two measures of minimal pair counts: (*a*) phoneme type contrast—the number of times an individual phoneme contrasts when each minimal phoneme pair is counted only once for any one suitable word pair; and (*b*) phoneme frequency contrast—the number of times an individual phoneme contrasts when each minimal phoneme pair is counted for all occurrences for any one suitable word pair. For example, /t/ and /d/ contrast in the final position in the minimal pair *bed—bet*; phoneme type contrast for /b/ and /t/ would be one. If each of these two words occurred twice, then the phoneme frequency contrast for /b/ and /t/ would be two.

We have tabulated both phoneme type contrast and phoneme frequency contrast with the frequency findings of Templin (1957). The procedure used here is the same as that described above, except that in this case the data for each phoneme were averaged for each of the three word positions. The following correlations (n = 24 phonemes) were obtained:

Phoneme type contrast versus Templin	.64[12]
Phoneme frequency contrast versus Templin	.37
Phoneme type contrast versus phoneme frequency contrast	.74

From these findings we may note that the rank order of the phonemes is fairly consistent for the contrasts of phoneme type and phoneme frequency. And that phoneme acquisition at age three seems to be more highly related to phoneme type contrast than to phoneme frequency contrast. Some additional correlations were made. First we looked at the relation between phoneme frequency obtained by Denes and the findings of Templin for children of three. A correlation of .47, which is somewhat lower than the correlations reported above for the initial and final positions, was obtained; this correlation suggests that phoneme frequency and phoneme acquisition are moderately related. Second, in order to be complete, we computed correlations between phoneme frequency and phoneme type contrast and between phoneme frequency and phoneme frequency contrast. The rho for phoneme type contrast and phoneme frequency was .87 and the rho for phoneme frequency contrast and phoneme frequency was .81. These high relations suggest that the rank order of the phonemes (both frequency and type) is fairly consistent for

---

[12] $r_{.05} = .34$ and $r_{.01} = .49$.

minimal pair words as well as for all words. This finding is surprising in view of the fact that the number of minimal pairs comprised only 4116 of the 20,052 words analyzed by Denes.

The discussion thus far has explicitly assumed that phoneme acquisition depends upon an environment that is ready to reinforce all correct responses. No mention was made of the fact that children may rehearse previously learned responses and also correct some of the errors they have made during the day. Weir (1962) reports that a young child may engage in sound practice by himself.

She recorded the monologues of a two-and-one-half-year-old child shortly before he fell asleep. In the following example, the young child had just been exposed to the word *raspberries*. The split between [æ] and [ɛ] was in the process of being developed, as is clear from the following transcript observed by Weir (1962, p. 108):

[bǽk] please[13]
[bérìz]
not [bǽrìz]
[bǽrìz]
[bǽrìz]
not [bærìz]
[bérì:z]
[bǽ]
[bǽ]

Weir indicates that such soliloquies were none too frequent; nevertheless, this wonderful little transcript adds an exciting dimension to future research in phoneme acquisition.

INFORMATION VALUE. Many of the child's early verbal utterances occur in contextual frames of reference. A single word may bear very little relation to the phonemic shape of the adult word, yet its meaning is clearly understood by an adult, because the meaning of adjacent words are understood and/or the physical environment itself restricts the possible range of meaning. However, when the contextual environment does not assist in the meaning of a word, the adult structure may be imposed upon the child.

Let us use the /r/ and /w/ contrast as an illustration. It is quite possible that a child will learn to pronounce /r/ correctly in one word and incorrectly in another word if in the first word /r/ functions as a contrast in a minimal pair. For example, /w/ for /r/ in *rabbit* may be acceptable to a parent because there is no such word as *wabbit* and, therefore, no confusion of understanding results. However, /w/ for /r/ in words such as *ring*

---

[13] ' refers to primary stress, ` to tertiary stress, and : to a lengthened vowel.

and *rest* would result in different English words: *wing* and *west*. In some contexts the /r/ for /w/ substitution may not interfere with understanding, but in other contexts it may seriously impair understanding. In those cases where understanding is impaired, we would expect that the parent would engage in sound correction procedures. If the parent is successful, the child may soon learn to utter /r/ in some words, but maintain his /r/ errors in other words.

The development of omission errors may also be viewed within this same framework. Many children, when they learn to say a word, will omit terminal members. If the words are understood the child may continue to omit final utterance units.

The comparative linguists tell us that in some cases phoneme omissions may lead to a change in the phonological structure of a language. Often this change is most common in the final position:

> Final positions of syllables, words and utterances are often conditioning factors for change, initial positions only rarely. Changes with final position as their conditioning factor are typically those which result in loss or merger. This, of course, results in fewer phonemes in these positions. We know of few languages which have more distinct phonemes in the syllable final than in the syllable initial position (Osgood and Sebeok, 1954, p. 148).

Omissions are not a frequent error for young children. They account for about 13 percent of all errors from ages three through eight (Templin, 1957). However, clinicians often report that errors of omission occur more frequently in the final position. Templin's data (1957) confirm this observation; her results reveal that omission errors occur with greater frequency in the final position that in the initial and medial positions of words. She reported the percentage of error types for each position and each age level separately. The percentage of omission errors in the initial position ranges from 0 (seven years) to 6.1 (three and a half years); in the medial position from 1.5 (seven years) to 9.7 (three years); in the final position from 5.4 (eight years) to 23.2 (three years). For age levels combined the percentages of omission errors for the initial, medial, and final positions are 3.1, 5.7, and 19.1, respectively. These findings may be interpreted to mean that children omit terminal sounds more than initial and medial sounds because terminal sounds are most redundant.

It is possible that in some cases the omission may be incorporated into the child's language system as a null contrast. Albright and Albright (1958, p. 259) have the following to say about sound omissions: ". . . the concept of zero [ɸ] is important to child language study, as the regular absence of a sound in its patterning in a sound system may be as much of a signal as the regular presence of a sound or other audible feature."

Phonetic Determiners of Phoneme Acquisition

In the previous section we discussed a group of variables that were thought to play a significant role in phoneme system learning.[14] It was assumed that the phonetic responses are available to the child and that what are learned or refined are the English phonemic rules for organizing these phonetic elements, a point stressed by Jakobson (1941). To a large extent this may be a true picture of articulatory acquisition, at least at the intermediate age levels of articulatory development, say, from two years to about four years for most children. In the early period of word learning the child is no doubt involved in a concerted effort to master both the phoneme system of English and certain phonetic productions (phoneme clusters and diphthongs) he has not made in the prelanguage period. The biographical studies indicate that most of the phonetic productions used in English are present when words are first learned. However, these studies usually describe children who are well into the language period.

Irwin's findings permit us to examine the phonemic utterances (the qualifications previously presented still hold in the present discussion, although no attempt will be made to review them again) of a large number of children who have learned a few English words. Prior to the first year of life practically no words were uttered by the children studied by Irwin and very few words were uttered in the first six months of the second year of life (Winitz and Irwin, 1958). Examination of the consonantal profiles up to the first year and for the following six months indicates that all but the /tʃ/ and /dʒ/ consonantal phonemes were uttered. Some phonemes, of course, occur very infrequently. Those phonemes occurring less than one percent at 17 and 18 months are /f/, /r/, /θ/, /ð/, /z/, /ʃ/, /ʒ/, and /ŋ/. Interestingly the list includes primarily "continuant" phonemes. In addition to the preceding eight unit phonemes and the /tʃ/ and /dʒ/ cluster phonemes, the many consonantal clusters of English (or the rules which govern them)—e.g., /tr-/, /kr-/, /-lt/, /-nd/, etc.—need to be learned (or at least strengthened) as utterance units in words.

Some of the same learning laws that apply to phonemic learning presumably apply to phonetic learning, especially discrimination, generalization, motivation, and frequency of reinforcement. In some cases it is difficult to disentangle phonetic learning from phonemic learning because attempts to make phonetic responses will impair phonemic learning. For example, if we assume a child possesses no [s] sound in his repertoire of responses and is confronted with a need to utter a word that begins

[14] We used the term mechanism rather than variable because the topic was not treated formally.

with [s], he may select the /θ/ response. He may be able to discriminate these two sounds, but since he has never uttered [s] before, he may select a sound, in this case the /θ/ sound, because it is similar to the [s] sound.[15] If the incorrect response is reinforced, the error will be uttered again. Thus the child will have developed both a phonemic (loss of a phoneme) and phonetic problem. However, if the child selected the retroflexed [ʂ], only a phonetic problem would have resulted.

Are there other ways in which phonetic variables may effect phoneme mastery? Perhaps there are; one will now be mentioned under the rubric of *fusion*.

Fusion

Fusion refers to phonetic changes that occur in a language. Heffner (1960, p. 175) defines fusion as "the unifying process by which the speech measure becomes a single configuration." When a sound in a configuration undergoes change that makes it more like its neighbor, the process is called assimilation. These changes may, in some cases, reflect physiological "ease," or rate of speech utterances, but not necessarily, for the changes are not always consistent or predictable. These resemble to a large degree the articulatory errors observed in young children and, therefore, are of interest to us. Also, fusion probably accounts for some of the phonetic differences found among adults. Such variations are not regarded as articulatory errors, although at times some variations may be considered substandard.

Several types of fusion follow (for more examples of each fusion type the reader is referred to Heffner (1960, pp. 175–200):

1. Assimilative changes as to voicing—e.g., [ð] and [θ] are often interchanged in the word *with*.
2. Assimilative changes of release—e.g., /tʃ/ for [tj] as in won't *you*.
3. Linking—e.g., omission of [r] as in [bʌtə] for [bʌtər] when *butter* is the final word in a phrase or is followed by forms beginning with a consonant.
4. Glides and intrusive sounds—e.g., [j] appears in the word *angel*, [ði jendʒəl].
5. Reduction, e.g., in *have various* the two [v] phones may fuse into one phone.
6. Assimilation of place of articulation—e.g., the [l] before [jʊ] becomes assimilated to the [j] as in *evaluate*, [ɪvæjʊet]; the [ŋ] becomes [n] as in *length;* the [t] may be released laterally in *atlas;* [t] for [k] and [d] for [g] may appear in the words *climb* and *glue,* respectively.

[15] We will define this type of generalization in Chapter 5.

Sometimes dissimilation occurs. Heffner states, "under some conditions of fusion the constituent sounds of a linguistic form suffer adaptive changes which make them less rather than more like their neighbor in the configuration" (Heffner, 1960, p. 198). He continues as follows:

> Whereas the phenomena of assimilation result from the anticipation of some portion of a movement required for a subsequent sound in the complex, or from the continuation of some feature of one sound into the articulation of a subsequent one, dissimilation is due to the avoidance of the difficulty of execution of two identical or closely similar movements within a very brief period of time. Every muscular movement has a minimum repetition time (or a maximum repetition rate), that is, a minimum period within which it cannot be successfully repeated. If new nervous impulses calculated to repeat the movement are initiated before this minimum interval has elapsed, the result is likely to be to lock the moving organ into its position rather than to repeat a movement. It appears to be possible to avoid this disturbance sometimes by what seem to be quite small modifications of the gross movements, if these are changes which involve a different array of neuromotor units in a different time pattern.[16]

Examples of dissimilation are also given by Heffner, but since this type of fusion is rare in English, no examples will be given.

Recall also the comments in Chapter 1 on phonological conditioning. The distinction between fusion and phonological conditioning should be clear; the former is used to identify a process, the latter to describe an already observable sequence. In any event assimilative principles based solely on phonetic environments cannot be used to predict changes that may occur in a language since so much more is involved, e.g., grammatical constraints. However, fusive principles may have some merit for understanding articulatory inconsistency and we shall illustrate one. The following examples pertain only to the /r/ and the /s/ sounds.

In the utterance of /pr/ the production of /r/ follows the labial sound /p/. As the child learns to produce this cluster he may initiate a glide-like sound in the labial position. The resulting cluster would be /pw/, a cluster which occurs infrequently in the initial position in English. On the other hand, the productions of /tr/, /kr/, /gr/, etc., are initiated from an alveolar position. The child is, therefore, much more likely to utter an /r/ variant, a vowel, or no sound at all.

This reasoning is not supported by the observations of Williams (1937) and Templin (1957). Williams reported the substitution errors for /r/ clusters obtained by Wellman and others (1931). Substitution of /w/ for /r/ occurred with about the same frequency in postlabial clusters, such as /kr/, /gr/, and /tr/, as in labial clusters, such as /pr/ and /br/. Templin (1957) found that /pr/ and /br/ are learned at about the same rate as other initial double /r/ clusters.

Nor is support for this speculation found in studies conducted with articulatory defective children. Buck (1948) studied the correct production of /r/ clusters for 91 children judged to be defective in /r/. The children were drawn from kindergarten, first, second, and third grades. For the initial position more correct responses were obtained for the/θr/, /gr/, /kr/, /tr/, and /dr/ clusters than for the /fr/, /br/, and /pr/ clusters. Curtis and Hardy (1959) studied 30 children between five years six months and eight years six months who were considered to have /r/ errors. For prevocalic /r/ clusters the rank order of correct production for the eight clusters studied by Buck were as follows: /pr/, /dr/, /tr/, /br/, /kr/, /gr/, /θr/, and /fr/. The findings obtained by Buck and by Curtis and Hardy are, for the most part, in disagreement.

Consider now the /s/ phoneme. Children may anticipate /k/ in /sk/ and, therefore, retract the tongue for an /sk/ cluster. We are assuming in this discussion that a retracted [s] would be classified as defective. According to Templin, /sk/ does not differ in learning rate when compared with other initial double /s/ clusters. However, Hale (1945) reports /sk/ more defective and /st/ less defective than other initial /s/ clusters. It should be noted that the place of articulation for the alveolar [s] is anticipated in the /st/ blend. It appears that, for the most part, the above analyses are unsatisfactory.

Concluding Remarks on Phoneme Development

In this treatment of phoneme acquisition, no clear distinction has been made between the child's passive understanding of the adult phoneme system and the active use of his own phoneme system. His understanding of the adult phoneme system, or a portion thereof, no doubt antedates any attempt by the child to utter language units. When the child begins to talk he has some understanding of the adult phoneme system but at the present time we do not know the level of passive development, either phonological or grammatical, that is necessary before attempts to talk are made. The developmental variance between these two systems is a topic of considerable interest.

First, as mentioned, we need to know something about the child's speech sound discrimination development. Is there, as Jakobson and Halle suggest, an orderly developmental sequence based on the degree of physical difference between the phonemes? Second, we need to know whether the active system develops at the same rate and in the same order as the passive system. Does the sequence of phonemic contrasts outlined by Jakobson and Halle, for example, apply only to passive learning (Berko and Brown, 1960) or to production learning as well? Third, since the passive and active systems are not the same at each age level, although there is probably only one underlying phonological system at each point in time, we need to know something about the transformation rules (mediational process) that bridge and translate a passive system into an active system. Fourth, we need to know whether or not the passive and active systems actively interact. That is, is the development of active and passive phoneme contrasts contingent on the simultaneous development of subsequences of these two systems? For example, children may not be able to discriminate the grave/acute contrast until the production of the nasal/nonnasal contrast is learned. If these two systems actively "interact," then, for example, the discrimination of adult phoneme contrasts cannot be fully described by the discrimination theories previously presented. The children's perceptions will be, in part, a function of previous categorizations. Retaining our example, the active learning of the nasal/nonnasal contrast will tend to make nasal and nonnasal perceptions categorical, and thus there will be little generalization between these two features. All subsequent nasal or nonnasal discriminations will then be "mediated" by the phonemes which are produced rather than by the absolute physical stimuli which are heard. The mechanism of mediation will be explained in Chapter 3 when the relation between discrimination and articulation is discussed. Here we shall also learn that in one instance a passive phoneme system developed correctly when physiological deficits prevented the acquisition of an active phoneme system; this suggests that the two systems need not interact.

The discussion of phoneme system learning presented here should at best be considered a poor sketch of an elegant process. For example, terms like *generalization* and *discrimination* have been used to cover a multitude of processes or rules that might be called phonological competence about which we know very little.

However, one significant point should be made. Although language use involves principles or rules (now generally called linguistic competence) rather than a probabilistic arrangement of items, language learning is most likely a function of the arrangement of stimulus and reinforcement events as well as a function of biological traits, predispositions or capacities, however they are characterized. Even if one is fully convinced that a stimulus event is a mere elicitor of a biologically inherited rule, or device which forms these rules (Lenneberg, 1967), the elicitation process is an interesting one and no doubt worthy of study. Further, such investigations may reveal among other things the way humans process, store, and produce language events, resulting in sentences that have a syntactic, semantic, and phonological description.

Are Articulatory Errors a Phonetic or a Phonemic Problem?

In the discussion of the descriptive studies on speech sound development it was mentioned that the results of these studies reflect, for the most part, phoneme system mastery rather than the acquisition of certain phonetic (motor) productions. This concept might now be extended to children with articulatory errors. It is possible to think of articulatory errors for children of about six to eight years of age simply as phoneme systems that are at variance with the adult phoneme system. For some reason the young child has acquired a phoneme system that is not the same as the adult phoneme system. The more the two phoneme systems differ, the more severe is the articulatory defectiveness of the young child.

A child may be said to have an articulatory error whenever the individuals of the culture demand a close if not exact correspondence to the adult phonological norm. For example, in the word *to* the English language does not permit the /t/ to alternate with the /d/, but it does in the medial position of many words like *latter* and *ladder*. (This medial sound is really a variant of the /t/ or /d/.) Let us assume, however, that for the child in question the /t/ and /d/ are in free variation, i.e., the /t/ and /d/ are allophones of the same phoneme, designated /D/, i.e., we can determine no linguistic rule for their alternation (just as in English we vary freely the allophones [kʰ] and [k] in the word-final position). Can we say that this child has a phonetic problem? He possesses the necessary motor productions, but he has yet to cleave the [t] and [d] into two separate phonemes.

Does a child who substitutes frequently /w/ for /r/, but whose [r] is an allophone of /w/, have a phonetic problem? Do all children with articulatory errors possess this kind of problem? Probably not. Conceivably there are many children, who, after exhautive testing, will not be found to produce the desired production. Recall the subject studied by Haas. He did not produce an [r] phone. However, it is difficult to determine whether the omission of [r] was a function of this child's inability to produce this phone, or simply that the subject's system as it developed did not for some reason require the /r/ contrast. The issue cannot be resolved by asking this child or children with similar phoneme systems to imitate the [r], in order to determine whether or not the child possesses the "ability" to pronounce the [r]. In much the same way, English adults would have difficulty uttering phones which are not variants of the phonemes of their language.

When one begins to teach this child the /r/ phoneme it is, of course, essential to teach the phonetic productions of the several /r/ variants.

Thus, for all practical purposes it can be said that the child has a phonetic problem. Even so, many of the phonetic features of the /r/ phoneme are present in the child's repertoire of responses (glide, resonant, voicing, etc.). A phonetic error does not mean, then, the inability to produce all of the phonetic features of a sound in error.

We would like to take the point of view that when obvious physical and mental abnormalities are not present, most if not all phonetic errors are the result of incorrectly learned phonemic systems. (In some cases articulatory errors may result in morphological "errors.") This statement may seem too general to prove to be operationally useful. Besides, we have already said that some phonemic systems may be determined by phonetic factors. Perhaps, then, the hypothesis should be qualified by suggesting that when obvious physical and mental impairments are not present, articulatory errors represent the incorrect learning of the phoneme system of the community language, which in some cases may have been partially a result of incorrectly learned phonetic productions. What the psychological variables are and how they contribute to articulatory mislearning are, of course, research questions for the present and future generations of speech pathologists. We have already made some hints. Perhaps the first step would be to obtain longitudinal data on many children so that the development of phoneme systems may be charted. In this way the development of phoneme systems that eventually prove to be at variance with the adult phoneme system can be studied.

In the following pages information will be presented that is both interesting and supportive of my hypothesis. The information is not a systematic or analytical development, but it does suggest that learning factors seriously need to be included when attempts are made to describe the development or etiology of articulatory errors.

PRELANGUAGE UTTERANCES. The consonantal phonemes for the English-speaking child are gradually learned from birth, and with the exception of the phonemes /dʒ/ and /tʃ/, they are acquired by two and one-half years of age (the terminal point of the Irwin investigations). That is, by two and one-half years of age children can utter to the satisfaction of English transcribers nonvocoid phones that are adequate instances of English consonantal phonemes, a point which Jakobson (1941) stressed. It is still possible, however, that some of the consonants judged as correct by Irwin might be considered defective if they occurred in the words of children.

LEWIS' SUBSTITUTION RULE. The observation by Lewis (1951) that 81 percent of substitution errors involve attempts to utter sounds already in the child's repertory would suggest that phonetic facility precedes phoneme system learning. Lewis states (1951, pp. 179–180) as follows:

> . . . Substitution is not usually a matter of replacing a
> consonant that the child cannot make by one that he

can. On the contrary, in the great majority of cases the three children were already able to produce the consonant now attempted. This is shown . . . by Stern and Deville and of those in my own record of K up to the age of 2; . . . Here, out of a total of 355 cases, no fewer than 81 per cent consist of attempts upon consonants already in the child's repertory.

Taking now these cases where the child attempts a consonant already present in his repertory, we find that of 286 substitutions, 77 per cent consisted in replacing the attempted consonant by one which had appeared *chronologically earlier* in the child's history, while in only 20 per cent of the cases did he substitute a sound chronologically later.[17]

In brief, the rule is this: substitution occurs when the child *replaces a heard consonant by one relatively more familiar,* one which has been longer established in his repertory. The child, when confronted with the necessity of carrying out a new, or relatively new, pattern of action, often produces one which has become more habitual to him.

PHONETIC FEATURES OF ARTICULATION ERRORS. The phonetic features of the incorrect sound resemble to a high degree the phonetic features of the correct sound. Van Riper and Irwin (1958) and Snow (1963) have reported the substitution errors of frequently misarticulated phonemes for American children. Some examples of frequent errors for the /s/, /l/, and /ʃ/ are as follows (Van Riper and Irwin, 1958, pp. 81–85): for /s/ the errors are /θ/, [ɬ], /ʃ/, /t/, /f/, and /z/; for the nonsyllabic allophones of the /l/ phoneme the errors are /j/, /w/, /r/, and [hw]; and for the /ʃ/ phoneme the errors are /s/, /tʃ/, /ʒ/, [ɬ], and /t/.

Kantner and West (1960, pp. 246–279) have grouped the English consonants according to the muscles involved in their production and the nerves that innervate these muscles. Utilizing this information, it may be noted that in many instances the error sound and the correct sound are produced by the same set of muscles which are innervated by the same cranial nerve.

INCONSISTENCY OF ARTICULATION ERRORS. The findings of the studies reported above suggest that errors for a particular phoneme occur inconsistently. Thus, children who misarticulate a phoneme may be found to utter the phoneme correctly (either the same or a different allophone) in some other context, indicating that the same or a similar production has been learned but has not generalized to all contexts.

COMPARISON OF FREQUENCY OF SOUND ERRORS FOR GERMAN AND AMERICAN CHILDREN. The order of difficulty of certain sounds appears to

[17] It should be emphasized that Lewis is referring to phones learned "chronologically earlier" in *words*.

vary for German and American children. The values for the German children are taken from Luchsinger and Arnold (1959, p. 260) and for American children from Roe and Milisen (1942). Luchsinger and Arnold report that Möhring in 1938 tested twenty consonants of 2102 defective-speaking schoolchildren. The sounds were grouped according to percentage of subject difficulty. Errors of Group I occurred in 1 to 11.1 percent of the cases, Group II in 17.9 to 28 percent of the subjects, and Group III in 33.5 to 54.5 percent of the cases. Group III consisted of the following six sounds: /s/, [ts], /z/, /ʃ/, [ç] (voiceless palatal fricative), and [r̃] (trilled alveolar [r]).

The order of difficulty of certain sounds in German and in English was compared by listing the frequency of defectiveness *in English* of the four most defective German sounds ([ç] and [ts] are excluded; the former because it does not "occur" in English and the latter because it is not a phonemic entity in English). The data for the English sounds were taken from the results of Roe and Milisen (1942); both the percentage of errors and the rank order of the errors are as follows:

	VOICELESS ERRORS INCLUDED		AFTER ELIMINATING VOICELESS FOR VOICED ERRORS	
Phoneme	Percent	Rank	Percent	Rank
/s/	19.9	6	19.9	2
/z/	45.8	1	12.4	5
/ʃ/	3.8	15	3.8	12
/r/	5.9	13	5.9	8

It is apparent that the /ʃ/ and /r/ phonemes are not frequently erred in English while they are in German.[18]

Second, Möhring found that the least defective sounds were the /b/, /p/, /v/, /f/, /d/, /t/, /l/, and /n/ sounds, occurring in 1.5 to 11.1 percent of the children tested. The results of Roe and Milisen are essentially in agreement with these findings with the exception of the /d/ and /t/ sounds. The /d/ was the fifth most defective sound (25 percent) and the /t/ the tenth most defective sound (14 percent). When voicelessness was not considered an error, the /d/ was the eleventh most defective sound (4 percent) and the /t/ the third most defective sound (14 percent).

Comparisons between the findings of Roe and Milisen and Möhring may not be completely justifiable. Möhring studied defective-speaking children while Roe and Milisen studied a group of children unselected as to speech production. However, this difference should not greatly alter the rank order of the defective sounds. In addition, sampling procedures, criteria

---

18 Comparisons between the two languages for the /r/ may be unfair, since the allophones are different.

of defectiveness, and reliability of estimates may have contributed to some of the differences.

Further research may indicate that certain sounds are frequently defective in some languages while the same sounds are not defective in other languages. It would be of interest, for example, to compare the frequency of articulatory errors for children from languages that differ widely in the number of phonemes. Hawaiian, for example, has only 13 phonemes while English has 45 (Hockett, 1958, p. 93).

SUBSTITUTION ERRORS FOR GERMAN, DANISH, AND AMERICAN CHILDREN. Some differences among American, German, and Danish children become apparent when substitution errors of defective sounds are considered. Luchsinger and Arnold (1959, pp. 476 and 479) and Abrahams (1957) report in detail the substitution errors for the uvular flap or rolled, [R], allophone of the /r/ phoneme for German- and Danish-speaking children, respectively. For [R] German children substitute /l/ (in 38 percent of the cases), /ʃ/, /d/, and /n/, and Danish children primarily substitute the [ʔ] (the /ʔ/ is phonemic in Danish). According to Van Riper and Irwin (1958), the [r] substitutions for American children are primarily /w/, /j/, /v/, [R] and /f/, in that order.

Cross-language comparisons of sound substitutions is an intriguing area of research. It is quite possible that substitution errors will show some universal regularities in that the substituted error may be phonetically similar to the correct sound and may conform to certain grammatical or phonological rules of the natural language. Detailed and precise information is needed here, but the foregoing findings for /r/ lead us to this conclusion. An organic hypothesis, on the other hand, would suggest that lawfulness would prevail between the substitution errors for the same or similar sounds of several different languages, even though the phonemic structure of the languages differs. That is, an error would be determined, for the most part, by physiological mechanisms.

ALLOPHONES OF PHONEMES IN CERTAIN LANGUAGES. The phonemic studies of languages indicate that the assignment of phones to phonemes varies considerably from language to language. For example, the following pairs of phones are allophones of a phoneme in some language: [pf], [bp], [sz], [tθ], [dθ], [sʃ], [řl] (ř = voiced alveolar flap [r]), [fv], [nŋ], [dř], [wv], [tř̥] ([ř̥] = retracted [ř]) (Gleason, 1961, p. 275; Pike, 1947, p. 70). It may be seen that the preceding pairing of phones resembles to a high degree the articulatory substitutions of English-speaking American children. It does not seem, therefore, that articulatory substitutions represent an "unnatural" condition. The substitutions are considered errors merely because the child's and the adult's phoneme systems are at variance.

FUSION. Phonetic variation in the speech of adults has been previously described. These phonetic changes show a resemblance to the articulatory errors of young children; that is, errors of omission and substitution are characteristic of speakers in general and are part of the normal speaking process. Since the variation is considered "normal," they are not viewed as articulatory errors.

ARTICULATION LEARNING ABILITY. In two separate investigations the sound learning ability of children with "functional" articulatory errors was examined. In both of these studies the hypothesis was that the present articulatory learning ability of children with "functional" articulatory errors does not differ from normal-speaking children as long as their impaired articulatory responses are not included in the learning task. In the first study (Winitz and Lawrence, 1961) this hypothesis was tested by comparing children with good and poor articulation on three sounds not present in their repertoire (non-English sounds). In the second study (Winitz and Bellerose, 1963b) the hypothesis was tested by controlling for response skills presumed to contribute to the learning of the experimental sounds. The test sounds were double phoneme clusters which occur infrequently in English. Response skill was equated by selecting subjects whose articulatory performance on the individual phonemes of the cluster was the same.

Experiment I. The subjects were 96 kindergarten children, 48 boys and 48 girls, serially selected from the enrollment lists of five classes. These children were given the Templin (1953) 50-item articulation screening test. On the basis of their scores on the Templin test, the upper 12.5 percent and the lower 12.5 percent of the children in each sex group were determined. Those subjects in the upper 12.5 percent were identified as having good articulation (high group), and those in the lower 12.5 percent as having poor articulation (low group). The sample included 6 boys and 6 girls at each of the levels, making a total of 24 children.

Three non-English sounds, [x], [œ], and [ç], were selected. Five independent blocks of sounds were prepared, with each block containing two instances of each sound randomly placed (six sounds to a block). For the final training tape the five blocks were repeated making a total of 10 blocks or 60 sounds. The children were brought to the examination room and asked to say the sounds they heard on the tape recorder. Correct responses were reinforced. The findings (Figure 2.11) revealed no significant differences between the two groups in the articulation acquisition curves.

Experiment II. Three groups of children were studied: Group I was composed of children who were not defective in articulation; Group II consisted of children who had errors of articulation for the /r/ phoneme; and Group III was composed of children who had errors of articulation for the /r/ and /ʃ/ phonemes and who, in addition, were generally defective in articulation. It was assumed that for the learning of a phoneme cluster composed of the /r/ phoneme Group I would be superior to Groups II

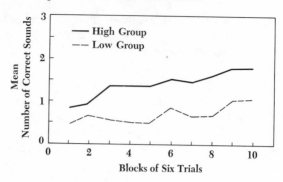

[Figure 2.11] Mean acquisition curves on the non-English sound learning task. High group, good articulation; low group, poor articulation.
SOURCE: Winitz and Lawrence, 1961.

and III, and Groups II and III would not differ from each other. It was further hypothesized that for the learning of a phoneme cluster composed of the /ʃ/ phoneme, Groups I and II would not differ from each other, and both groups would perform better than Group III. The subjects were 36 kindergarten children, 18 boys and 18 girls. Subjects were assigned to the three groups on the basis of their scores on the Templin-Darley Test (1960) as follows:

Group I—perfect articulation. Subjects who achieved perfect scores (50 correct responses) on the Templin-Darley Test were designated as perfect articulators.

Group II—/r/ errors of articulation. The Templin-Darley Test contains 15 items in which allophones of the /r/ phoneme and 4 items in which allophones of the /ʃ/ phoneme are tested. Subjects designated as having only errors of the /r/ phoneme were children who had /r/ errors on at least 12 of the 15 /r/ items and who missed not more than 6 other items. None of these additional 6 items were errors of the /ʃ/ phoneme.

Group III—defective articulation. Subjects in this group were children who obtained no more than 20 correct responses on the Templin-Darley Test, had at least 12 of the 15 /r/ items defective, and had all of the 4 /ʃ/ items defective.

Two phoneme clusters, /vr/ and /ʃm/, were selected as test stimuli. These two blends occur infrequently in English words. The /vr/ occurs in words like *every* and *everyone* (Kenyon and Knott, 1949) and never appears in the initial position (Trager and Smith, 1962, p. 35). The /ʃm/ also does not occur as an initial cluster in English (Trager and Smith,

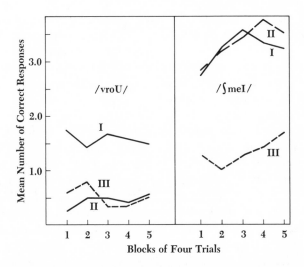

[Figure 2.12] Mean acquisition curves for learning of /vroʊ/ (left panel) and /ʃmeɪ/ (right panel) for all three groups: Group I, perfect articulation; Group II, defective /r/ articulation; and Group III, defective articulation.

SOURCE: Winitz and Bellerose, 1963b.

1962, p. 35), but it occasionally occurs in nonstandard English words, such as *shmoo*. It was assumed that this blend was not familiar to these children. Thus, the two phoneme clusters were considered to be essentially new sound stimuli for the subjects in this study. The /vr/ cluster was combined with the diphthong /oʊ/ to form the syllable /vroʊ/, and the /ʃm/ cluster was combined with the diphthong /eɪ/ to form the syllable /ʃmeɪ/.

The subjects in each group were asked to repeat the sounds they heard on the tape recorder. There were 20 successive instances of the /vroʊ/ and /ʃmeɪ/ syllable grouped into five blocks of four trials. All correct responses were reinforced.

The results are presented in Figure 2.12. The findings indicated that learning took place for the /ʃmeɪ/ syllable but not for the /vroʊ/ syllable. Generalizations derived from this study are, therefore, limited to the /ʃmeɪ/ syllable. The findings for the /ʃmeɪ/ syllable appear to indicate that learning of the /ʃm/ cluster is related to present ability to articulate the individual phonemes of the cluster; learning of the /ʃm/ cluster does not appear to be related to the missing of articulation items that test for phonemes which are not part of the /ʃm/ cluster.

The findings for Groups I and II on the /ʃmeɪ/ syllable seem to support the hypothesis that the articulatory learning ability of children with "functional" articulatory errors is not different from normal-speaking children as long as their impaired articulatory responses are not included in the learning task. However, the hypothesis needs additional empirical support. Further testing should be done with children from different age levels and with a variety of sounds.

This, then, concludes the list of supporting "evidence." It is my contention that an articulatory error which has persisted beyond what is generally considered to be normal is the result of an incompletely developed phoneme system. It is incomplete in the sense that it does not correspond in a one-to-one fashion with the adult system. We have speculated about some of the psychological variables that may account for phoneme system learning. Greater understanding of this process may provide us with the necessary variables that account for phoneme system mislearning.

SUMMARY

The focal point of this chapter was the development of speech sounds in words. First, a distinction was made between phonetic and phonemic development. Second, the studies on phonetic achievement were summarized, giving an account of the developmental mastery of speech sounds with age and of the most frequently occurring articulatory errors. Third, the process of phonemic mastery was considered. The concept of distinctive features was introduced first. Then, studies of the phoneme systems of children, both normal and defective, were summarized. This section was followed by a discussion of "inconsistency" of misarticulations.

The relevancy of the psychological concepts of discrimination, generalization, and classification learning were considered. Also the importance of motivation in speech sound learning was stressed.

Lastly the author's thesis that articulation errors represent, for the most part, the incorrect learning of the phoneme system of the language was developed. Evidence was garnered from a variety of sources and included experimental investigation as well as cross-cultural data.

REFERENCES

Abrahams, H. Konsonant i forlyd foran vokal. *Tale òg Stemme,* 1957, *17.*

Albright, R. W., and Albright, J. B. The phonology of a two year old child. *Word,* 1956, *12,* 382–390.

Albright, R. W., and Albright, J. B. Application of descriptive linguistics to child language. *Journal of Speech and Hearing Research,* 1958, *1,* 257–261.

Applegate, J. R. Phonological rules of a subdialect of English. *Word,* 1961, *17,* 186–193.

Berko, J. The child's learning of English morphology. *Word,* 1958, *14,* 150–177.

Berko, Jean [Gleason], and Brown, R. Psycholinguistic research methods. In P. H. Mussen (Ed.), *Handbook of research methods in child development.* New York: Wiley, 1960.

Buck, M. W. A study of the misarticulation of [r] in children from kindergarten through third grade. M.A. Thesis, State University of Iowa, 1948.

Carroll, J. B. *Language and thought.* Englewood Cliffs, N.J.: Prentice-Hall, 1964.

Chomsky, N. Current issues in linguistic theory. The Hague: Mouton & Co., 1964.

Contreras, H. W. The phonological system of a bilingual child. Ph.D. Dissertation, Indiana University, 1961.

Curtis, J. F. Personal communication. 1963.

Curtis, J. F., and Hardy, J. C. A phonetic study of misarticulation of /r/. *Journal of Speech and Hearing Research,* 1959, *2,* 244–257.

Curtis, J. F., and Hardy, J. C. Letter to the editor. *Journal of Speech and Hearing Research,* 1961, *4,* 197–199.

Davis, I. P. The speech aspects of reading readiness. *Newer practices in reading in the elementary school, 17th Yearbook of the Department of Elementary School Principals,* NEA, 1938, 17 (7), 282–289.

Denes, P. B. On the statistics of spoken English. *Journal of the Acoustical Society of America,* 1963, *35,* 892–904.

Ervin, S. M. and Miller, W. R. Language development. In H. W. Stevenson (Ed.), *Child psychology, The Sixty-second Yearbook of the National Society for the Study of Education,* Part I. Chicago: The University of Chicago Press, 1963.

Estes, W. K. The statistical approach to learning theory. In S. Koch, *Psychology: A study of a science,* Vol. 2. New York: McGraw-Hill, 1959.

Fant, G. M. Descriptive analysis of the acoustic aspects of speech. *Logos,* 1962, *5,* 3–17. (a)

Fant, G. M. Sound spectography. Pp. 14–33 in A. Sorijarvi, and P. Aalto (Eds.), *Proceedings of the Fourth International Congress of Phonetic Sciences.* The Hague: Mouton & Co., 1962. (b)

Francis, W. N. *The structure of American English*. New York: Ronald, 1958.

French, N. R., Carter, C. W., Jr., and Koenig, W., Jr. The words and sounds of telephone conversations. *Bell System Technique Journal*, 1930, *9*, 290–324.

Gemelli, A., and Black, J. W. Phonetics from the viewpoint of psychology. In L. Kaiser (Ed.), *Manual of phonetics*. Amsterdam: North-Holland Publishing Co., 1957.

Gleason, H. A. *An introduction to descriptive linguistics*. Revised. New York: Holt, Rinehart and Winston, 1961.

Guttman, N., and Kalish, H. I. Discriminability and stimulus generalization. *Journal of Experimental Psychology*, 1956, *51*, 79–88.

Haas, W. Phonological analysis of a case of dyslalia. *Journal of Speech and Hearing Disorders*, 1963, *28*, 239–246.

Hale, Anita R. A study of misarticulation of [s] in combination with selected vowels and consonants. M.A. Thesis, State University of Iowa, 1945.

Hall, Margaret E. Auditory factors in functional articulatory speech defects. *Journal of Experimental Education*, 1938, *7*, 110–132.

Halle, M. On the bases of phonology. In J. A. Fodor and J. J. Katz (Eds.), *The structure of language*. Englewood Cliffs, N. J.: Prentice-Hall, 1964. (a)

Halle, M. Phonology in generative grammar. In J. A. Fodor and J. J. Katz (Eds.), *The structure of language*. Englewood Cliffs, N. J.: Prentice-Hall, 1964. (b)

Heffner, R.-M. S. *General phonetics*. Madison: The University of Wisconsin Press, 1960.

Hockett, C. F. *A course in modern linguistics*. New York: Macmillan, 1958.

House, A. S. Letter to the editor. *Journal of Speech and Hearing Research*, 1961, *4*, 194–197.

Hunt, E. B. *Concept learning: An information processing problem*. New York: Wiley, 1962.

Jakobson, R. *Kindersprache, Aphasie und Allgemeine Lautgesetze*. Uppsala: Almqvist and Wiksell, 1941.

Jakobson, R., Fant, G. M., and Halle, M. *Preliminaries to speech analysis*. Acoustics Laboratory, Massachusetts Institute of Technology, Tech. Rep. No. 13, 1952.

Jakobson, R., and Halle, M. *Fundamentals of language*. The Hague: Mouton & Co., 1956.

Jakobson, R., and Halle, M. Phonology in relation to phonetics. In L. Kaiser (Ed.), *Manual of phonetics*. Amsterdam: North Holland Publishing Co., 1957.

Jones, D. *Phonetic readings in English*. Heidelberg: Winter, 1929.

Jordan, E. P. Articulation test measures and listener ratings of articulation defectiveness. *Journal of Speech and Hearing Research*, 1960, *3*, 303–319.

Kantner, C. E., and West, R. *Phonetics*. Rev. ed. New York: Harper & Row, 1960.

Kenyon, J. S., and Knott, T. A. *A pronouncing dictionary of American English*. Springfield, Mass.: Merriam, 1949.

Ladefoged, P. Linguistic Phonetics, Working papers in phonetics, 6, Los Angeles: UCLA, 1967.

Lenneberg, E. H. *Biological foundations of language*. New York: Wiley, 1967.

Leopold, W. F. *Speech development of a bilingual child*. (4 Vols.) Evanston: Northwestern University, 1947.

Leopold, W. F. Patterning in children's language learning, In *Psycholinguistics, a book of readings*. S. Saporta (Ed.), New York: Holt, Rinehart and Winston, 1961.

Lewis, M. M. *Infant speech, a study of the beginnings of language*. New York: Humanities Press, 1951.

Luchsinger, R., and Arnold, G. E. *Lehrbuch Der Stimm- und Sprachleikunde*. Wien: Springer-Verlag, 1959.

Menyuk, P. Syntactic rules used by children from preschool through first grade. *Child Development*, 1964, *35*, 533–546.

Menyuk, P. The role of distinctive features in children's acquisition of phonology, *Journal of Speech and Hearing Research*, 1968, *11*, 138–146.

Miller, G. A., and Nicely, P. E. An analysis of perceptual confusions among some English consonants. *Journal of the Acoustical Society of America*, 1955, *27*, 338–352.

Osgood, C. E., and Sebeok, T. A. (Eds.). Psycholinguistics, a survey of the theory and research problems. *International Journal of American Linguistics*, 1954, (Supplement) 29, 1–203.

Perkins, W. H. Methods and materials for testing articulation of [s] and [z]. *Quarterly Journal of Speech*, 1952, *38*, 57–62.

Peters, R. W. Dimensions of perception for consonants. *Journal of the Acoustical Society of America*, 1963, *35*, 1985–1989. (a)

Peters, R. W. Structure of auditory space for five and six year old children. Unpublished study, 1963. (b)

Pike, K. L. *Phonemics, a technique for reducing languages to writing*. Ann Arbor: The University of Michigan Press, 1947.

Poole, I. Genetic development of articulation of consonant sounds in speech. *Elementary English Review*, 1934, *11*, 159–161.

Postal, P. M. *Aspects of phonological theory*. New York: Harper & Row, 1968.

Roe, V., and Milisen, R. The effect of maturation upon

defective articulation in elementary grades. *Journal of Speech Disorders,* 1942, *7,* 37–45.

Saporta, S. Frequency of consonant clusters. *Language,* 1955, *31,* 25–30.

Sayler, Helen K. The effect of maturation upon defective articulation in grades seven through twelve. *Journal of Speech and Hearing Disorders,* 1949, *15,* 202–207.

Scott, N. C. *English conversations.* Cambridge: Heffer, 1942.

Shepard, R. N., and Chang, J.-J. Stimulus generalization in the learning of classifications. *Journal of Experimental Psychology,* 1963, *65,* 94–102.

Siegel, G. M., Winitz, H., and Conkey, H. The influence of testing instruments on articulatory responses of children. *Journal of Speech and Hearing Disorders,* 1963, *28,* 67–76.

Snow, K. A detailed analysis of articulation responses of "normal" first grade children. *Journal of Speech and Hearing Research,* 1963, *6,* 277–290.

Spence, K. W. The basis of solution by chimpanzees of the intermediate size problem. *Journal of Experimental Psychology,* 1942, *31,* 257–271.

Spence, K. W., *Behavior theory and conditioning.* New Haven: Yale University Press, 1956.

Spiker, C. C. The hypothesis of stimulus interaction and an explanation of stimulus compounding. In L. P. Lipsitt and C. C. Spiker (Eds.), *Advances in Child Development and Behavior.* New York: Academic Press, 1963.

Spriestersbach, D. C., and Curtis, J. F. Misarticulation and discrimination of speech sounds. *Quarterly Journal of Speech,* 1951, *37,* 483–491.

Stevens, K. N., and Halle, M. Remarks on analysis by synthesis and distinctive features. In W. Wathen-Dunn (Ed.) *Models for the perception of speech and visual form.* Cambridge: M.I.T. Press, 1967.

Taylor, J. A. A personality scale of manifest anxiety. *Journal of Abnormal and Social Psychology,* 1953, *48,* 285–290.

Templin, M. C. Norms on a screening test of articulation for ages three through eight. *Journal of Speech and Hearing Disorders,* 1953, *18,* 323–331.

Templin, M. C. Certain language skills in children, their development and interrelationships. *Institute of Child Welfare, Monograph Series,* No. 26. Minneapolis: University of Minnesota Press, 1957.

Templin, M. C., and Darley, F. L. *The Templin-Darley tests of articulation.* Iowa City, Iowa: Bureau of Educational Research and Service Extension Division, 1960.

Torgerson, W. S. *Theory and methods of scaling.* New York: Wiley, 1958.

Trager, G. T., and Smith, H. T. An outline of English structure. *Studies in Linguistics: Occasional Papers,* 3, American Council of Learned Societies, 15th printing, 1962.

Travis, L. E. *Speech pathology.* New York: Appleton-Century-Crafts, 1931.

Van Riper, C. and Irwin, J. V. *Voice and articulation.* Englewood Cliffs, N.J.: Prentice-Hall, 1958.

Velten, H. V. The growth of phonemic and lexical patterns in infant language. *Language,* 1943, *19,* 281–292.

Voegelin, C. F., and Adams, S. A phonetic study of young children's speech. *Journal of Experimental Education* 1934, *3,* 107–116.

Voelker, C. H. Phonetic distribution in formal American pronunciation. *Journal of the Acoustical Society of America,* 1934, *5,* 242–246.

Weir, R. H. *Language in the crib.* The Hague: Mouton & Co., 1962.

Wellman, B. L., Case, I. M., Mengert, I..G., and Bradbury, D. E. Speech sounds of young children. *University of Iowa Studies in Child Welfare,* Vol. 5, No. 2, 1931.

Williams, H. M. A qualitative analysis of the erroneous speech sound substitutions of preschool children, Part II, Development of language vocabulary in young children. *University of Iowa Studies in Child Welfare,* 1937.

Winitz, H. Temporal reliability in articulation testing. *Journal of Speech and Hearing Disorders,* 1963, *28,* 247–251.

Winitz, H., and Bellerose, B. Phoneme generalization as a function of phoneme similarity and verbal unit of test and training stimuli. *Journal of Speech and Hearing Research,* 1963, *6,* 379–392. (a)

Winitz, H., and Bellerose, B. Learning of certain phoneme clusters by children with specific articulation errors. Unpublished study, 1963. (b)

Winitz, H., and Irwin, O. C., Syllabic and phonetic structure of infants' early words. *Journal of Speech and Hearing Research,* 1958, *1,* 250–256.

Winitz, H., and Lawrence, M. Children's articulation and sound learning ability. *Journal of Speech and Hearing Research,* 1961, *4,* 259–268.

3

VARIABLES RELATED TO ARTICULATORY DEVELOPMENT AND PERFORMANCE

The relation between articulatory performance and a number of somatic, psychological, and behavioral variables has engaged continually the ingenuity of speech pathologists. Two experimental procedures, for the most part, have been employed in these studies. In some studies correlations were computed between articulatory scores and the variables under study, and in others comparisons were made between normal children and articulatory defective children.[1] The difference between these two procedures will become clear below.

Since our interest is in children generally designated as functionally defective in articulation, only those studies are reported whose subjects were physically and mentally normal. The criteria of normalcy varied somewhat from study to study, but most investigators were consistent with regard to the following: the exclusion of children with severe organic involvements, such as cleft palate or cerebral palsy; the exclusion of children who stuttered; the inclusion of children with normal intelligence (IQ's above 70, although many studies excluded subjects with IQ's below 90); the inclusion of only those children from monolingual homes; and the inclusion of only those children who had normal hearing. Normal hearing was usually defined as no loss greater than 20

---

[1] Throughout this chapter children without articulatory defects will be referred to as either normal, normal-speaking, or control subjects. Children with articulatory defects will be referred to as either articulatory defective, defective-speaking, or experimental subjects.

decibels ASA for the frequencies 500, 1000, 2000, and 4000. The authors do not always indicate the race of the subjects, but in most instances the subjects were white.

Several additional criteria were used in deciding the acceptability of an article. The subjects had to have no additional speech impairments such as a voice disorder or a serious delay in language development. The data for the control group needed to be collected at the time the study was made. In some studies the scores of the experimental subjects were compared with available norms. Despite the fact that experimenters try to duplicate methods of test administration and subject sampling procedures, differences in experimental procedures probably exist when investigations are carried out on two separate occasions. Therefore, when no control group was used, the study was excluded. Finally, our discussion is restricted to published studies. Publication does not necessarily mean, of course, that a study has achieved a certain standard of excellence. However, those articles that have passed the scrutiny of an editorial board seem to merit initial consideration more often than not. In all cases differences between control and experimental groups are reported as statistically significant when the level of confidence reached or exceeded .05. In some studies statistical tests were not applied, in which case only those differences that appear meaningful will be mentioned. When a significant difference was found, it seemed purposeless, except in a few cases, to report the magnitude of the difference, since this would require a detailed description of the test items. Finally, the correlational coefficients will be reported for only those items found to be significantly different from zero at or beyond the .05 level.

The studies will be reviewed in chronological order except that the studies conducted with children will precede those conducted with adults. A fairly detailed description of the subjects, sampling procedures, and tests is given when the study is first cited. Later citations of the study are necessarily brief.

Before beginning our detailed review it is of interest to mention that the studies have been motivated by at least two different orientations. In some instances misarticulation was studied as one of many symptoms indicative of developmental immaturity. In other studies the purpose was simply to describe the relationship between articulation and some other variable. For this reason, a variety of physical and mental measures were investigated. Some measures like rapid eyebrow movement, could by no stretch of the imagination be thought of as causing articulation defectiveness. Yet many of these measures are still retained as diagnostic tests (Van Riper and Irwin, 1958, pp. 11–47).

Variables Related to Articulatory Acquisition

The following variables will be discussed:

(a) chronological age
(b) intelligence
(c) cultural variables: socieconomic status, sex, and sibling status
(d) general motor skills
(e) oral and facial motor skills
(f) laterality
(g) kinesthetic sensibility
(h) dentition
(i) oral structure
(j) tongue thrust
(k) development and physical health
(l) auditory memory span
(m) speech sound discrimination
(n) discrimination of pitch, intensity, and rhythm
(o) personality and adjustment
(p) lexical and grammatical measures
(q) fluency
(r) educational achievement: reading, spelling and academic evaluations

Chronological Age

In Chapter 2 several studies on phoneme mastery and age were reviewed. It was evident from the results of these studies that with increasing age the phoneme system of a child shows greater and greater correspondence to the phoneme system of the community language. Although chronological age may be thought of as the variable that makes this process possible, more than likely age is a macrovariable—a variable formed from several other variables. No doubt some of the variables to be discussed are elements of this macrovariable.

Intelligence

In five studies (Wellman and others, 1931; Williams, 1937a, 1937b; Schneiderman, 1955; Templin, 1957; Winitz, 1959b) intelligence and articulation were related for subjects of normal intelligence. In two investigations (Reid, 1947a, 1947b; Yedinak, 1949) intelligence and articulation were correlated for subjects who were selected, among other reasons, because they had defective articulation. The first group of studies is designated as "developmental" and the second group as "clinical."

DEVELOPMENTAL STUDIES. In 1931 Wellman and others elicited 133 speech sounds, vowels and consonants, from 204 children attending the Iowa Child Welfare Preschool. The children ranged in age from two to six years and had a mean Stanford-Binet IQ of 115. For 55 children for whom articulation and MA scores were available, an r of .71 was obtained between these measures. However, when chronological age was held constant by means of a partial correlation procedure, a nonsignificant coefficient was obtained.

Williams (1937a, 1937b) studied the articulatory responses of 70 children from three to four years of age on a 104-item test. For 38 children for whom articulation and MA (Stanford-Binet) scores were available, a nonsignificant correlation was found between MA and articulation.

In an investigation relating language and articulation ability Schneiderman (1955) studied 70 first-grade children who ranged in age from six years to seven years and one month. An MA was obtained from the Chicago Non-Verbal Examination. Articulatory ability was measured by the Bryngelson-Glaspey Speech Improvement Cards (51 items) and was found to relate to MA .35.

The articulatory skills of 480 singletons, 60 at each of eight age levels from three to eight years, was studied by Templin (1957). Articulation was measured by a 176-item test, and IQ was determined by the Ammons Vocabulary Test at ages three through five and by the Stanford-Binet test at ages six through eight. The individual IQ's for all age levels ranged from 74 to 172, and the mean IQ's for the eight age levels ranged from 107 to 123. The obtained r's ranged from nonsignificant to .48.

Winitz (1959a, 1959b) studied the articulation responses of 150 kindergarten children on the Templin 50-item Screening Test of Articulation. The mean CA was 63.5 months, and the mean IQ obtained from the Full Scale WISC was 100.5. The IQ scores ranged from 72 to 133. A correlation of .34 was found between the Templin Test and the WISC IQ.[2]

CLINICAL STUDIES. Reid (1947a, 1947b) tested 38 children in grades one through eight (mean CA = 8 years and 8 months) who were judged to have articulatory defects and who had a mean IQ of 106.8. Test scores were made available from school records. When test scores were not available the California Short Form Test of Mental Maturity was administered. Children with IQ's below 75 were excluded. The articulation test consisted of 23 consonant items (weighted according to develop-

---

[2] The index of correlation (η) for evaluation of the relationship between the WISC IQ and the Templin Test is .64 (N = 150, k = 45). This value of eta was employed in testing linearity of regression. An F value of 1.193 was not significant (F .05 = [nearest tabled df = 24 and 120] 1.61) indicating that the hypothesis of linearity may be retained.

mental order). Nonsignificant correlations were obtained between the weighted score and MA, and the weighted score and IQ.

Correlations between IQ and articulation errors for 42 second-grade children judged to have an articulatory problem and 27 children judged to have both a reading and an articulatory problem were obtained by Yedinak (1949). An articulatory problem was defined as one in which at least one phoneme of frequent occurrence was defective as tested in a modification of the McCarthy Articulation Test. This modification contained 70 items (23 consonants and 20 blends tested in several positions). An articulatory and reading problem was defined as an articulatory problem plus a minimum reading retardation of one year as tested by the Gray's Standardized Oral Reading Paragraph Test. The mean age of both groups was 93 months. All children had IQ's of 76 and above as measured by the Pintner-Durost Elementary Test. The mean IQ's of the articulation disability group and the articulation-reading disability group were 98 and 94, respectively. Nonsignificant correlations were obtained for both groups, those without a reading problem and those with a reading problem.[3]

The correlations cited above and summarized in Table 3.1 indicate a low, positive relationship between articulation and intelligence. This finding suggests that intelligence is a poor predictor of articulation and also that intelligence is of limited importance as an etiological consideration in articulation disorders.

It should be pointed out that intellectual functioning has often been cited as an important determinant of articulatory development (see the summary by Powers, 1957). This generalization has probably been derived from the fact that the proportion of articulatory errors is greater for the children with IQ's below 70 than for children with IQ's above 70 (Bangs, 1942; Sirkin and Lyons, 1941; Goodwin, 1955; Schlanger, 1953). The relationships cited above pertain to populations of children within the normal range of intelligence and who, in addition, are without psychological and organic involvements.

Cultural Variables

SOCIOECONOMIC STATUS. Socioeconomic status as used here refers to either socioeconomic class ratings, paternal occupation, or maternal education. Socioeconomic class ratings are usually derived from several social and economic measures, such as years of parental education, source of income, occupation, and residential area.

Several studies have been devoted to the relationship between socio-

---

[3] The mean IQ of the articulation-disability group was not significantly different from a control group of subjects. The control group is described in the section on reading.

[Table 3.1] Summary of Studies Relating
Articulation and Intelligence, Arranged
According to Type of Study

Study	Age of Subjects	N	IQ Test	Results (r)
DEVELOPMENTAL STUDIES				
Wellman and others (1931)	2 to 6 yrs. (range)	55	Stanford-Binet	MA = .71[a] MA = −.05 (CA constant)
Williams (1937a, 1937b)	3 to 4 yrs. (range)	104	Stanford-Binet	MA = .12
Schneiderman (1955)	6 to 7 yrs. 1 mo. (range)	70	Chicago Non-Verbal Examination	MA = .35[a]
Templin (1957)	3 yrs. (mean)	6	3 to 5 yrs.	IQ = .47[a]
	3½ yrs. (mean)	6	Ammons	IQ = .48[a]
	4 yrs. (mean)	6		IQ = .24
	4½ yrs. (mean)	6		IQ = .41[a]
	5 yrs. (mean)	6		IQ = .27[a]
	6 yrs. (mean)	6	6 to 8 yrs.	IQ = .37[a]
	7 yrs. (mean)	6	Stanford-Binet	IQ = .39[a]
	8 yrs. (mean)	6		IQ = .29[a]
Winitz (1959b)	5 yrs. 3 mos. (mean)	150	WISC Full Scale	IQ = .34[a]
CLINICAL STUDIES				
Reid (1947a, 1947b)	8 yrs. 8 mos. (mean)	38	School Records and California Mental Maturity Test	IQ = .16 MA = .29
Yedinak (1949)	7 yrs. 9 mos. (mean)	42	Pintner-Durost Elementary Test	IQ = .06

[Table 3.1 (Continued)]

Study	Age of Subjects	N	IQ Test	Results (r)
Yedinak (1949)	7 yrs. 9 mos. (mean)	27	Pintner-Durost Elementary Test	IQ = −.15

a Significant at or beyond the .05 level.
SOURCE: Winitz (1964), *Child Development*.

economic status and articulation scores. In 1937 Davis examined the articulatory skills of 436 children at 5.5 (N = 248), 6.5 (N = 63), and 9.5 years (N = 125). The subjects were selected so as to represent the occupational proportions, excluding the farmer category, of the 1920 Minneapolis population as determined by the Minnesota Scale of Paternal Occupations. The upper three classes (professional; semiprofessional and managerial; and clerical, skilled trades, and retail businesses) constituted the upper occupational group and the lower three classes (semiskilled, slightly skilled, and day laborers) constituted the lower occupational group. The number of boys and girls in each group was approximately equal. Within each socioeconomic group only children, twins, and singletons with siblings were represented. The sibling categories are described later.

Articulatory proficiency was evaluated by a rating scale ranging from "1," articulation perfect, to "7," speech almost incomprehensible. Subjects were then dichotomized as either perfect articulators, a rating of "1," or defective articulators, ratings of "2" to "7." The percentage of children with perfect articulation was given by sex, sibling status, and occupational group for the 5.5 year group. Significance tests were not applied; however, a greater percentage of perfect articulation scores was found in the upper occupational group than in the lower occupational group with the exception of the male singleton category.

Everhart (1956) studied the relationship between articulation and paternal occupation as measured by the Minnesota Scale for Paternal Occupations for 78 boys and 30 girls with articulation errors and 70 boys and 28 girls possessing "articulation patterns within the normal range." The subjects were selected from grades one through six. The occupational class of the subjects was found to be independent of their speech category.

Templin (1957) related the child's articulation score to the occupation of his father. The subjects were selected according to their fathers' occupations, and the occupational categories were representative of the United States' 1940 urban population. Occupation was determined by the Minnesota Scale for Paternal Occupations. Eight age levels, 3, 3.5, 4, 4.5, 5, 6, 7, and 8 years, were employed, 60 subjects at each age level. The three upper socioeconomic ($N = 18$) groups were combined to form the upper socioeconomic group, and the three lower ($N = 42$) socioeconomic groups were combined to form the lower socioeconomic group. A 176-item articulation test was administered to all children. At each age level the upper occupational group achieved higher articulation scores than the lower occupational group. The differences were significant at three age levels (4, 4.5, and 7 years).

Articulation differences between groups were the largest in the age range from 4 to 7 years. These differences ranged from 14 to 18 test sounds. At the early ages, 3 and 3.5 years, the difference in articulation scores was about five. At the last age level the difference was about four, despite the fact that the upper socioeconomic group had not yet achieved perfect performance. Their mean score at this last age level was about 170. Thus, between 7 and 8 years the lower occupational group achieves a rapid rate of growth and appears to "catch up" with the upper occupational group.

Using a modified version of the Templin Test, the Templin Screening Test of Articulation, Winitz (1959a, 1959b) obtained a nonsignificant correlation between articulation and socioeconomic status. In that study the socioeconomic class of the child's family was estimated through the use of the Warner, Meeker, and Eells Index of Status Characteristics.

Weaver and others (1960) investigated the relationship between paternal occupational class and articulation. A number of first-grade classrooms were selected from each elementary school. The authors report that care was taken to select sections representative of each school population in socioeconomic level, race, intelligence, and age. An articulation test consisting of 96 items was administered to each child. The sample included 437 children with at least one articulation error and 157 children without any errors. The teachers administered the Minnesota Scale for Paternal Occupations.

A significant relationship was found between paternal occupational class and the distribution of subjects in each of the six classes (farmers were not included). Inspection of the frequency distribution revealed a greater percentage of defective-speaking subjects (at least one error) in the last three categories. The mean number of errors for each of the experimental subjects was as follows: professional, 7.6; semiprofessional and management, 11.3; clerical, skilled trades, and retail businesses, 9.6; semiskilled, 9.1; slightly skilled, 12.1; and day laborers, 13.1. With the exception of the semiprofessional and management group, articulation errors generally increase in frequency as the occupational class rating of the father decreases. The reversal noticed for the semiprofessional and managerial groups may prove to be a reliable one and, thus, appears worthy of future research. It is entirely possible that the articulatory errors of the children in this group reflect the psychological "stresses" of their parents, who are striving for social and economic advancement. A similar "hypothesis" is presented by Morgenstern (1956) with regard to the relation between frequency of stuttering and certain upper socioeconomic groups.

Prins (1962a, 1962b) related articulation and socioeconomic status for a group of articulatory defective children who were also divided into several articulation-error subgroups. The articulation measure was determined from a test containing 59 consonantal items, and the socioeconomic measure was determined by the Minnesota Scale for Paternal Occupation. The subjects (N = 92 children) ranged in age from three to six years. First, he correlated articulation and socioeconomic status and obtained a correlation coefficient of .23. Second, he divided his experimental group into three subgroups on the basis of their articulation errors. The three groups were described as a lisping group (N = 20), an omission group (N = 14), and a phonemic substitution group (N = 19); 39 subjects presented "mixed" errors and were not included in this analysis. A control group composed of 71 children was included. Multiple comparisons between the groups revealed that the experimental groups came from significantly lower socioeconomic circumstances than did the control children.

A summary of the findings relating articulation and socioeconomic status is given in Table 3.2. As can be observed from this table, more misarticulating children and more articulatory errors are found in the lower socioeconomic groups than in the upper socioeconomic groups. However, when a correlational index is used, the relationship is low or nonsignificant. It is therefore clear that the relation between articulation and socioeconomic status is about the same as that between articulation and intelligence, and the conclusions made in the section on intelligence seem to apply here.

Socioeconomic class structure, like chronological age, may be considered a macrovariable. Presumably, socioeconomic class differences reflect differences in language stimulation and reinforcement. Templin's data seem to suggest that these differences occur between the ages of four and seven years.

SEX. Girls are, in general, considered to attain language skills at an earlier age than boys. In a number of investigations (Winitz, 1959a) differences in language scores have favored girls, but in most instances these differences have failed to achieve statistical significance. However, in many survey studies on school-age children (Milisen, 1957; Powers, 1957) more boys than girls are reported to have defective articulation. In

[Table 3.2] Summary of Findings Relating
Articulation and Socioeconomic Status

Investigation	Age	Results
Davis (1937)	5.5, 6.5 and 9.5 yrs. (means)	Greater percentage of children with perfect articulation in the upper occupational group than in the lower occupational group excluding the male singleton category
Everhart (1956)	Grades 1 through 6 (range)	No relationship
Templin (1957)	3, 3.5, 4, 4.5, 5, 6, 7, 8 yrs. (means)	Higher articulation scores for the upper occupational group than for the lower occupational group; the differences were significant at three of the age levels studied
Winitz (1959a, 1959b)	5 yrs. 3 mos. (mean)	No relationship
Weaver, Furbee, and Everhart (1960)	First grade (mean)	A significantly greater proportion of non-articulatory defective subjects in the upper occupational categories
Prins (1962a, 1962b)	3 to 6 yrs. (range)	Low relationship (r = .23)

some cases twice as many boys as girls were found to have defective articulation. Despite this fact significant differences favoring girls, as we shall see, are rarely reported in well-controlled studies. In most cases the differences are very small and are not consistent with regard to age level.

Wellman and others (1931) report means according to sex for vowels and consonants for subjects tested at 2, 3, 4, 5, and 6 years. For the consonants the girls surpassed the boys at three age levels, and the boys surpassed the girls at two age levels; the differences favoring the girls were statistically significant at 3 and 4 years. For the vowels the boys surpassed the girls at four age levels, and the girls surpassed the boys at one age level. None of the differences for vowels was significant.

Poole (1934) and later under the married name of Davis (1938) established the age at which each consonant sound was correctly produced by 100 percent of the subjects tested. With regard to sex differences she states, "Boys and girls develop efficiency of articulation at about the same rate from 2½ to 5½ years of age. From this point girls show slightly more rapid growth. . . . At 6½ years, girls approach efficiency in articulation, while the boys require another year, until 7½ years of age, to reach the same degree of perfection" (Poole, 1934, p. 159).

According to Davis (1937) a greater percentage of girls than boys of

5.5 years of age have perfect articulation. Perfect articulation, as you may recall, was determined by a rating scale procedure. This finding by Davis is an average score for all occupational groups, upper and lower, and for all sibling status groups—twins, singletons, and only children.

Roe and Milisen (1942) and Sayler (1949) compared the mean number of errors for boys and girls in grades one through twelve. Roe and Milisen (1942) found no significant difference between boys and girls for grades one through six, and Sayler (1949) found no significant difference between boys and girls in grades seven through twelve.

Wilson (1954) compared 122 male and 120 female kindergarten children on 12 sounds tested in three word positions (36 items). Subjects in both groups had a mean age of about 66 months. A significant difference was not obtained between the sexes. Koch (1956), in a study to be reported in detail in the section on sibling status, found that girls were rated as articulating significantly better than boys when the age difference of the sibling was less than two years, but not when the age difference of the sibling was two to four years or four to six years. The overall sex difference was not significant.

Sex comparisons were also included in Templin's study (1957). Using the 176-item test, she found that girls achieved higher scores than boys on five of eight age levels studied. Only one of eight comparisons was significant. This difference was in favor of the girls at seven years. Boys surpassed girls at three years (by ten test sounds), four years, and eight years. Winitz (1959a) reported no difference between five-year-old boys and girls on the Templin 50-item Screening Test.

In two articulatory learning studies, mentioned in detail elsewhere in this book, Winitz and Lawrence (1961) and Winitz and Bellerose (1965) report conflicting findings. In the first study a significant difference favoring the girls was found, and in the second study a significant difference between the sexes was not found. In the Winitz and Lawrence investigation the children were taught three non-English sounds ([x], [ç], and [œ]), and in the Winitz and Bellerose study the children were taught a non-English phoneme cluster (/sr/). In both cases the examiner was a female.

The results of the above reviewed studies indicate that girls surpass boys more times than boys surpass girls (see Table 3.3). However, very few of the differences are significant. It is interesting to note that in the studies of Roe and Milisen, Snow, Wilson, and Winitz, in which a large number of subjects were available at each age level, significant differences between boys and girls were not obtained.

How can we explain, then, the fact that a greater proportion of elementary school males are most often reported as articulatory defective? One explanation may be that boys more often than girls have very high or very low scores, making the average score about the same as that for

[Table 3.3] Summary of Findings Testing
Differences Between Sexes on
Articulation*

Investigation	Age Levels Studied	Superior		Significantly Superior	
		BOYS	GIRLS	BOYS	GIRLS
Wellman and others (1931)					
consonants	5	2	3	0	2
vowels	5	4	1	0	0
Poole (1934)	6	0	1	NT[a]	
Davis (1937)	1	0	1	NT[a]	
Roe and Milisen (1942)	6	1	5	0	0
Sayler (1949)	6	1	5	0	0
Wilson (1954)	1	NR[b]		0	0
Koch (1956)	1	0	1	0	0
Templin (1957)	8	3	5	0	1
Winitz (1959a)	1	0	1	0	0
Winitz and Lawrence (1961)	1	0	1	0	1
Winitz and Bellerose (1965)	1	NR[b]		0	0

* The age of the subjects varied from study to study; the overall range was from 2 to 18 years.
[a] NT = Statistical test not applied.
[b] NR = Differences not reported.

the girls. This conclusion is probably not true, since the variances for boys and girls are generally similar.

No further explanations for the generally accepted fact that young females outstrip their male companions in articulatory development can be offered. However, it seems that in the past undue emphasis has been placed on sex as a critical variable in language and articulatory development (McCarthy, 1954), despite the fact that in one case a detailed theory purported to explain female superiority was constructed (McCarthy, 1953). Templin (1963) has suggested that this variable is probably of little significance for a general theory of language development. According to Templin many of the recent studies do not show sex differences because of the increasing equanimity of the "speech environment" for American boys and girls. This conclusion appears tenable. However, it should be noted that the Roe and Milisen study was conducted prior to World War II when, presumably, the "language environments" of the sexes were different.

SIBLING STATUS. The number of siblings a child has and the ordinal position of a child among his siblings have been matters of some interest. Wellman and others (1931) found no relation between the number of older siblings and consonant elements at three years (N = 19) and for all age levels combined (N = 85).

Davis (1937), using the Minnesota Scale for Paternal Occupations, found that the proportion of 5.5-year-old children with perfect articulation was greater among only children than among twins or singletons in all occupational and sex groups studied, with the exception of the male, lower occupational group.[4] Singletons with siblings surpassed twins in articulation in both sexes for all occupational groups. Significant differences were not computed.

A comprehensive investigation of sibling influence on articulation was conducted by Koch in 1956. The author selected 384 five- and six-year-old subjects who were from white, urban, native-born, intact, two-children families. Three levels of intersibling age differences were studied (under two, two to four, and four to six years) for each of eight sibling classes (N = 16 in each of the 24 groups): boys with an older brother, boys with a younger brother, boys with an older sister, boys with a younger sister; girls with an older brother, girls with a younger brother, girls with an older sister, and girls with a younger sister. For these eight sibling-sex groups there were, thus, four groups for each of the three intersibling age groups in which the subjects were first-born and four groups in which the subjects were second-born, denoted as the ordinal position factor. The subjects were matched on the basis of age, father's occupation, and residence neighborhood. With the careful controls exercised, it is unfortunate that the articulatory measure was derived from the ratings of teachers ("1" to "9" scale).

The findings indicated significant differences for ordinal position (in favor of the first-born children) and intersibling age differences (articulation improved as the age spacing increased). In addition, as reported above, a significant sex by spacing interaction was found; when the groups were combined for sibling-sex and ordinal position, the girls at the under two-year spacing interval articulated better than the boys.

The findings of the preceding three studies suggest a relationship between sibling status and articulation. The factors found to be significant (only children, intersibling age differences, and first-born children) suggest at least two explanations. One may be the time spent by the parents with the child—i.e., the number of opportunities or trials for language learning. Children who have siblings similar in age must be content with only a portion of the parents' time. Twins represent the limiting case. They

---

[4] In this study an only child was defined as a child who had no living brothers or sisters or other children (adopted) within nine years of age who were members or had been members of the same household. Twins included both like and unlike sex pairs. Singletons were children with siblings.

are continually confronted with each other's presence and thus may develop speech patterns (special phonological rules) that are deviant from their parents. Another explanation would suggest a second force acting at times in concert with the first one. Children who have siblings similar in age may be reinforced, for the most part, by their siblings. Young children may also mold their language after siblings. It would seem, then, that the variable of sibling status would appear to be another macrovariable— simply reflecting the language experience of the child.

Motor Skills

The hypothesis that poor motor coordination is related to defective articulation has motivated a number of studies. In some investigations motor coordination was measured by performance on a general motor test and in others by examination of the oral and facial structures.

GENERAL MOTOR SKILLS. Wellman and others (1931) related total articulation score to two measures of motor skill, the perforation test and the Wellman Tracing Path Test. In the perforation test the child attempts to punch perforated holes with a stick as rapidly as possible. In the tracing path test the child is requested to draw a line on a sheet of paper between two printed lines. The obtained correlations were .52 (N = 34) between articulation and the perforation test and .67 (N = 36) between articulation and the tracing path test. These correlations no doubt reflect the influence of age. Wellman and others report a correlation of .71 between chronological age and the perforation test. Wellman (1926) had previously reported a correlation of .81 between age and the tracing path test.

A careful investigation of general motor skills and articulation was conducted by Mase in 1946. He selected 53 fifth- and sixth-grade males who evinced "two or more sound substitutions or omissions exclusive of lisping" in reading to and conversing with the examiner. Each of the 53 boys was matched with a control subject on mental and chronological age, IQ, academic achievement, racial background, socioeconomic status, and, for a large number of cases, classroom and school. The subjects ranged from 9 to 15 years of age with a mean of about 11 years and 3 months. The 26 subjects with the greatest frequency of errors were designated as severely defective. All subjects in this group possessed "three or more sound substitutions or omissions." This latter group of subjects was used in some of the comparisons.

Motor performance was measured by the Heath Rail-Walking Test. In this test the subject is required to walk a narrow board, toe to heel, without outside support. The number of completed steps is his score. Significant differences were not obtained when the mild and severe subjects were compared with their respective control groups.

Reid (1947) related pencil-tapping with articulation. With chronological age held constant, a nonsignificant r was obtained.

Clark (1959) compared articulatory defective and nonarticulatory defective children on several motor tests. The 50 experimental children were selected from cases attending a speech clinic. They were matched with a control group of 55 children on age, sex, IQ, and socioeconomic status. Clark reports that in order to match the groups statistically, five more children were needed in the control group than in the experimental group. She also mentions that 39 children in the control group were siblings of children in the experimental group. This comment would seem to imply that the subjects were not matched closely in age. Subjects for both groups ranged in age from 4 to 6 years.

Significant differences favoring the control subjects were found on the following motor tests: hand coordination (rapid marking of pencil dots in three different circles while alternating the dominant and nondominant hand); hopping on one foot; and a rail-walking test.

Prins (1962a, 1962b) studied three different experimental groups: Group I—interdentalization errors of /s/ and /z/ (N = 20); Group II—omission errors (N = 14); and Group III—phonemic substitutions involving a change in one articulatory feature (N = 19) (Miller and Nicely, 1955). The control group subjects (N = 71) were randomly selected from the same classrooms as the experimental subjects. In addition they were similar to the experimental group in socioeconomic status, sex, and age. The subjects ranged in age from three through six years. Some differences in the mean IQ's of the four groups were found. However, no difference was greater than 11 IQ points.

The distinguishing difference between Groups I and III seems to be determined by the transcription procedures of American speech pathologists. The sound errors of Group I are transcribed generally as distortion errors, while the errors of Group III are transcribed, for the most part, as phonemic (substitution) errors. This is because the errors of the /s/ and /z/ sounds are not generally considered to be allophones of other English phonemes. If one's frame of reference is phonetic rather than phonemic, phones such as [s̪] (dentalization), [sʰ] (aspiration), or [ṣ] (retroflexion) can be considered to be substitution errors. To be consistent, then, many but not all of the errors of Group III would need to be transcribed as distortions rather than phonemic substitutions, since phones such as the labiovelar allophone of /r/, transcribed [ɹ̈], no doubt occurred. The subjects in the omission group may also have uttered substitution errors such as a lengthened vowel or a glide (/w/, /h/, or /j/). (They may have uttered distortion errors as well, e.g., [ʔ].) Thus Prins' subgroups are, for the most part, a function of his transcription procedures. In addition, they are also a function of the sounds that were tested. For example, Group I, which is described as an interdental lisp group, could just as easily be described as an /s/ and /z/ defective group, since American speech pathologists do not usually define distortions as lisps unless they occur on the /s/ and /z/ sounds and perhaps on the /ʃ/, /tʃ/, /ʒ/, and /dʒ/ sounds. Similarly, the omission group might be described as a glide defective group. Finally, since the errors of groups II and III involved more than two sounds, they may have had considerably more articulatory errors than Group I. Thus, the error classifications are confounded with severity.

Prins used two tests of general motor ability, tandem-walking and the Gesell Pellet and Bottle Test. In the first test the subject walks forward, touching heel to toe on every step; the examiner records the number of completed steps taken without loss of balance. In the second test the subject places 10 pellets in a container, using both the preferred and nonpreferred hand; the examiner records the time it takes for the completion of these two tasks. Only one difference was significant—for the pellet test with the preferred hand. The mean for the control group fell below the mean for Group III (phonemic substitution).

Using the Oseretsky Tests of Motor Proficiency, with some modification, Jenkins and Lohr (1964) compared the motor skills of 38 normal and 38 articulatory defective first-grade children.[5] The mean number of articulatory errors for the experimental children was about six. A significant difference favoring the normal-speaking children was found. The mean age of both groups was about 80 months.

In one investigation the subjects were adults. Albright (1948) compared 31 control and 31 experimental college students (average age about 19.5 years) on several tests of motor coordination. A five-point rating scale (very poor, poor, fair, good, and excellent) was used to assess articulation. Judges were instructed to base their ratings on articulation ability—"the series of movements involved in producing speech sounds." Factors such as posture, audience contact, voice quality, etc., were to be ignored. Sub-

---

[5] The Oseretsky Tests are grouped into six categories (See Chapter 4, p. 266). Each category contains items appropriate for subjects from 4 to 16 years. Only five of the six tests were used by Jenkins and Lohr.

They were as follows:

1. General Status Coordination, maintaining balance in a given body position for a given period without gross movement of the limbs or torso, for example, standing on tiptoe or one leg.

2. Dynamic Manual Coordination, performing coordinated hand activities as directed within a given time and with accuracy, for example, cutting paper or throwing a ball.

3. General Dynamic Coordination, maintaining balance while performing a given movement for the whole body, for example, running and hopping.

4. Simultaneous Voluntary Movements, executing given patterns of movement simultaneously with both hands and/or feet, for example, tapping alternately the left and right foot.

5. Synkinesia, performing a given muscular activity without showing any extraneous (overflow) movements, for example, clenching the teeth without wrinkling the forehead (Jenkins and Lohr, 1964, p. 287).

jects rated very poor or poor were assigned to the experimental group, and subjects rated good or excellent were assigned to the control group.

The motor tests administered to the subjects were (a) rhythm (subjects were to tap in time with a sound pattern), (b) Miles Speed Rotor Test (following a pattern with a hand drill), (c) speed of tapping with a stylus, (d) Whipple Steadiness Test (inserting a stylus in three holes of different diameters without touching the side), (e) writing speed (speed of writing first stanza of "Mary Had a Little Lamb"), and (f) rail-walking (one thin board was used and subjects were to walk the board without falling). Significant differences favoring the control group were obtained for the rhythm and speed rotor tests.

The results of the preceding studies are summarized in Table 3.4. Of the six studies involving children, only three (Clark, 1959; Prins, 1962b; and Jenkins and Lohr, 1964) showed significant differences. In two of the studies the differences favored the control group and in one the experimental group. For the one study with adults the findings indicate that differences on two of the motor tests were significant. These differences favored the normal-speaking group. In general the studies do not indicate that articulatory defectives are retarded on any specific measure of general motor ability. Sufficient evidence is also lacking to support the hypothesis that articulatory defectives demonstrate a general retardation in motor skills. This is not a surprising finding in view of the fact that individual motor skills show a low intercorrelation (Goodenough and Smart, 1935).

ORAL AND FACIAL MOTOR SKILLS. Tests involving the oral and facial musculature have also been used to assess the motor ability of the articulatory defective individual. These tests involve measurement of maximum muscle rate. They are administered by having the subject repeat a certain movement as rapidly as possible until he is asked to stop. Generally the time intervals are for less than a minute, e.g., five seconds. The subject is usually given several trials in addition to a practice trial. These speed tests are often referred to as tests of diadochokinesis.

Mase (1946) employed several tests of diadochokinesis. They were (a) tongue tip movement from one corner of the mouth to the other, (b) opening and closing of the mouth, (c) extension of the tongue (opening of the mouth, extension of the tongue, and closing of the mouth), (d) lip rounding with mouth closed, and (e) repetition of *daddy*. Mase remarks that when a sound in *daddy* was omitted or slurred, the subject was instructed to begin again. Also, he indicated that no subjects in the study had difficulty with the sounds in this word. Significant differences were obtained on test (d), lip rounding with mouth closed, for all subjects and for the 26 severe subjects in favor of the control groups.

Several measures of diadochokinesis were used by Reid (1947a, 1947b). They were (a) clicking teeth together, (b) uttering *boy* as rapidly as possible, (c) rapid sucking of seven ounces of water from a cup with a straw,

(d) rapid drinking of seven ounces of water from a cup, and (e) raising and lowering the eyebrows. With chronological age held constant the r's were nonsignificant.

Clark (1959) reports significant differences favoring a control group on two tests of diadochokinesis. The tests were tongue movement (open lips, touch a lollipop approximately one third of an inch in front of the mouth,

[Table 3.4] Summary of Findings on Tests
of General Motor Ability

Investigation	Test	Results
CHILDREN		
Wellman and others (1931)	Perforation Test	$r = .52$
	Wellman Tracing Path Test	$r = .67$ Computed over wide age range
Mase (1946)	Heath Rail-Walking Test	Differences nonsignificant for mild and severe cases
Reid (1947)	Pencil tapping	$r =$ nonsignificant
Clark (1959)	Hand coordination	Significant difference favoring control group
	Hopping	Significant difference favoring control group
	Rail walking	Significant difference favoring control group
Prins (1962a, 1962b)	Tandem walking	Nonsignificant difference between control group and three experimental groups
	Gesell Pellet and Bottle Test (Preferred and Nonpreferred Hand)	One significant difference—the phonemic substitution group outperformed the control group with the preferred hand
Jenkins and Lohr (1964)	Oseretsky Motor Test	Significant difference favoring control group
ADULTS		
Albright (1948)	Rhythm	Significant difference favoring control group
	Miles Speed Rotor Test	Significant difference favoring control group
	Stylus tapping	Nonsignificant
	Whipple Steadiness Test	Nonsignificant
	Writing speed	Nonsignificant
	Rail walking	Nonsignificant

draw the tongue back into the mouth, and close the lips) and teeth to lip movement (bite lower lip lightly with upper teeth, purse lips, and say oo).

A graded series of diadochokinetic tests were employed by Prins (1962a, 1962b). They were repetitions of the following individual and combined syllables: [pʌ], [tʌ], [kʌ], [pʌtʌ] and [pʌtʌkʌ].[6] (Although Mase indicated that none of his subjects had difficulty articulating the sounds in his test item, Prins does not make a similar statement.) He used three experimental groups, as you may recall, and one control group.

For [pʌ] and [kʌ] significant differences were not found between the control group and each of the experimental groups. For [kʌ] and [pʌtʌ] the control group was significantly better than Group II (omission errors), but, with the exception of [pʌtʌkʌ], all other control and experimental group comparisons were not significant. For [pʌtʌkʌ] the control group was significantly better than all three experimental groups. Some of the differences between the experimental groups were significant. For [kʌ], [pʌtʌ], and [pʌtʌkʌ] Group III (phonemic substitutions) performed significantly better than Group II, and Group I (interdentalizations) performed significantly better than Group II; Groups III and I did not differ from each other. For [tʌ] only one difference was significant; the difference favored Group III over Group II.

Speculating that a number of physiological factors may contribute to the etiology of functional articulation errors, that these may not be the same for all individuals, nor monotonically related to articulation errors, Shelton and others (1966) stressed the need for a reevaluation and a revision of measures of physiological competence. (See the discussion in the section on Physiological study of articulatory errors, pp. 218–221.) Unfortunately they selected traditional motor tasks: elevation of the tip of the tongue behind the upper central incisors for five to seven seconds on three consecutive trials, and movement of the tongue from one corner of the mouth to the other. The second motor task was passed by all subjects and, therefore, was excluded from analysis. Three age levels were included: four, five, and six years; this resulted in a total of 106 subjects.

Articulation was assessed in the standard way. A single score was derived from the performance of subjects on a 69-item consonantal test. The investigators first noted that, since a great proportion of the children without articulation errors failed to hold the linguo-alveolar position for five seconds for all three trials, the test was diagnostically unimportant. However, when those subjects who passed all three trials were compared with those subjects who failed all three trials (The number of subjects was kept constant for all three age levels, N = 28 in each group) significantly fewer articulatory errors were found for the former group. A subsequent

---

[6] The author's use of [ʌ] for [pʌtʌ] and [pʌtʌkʌ] suggests that all syllables were uttered with the same stress. In all probability, there was only one syllable with primary stress for [pʌtʌ] and one or two for [pʌtʌkʌ].

analysis revealed no age level differences on the physiological measure of tongue elevation. This finding is difficult to explain since articulatory scores were found to increase with age. It seems to suggest that the physiological variable does not relate to articulatory increments by age after four years, but does distinguish between articulatory differences within an age level. We infer that other factors, such as examiner bias and/or apico-alveolar skill, a possible by-product of speech sound learning, were operating.

In two studies, using adult subjects, the relation between articulation and oral and facial motor skills was examined. In the first study (Albright, 1948) five measures of diadochokinesis were employed. They were (a) speech rate (subjects recited the first stanza of "Mary Had a Little Lamb" as fast as possible), (b) rapid utterance of [lɑ], (c) rapid utterance of [tʌkə], (d) rapid utterance of [mu], and (e) teeth clicking. On all but the teeth-clicking test a significant difference favoring the group with good articulation was found.

In the second study (Fairbanks and Spriestersbach, 1950) electronic devices were used to measure the movements of the following: (a) approximation of upper and lower lips, (b) vertical movement of the mandible, (c) contact between the tongue and alveolar ridge, (d) protrusion of the tongue, and (e) vertical movement of the eyebrow. The subjects were 30 superior- and 30 inferior-speaking college students.[7] They were first identified from speech class records which contained evaluations of pronunciation and voice control. The subjects were then rated on 25 sound elements, employing the procedures of Fairbanks (1940). Each consonant was rated on a "1" (inferior) to "5" (superior) scale by two speech pathologists. Subjects selected for the superior group had (a) no mean rating (average of both judges) lower than 3.0 and (b) at least 20 of the 25 mean ratings higher than 3.0. Subjects selected for the inferior group had at least one mean rating of 1.0. The mean ratings per consonant for each of the subgroups (N = 15) was as follows: superior males, 4.6; inferior males, 3.9; superior females, 4.7; inferior females, 4.1. Only one difference, lip rate, was significant. The superior-speaking males performed significantly better than the inferior-speaking males.

The results of the preceding studies are summarized in Table 3.5. As may be observed from this table, those differences found to be significant involved, for the most part, measures of speech movements. It seems unfair to compare an articulatory defective group with a control group on a diadochokinetic test of speech sounds. Subjects without articulatory errors have a long history of success with speech sounds and, therefore, have a decided advantage over subjects with articulatory errors. For

---

[7] These subjects are the same as those used by Fairbanks and Bebout (1950), Fairbanks and Green (1950), and Fairbanks and Lintner (1951).

example, American speakers could not repeat the /dl/ and /zkr/ phoneme clusters as rapidly as foreign speakers who have these clusters in their language. In order to test the hypothesis that articulatory defectiveness is a function of inferior motor ability, speech measures need to be selected (or developed) which are free of speech sound experience. The measures might involve nonbehavioral neurological tests of the speech muscles or of the nerves that innervate these muscles.

Laterality

In the early years of speech pathology, handedness theories of speech disorders were very prevalent. Today these theories are less popular. Their decline can be attributed, for the most part, to the low or zero correlation found between this variable and speech disorders in general, rather than to any advanced knowledge of the role of the cerebral hemispheres in the development of speech and language.

Functional articulatory disorders have rarely been considered "cerebral" in origin. Most of the physiological theories have been centered around peripheral and oral facial mechanisms. Thus, only two experimental studies on laterality and articulation have been reported.

Johnson and House (1937) matched 33 control and experimental children on sex, age, and IQ. The articulatory defective children were selected from children enrolled in speech correction classes. The control children were selected from children attending either a juvenile, orphan, or elementary school. The age range for the speech-defective children was 6 years 8 months to 12 years 10 months, and for the normal-speaking children the age range was 7 years to 12 years 11 months. The articulation errors of the experimental children were described as serious. The subjects had at least one sound error in at least two of the following three sound groups: (a) /s/, /ʃ/, /tʃ/, and /dʒ/; (b) /r/ and /l/; (c) any other sound except /θ/.

Two tests of laterality were employed—ocular dominance and an adaptation of the Van Riper simultaneous vertical writing test.[8] The findings for ocular dominance revealed no significant difference between the groups in the proportion of left-eyed and right-eyed dominance. Amphiocular subjects made up only a small percentage of the cases, no more than 6 percent, in the two groups. On the vertical writing test a significantly greater number of the experimental cases scored within the ambidextrous and left-handed range.

Everhart (1953) reports no significant differences between groups of control and experimental children analyzed separately with regard to sex

---

[8] In the test of ocular dominance the subject looks at the examiner's nose through a small hole, arm's length from the subject. Only one eye, presumably the dominant eye, is used. In the test of simultaneous writing the nondominant hand mirrors the image of the dominant hand.

[Table 3.5] Summary of Findings on Oral
and Facial Diadochokinetic Tests

Investigation	Test	Results
CHILDREN		
Mase (1946)	Tongue tip to corner	Nonsignificant
	Mouth opening and closing	Nonsignificant
	Tongue extension	Nonsignificant
	Lip rounding	Significant in favor of control over severe and mild groups
	Repetition of *daddy*	Nonsignificant
Reid (1947a, 1947b)	Clicking teeth	Nonsignificant r
	Repetition of *boy*	Nonsignificant r
	Sucking	Nonsignificant r (CA held constant for all measurements)
	Drinking	Nonsignificant r
	Eyebrow movement	Nonsignificant r
Clark (1959)	Tongue extension	Significant differences favoring the control group
	Teeth to lip movement	Significant differences favoring the control group
Prins (1962a, 1962b)	[pʌ]	Nonsignificant
	[tʌ]	Nonsignificant
	[kʌ]	Control group significantly better than omission group
	[pʌtʌ]	Control group significantly better than omission group
	[pʌtʌkʌ]	Control group significantly better than all three experimental groups
Shelton and others (1966)	Elevation of the tip of the tongue behind the upper central incisors for five seconds	Significant difference favoring the control group
ADULTS		
Albright (1948)	Speed of short poem	Significant in favor of control group
	[lɑ]	Significant in favor of control group
	[tʌkə]	Significant in favor of control group

[Table 3.5 (Continued)]

Investigation	Test	Results
ADULTS (CONT.)		
	[mu]	Significant in favor of control group
	Teeth clicking	Nonsignificant
Fairbanks and Spriestersbach (1950)	Lower lip to upper lip	Significant in favor of superior males
	Vertical movement of mandible	Nonsignificant
	Tongue to alveolar ridge	Nonsignificant
	Tongue protrusion	Nonsignificant
	Eyebrow movement	Nonsignificant

on an undefined measure of handedness. This finding does not support Johnson and House's results. Everhart's data, as previously mentioned, were abstracted from a questionnaire sent to the parents of the control and experimental children. Data gathered in this way are not often reliable. In addition, the operational definition of handedness is not given. Further research is needed before conclusive statements can be made about the relation between laterality and articulatory defectiveness.

Kinesthetic Sensibility

Kinesthetic sensibility—muscular sensitivity to position, movement, and tension—has been tested for normally speaking and articulatory defective individuals. The first study was conducted by Patton in 1942. She compared experimental and control groups on a kinesthetic test which included the following measures: (a) end of nose touched with right index finger with eyes closed; (b) end of nose touched with left index finger with eyes closed; (c) tip of right and left index fingers touched together with eyes closed; (d) tip of right index finger and tip of left thumb touched together with eyes closed; (e) tip of right index finger and tip of left little finger touched together with eyes closed; (f) right index finger touched to end of big toe of left foot with eyes closed; and (g) left index finger touched to end of right big toe with eyes closed. Each subject was given two trials for each of the seven tasks and received two points for correct responses on the first trial and one point for correct responses on the second trial. A total score was obtained from these seven tests.

The experimental and control subjects (N = 214 in each group) ranged in age from 5 to 12 years. The experimental subjects were drawn from children enrolled in speech correction classes. The subjects in the control group were matched for sex and age. A significant difference favoring the normal-speaking group was obtained.

Clark (1959) used two tests of kinesthetic sensibility. The first measure was derived from two of Patton's tasks, measures (f) and (g) above. The second measure involved touching the tongue tip to the alveolar ridge. A significant difference favoring the control children was obtained for the tongue tip task but not for Patton's finger-to-toe test.

Fairbanks and Bebout (1950) studied the ability of inferior- and superior-speaking college students to duplicate a tongue position. The subjects extended their tongues to a stop which was placed one-half the length of their individual maximum tongue protrusion. This task was practiced ten times. The stop was then removed and the subject was asked to perform the task again. Experimental and control subjects did not differ significantly on this task.

The findings for kinesthetic skill appear to be inconclusive in that disagreement was obtained for measures involving the tongue as well as for other body parts. It is quite possible that oral kinesthetic responses reflect the speech sound experiences of young children. That is, if we assume that articulatory errors reflect, in part, a truncation of the "usual" number of learning trials, then some positive relation between oral kinesthesia and articulatory performance would be expected. When the phonemes of the speech community are acquired we would expect no relation between oral kinesthesia and articulation.

Dentition

Poor dentition is another variable often considered to be one cause of an articulatory disorder. Dental factors—such as malocclusion, missing teeth, open bite—and their relation to articulation have been investigated in a number of studies. They are summarized in this section.

Reid (1947a, 1947b), holding chronological age constant, found no relation between the number of permanent teeth erupted and articulation. She tested 38 subjects enrolled in grades one to eight. Hanley and Supernaw (1956) investigated the relation between articulation and two orthodontic variables, open bite and malocclusal classification. The 25 subjects ranged in age from 9 to 18 years and averaged 13.2 years, and were selected from approximately 300 children who were considered as possible candidates for orthodontic treatment. (The investigators apparently observed that many of the subjects had normal articulation.) "Only subjects for which [sic] no etiologic factor, other than dental malocclusion, could be found were selected . . ." (Hanley and Supernaw, 1956, p. 24).

Open bite was usually measured between anterior segments but occasionally at the level of the first molars. Twelve of the subjects were found to have a Class I malocclusion (neutroclusion—normal anteroposterior relationship between the maxilla and mandible with malalignment of anterior teeth) and 13 subjects had a Class II, Division 1, malocclusion (distoclusion—mandible is distal in relationship to the maxilla).

The articulation tester was aware that the subjects had dental abnormalities but was not informed of the severity of the defects. The articulation examination revealed errors of /s/, /z/, /ʃ/, /tʃ/, /ʒ/, and /dʒ/. The subjects were then divided into three groups: (a) normal speech (N = 8); (b) compensatory speech (N = 8)—the sounds were auditorily correct but compensatory movements of the oral structures occurred; and (c) defective speech (N = 9)—articulatory errors for the six sounds indicated above. A biserial correlation was computed between open bite (continuous variable) and speech defect (dichotomous variable) for each of the three groups. (It is unclear from the procedures of the article how two speech defective groups were derived for each of the three groups described above.) None of the three correlations was significantly different from zero. Also, no significant difference for mean open bite was found among the three speech groups, nor was a significant relationship (tetrachoric r) found between malocclusal class and the presence or absence of speech errors.

Another investigator, Snow (1961), was interested in determining whether or not the absence of the upper incisors would affect the articulatory production of the following six consonants: /f/, /v/, /θ/, /ð/, /s/, and /z/. Each sound was tested in six different words (twice in each word position) and elicited by picture cards. The testing involved 438 first-grade children. The 99 children with one or both of the upper central incisors missing, decayed nearly to the gum line, or malpositioned were designated as the experimental group.

It can be noted from Snow's table of results (Snow, 1961, Table 1, p. 210) that the percentage of correct responses is tallied for each sound separately. Of a total of 2628 (6 × 438) possible responses for each sound, the percentage of correct responses is indicated separately for the control and experimental children. For example, for the /θ/ sound 2022 responses were elicited from the control group and 593 responses were elicited from the experimental group, a total of 2615 responses. A few children probably did not respond to the pictorial stimulus for this sound. For the control group about 72 percent of the responses were correct, and for the experimental group 64 percent of the responses were correct. Although more correct responses, about 8 percent, were obtained for the control than for the experimental group, the findings clearly indicate that many of the subjects in the control group had difficulty with the /θ/ sound.

Another interesting consideration is that of the error consistency. From Snow's table of results it cannot be determined whether or not the articulatory errors for the experimental group were consistently in error—i.e., in error six out of six times. It is possible that many subjects missed the sound in only one or two of the positions tested. Assuming this to be true, it might indicate that incisal deviations do not prevent, but simply retard, the consistency of correct articulatory productions.

The percentage differences between groups for the six sounds ranged from 3 percent (/f/) to 12 percent (/z/). In all cases a greater percentage of errors occurred for the subjects in the experimental group. For each of the cognate pairs the difference between groups was greater for the voiced than for the voiceless sound. This directional difference was found to be significant.

Does the loss of deciduous teeth alter previously acquired sound productions? Bankson and Byrne (1962) directed their attention to this topic. The subjects were 304 kindergarten and first-grade children; the mean age was 73 months. The children were first tested in May and were tested again four months later. Pretest and posttest evaluations were made of the /f/, /ʃ/, /s/, and /z/ phonemes. With the exception of the /z/ phoneme all sounds were tested in all three word positions; pictorial stimulation was used. Visual cues may have been utilized in the evaluation, as the subject was seated across a table from the examiner. Following the articulation test the dental evaluations were made. Subjects designated as having missing teeth were those who had one or more of the following 12 teeth missing: upper and lower central and lateral incisors, and upper and lower canines. None of the subjects was enrolled in speech correction classes.

The 304 children selected for the pretest examination were those who in May had all of the above-mentioned teeth present and who in addition articulated correctly one or more of the above ten test sounds. Thus, the number of subjects available for study ranged from 246 to 302, depending upon the test sound analyzed. The findings indicated that a significant change occurred for only one of the four phonemes, /s/. The difference was significant in all three word positions.

The fact that Bankson and Byrne obtained a significant difference for the /s/ phoneme but not for the /z/ phoneme is difficult to understand. This finding seems to suggest that apical tongue positioning was not affected by the loss of teeth but that the voiced/voiceless contrast was in some way related to the evaluations.

It would be of interest to know if the subjects in this study retained their incorrect production of /s/ following the eruption of their permanent teeth. Davis (1938) reported that the /s/ and /z/ phonemes develop consistently in words at four or five years and then become distorted with a loss of the upper anterior teeth. Davis found that these distortions were eliminated following the eruption of the permanent, anterior teeth at about eight years.

Fymbo (1936) evaluated the dentition of three groups of college students —superior speech (N = 100), defective speech (N = 111), and average speech (N = 199). Speech evaluations were made by members of the department of speech; they included rating scales and articulation evaluations. A rating of "1" and "2" was considered defective, "3" and "4" average, and "5," "6," and "7" superior. For some of the comparisons the subjects were regrouped as follows: ratings of "1," "2," and "3" were considered unsatisfactory speech; and ratings of "5," "6," and "7" were considered satisfactory speech. Four occlusion measurements were made: (a) normal occlusion, (b) slight malocclusion—minor rotations and malalignments of the teeth and very slight medial and distal discrepancies of the arches, (c) severe malocclusion—serious anomalies in the formation of the dental arches and in the relation of one arch to the other, and (d) facial deformity—most severe malocclusion which manifests itself in an unpleasing contour of the face, particularly of the lower one third. These measurements, as well as all other facial measurements, were made by the author, an orthodontist.

Table 3.6 is a summary of Fymbo's findings. A greater percentage of the subjects with average and superior speech is found in the normal occlusion group. In the slight malocclusion group there is a greater percentage of average than defective speakers. In the severe malocclusion group there is little difference between the percentage of defective and average speakers. More than half of the subjects with facial deformity were defective speakers. These trends are supported statistically by a significant chi-square computed by this author from the data presented in Table 3.6.

One wonders whether the appearance of malocclusions or the presence of other speech disorders affected the raters' scoring. It is possible that some of the subjects with facial deformities developed deviant social and language patterns during childhood. Also, many of the articulatory prob-

[Table 3.6] Summary of Fymbo's Findings*

	Speech Group		
Occlusal Group	% DEFECTIVE	% AVERAGE	% SUPERIOR
Normal occlusion	9.1	48.7	42.2
Slight malocclusion	21.0	66.0	13.0
Severe malocclusion	46.0	39.8	14.2
Facial deformity	55.8	30.2	14.0

* Subjects are classified into four occlusion groups and the percentage of subjects in each of these four groups with defective, average, or superior speech is given.

lems of the facial deformity group would be considered, by present-day standards, organic rather than functional.

The malocclusion groups (slight and severe malocclusion groups and facial deformity group) showed a greater percentage of articulatory errors than the normal occlusion groups. The defective sounds, ordered according to frequency of error, for the malocclusion groups were as follows: /s/, /z/, /θ/, /ð/, /ʃ/, /ʒ/, /tʃ/, and /dʒ/.

Another comparison by Fymbo involved the vertical relation of the jaws and the speech ratings. He found that 58 percent of the subjects with normal vertical relations, 29 percent of the closed bite subjects, and 21 percent of the open bite subjects had satisfactory speech. Finally, Fymbo found a greater proportion of upper anterior teeth (the upper third molar was not included in this analysis) were reported as missing for the defective-speaking group. Significance tests were not applied to these last two findings.

Fymbo's finding that the /s/ and /z/ phonemes were most frequently misarticulated was corroborated by Snow (1961). However, Snow's data show that the voiceless cognates were more defective than the voiced cognates.

In the final study, Fairbanks and Lintner (1951, p. 275), to be reported in this section, the following dental measurements were used:

> (1) Molar occlusion, . . . in which the antero-lateral cusp of the upper first molar is aligned with the buccal groove of the lower first molar; (2) occlusion of the upper and lower anterior teeth in both antero-posterior and infero-superior planes; (3) alignment of the individual upper and lower incisors and cuspids; (4) spaces (failures of proximal contact) anterior to the bicuspids, both upper and lower. Each of these four items was rated on a Normal-Slight-Marked deviation scale . . .

Superior and inferior college speakers were rated as deviant or nondeviant on each of these four dental measurements. Individual analyses of the four dental measurements revealed no significant difference in the proportion of superior and inferior speakers rated deviant or nondeviant.

The data were then grouped into two categories "no marked deviations in any of the four dental evaluations" and "one or more marked deviations in any of the four dental evaluations." Using this broader categorization, a significantly greater proportion of inferior speakers had one or more marked deviations.

No significant relation was found between the speech categories (superior and inferior) and occlusal class. For this analysis subjects were categorized as either normal occlusion or malocclusion (neutroclusion, distoclusion, and mesioclusion).[9] There was, however, a tendency for neutroclusion to predominate in the superior group, while distoclusion and mesioclusion were more frequent in the inferior group. This relationship, was not significant.

The occlusion of the upper and lower anterior teeth was further examined. Although a nonsignificant relation between class of speakers and anteroposterior measurements (normal, and overjet or undershot) was found, a significant relation between inferosuperior measurements (normal, and open bite or closed bite) and class of speakers was found. A significantly greater proportion of inferior subjects had open or closed bites in contrast to normal bites. A further breakdown of those subjects with poor inferosuperior relationships revealed that the occurrence of closed bite was similar for both speech groups but that open bite ($N = 9$) was only found to occur in the inferior group.

For the children the studies as a whole (see Table 3.7) do not reveal a high or consistent relation between the frequency of articulatory errors and dental irregularities. However, the careful study of Snow seems to suggest that further research is necessary before conclusive statements of this kind can be made. In the two adult studies articulation was found to be related to dental irregularities in that marked dental deviations were more numerous among inferior speakers. One finding that seems to be supported by both the Fymbo and the Fairbanks and Lintner investigations is that superior speakers showed less frequency of open and/or closed bites. A finding common to both children and adults is that malocclusions and dental deviations were frequent among good speakers. Thus, the results of these studies do not provide the speech clinician with definitive diagnostic guidelines for identifying those occlusal deviations associated with articulatory errors. Finally, we cannot ignore the findings of Davis (1938) and Bankson and Byrne (1962) which indicated that loss of teeth does not seem to impair the production of sounds already learned.

More precise and comprehensive investigation needs to be made of the relation between dental irregularities and articulatory errors. In addition, dental deviations should be related to specific types of articulatory errors. The precise measurements employed by Fairbanks and Lintner could be used for this purpose. Another point of view might be to assume that dental deviations are in some cases related to certain linguo-dental, labio-dental and linguo-alveolar sound errors. Proceeding from this frame of reference (assuming that the necessary orthodontia is provided) two dif-

[9] The authors report that "Normal occlusion implies the molar relationship described above [see quote above] . . . plus normal alignment and occlusion of the anterior teeth; in neutroclusion the molar relationship is normal, but there are anterior irregularities; in distoclusion the upper first molar is anterior to its normal position, and in mesioclusion it is posterior" (Fairbanks and Lintner, 1951, p. 277).

[Table 3.7] Summary of Studies Relating Dental Deviations and Articulation

Investigation	Results
CHILDREN	
Reid (1947a, 1947b)	No relationship between number of permanent teeth erupted and articulation
Hanley and Supernaw (1956)	No relationship between articulation and open bite or malocclusion class (neutroclusion and distoclusion)
Snow (1961)	Significantly greater proportion of articulatory errors for children with missing upper incisors
Bankson and Byrne (1962)	Significantly greater proportion of /s/ errors following loss of one or more upper and lower anterior teeth
ADULTS	
Fymbo (1936)	Greater proportion of defective and average speakers had malocclusions, and open and closed bites
Fairbanks and Lintner (1951)	No relationship between the proportion of inferior and superior speakers for occlusion of the molar and anterior teeth, alignment of incisors and cuspids and dental spaces. No relationship was found between class of speakers and class of occlusion (malocclusion and normal occlusion). However, inferior speakers had a greater proportion of one or more marked dental deviations and showed a greater proportion of open or closed bites

ferent kinds of problems may be studied: first, an investigation of tongue, lip, and jaw placement associated with various types of dental irregularities; second, if the above findings prove to be of value, the development of specialized teaching procedures. Subtelny and others have made a giant step in this direction. Their cephalometric observations (1964, pp. 277–278) revealed, for example, that:

> Normal speakers with malocclusion positioned the tongue tip slightly posterior to the lower incisors. . . . In contrast, the group with defective speech [and malocclusion] fronted the tip of the tongue to a significantly greater extent. In the defective speakers, the tongue tip closely approached the lower incisors at rest and protruded beyond the lower incisors during /s/ production. The tongue tip of the defective speakers thus tended to approach the lingual surfaces of the protruded upper incisors."

One final point needs to be made. In the studies on occlusion and articulation, evaluations were generally not made independently of the occlusal evaluations. In the studies conducted with children, the examiners made both the speech and dental evaluations. In thé adult studies, speech ratings were made by individuals who may have been influenced by the general facial expressions of the subjects. In future investigations it seems important to control for such bias.

The major purpose of this chapter is to report the relation between articulation and a great many other variables. When substantial relationships are found or when significant differences between control and experimental subjects are frequently found for a single independent variable, a cause-and-effect relation has not been assumed. Some investigators, however, make this inference. Articulatory defectiveness is assumed to be the "effect" of a second variable, the "cause." However, statements can be found occasionally in the literature that suggest that articulatory behavior may be the cause of the second variable, or that both variables are related to a third variable. Thus it is no surprise to find that articulatory errors have been suggested as a cause for open bite (Froeschels and Jellinek, 1941, pp. 162–163). "Cause-and-effect" inferences will be discussed in great detail in the concluding pages of this chapter.

Oral structures

In addition to dental structures, several other structures of the oral cavity have been related to articulatory production. In this section four studies shall be summarized in which measurements of the tongue, palate, and lips have been related to articulatory production. In all of these studies the subjects were adults.

Fymbo (1936) studied palatal dimensions and articulation. All of the 154 subjects had normal occlusion. The palatal dimensions were height,[10] cuspid width, and molar width (between first molars). Only palatal cuspid width showed a monotonically increasing relationship to speaking ability; for sexes considered separately, cuspid width increased as speaking ability increased. Successive differences between groups were less than one millimeter. Significance tests were not applied. Fymbo also reports that 70 percent of the cases with a high palate (21 to 28 mm.) in contrast to 57 percent of the subjects with a low palate (15 to 20 mm.) had /s/ and /z/ errors.

Palatal dimensions and articulation were investigated in a second study

---

[10] Fymbo does not describe where the palatal height measurement was made. However, Fairbanks and Lintner (1951) indicate that they used Fymbo's procedure. They measured the midline, vertical palatal distance from the plane of the occlusal surfaces of the first molars to the hard palate.

by Fairbanks and Lintner (1951). Three dimensions of the hard palate as well as maximum mouth opening were examined. The three measurements of the hard palate were those described by Fymbo (1936): (a) cuspid width, (b) molar width, and (c) palatal height. None of the palatal differences between articulation groups was significant. For sexes combined, the difference for mouth opening measured at the level of the incisors with the mandible depressed was significant in favor of the inferior speakers. Inferior males averaged 4 mm. more than superior males and inferior females averaged 2.2 mm. more than superior females. The authors speculate that the significant difference obtained for maximum mouth opening in favor of the control subjects may be related to the high incidence of open bite found in the inferior group. (This finding was reported in the preceding section.) However, Fairbanks and Lintner do not indicate if the subjects with open bite were also the same subjects who obtained high scores on the maximum mouth opening measurement.

In one study (Fairbanks and Bebout, 1950) lingual measurements of control and experimental adults were compared. The major measurements were maximum length of tongue protrusion from the incisors and length of the tongue tip (relaxed) from the lingual frenulum. No significant differences were obtained between experimental and control groups for these two measures. The size (in relation to the lower dental arch) and shape of the tongue were also assessed. Small frequencies prevented statistical analysis; observations of the findings appeared to be essentially negative.

In one study lip measurements and articulation were related. Fairbanks and Green (1950) compared (a) the maximum thickness of the free border of the upper lip in the midline, (b) the maximum thickness of the free border of the lower lip in the midline, (c) the horizontal spread of the lips during relaxed occlusion, from corner to corner, and (d) the vertical length of the skin-covered portion of the upper lip in the midline. No significant differences between speaker ability groups were found for the four lip measurements. Observation was also made of the anteroposterior positioning of the lips in profile and the uniformity of the inferosuperior contact between the two lips in the frontal position. The findings for the profile and frontal lip observations revealed similar results for both groups; the frequencies in the separate cells were too small for statistical evaluation.

The foregoing studies are summarized in Table 3.8. The findings do not seem to indicate that measurements of the palate, tongue, and lips can be used to distinguish between normally speaking and articulatory impaired individuals. One of the two significant results, Fymbo's finding for cuspid width, was not sustained by the later study of Fairbanks and Lintner. The second significant finding, maximum mouth opening, may simply be, as was discussed, another measure of open bite.

[Table 3.8] Summary of Studies Relating Articulation
and Oral Measurements

Investigation	Results
Fymbo (1936)	No differences between speaker groups on palatal height and palatal molar width; size of palatal cuspid width increased as speaking ability increased
Fairbanks and Lintner (1951)	No significant difference between superior and inferior speakers for palatal height and palatal cuspid and molar widths. Inferior speakers showed significantly greater maximum mouth opening than superior speakers
Fairbanks and Bebout (1950)	No significant differences between superior and inferior speakers on maximum tongue protrusion and length of relaxed tongue tip
Fairbanks and Green (1950)	No significant differences between superior and inferior speakers for thickness of upper and lower lip, horizontal spread of the lips and vertical length of upper lip

Tongue Thrust

In 1940 Palmer and Osborn advanced the hypothesis that articulatory errors may result from too little tongue force. Their study is not included in this chapter because some of the experimental subjects had speech errors other than articulation. However, in 1950 Fairbanks and Bebout examined maximum tongue force for a group of superior and inferior college students. Maximum tongue force was measured 5 mm. from the lower incisors toward the labial surface. A significant difference in maximum tongue force was not obtained between the inferior- and superior-speaking college students. Recently a hypothesis has been advanced that articulatory errors may result from excessive tongue pressure or from frequent frontal excursions of the tongue. This disorder has been given the nomenclature of tongue thrust or abnormal swallow.

Tulley (1956, p. 805) describes tongue thrust as follows, ". . . the tongue rests constantly against the lower lip and thrusts or spreads forward to meet the contracting lower lip in swallowing and speech."

According to Straub (1960) individuals with the abnormal swallow habit do not bring the jaws tightly together during swallow, thrust the tongue forward between the teeth, and use facial muscles to help in swallowing. The excessive and frequent excursions of the tongue have been suggested as a cause for errors of the linguo-dental, linguo-alveolar, and labio-dental sounds. Speculations about the etiology of tongue thrust and its relationship to malocclusion and other oral facial deformities have been provided by Francis (1958, 1960), Shelton and others (1959), Jann (1960), Straub (1960, 1961), and Palmer (1962).

In three experimental studies tongue thrust and articulatory errors have been related. Fletcher and others (1961, pp. 201–202) conducted the first study. They described the tongue-thrust swallow pattern as including: "(a) extreme tension in the mouth-enclosing musculature, (b) diminution or absence of palpable contraction in the muscles of mastication during the swallowing act, and (c) forward thrust of the tongue causing it to protrude between the incisors."

The relationship between the tongue-thrust swallow pattern and articulatory behavior was studied from data collected from 1615 subjects from ages 6 through 18. All subjects were enrolled in one school district and represented socioeconomic and urban-rural cross sections. The authors report that articulatory evaluations were made of two sibilant sounds, the /s/ and /z/ phonemes, since Fletcher and others (1961) and Francis (1958) report that these sounds are "acoustically most affected by an anterior lingual-placement shift."[11]

One more point should be mentioned before we continue. The number of children found by Fletcher and others to have sibilant errors far exceeds nationally reported figures based on errors of all sounds (Powers, 1957; Milisen, 1957). For example, the percentages of sibilant distortion at 6, 8, 16, and 18 years were about 19 percent, 14 percent, 13 percent, and 18 percent, respectively. The authors are cognizant of this fact and state, "The frequencies of sibilant distortion which are reported should not be construed to represent frequencies of children in need of speech treatment. Some of these distortions were minimal and would be noted only by the speech specialist. Therefore, the frequencies would be expected to exceed nationally reported incidence" (Fletcher and others, 1961, p. 204).

The tongue-thrust evaluation followed the articulation test. Deviant swallowers were those subjects who evidenced all three of the above-mentioned criteria. Each subject was tested by asking him to swallow while the examiner depressed the lower lip in order to expose the tongue. Examiners were found to make these observations reliably.

The tongue-thrust swallow, but not the sibilant distortion, decreased with age. When the tongue-thrust and nontongue-thrust groups were examined separately, distortions did not decrease with age for the tongue-thrust group, but they did decrease with age for the nontongue-thrust group. Finally, when age levels were combined, a significant relationship (chi-square) was found between tongue-thrust and sibilant distortions.

Several criticisms may be leveled against the procedures of this article.

[11] Fletcher, in a personal communication, indicated that /ʃ/ and /ʒ/ productions were not tested, although the original study reports that all English sibilant phonemes were evaluated.

The primary criticisms involve the behavioral definition used to assess sibilant distortion, and the lack of independence between the observations of speech and swallowing.

In a second study on tongue thrust and articulation (Ward and others, 1961) two types of swallowing—somatic or typical swallowing and visceral or atypical swallowing—were observed. They are described as follows:

> . . . visceral swallowing is characterized in the following way: During the mylohyoid stage of swallowing, the posterior teeth are not brought together. The orbiculoris [sic] oris and other circumoral muscles exhibit a sphincteric or peristaltic form of behavior. The tongue *thrusts forward,* spreading out between the anterior incisors. . . . somatic swallowing [is a] . . . more highly selective activity of the orofacial muscles. The contraction of the masseter and the temporalis muscles brings the posterior teeth firmly together while the lips and cheeks remain in a relatively passive state. The tongue *remains within the oral cavity* (Ward and others, 1961, p. 335).

The above criteria were used by Ward and others (1961) in their observation of 358 children from grades one through three. The children were from two schools which did not have a speech correction program.

Each child was asked to swallow, and circumoral lip action was noted. During the beginning stage of swallowing the lips were parted to determine whether or not the teeth were separated, and the tongue was spread between the anterior incisors. Malocclusion was determined by Angle's classification as given by Salzman (1957, pp. 245–247). Examiner reliability was demonstrated for the swallowing and occlusal assessments. The reliability ratings were made on the first 99 children by four examiners—one dentist and three speech pathologists. The remaining 259 children were examined by the three speech clinicians, presumably at the time the tongue-thrust evaluations were made.

Eleven consonants were evaluated in all three positions. However, in the final analysis some of the sounds were grouped (such as /s/ and/z/), making a total of eight test sounds. The percentage of errors occurring for each sound for subjects who had visceral swallowing and malocclusion (91 percent according to the authors) and for subjects who had none of these disorders is reported. However, there are a number of inconsistencies and errors in the results section of this article. Often the findings in their table of results do not agree with statements made in the text. For example, from values presented in one of their tables of results, the percentage of errors is less for all eight of the sounds or sound pair tests (/t/ and /d/; /l/; /n/; /θ/ and /ð/; /ʃ/ and /ʒ/; /tʃ/ and /dʒ/; /s/ and /z/; and /r/) when malocclusions and visceral swallowing are present.

In 91 percent of the subjects, malocclusion and visceral swallowing were both present. This fact suggests that these coincidental conditions are probably too frequent to act as discriminating variables in articulatory assessment. It should be mentioned that the 91 percent figure is probably somewhat high as it does not agree with figures given elsewhere in the article. (In one case the figure of 44 percent is given.)

The frequency of articulatory errors is not as great as the frequency of malocclusion and visceral swallowing. With the exception of two test sounds (/l/, and /s/ and /z/) the frequency of articulatory errors for the experimental children (presence of a malocclusion and visceral swallowing) was no greater than 19 percent. The frequency of errors for the /l/ and for the /s/ and /z/ was 48 percent and 29 percent, respectively. Thus, many of the children with deviant swallowing and poor occlusion did not have articulatory errors.

Ward and others also found that neither atypical swallowing nor articulatory errors decreases with age. In fact, for subjects with normal swallowing and dentition, the articulation errors of seven of the eight test sounds actually increase with age. For the /l/ phoneme the increase in errors from the first to the second grade is 22 percent.

Subtelny and others (1964) related tongue-thrust and /s/ production for a group of 48 adolescent subjects who had a Class II, Division 1, malocclusion (distoclusion); 20 subjects had /s/ errors (noticeable lisping) and 28 did not have /s/ errors. The proportion of subjects with /s/ errors was not significantly higher for the tongue-thrust group. (A chi-square using Yates' correction was computed from data reported by Subtelny and others.)

Because of the way it has been studied, no definitive statement can be made about the relation between articulation and tongue thrusting. Careful consideration of the experimental design of two of the studies (Fletcher and others, 1961; Ward and others, 1961), wherein the relation between tongue thrust and articulatory errors was reported as positive, makes conclusions impossible. In a third study (Subtelny and others, 1964) no relation between tongue thrusting and /s/ "lisping" was found.

In exploratory studies, such as these, it is important that every experimental principle be adhered to, especially that of independency of measurements. That this kind of bias is real can be shown by examining a study by Kortsch (1963). He reports that in September, 1962, 660 grade school children were examined for the tongue-thrust reflex and for articulatory defects. Articulatory defects were found in 41 (6.2 percent) of the children and tongue thrusting was found in 134 (20.3 percent) of the children. Two months later the 134 children found to have a tongue thrust were reexamined, and 64 (47.76 percent) were found to have an articulatory defect and only 70 were not found to have a defect!

Development and Physical Health

The developmental status of the articulatory defective child has interested some investigators. The term "developmental" as used here includes the following: the acquisition time of certain physical and motor attributes, the presence or absence of certain childhood diseases, parental reports of personality behaviors, and the present physical health of the child. The foregoing variables have been thought to play a role in the impairment or retardation of articulatory acquisition.

Wellman and others (1931) obtained correlations between total articulation and the following developmental variables: height, .59; sitting height, .50; standing height, .52; weight for boys separately, .72; weight for girls separately, .28; weight-height index, .28; and weight–sitting-height index, nonsignificant. The number of subjects for these correlations ranged from 30 to 48. The relatively high height and weight correlations result from the fact that height, weight, and articulation increase with age; the correlations of articulation with height and articulation with sitting height were found to be nonsignificant when computed separately for ages four and five (N = 14 or 15 at the two age levels). However, these two correlations may have been attenuated for a number of reasons: sampling errors, unreliability, and restriction in the spread of scores.

Reid (1947a, 1947b), holding chronological age constant, found nonsignificant r's between articulation and height, weight, and grip strength. Everhart (1953) selected a group of 110 children enrolled in grades one through six who misarticulated a consonant in any of the three word positions. The control group of 110 children was matched on sex, grade, and race. Most of the physical and growth factors (factors a to g below) were obtained from a questionnaire filled out by the parents. Height and weight measures were secured from school records. No significant differences were found between the groups in the onset or occurrence of the following factors: (a) holding head up, (b) sitting alone, (c) crawling, (d) walking, (e) talking, (f) voluntary control of bladder, (g) eruption of first tooth, (h) height, and (i) weight. Everhart also reports no significant differences between the experimental and control groups for grip strength, as measured by the Smedley dynamometer.

In a study by Nelson (1953) a significant difference was not found in the health records of normal- and defective-speaking children. The 35 control and experimental subjects were from the third, fifth, and seventh grades and were matched on sex, IQ, grade, and school. The information was gleaned from pupils' health and medical cards and from interviews with school nurses. A composite score for each subject was obtained by rating each subject's datum on a "1" to "3" scale.

FitzSimons (1958) compared 70 articulatory defective and 70 children with normal articulation on several developmental variables. The experimental and control subjects were selected from a group of first-grade children. The subjects ranged in age from approximately six years to seven and a half years. The experimental subjects were children considered to have articulatory problems. The matching variables were IQ, age, sex, and school locale. The developmental data were obtained from interviews with the mothers of the subjects.

In comparison to the nonarticulatory defective group, a significantly greater number of experimental subjects were reported to have had abnormal births, were bottle fed, were weaned before six months, began toilet training before nine months, completed toilet training before two years, and had a greater number of childhood illnesses before three years. Also, the articulatory defective children lagged behind the normal-speaking children in beginning to walk and were behind them in language responses as measured by the appearance or nonappearance of words at 12 months and phrases at 18 months.

The experimental group demonstrated a greater frequency of childhood problems (we would say parent-child interaction problems); 10 of 15 comparisons were significant. Examples of these problems were destructiveness, difficulty in eating, fears, jealousy, temper tantrums, and thumb sucking. Many of the developmental factors and childhood habits were obtained from the Vineland Social Maturity Scale. However, the author reports that the groups did not differ significantly on this scale.

An examination of the relation between thumb sucking and frontal lisping yielded negative findings for a group of 76 elementary school children ranging in age from 8 to 12 years (Mims and others, 1966). Hypothesizing an historical relationship between open bite and thumb sucking the investigators were careful to select only those children who demonstrated an open bite, as diagnosed by a dentist. Thumb-sucking was defined as persisting beyond the age of six, daily in occurrence, and having lasted at least four years, as judged by the child's parents. The frequency of lisping was no greater for thumb suckers than for those children who did not have a history of thumb sucking.

The findings of these six studies appear to be in disagreement (see Table 3.9). For example, Everhart found no differences between the articulatory defective and nonarticulatory defective groups on a variety of developmental measures, but FitzSimons found many differences. Wellman and others obtained fairly high correlations, but their results, as the findings of Reid would suggest, are confounded with age. The studies of Nelson and FitzSimons are carefully done, yet the findings pertaining to health measures are not in agreement. FitzSimons' study is more carefully done than Everhart's in that the parents were questioned by an interviewer. An interviewer can clarify the questions and can recheck many of the

[Table 3.9] Summary of Findings Relating Developmental
Variables to Articulation

Investigation	Age	Results
Wellman and others (1931)	2 to 6 yrs. (range)	Positive correlations for measures of height, weight, sitting height, etc., computed over a wide age range. These relationships reflect the fact that articulation and these developmental variables covary as a function of age.
Reid (1947a, 1947b)	8 yrs. 8 mos. (mean)	No relation between articulation and height, weight, and grip strength with CA held constant
Everhart (1953)	Grades 1 through 6 (range)	No significant difference between control and experimental children on a variety of measures, like height, weight, crawling, walking, etc.
Nelson (1953)	Grades 3, 5, and 7 (range)	No significant difference in the health records of control and experimental children
FitzSimons (1958)	6 to 7.5 yrs. (range)	Significant differences between control and experimental children on a variety of measures, such as birth condition, bottle feeding, weaning, toilet training, "childhood" problems, and childhood illnesses. No significant differences between control and experimental groups on the Vineland Social Maturity Scale.
Mims and others (1966)	8 to 12 yrs. (range)	Thumb sucking and frontal lisping not related for children with open bites

responses. Still, FitzSimons' data were gathered from parents, whose responses are subject to the vagaries of the human memory. Also, the parents of articulatory defective children may be more concerned about their children's general behavior than the parents of nonarticulatory defective children. The parents of articulatory defective children may judge their children's growth patterns as slow and their illnesses as frequent in order to assist the examiner in detecting some cause of the articulatory defect. Nelson's study is probably not biased in this way, since the data were gathered from documents routinely administered to the parents of school-aged children. However, the data used by Nelson may not have been an accurate report of early childhood diseases. Ultimately, longitudinal research may help answer the queries one has about the relationship between developmental factors and articulatory acquisition.

Auditory Memory Span

The ability to store and recall recent information has been considered by some to be an important prerequisite for speech and language learning. This "ability" has been tested by having the subject repeat a series of stimulus units. The experimenter utters each unit in the series at about one-second intervals; the subject is then requested to repeat the series. About five or six units can be recalled by most adults with average intelligence.

In order to determine whether or not children with articulatory errors are less skilled in the immediate recall of items than nonarticulatory defective children, several investigations have been conducted. The hypothesis is, of course, that nonarticulatory defective children will recall series that are longer in length than articulatory defective children. We have no idea of the number of items in a series that needs to be recalled in order to assure one of adequate articulation. Very young children can recall a series of no more than two or three digits, yet they utter many sounds correctly and often speak in sentences of four or five words.

The first study on auditory memory span and articulation was conducted by Hall in 1938. She compared 21 children designated as articulatory defective by their scores on the Detroit Articulation Tests with 64 children not so designated by this test. Each experimental child was matched in age, sex, and IQ, with from two to five control group children. The age range for both groups was 7 years 2 months to 13 years 5 months. The test included both vowel and consonant series. The vowel series ranged from three to six, and the consonant series from two to four. A significant difference was not obtained between the groups on the auditory memory span test.

Metraux (1942) matched 34 normal-speaking and 34 children from speech classes on age, sex, grade, and IQ. Two tests were administered, a vowel and a consonant test. The number of items for the vowel and consonant tests ranged from one to seven. The subjects were given considerable preliminary practice, so that the examiner could become aware of the child's closest "approximation" to the test sound. The normal group was found to perform significantly better than the articulatory defective group on the consonant test, but not on the vowel test.

Mase (1946) used the digit span test of the Stanford-Binet IQ Test as his criterion measure. The differences between experimental and control subjects for the mildly articulatory defective group and the severely articulatory defective group were nonsignificant.

Holding chronological age constant Reid (1947) found no correlation between articulation and auditory memory span for vowels (the items in each series ranged from two to seven). She used an auditory memory test designed by Fontaine (1940).

Clark (1959) compared experimental and control subjects on two tests of auditory memory span: memory for short sound patterns tapped by a pencil and memory for digits (four and five digits). Control subjects performed significantly better than experimental subjects on both tests of auditory recall.

Using a modification of the Wechsler digit span test, Prins (1962a) compared the retention span of a control group with three different experimental groups. Of the three comparisons, two were significant—the difference between the lisping group and the control group, and the difference between the omission group and the control group. The first difference favored the lisping group, and the second favored the control group.

Using three verbal tasks and one performance task, Smith (1967) compared the scores of 12 normal speaking children and 12 mild to severe articulatory defective children whose mean age was 7.4 years. The three verbal tasks were: single digit sets (Three units of three to six numbers were presented to the left ear for half of the subjects and to the right ear for the other half of the subjects.); sequential digit sets (Two series, three to six in number, were presented at a time and the subject was asked to recall the first series. Ears were counterbalanced.); simultaneous digit sets (Three to six in number, the digits were presented to both ears simultaneously. Half of the subjects were requested to report only those stimuli presented to the left ear and half those stimuli presented to the right ear.) The performance task was a bead pattern. (The subject was asked to duplicate a pattern of seven beads formed from a set of uni-color, three-form beads.)

Immediate and delayed recall measures were used. The delay interval was five seconds for the digit series and ten seconds for the bead series. This resulted in eight comparisons. All of the six digit differences favored the children without articulatory errors. For the two bead measures, however, the differences were not significant.

In one study (Hall, 1938) the control and experimental subjects were adults. A vowel series ranging from five to seven units and a consonant series ranging from four to eight units were used. A seven-point rating scale was employed to identify control and experimental subjects, "1" indicating extreme articulatory inferiority and "7" indicating extreme articulatory superiority. All subjects were rated by two experienced judges. Experimental subjects (N = 83) were those whose scores totaled six or less with at least one rating no higher than two. Control subjects (N = 83) were those whose scores totaled eight or more with both ratings not less than four. The control and experimental subjects were matched on age, sex, and college ability (percentile score of the Iowa Qualifying and

Placement Examinations). From the experimental group of 83 subjects, 25 subjects were selected as the most serious in defect. This group had a mean articulatory rating of 3.0 in comparison to a rating of 4.3 for all 83 experimental subjects. The 83 control subjects and the control subgroup of 25 subjects had mean articulation ratings of about 8.3. No significant differences were found between the control and experimental group or between the control and experimental subgroup.

That children with articulatory errors are retarded in the immediate recall of items has not been consistently demonstrated. In four of the seven studies (see Table 3.10), significant differences were found. Metraux reports differences favoring the control group on a consonant test. Clark and Smith report differences favoring a control group on digits and sound patterns. Prins reports differences that both favor and disfavor a control group.

Metraux's findings hint at a partial explanation for these inconsistencies. Her groups differed in the recall of consonants but not of vowels. Possibly, subjects who have not learned to utter consonant sounds well, might have difficulty coding the sounds they hear, especially if the auditory recall test involves sounds that are defective for the subjects. A similar situation would obtain for English speakers, were they asked to recall the voice quality, words, or sounds uttered by speakers of unfamiliar tongues. In such situations it is difficult to code the stimuli into familiar symbols (acoustic bins) for recall. This "coding" factor should be eliminated in tests of auditory recall. Clark's tapping test and Smith's bead pattern tests were probably free of such bias. However, in view of the negative findings for many of the studies employing speech sound stimuli, further research is necessary before conclusive statements, either positive or negative, can be made.

Auditory Discrimination

It seems logical that the learned discriminations among different speech sounds must occur prior to or simultaneously with the phonetic and phonemic learning processes. However, little is known about this process. We have only the tentative formulations of Jakobson (see pp. 88–96). It has been assumed by some that articulatory errors reflect a retardation or impairment in the development of speech sound discrimination. To test this hypothesis, the relationship between articulatory performance and discrimination (speech sounds, pitch, loudness, etc.) has been investigated. Although it has been recognized that individuals with functional articulatory errors make many correct sounds and that many of the "incorrect" sounds are uttered correctly in some contexts, some speech pathologists have continued to assume that the discrimination deficit is a general rather than a specific one. Accordingly, articulatory defective subjects have, for the most part, been studied as a group without regard to the specific sounds in error.

SPEECH SOUND DISCRIMINATION. The usual speech sound discrimination test consists of a list of word or nonsense syllable pairs. Each pair of test

[Table 3.10] Summary of Studies Relating Auditory Memory Span and Articulation

Investigation	Test	Results
CHILDREN		
Hall (1938)	Consonants and vowels	No significant difference between experimental and control groups
Metraux (1942)	Consonant and vowels tested separately	A significant difference favoring the control subjects on a consonant test. No significant difference on a vowel test.
Mase (1946)	Digit span test of Stanford-Binet	No significant difference between the control and experimental subjects for both the articulatory defective group and the severely articulatory defective group
Reid (1947)	Vowels	No relation between articulation and auditory memory span, holding CA constant
Clark (1959)	Digit span and tapping	Significant differences between control and experimental subjects favoring the control children on both tests.
Prins (1962a)	Modification of Wechsler digit span test	A significant difference favoring a lisping group over a control group; a significant difference favoring a control group over an omission group; no difference between a phonemic group and the control group.
Smith (1967)	Single, simultaneous and sequential digit sets, and bead pattern, immediate and delay measures used	Control group performed significantly better on all six digit test measures but not on the bead test.
ADULTS		
Hall (1938)	Vowels and consonants	No significant differences between a control group and an articulatory defective group, and a control group and a severe articulatory defective group

items consists of short sequences of phonemes, identical in number. The test items are varied, so that some pairs contain the same phonemes and other pairs show a difference of one phoneme. When the pairs differ by one phoneme, the position of the contrasting phoneme is kept constant. Examples are /kɪm/ and /kɪm/, and /kɪm/ and /pɪm/; /koʊt/ and /koʊt/, and /koʊt/ and /boʊt/. The subject is asked whether the two response pairs are the same or different.

The first investigation comparing defective and normal subjects was conducted by Travis and Rasmus in 1931. They studied three paired groups of defective- and normal-speaking subjects: fourth and fifth grade normals (N = 50), and fourth and fifth grade defectives (N = 40); second and third grade normals (N = 60), and second and third grade defectives (N = 36); junior primary and first grade normals (N = 50), and junior primary and first grade defectives (N = 27). The authors report that the majority of defective cases had mild disorders of articulation. The discrimination test consisted of 366 paired nonsense syllable items. For all three pairs of groups the normal group performed significantly better than the defective group.

Hall (1939) compared control and experimental children on two tests of discrimination. The children received the Travis-Rasmus Speech Sound Discrimination Test and a complex speech sound discrimination test, the latter consisting of 40 items composed of sentences which included a nonsense item, such as "A *vestik* radio." The subjects then heard two (10 items) or three (30 items) sentences, one of which contained an exact replication of the nonsense item, and they were to select the sentence which contained this exact replication. The nonsense items were devised to be one of five errors: vowel and consonant substitution, transposition of a sound, omission of a sound, and addition of a sound. For example, the errors for "A *vestik* radio" were "ve–tik" (omission of a sound) and "hestik" (consonant substitution). Significant differences between control and experimental subjects were not obtained for the two discrimination tests.

Two different discrimination tests were employed by Mase (1946). The first test consisted of sentences, such as "*shoe* your food well," which were printed on standard forms with the test word absent. The subjects were to check the blank space if the test word was mispronounced. The second test consisted of a paired list of word similars and word contrasts. Two forms of each test were developed, each test containing 50 items. Both tests were played from phonographic recordings. When the scores for the separate forms were analyzed, significant differences were not obtained. However, a significant difference favoring the control subjects was obtained for the sentence test when the scores on both forms (100 items) were combined.

Reid (1947a, 1947b), holding chronological age constant, found a correlation of .48 between articulation and discrimination as measured by the Templin Speech Sound Discrimination Test. This discrimination test con- sists of 70 pairs of nonsense syllable items.

Carrell and Pendergast (1954) matched 33 control and experimental subjects on sex, age (8 to 13 years), intelligence and/or tester's estimate of academic achievement, personality traits, and home background. The test consisted of 60 nonsense pairs. A significant difference favoring the control group was found.

Kronvall and Diehl (1954) compared 30 articulatory defective (four or more sound errors) elementary grade children with 30 normal-speaking children ranging in age from 6 to 9 years. They were matched on the basis of age, sex, grade, and intelligence. The Templin Speech Sound Dis- crimination Test was administered to all subjects. A significant difference favoring the control group was found.

Correlations between sound discrimination and a 176-item articulation test for 480 children from 3 to 8 years of age were reported by Templin (1957). For ages 3, 3.5, 4, 4.5, and 5 a picture discrimination test was given. This test contained 59 items; one like pair of items or one unlike pair was depicted pictorially on a card. The subjects were required to point to the like or unlike picture pair. For ages 6, 7, and 8 the test con- sisted of 50 items of paired nonsense syllables. The correlations ranged from .41 (4.5 years) to .69 (7 years).

An interesting set of tests was developed by Schiefelbusch and Lindsey (1958) in order to determine whether there were sound discrimination differences between normal and articulatory defective children for sounds (a) uttered by the examiner, (b) spoken by the subject, and (c) evaluated silently by the subject. Eleven consonant sounds were included. For each of these three conditions, three discrimination tasks were tested: (a) rhyming of words, (b) discrimination of initial consonants, and (c) dis- crimination of final consonants. The procedure called for 30 items for each of the three discrimination tasks (90 items for each of the three discrimination conditions). Each item consisted of a card with three pictures, and each picture represented a word. Subjects were instructed to select the two pictures which sounded alike.

Twenty-four experimental and 24 control children from the first and second grades were matched for intelligence and age. The experimental children had a mean number of 11.6 consonant errors as determined by a 30-item articulation test. For all three conditions, significant differences were obtained in favor of the nonarticulatory defective group. Also, the differences between each of the three conditions for both the experimental and control group children were very small. This latter finding suggests that the three conditions were of equal difficulty.

Clark (1959) reports that articulatory defective children perform sig- nificantly poorer than nonarticulatory defective children on the following discrimination tests: vowels, consonants, and words and phrases. The first two tests consisted of pairs of same or different items. The vowel and consonant tests had 12 items. The word and phrase test consisted of a series of 15 cards, each card having two pictures on it. The pictures represented objects or events whose names had common sound elements; the subject was to identify one of the two pictures by name in response to a word or a phrase.

The Templin Speech Sound Discrimination Test was administered again by Cohen and Diehl in 1963. The subjects were 30 experimental children and 30 control children in grades one, two, and three. The articulatory defective children had at least 5 of 24 consonants in error. The groups were matched for age, sex, grade, and intelligence. In order to avoid visual cues the subjects were seated with their backs to the examiner. The control subjects performed significantly better than the experimental children.

Prins (1963) compared a group of experimental and control first-grade subjects on a word discrimination test designed by Wepman (1958). This test contains 40 pairs of items. There were 26 children in the articulatory defective group and 19 children in the control group. A significant difference was not obtained between control and experimental groups.

Articulatory defective children scored below normal-speaking children on two tests of discrimination, "filtered speech" test and "binaural summation" test, in a study conducted by Costello and Flowers (1963). The subjects were 30 control and 30 experimental grade school children. The articulatory defective children were considered to have a severe articulatory problem, determined, in part, by the Templin-Darley Test.

In the "filtered speech" test energy below 960 cycles per second was delivered 40 decibels above the subject's speech reception threshold; in the "binaural speech" test the distorted stimulus was presented to the left ear while the right ear received an undistorted signal 5 decibels above the speech reception threshold for that ear. The stimulus materials consisted of 50 pictures. A corresponding list of 50 different monosyllabic words was compiled; each word was either the name of the object in the picture or the name of an object whose name was similar (a difference of one or two phonemes) to the object in the picture. Discrimination was tested by having the subject answer Yes or No to the question: "Is this a picture of ————?" On both auditory tests the control group significantly outperformed the experimenal group.

Taking a different experimental strategy, Sherman and Geith (1967) categorized subjects on the basis of discrimination scores and then made articulatory measurements. The Templin (1957) 50-item discrimination test was administered to a large number of kindergarten children from whom 18 high ranking subjects (scores of 48 to 50) and 18 low ranking subjects (scores of 19 to 28) were selected. Subsequent to this testing the children were administered the 176-item Templin and Darley diagnostic test (see Chapter 4, p. 250). The high ranking subjects articulated correctly about 36 more sound items.

In three studies the discrimination of adult subjects with varying levels of articulatory proficiency was tested. In the first study Travis and Rasmus (1931) compared 223 adult normals with 62 defective adults on a 366-item discrimination test. The normal adults performed significantly better than the defective adults.

In a second study (Hall, 1938) college freshmen were used as subjects. The subjects were assigned to control or experimental groups on the basis of their articulation ratings, as discussed previously. The auditory test battery consisted of the Travis-Rasmus Speech Sound Discrimination Test and a complex speech sound discrimination test, the latter consisting of 38 items composed of sentences which included a nonsense item, such as, "my *per'sa lent* friend." These nonsense items were described above. Each sentence was read twice followed by a reading of five sentences. One of these five sentences contained an exact replication of the nonsense item. The subjects were to indicate the replicated sentence. No significant differences were found with either discrimination test between the control group and the mild group or between the control group and the severe group.

In a third study (Hansen, 1944) three groups of college male students (N = 13 in each group) were tested on a 50-item vowel discrimination test and on a 108-item nonsense syllable discrimination test (Travis-Glaspey Test). The tests were prerecorded. The first two groups consisted of subjects with known defectiveness of articulation, as judged in the reading of a passage (Group I) and as determined by their enrollment in articulatory correction classes (Group II). The third group contained subjects "classified as normal speakers." All subjects were matched on the basis of their percentile scores on the American Council Psychological Examination. No significant differences were found between any of the two groups for both discrimination tests.

For the tests of speech sound discrimination involving children, nine of the eleven studies (summarized in Table 3.11) employing control and experimental children indicate significant differences favoring the control groups for at least one of the tests employed. In the two investigations in which correlational procedures were used, moderate to moderately high correlations were obtained. The interesting approach taken by Sherman and Geith further suggests that children with poor discrimination scores will also have less than adequate articulation. For the adult studies, two of the three investigations revealed a non-significant difference. Therefore, for children at least, the evidence overwhelmingly supports the point of view that articulatory defective children score below nonarticulatory defective children on tests of speech sound discrimination.

DISCRIMINATION AS A FUNCTION OF LEARNING. Anderson (1949), in a

[Table 3.11] Summary of Studies Relating Speech Sound
Discrimination and Articulation*

Investigation	Results
CHILDREN	
Travis and Rasmus (1931)	Significant difference favoring three control groups over three experimental groups
Hall (1938)	No significant difference between control and experimental groups on a sentence test and a word test
Mase (1946)	Significant difference favoring the control group on a sentence test, but not on a word test
Reid (1947a, 1947b)	$r = .48$ between articulation and discrimination when CA was held constant
Carrell and Pendergast (1954)	Significant difference favoring the control group
Kronvall and Diehl (1954)	Significant difference favoring the control group
Templin (1957)	r ranged from .41 to .69 for age levels 3 to 8
Schiefelbusch and Lindsey (1958)	Significant difference favoring the control group was found when discrimination was tested in the usual way and when the child uttered the sounds or evaluated them silently.
Clark (1959)	Significant differences on vowels, consonants, and words favoring the control group
Cohen and Diehl (1963)	Significant difference favoring the control group
Prins (1963)	No significant difference between control and experimental subjects
Costello and Flowers (1963)	Significant difference favoring the control group on a filtered speech and a binaural summation test
Sherman and Geith (1967)	Significantly better articulation scores for subjects with good discrimination
ADULTS	
Travis and Rasmus (1938)	Significant difference favoring the control group
Hall (1939)	No significant differences were found between a control and an articulatory defective group or between a control and severely articulatory defective group on a sentence test and on a word test.
Hansen (1944)	No significant differences between control and experimental groups on a vowel test and a nonsense syllable test

* Unless otherwise indicated, the discrimination test was a word or nonsense syllable test.

study reported by Spriestersbach and Curtis (1951), found that a greater percentage of /s/ discrimination errors occurred in contexts in which the subjects themselves misarticulated the /s/ sound than in contexts in which they had no /s/ articulatory difficulty. The subjects were 31 children in the kindergarten through the fourth grade who had errors of the /s/ phoneme. This phoneme was tested in 58 items, blends and singles. The discrimination test followed the articulation test. The examiner pronounced each of the words used in the articulation test three times. In one of the three instances the sound was produced incorrectly; the error was a simulation of each subject's articulatory error. For those items produced correctly by the subject, the most "common" type of /s/ error was uttered. The correlation between the number of /s/ errors and the total number of discrimination errors was .25, and the correlation between the number of discrimination errors in contexts in which /s/ misarticulations occurred was .38. A correlation of .66 was obtained between the number of omission errors and the number of discrimination errors for items involving sound omissions, and a correlation of .48 was found between the number of substitution errors and the number of discrimination errors for items involving sound substitutions. These findings seem to suggest that subjects, for the most part, have difficulty discriminating /s/ items (a) in contexts in which the articulation errors occur and (b) when the type of articulation error is used in the discriminative comparison.

More recently Prins (1963), Aungst and Frick (1964), and Snow (1964) have presented evidence that seems to support the findings of Anderson. Prins, using procedures described previously (Prins, 1962a, 1962b), correlated specified articulatory responses with scores obtained on a discrimination test devised by Wepman (1958). The Wepman test consists of 40 word pairs of contrasts and similars. The experimental subjects were 26 first-grade children with functional defects of articulation, who were selected from 92 experimental subjects (Prins, 1962a).

Prins (1963, p. 383) developed the following classificatory system for categorizing articulation errors:

> Articulatory deviations were divided into three error classes: I, phonemic sound substitutions; II, non-phonemic substitutions; and III, sound omissions. Class I and II errors were subdivided further depending upon whether the intended phoneme was altered in manner of articulation (M), place of articulation (P), or voicing (V); whether these alterations occurred singly (1) or in combination (2, 3); and the degree to which place of articulation was changed (1d, 2d, 3d). A maximum of three degrees of articulatory place change was possible with all phonetic elements being categorized in one of four places: front (bi-labial, labio-dental), middle (linguo-dental and alveolar), back (linguo-palatal and velar), and glottal.

This classificatory system resulted in 22 categories for sound errors, including a category for total articulation errors.

Of the 22 correlations with the Wepman test, only 3 were found to be significant; all 3 involved phonemic sound substitutions. They were alteration of place of articulation, —.46; alteration of one degree of place of articulation, —.47; and alteration of one feature of the intended phoneme, —.43. (In Prins' first study, phonemic substitutions involving a change of one articulatory feature correlated .70 and .75 with articulatory place change and one degree of articulatory place change, respectively. Thus we might conclude that "alteration of one feature" involved primarily changes in place of articulation.) In addition, the correlation between discrimination scores and total articulation errors was nonsignificant.

The contrastive elements of the Wepman test involve changes in place of articulation, while manner and voicing are kept constant. The contrastive elements include both consonants and vowels. Thus, the findings for this study lend support to the hypothesis that discrimination and articulatory sound errors are related when the measurements involve similar phonetic or contextual dimensions.

In the Aungst and Frick (1964) investigation the relation between the production and discrimination of the /r/ phoneme was studied. The subjects, numbering 27 clinical clients, ranging in age from about eight to ten years, were tested. The discrimination test consisted of 30 items, each containing a variant of the /r/ phoneme. The /r/ production test (articulation test) consisted of 50 items in which allophones of the /r/ phoneme were tested. Discrimination was tested for the /r/ phoneme in a variety of ways: (a) the subject's immediate evaluation (right or wrong) of his own response (instantaneous judgment), (b) the subject's evaluation of his own response (right or wrong) when heard from a tape recording (delayed judgment), and (c) the subject's evaluation of his own response (right or wrong) in comparison to the experimenter's correct response (comparison judgment) when heard from a tape recording. In addition, the Templin 50-item discrimination test was administered. The tests were administered in two separate sessions, about three days apart. At the first session the Templin test and the instantaneous judgment test were given, and at the second session the delayed and comparison judgment tests were administered.

On the /r/ articulation test the subjects averaged 23 errors out of 50, and about 19 errors on each of the three /r/ discrimination tests. On the Templin test the mean number of correct responses was about 45 correct out of 50; the standard deviation was about 5. This latter result suggests that the majority of the subjects were able to discriminate a large proportion of the items on the Templin test. Therefore, the items on this test were not of sufficient discriminability, in the statistical sense, for the subjects of this study.

Correlations among the three /r/ discrimination tests were in the .90's; however, the Templin test did not correlate significantly with any of the three /r/ discrimination tests, no doubt due to the restricted range of scores. The correlations between each of the three /r/ discrimination tests and the /r/ articulation test ranged from .59 to .69. The Templin test, as would be expected, did not correlate significantly with the /r/ articulation test. These findings suggest that the production of /r/ and the discrimination of /r/ variants are related. We would like to conclude that the production of /r/ sounds is not related to discriminations involving other sounds, but this would seem unwise, because most of the subjects achieved high scores on the Templin test. On the other hand, the subjects in the study performed as well as the subjects in Templin's normative study, children who were not distinguished on the basis of /r/ errors. Templin (1957) reports that the average discrimination score at eight years of age was 46.1. This finding seems to suggest that /r/ errors are not related to a "general discrimination ability."

Snow (1964) examined the sound substitutions of a large number of first-grade children. The test included all of the English consonants. In many instances the sound substitutions of the children closely corresponded to the sound confusions frequently made by adults in quiet and relatively quiet conditions (Miller and Nicely, 1955). The adults had been tested by asking them to identify the consonants when uttered in a nonsense syllable.

It is possible that the sound discrimination difficulties of children with articulatory impairments have resulted from the articulatory errors themselves. Winitz and Bellerose (1962, 1963) have theorized that the learning of an incorrect articulatory response may affect subsequent discrimination between the correct sound and the incorrectly learned sound. This hypothesis is in accord with findings predicated on the stimulus-response theories of acquired distinctiveness and equivalence of cues (Dollard and Miller, 1950, pp. 97–105; Goss, 1955, 1961). According to the former theory the learning of distinctive verbal responses to similar stimuli facilitates subsequent discrimination between the stimuli; and according to the latter theory, the learning of the same verbal response to two distinctive stimuli impairs subsequent discrimination between the stimuli by giving the two distinctive stimuli a certain learned equvalence. According to these two theories, speech sound discrimination would be more difficult after conditions which permit the incorrect learning of a sound than after conditions which permit the correct learning of a sound.

Before reporting the findings of the two Winitz and Bellerose studies, it might be desirable to describe these two theories more completely. Illustrations will include syllables from an experiment to be reported shortly. As we know, the /vr/ phoneme cluster does not occur in the initial word position in English. However, the /br/ cluster does. The question is this:

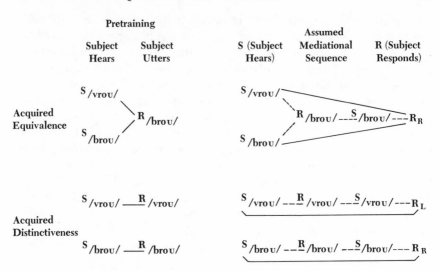

[Figure 3.1] Graphic illustration of the pretraining and testing conditions used to generate acquired equivalence and acquired distinctiveness of sounds. Each stimulus is denoted by S and each response by R. The speech stimuli are /vroʊ/ and /broʊ/. R_R and R_R refer to the right bar and to the left bar, respectively, of the discrimination apparatus.

Would English-speaking children have more difficulty hearing the difference between /vr/ and /br/ if they have learned to utter /br/ when they hear either the stimulus /br/ or /vr/ than children who have learned to utter /br/ when they hear /br/ and have learned to utter /vr/ when they hear /vr/? The models (see Goss, 1955) that have helped us generate this question are diagrammed in Figure 3.1.

In the acquired equivalence paradigm the subject is first trained to utter the same verbal response, /broʊ/, to two physically different stimuli, /vroʊ/ and /broʊ/. The subject is then placed before a discrimination apparatus (described later) and told to press one bar when he hears one "sound" and a second bar when he hears a second "sound." (The instructions include practice with two neutral sounds or syllables.) Presumably subjects pretrained in the acquired equivalence condition will have difficulty discriminating between these two stimuli because they both evoke the same mediational sequence, ^{R}/broʊ/ . . . ^{S}/broʊ/, which in turn elicits the same external response R_R, the pressing of the right bar.

In the acquired distinctiveness paradigm the subject utters a different verbal response to two physically different stimuli. In this example (see Figure 3.1) the response is simply the correct imitation of the stimulus. The subject is then asked to press one bar when he hears one "sound" and a second bar when he hears a second "sound." Since the subject has been pretrained in the acquired distinctiveness condition, he will mediate each of the two physically different stimuli by two different mediational chains (see Figure 3.1). This will enable him to press R_L when he hears /vrou/ and R_R when he hears /brou/. It is assumed, therefore, that the probability of correct bar responses for each trial is greater for the subject pretrained with the acquired distinctiveness condition than for the subject pretrained with the acquired equivalence condition. However, it is important to note that the studies to be described were directed toward investigating "pretraining" processes, and mediational concepts were used only as a guide. The results do not in any way support a mediational explanation. Further study is definitely indicated before we can describe adequately and clearly the perceptual processes involved, and whether or not labeling is critical to effect phonemic distinctiveness and equivalence.

The hypotheses described above were examined in two separate investigations. In the first investigation (Winitz and Bellerose, 1962) children from the fourth grade were assigned to one of three pretraining groups, I, II, and III; following this pretraining, all groups participated in a speech sound discrimination task.

For the pretraining condition the subjects in each group participated as follows: Group I repeated /ʃa/ for 40 trials; Group II uttered /ʃa/ in response to [ça] for 40 trials (/ʃ/ for [ç] is the usual response for English-speaking children; the error is maintained by reinforcement); and Group III served as a control group.

All subjects then participated in a successive sound discrimination task. One of two stimuli was presented on each trial, and the subject was asked to make one of two spatial responses, left or right bar-pressing. The apparatus, as pictured in Figure 3.2, has been described in detail in the Winitz and Bellerose study (1962). It consisted of a panel 24 inches square with two bars extending 4.5 inches from the panel and separated from each other by 3.5 inches. A silver strip extended from the left bottom corner of the panel to the top right panel. In the middle of the strip a blue toy car extended from the panel. The base of the car was attached to a movable pulley, which was not visible to the subject. The car was raised 0.5 inches when the child pressed the correct bar and lowered the same distance when he pressed the wrong bar. Movement (forward or backward) was actuated by two solenoids which placed the pulley into contact with a continuously running quiet motor. There were approximately 50 forward (or backward) movements with a setting of 0.5 inches.

The results are presented in Figure 3.3. Although it appears that group

[Figure 3.2] Discrimination apparatus.

II did not discriminate as well as the other two groups, the differences were not significant. Also, a nonsignificant trials effect indicated that the discrimination task was too difficult for the subjects.

In a subsequent study, Winitz and Bellerose (1963) investigated again the effects of pretraining conditions on sound learning. The subjects were first- and second-grade children. Three of the major changes made in this second experiment were the following: (a) a group was included which was to learn a new sound that contrasted with an acquired sound, (b) the

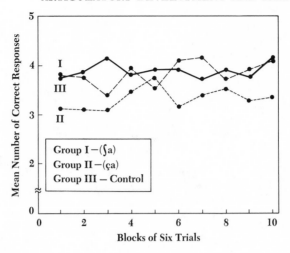

[Figure 3.3] Mean discrimination learning curves for the /ʃa/ — /ça/ contrast.
SOURCE: Winitz and Bellerose, 1962.

car was arranged to move upward only, (c) the experimental syllables were /vroʊ/ and /broʊ/.

For the pretraining condition the subjects responded to 60 trials of /vroʊ/ or /broʊ/ or both, as follows: (a) constant training (subjects in group I learned to say /vroʊ/ for /vroʊ/ and /broʊ/ for /broʊ/); (b) varied training with two syllables (subjects in group II learned to say /broʊ/ for /vroʊ/ and /broʊ/ for /broʊ/); (c) varied training with one syllable (subjects in group III learned to say /broʊ/ for /vroʊ/); (d) control condition (subjects in group IV learned to say /troʊ/ for /troʊ/ and /droʊ/ for /droʊ/. A fifth group was included but it will not be discussed here.

Immediately after the pretraining condition, all subjects participated in a 60-trial successive discrimination task involving /vroʊ/ and /broʊ/. The results are presented in Figure 3.4. Significant differences were obtained between the constant group and the varied group pretrained with two syllables and between the control group and the varied group pretrained with two syllables. The difference between the constant group and the varied group pretrained with one syllable fell short of significance.[12] The performance of the control group appeared to occupy a position intermediate to the constant group and the two varied groups in the following order: the constant group, next the control group, and finally the two

[12] This difference was erroneously reported as being significant in the original article (Winitz and Bellerose, 1963). It was due to a computational error.

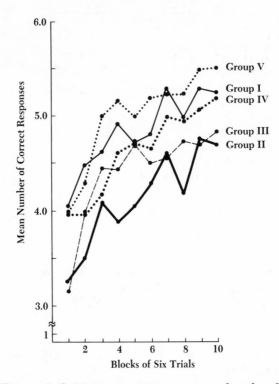

[Figure 3.4] Mean acquisition curves for the discrimination of /vroʋ/ and /broʋ/ for four pretraining groups: Group I, constant pretraining (/vroʋ/ for /vroʋ/, and /broʋ/ for /broʋ); Group II, varied pretraining with two syllables (/broʋ/ for /vroʋ/, and /broʋ/ for /broʋ); Group III, varied pretraining with one syllable (/broʋ/ for /vroʋ/); and Group IV, control pretraining (/troʋ/ for /troʋ/, and /droʋ/ for /droʋ/).
SOURCE: Winitz and Bellerose, 1963.

varied groups. As a tentative developmental interpretation of these findings, it might be suggested that constant pretraining improves discrimination learning above a control or innately given level and that varied pretraining reduces discrimination below a control or innately given level. However, these interpretations are mitigated by the fact that not all of the differences in the preceding study were statistically significant. It is possible, of course, that acquired equivalence of cues is the primary consideration for children who have developed articulatory errors.

An investigation by White (1961) in which visual stimuli were used also seems to support the hypothesis that discriminatory equivalence and distinctiveness can be pretrained. White found that a group pretrained to a constant stimulus performed better than a group pretrained to varied stimuli. Visual stimuli were red-orange for the constant group; red-orange, white, and yellow for the varied group; and gray for the control group. The subjects were then trained to discriminate between red-orange and red. The discrimination performance of the control group was inferior to the constant group but superior to the varied group. However, only the latter difference was significant. It should be mentioned that psychological literature contains numerous articles, like the White article, that are relevant, but space does not permit a summary of this work.

There is other evidence to indicate that sound pretraining may be related to sound discrimination. Lotz and others in 1960 found that the language background (Puerto Rican, Spanish, Hungarian, Thai, and English) of subjects was an important factor in their identification of stops. Also we know that phonemic discriminations are categorical (Liberman and others, 1961a and 1961b, for example); that is, subjects will not respond differentially to a range of stimuli within the phoneme boundary (when morphological and phonological contexts are held constant), but will respond differentially to a small stimulus change between phoneme boundaries. This is true for small as well as large stimulus differences between phonemes.

Liberman and others (1961a, 1961b), from their research on synthetic consonantal speech patterns, suggest that speech discrimination (the sharpening of discrimination at the phoneme boundary) may reflect the effects of a large amount of learning and may be interpreted as acquired distinctiveness of cues. In the first investigation (Liberman and others, 1961b) the data did not allow a statement regarding acquired equivalence of cues. In the second investigation (Liberman and others, 1961a) there was no evidence for acquired equivalence of cues. Liberman and others (1961a) suggest that this is a possibility but that their data do not tend to support it. (Although allophones of phonemes are learned as equivalent sounds, some "level" or "kind" of discrimination is learned within the phoneme boundary. If this were not so, phones occurring in complementary distribution could not be learned as articulatory units.)

On the basis of their findings, Liberman and his colleagues have developed a tentative hypothesis about speech perception. It has been dubbed the motor theory of speech perception, and it is stated by the authors in condensed form below as follows (1961b, p. 177):

> We believe that in the course of his long experience
> with languages, a speaker (and listener) learns to con-
> nect speech sounds with their appropriate articulations.
> In time, these articulatory movements and their sensory
> feedback (or, more likely, the corresponding neuro-

logical processes) become part of the perceiving process, mediating between the acoustic stimulus and its ultimate perception. When significant acoustic cues that occupy different positions along a single continuum are produced by essentially discontinuous articulations (as, for example, in the case of second-formant transitions produced for /b/ by a movement of the lips and for /d/ by a movement of the tongue), the perception becomes discontinuous (i.e., categorical), and discrimination peaks develop at the phoneme boundary. When, on the other hand, acoustic cues are produced by movements that vary continuously from one articulatory position to another (as, for example, the frequency positions of first and second formants produced by various vowel articulations), perception tends to change continuously and there are no peaks at the phoneme boundaries.

Lane (1965), in a lengthy article, criticizes the motor theory on theoretical, methodological, and empirical grounds. Although he makes several cogent points about the lack of theoretical and methodological support for the motor theory, we will direct our attention to his empirical findings.[13] In several studies Lane and his colleagues have provided preliminary evidence that would seem to show that the motor theory is an unnecessary assumption for the learning of categorical perceptions (e.g., phoneme contrasts); that is, one need not assume that the articulatory mechanism acts as a mediator in the perception of sounds. Stated in another way, the motor theory considers the perception of phonemes to be determined primarily by articulatory movements rather than by acoustic signals. In these experiments (Lane, 1965, and Cross and others, 1965) nonspeech stimuli (e.g., deleted sectors of circles) were employed; the results show a relation between labeling and discrimination. The labeling responses were linguistic rather than motor, suggesting that the acquisition of distinctive auditory visual cues (categorical labeling responses and the predictions from these of discrimination functions) can occur when stimuli and responses are grossly invariant. (This situation is usually the case in psychological experiments which relate perception to labeling.) In a certain way, then, these experiments seem to support that part of the motor theory which contends mediators (linguistic abstracts) are at work, "since acoustic (and visual) cues that occupy different positions along a single continuum are 'labeled' by essentially discontinuous productions." In another way they do not support the motor theory since nonlanguage stimuli were employed, stimuli which could not be imitated. Finally it should be mentioned that mediation theorists say nothing about the "epistemological status" (Kendler and Kendler, 1962) of the mediated events, i.e., where the "chain of events" takes place.

---

[13] See Eimas (1963) for a theoretical discussion in support of the motor theory.

Philosophical considerations aside, experiments directed toward assessing the relative difference between "motor" responses and "language" responses as labelizers in effecting discrimination functions are desperately needed.

Perhaps one way to discover whether or not speech is a special kind of decoder is to find a person who hears but cannot speak. MacNeilage, Rootes and Chase (1967) seem to have almost done this. They gave detailed study to a 17-year-old female who had chronic difficulties in swallowing, chewing and speaking, but whose hearing and intelligence were normal. Her inabilities were apparently related to a loss of somesthetic sensation rather than to damage of the systems governing motor activity.

The detailed inventory of the subject's phonemic perception, using the well-known synthetic patterns of the Haskins laboratory, gave data which are consistent with that found for normal subjects. Preclusion of articulatory information for the child who acquires speech normally is, of course, not directly confirmed by the finding of this study.

Rejection of Liberman's motor theory in no way implies a formal criticism of his work in acoustic phonetics, nor of his perceptive statements and hypotheses about the speech code, only that articulatory information, of the peripheral sort, is not critical to the development of the neural signals which govern both perception and production of speech.

Since phonemic discriminations seem to be discontinuous, we can now see why binary-valued stimulus models seem to have great appeal for psychological inquiry. It should be noted here, however, that recent developments in linguistics posit a binary phonemic level, far more abstract than suggested throughout this book, and a phonetic level, which in most instances is continuous (see Postal, 1968). The new developments in linguistics which specify phonological-phonetic and morphological-phonological relations (systematic phonemics) are of great significance for psychological theories of phonemic and phonetic acquisition and discrimination, as well as for the research in instrumental phonetics which has focused on the perception of the speech wave.

Since discrimination skills have been found to increase with age (Templin, 1957), and since the discrimination scores of articulatory defective children are lower than the discrimination scores of nonarticulatory defective children, it might be inferred that speech sound discrimination is a maturational process which is often delayed. In view of the preceding discussion, an alternate inference might be made. After some point in time (probably by two years of age) speech sound discrimination scores reflect the speech sound experience (phoneme systems) of children. A supplemental inference would be: the results of speech sound discrimination tests that are administered to articulatory defective children may reflect primarily the effect of a large amount of faulty speech sound learning (an incompletely developed or idiolectal phoneme system when viewed from the standpoint of the community language). Thus we are not saying that phonemic distinctions cannot be learned before articulatory productions are learned only that articulatory experience will affect later discriminations.

It would seem, then, that the following questions might be asked: (a) At what age can children learn to discriminate all English sounds? (b) After what age is sound discrimination learning unrelated to age?[14] (c) What are the relevant distinctive features and how are they manipulated? (d) Is discrimination of speech sounds related to the verbal units (word or syllable) in which sounds appear? (e) Is discrimination related to other linguistic variables, such as vocabulary level (Templin, 1957), meaningfulness (Underwood and Schulz, 1960), and the frequency of sounds, words (Brown and Hildum, 1956), or minimal pairs (Denes, 1963) in the English language? (f) Can discrimination skills generalize to verbal units not as yet learned? The answers to these questions may help to reveal the role of speech sound discrimination in articulatory learning.

Other Tests of Discrimination—
Pitch, Intensity, Rhythm

In addition to speech sound discrimination tests, several additional measures of discrimination have been utilized to test differences between normal and articulatory defective children. These measures include tests of frequency, rhythm, intensity, etc. Experimentation in this area was initiated by Mase in 1946. He employed the Seashore Tonal Memory and Rhythm Tests. In the tonal test the subject hears several different series of tones. Each series is played twice, and after each pair of series the subject is asked to indicate the number of changed notes. In the rhythm test a series of patterns is played. The subject is requested to indicate whether pairs of patterns are the same or different. No significant differences were obtained between experimental and control children on either of these tests.

Clark (1959) reports that articulatory defective children perform significantly poorer than nonarticulatory defective children on a test of tunes. The test consisted of seven pairs of tunes which were played for the subjects; they were to indicate whether they were the same or different.

In one study (Bradley, 1959) a just noticeable frequency difference was used as a test of discrimination. The subjects were 11 normal-hearing and -speaking children and 11 children with normal hearing but with articulatory defects severe enough to require speech therapy. The subjects ranged

---

[14] Answers to the first three questions might be obtained from procedures developed by Lipsitt (1963). He has employed operant discrimination procedures to study visual discrimination in infants of eight months.

between 9 and 14 years of age. Frequencies of 500, 1000, and 2000 were tested at 50 decibels above the subject's threshold. Both the ascending and descending techniques were used, and increments of one cycle were tested. Just noticeable differences in cycles per second were obtained for all three frequencies and for each ear separately, making 12 comparisons. All 12 differences favored the normal-speaking children, ten of which were significant.

Mange (1960) compared a group of 35 children with /r/ errors with a control group of 35 children on five auditory tests. The experimental group had errors in addition to the /r/ phoneme. However, none of these children had errors of the /s/ phoneme. The subjects were matched on the basis of IQ, age, sex, and classroom attendance. The five tests included three Seashore tests (pitch, loudness, and timbre), an auditory flutter fusion test, and a word synthesis test. The Seashore tests measure discrimination between pairs of stimuli, *higher* or *lower*, for example. The auditory flutter fusion test consists of a white noise signal whose interruption rate can be varied. The subject's score is the frequency at which he hears the continuous noise fuse. A low interruption rate was considered a good score. For the auditory synthesis test three sounds, produced in isolation, were spliced together to form a familiar word. A significant difference in favor of the control group was obtained only for the pitch test.

Sommers, Meyer, and Fenton (1961) compared a group of 65 children with /r/ or /s/ errors with a control group of 65 children on a pitch test taken from the Tilson-Gretsch Musical Aptitude Test. In this test 25 pairs of tones are presented; the subjects are asked to indicate whether or not the second tone is higher or lower than the first. The 65 experimental children included 27 subjects who misarticulated only the /r/ phoneme and 38 subjects who misarticulated only the /s/ phoneme. Both the control and experimental subjects were selected from grades 3 through 12. The matching variables were IQ, sex, and grade level. A significant difference was obtained between the experimental and control groups in favor of the control groups. No significant differences were found between the children with /r/ errors and the children with /s/ errors.

Only one investigation provides information on adults. This was the previously cited study by Hansen (1944). He reports no significant differences among three groups of college subjects—trained defectives, defectives, and normals—on the Seashore Test of Timbre.

The one measure that seems to favor consistently the control children is frequency discrimination (see Table 3.12). Since this finding is such a consistent one, and since it seems to involve a measure essentially free from the necessary perceptions imposed by the English language, it has appeal for the physiologically minded speech pathologist. The acquired equivalence and distinctiveness models can, of course, be used to nurture an entirely different hypothesis. One might speculate that because the

[Table 3.12] Summary of Findings on Discrimination Tests
Involving Nonspeech Stimuli

Investigation	Results
CHILDREN	
Mase (1946)	No significant differences between control and experimental subjects on tonal memory and rhythm tests
Clark (1959)	Significant difference favoring the control group on a test of tunes
Bradley (1959)	The frequency "just noticeable differences" are smaller for nonarticulatory defective children.
Mange (1960)	No significant differences on tests of loudness, timbre, fusion, and synthesis. A significant difference favoring a control group on pitch.
Sommers, Meyer and Fenton (1961)	Significant differences favoring a control group over an /r/ defective group and an /s/ defective group on a test of pitch discrimination
ADULTS	
Hansen (1944)	No significant differences among trained defectives, defectives and normals on timbre

phoneme boundaries of articulatory defective children show greater overlap than nonarticulatory defective children, frequency discriminations are more difficult for the former group than for the latter group. However, before any energy is expended in this direction, additional comparative data are needed.

Personality and Adjustment

Some investigators have speculated that articulatory errors may be related to personality maladjustments. Although most investigators have concentrated on the personality of the child, one study, to be discussed later, examined the personality of mothers of articulatory defective children.

It is difficult to think of a child's personality traits as behaviors which develop independently of the parent. In most cases, as discussed in child development texts, a child's personality behaviors reflect to a considerable degree the interaction between child and parent. It is also difficult to think of personality maladjustments as the cause of an articulatory error. They can just as easily be the result of the articulatory error or one of the traits that often accompany a personality or emotional disturbance. With these considerations in mind, we shall review several studies on personality and articulation.

Wellman and others (1931) obtained no relationship between articulation and the Marston Introversion-Extroversion Scale (N = 56). Davis (1937) found that a greater percentage of children with defective articulation were rated as shy, negative in attitude, and less distractible. The percentage differences ranged from about 4 to 9 percent: the differences were not tested for statistical significance. These results should be accepted with reservation, as the ratings were made following an articulation and language examination, and thus the examiner may have been influenced by the child's language performance during the test session. Reid (1947), holding chronological age constant, found no relation between articulation and personality. Personality scores were derived from the California Test of Personality.

Two tests of personality were used by Nelson (1953) in his comparison of 35 control and 35 experimental subjects. On the first test, the California Test of Personality, the difference between the experimental and control groups was not significant. However, on the second test, the combined Haggerty-Olson-Wickman Behavior Rating Schedule, a significant difference was found in favor of the control subjects. Scores on this test are derived from teachers' ratings, and in this case are interpreted to mean that articulatory defective children are rated as having more undesirable behavior than nonarticulatory defective children.

FitzSimons (1958), using the Children's Apperception Test, found that first-grade articulatory defective children exceeded first-grade normal children in aggression, fears and anxieties, perception of parents as authoritarian, and, in addition, had less positive outcomes (stories that have "happy" endings). An expanded form of the Wechsler digit-symbol test was used by Trapp and Evans (1960) to assess the anxiety level of two groups of articulatory defective children, mild and severe, and a nonarticulatory defective group (N = 18 in each group). The subjects in each group were matched for age, sex, intelligence, and socioeconomic background. The children ranged in age from eight to ten years with a median age of nine. On the Templin Screening Test the mild group had articulation scores ranging from 40 to 46, with a median of 43; the severe group had scores ranging from 6 to 35, with a median of 28. The mild group was found to be significantly more anxious than both the severe group and the normal group. The severe group and the normal group did not differ from each other.

Solomon (1961) matched 49 children who evidenced consistent defectiveness on at least one sound with 49 control children on the basis of age, intelligence, sex, and grade. The age range of the subjects was not given. Personality differences were assessed by interviewing the mothers of the children in several areas of personality and child development. The interviews were tape recorded and later rated independently by two judges. All of the behavior areas were rated separately (on a "1" to "5" scale) and, in addition, a rating of "overall adjustment" was made. Control and experimental subjects were rated in a random order. Significant differences were found between the groups on the following behavioral measures: sleeping behavior problems, fears, anxieties, tensions, peer relations, and overall adjustment. In all of these areas the experimental group exhibited greater "disturbances" than the control group.

In one study the personality of mothers of articulatory defective children was tested. Moll and Darley (1960) administered two questionnaires of maternal attitude—Parental Attitude Research Instrument (PARI) and Wiley's Attitudes Toward the Behavior of Children (ATBC)—to mothers of articulatory defective and nonarticulatory defective children. The children of the mothers (N = 26) of the articulatory defective group had been diagnosed as having a functional articulatory disorder. Mothers of the control group (N = 60) had at least one child 3 to 12 years of age. Mothers of this group answered "No" to the question, "Do any of your children have speech defects?" The mothers of the two groups did not differ on maternal age, maternal education (number of school years completed), and socioeconomic status. On the PARI scale, significant differences were obtained on only 2 of 23 measures. The measures were "Breaking the Will" and "Approval of Activity." These findings suggest that the mothers of articulatory impaired children express more agreement with "undesirable" attitudes related to breaking the child's will and "taking the natural meanness out of the child," and indicate more agreement with items expressing disapproval of children's activities than do mothers of the control group. On the seven ATBC scales, significant differences were not obtained between the two groups. The PARI differences, as indicated by the authors, could well have been chance differences.

The studies on the personality behavior of children, although not entirely consistent, tend to indicate that children with articulatory errors have a greater proportion of adjustment and behavioral problems than nonarticulatory defective children (see Table 3.13). However, the differences are only significant for those studies in which a nonstandardized personality inventory was used. Finally we might note that the one study on parental attitudes revealed essentially negative findings.

In two excellent reviews of both published and unpublished studies on personality and articulation, Spriestersbach (1956) and later Goodstein (1958a) concluded that a relation between personality factors and articulation disorders has not been clearly demonstrated.

In addition, Goodstein summarized a number of methodological considerations that should be carefully considered in future investigations. Among these were: adequate sample size, need for cross validation and appropriate control groups, grouping of subjects with regard to the severity of the articulatory disorder, consideration of the age of the subjects, need for reliability and validity of many of the tests used, and

[Table 3.13] Summary of Studies Relating Articulation
and Personality

Investigation	Results
CHILDREN	
Wellman and others (1931)	No relation between articulation and Marston Introversion-Extroversion Scale
Davis (1937)	A small but greater percentage of articulatory defective children were rated shy, negative in attitude, and less distractible.
Reid (1947)	No relation between articulation and scores on the California Test of Personality
Nelson (1953)	No difference between control and experimental children on the California Test of Personality; the experimental children were rated as having less desirable behavior on the Haggerty-Olson-Wickman Behavior Rating Schedule.
FitzSimons (1958)	On the Children's Apperception Test experimental children were judged (a) to be more aggressive, (b) to be more fearful and anxious, (c) to view parents as authoritarian, and (d) to view stories with less happy endings.
Trapp and Evans (1960)	Using the Wechsler digit-symbol test as a measure of anxiety a mild articulatory defective group was more anxious than a severe articulatory defective group and a nonarticulatory defective group. The latter two groups showed similar performance on this test.
Solomon (1961)	Experimental children were rated to have more disturbances, e.g., sleeping problems, fears, anxieties, tensions, poor peer relations, and poor overall adjustment.
PARENTS	
Moll and Darley (1960)	Parents of articulatory defective children were not found to be very different from parents of nonarticulatory defective children on two tests of parental attitudes, Parental Attitude Research Instrument and Wiley's Attitude Toward the Behavior of Children.

consideration of the bias of the examiner. With regard to this latter point
Goodstein (1958b, p. 380) states as follows:

> Many techniques of personality measurement, such
> as projective tests and interviews, involve the direct
> observation of the oral behavior of the subject. The

individual with speech problems is placed at a particular disadvantage in such a procedure and his difficulties are frequently magnified by the necessity for oral productivity. In any event, these procedures permit the tester or interviewer to identify the speech-handicapped individual as such and this knowledge may tend to maximize experimenter bias, for example, systematic tendencies to judge those who are thus handicapped as less well adjusted than those who are not. Much the same criticism can be made of teachers' and parents' ratings of the adjustment of the child with speech problems . . .

Spriestersbach and Goodstein offer one final and important point. They note that many of the studies on personality and articulation were conducted without any overall concept or theory about the effect of personality variables on articulatory disorders. Tests were generally applied without a specific hypothesis to guide the investigator in the selection of tests or in the circumscription of subject populations. It seems essential, then, that investigators doing research in this area develop a set of hypotheses that can serve as guidelines for their experimental endeavors in order to assure them some chance of success.

Lexical and Grammatical Measures

For many investigators an articulatory disorder, whether the result of environmental deprivation and/or physical or mental inability, is simply one of several responses which reflects a general language impairment. Accordingly, a delay in articulatory development would be accompanied by a delay in grammatical and lexical achievement. It is possible, of course, for one language system to develop faster than a second one and thus interfere measurably with the second language system's development. A hypothesis such as this has been tentatively proposed by Ervin and Miller (1963). They theorize that young children with large vocabularies have more articulatory errors than children with small vocabularies because children of the former group are continually being exposed to new vocabulary units and, thus, all of their efforts must be directed toward understanding these new items. In doing so they neglect to learn the (adult) phoneme contrasts of many of the words.

In any event it seems most plausible that phonology and syntax are formally related. (See pp. 71–76.) In this section we shall report the findings of a number of studies, which had as their aim, empirical assessment of the relationship between phonetic accuracy and syntactic and lexical development/

The first investigation relating articulation to a language measure was conducted by Wellman and others in 1931. They found no relation between the Smith Vocabulary Test and the articulation of single consonants ($N = 24$). In the Smith test knowledge of vocabulary items is tested by the identification of single pictures or the answering of questions about pictures.

Davis (1937) found that 5.5-year-old children with faulty articulation achieved significantly lower scores than children with perfect articulation in mean length of response, time required to elicit the responses (a higher score was obtained in this case), number of different words, and number of spontaneous remarks (remarks not elicited by the examiner). This last measure was computed for the boys and girls separately; the difference for the boys fell short of significance. No differences were found in the number of questions asked. Davis, however, found that for the 6.5 and 9.5 year groups mean length of response was longer for the children with articulation errors than for the children with perfect articulation. Statistical tests were not applied to the differences found at these latter two age levels.

Substantial relationships between articulation and language measures were found by Williams (1937). He related the articulation and language performance of 38 three- and four-year-old children who were examined on a 98-item articulation test. The following correlations were obtained: number of correct (grammatical) words used in 50 consecutive words (probably the first 50 words), .64; mean length of response based on 40 responses, .60; number of complete sentences (weighted as follows: $0 =$ unintelligible, $1 =$ incomplete, and $2 =$ complete, i.e., subject, predicate, and object present), .61; sentence complexity (based on the following index: $0 =$ unintelligible sentence, $1 =$ simple sentence, $2 =$ complex sentence, $3 =$ compound sentence, and $4 =$ compound-complex sentence), .62; Van Alstyne Vocabulary Test (picture identification), nonsignificant; Smith-Williams Vocabulary Test (naming or identifying single pictures), nonsignificant. When mental age and chronological age were held constant, the correlations were similar except that the coefficient for the Van Alstyne Test increased from a nonsignificant .16 to a significant .57.

Yedinak (1949) reported no significant differences between a control and experimental group on vocabulary (picture identification as measured by the Word Meaning part of the Durrell-Sullivan Reading Capacity Test), length of response, complexity of remark (a rating of 0 to 3), and completeness of response (mean number of complete remarks).[15]

Carrell and Pendergast (1954) found no significant difference between experimental and control groups on vocabulary as measured by the vocabulary subtest of the Wechsler Intelligence Scale for Children.

Schneiderman (1955) examined the relation between articulation and a combined language score obtained from three language measures: spoken vocabulary (the Van Alstyne Picture Vocabulary Test was used

[15] The Yedinak study is described in detail in the next section.

to elicit words), sentence length, and teachers' ratings of language ability. Each language measure was weighted equally; subjects were then assigned to one of three language groups according to their level of language ability. The three language groups were designated as high, medium, or low ($N = 23$ or 24 in each group). A significant difference was found among the three groups (the three between-group differences were not analyzed): articulation errors were found to increase as the combined language scores decreased. The subjects in each group were then reduced to 19 in order to eliminate those individuals representing the extremes in mental ages, resulting in similar mean CA's and MA's for the three groups. The same relation between articulation and language skills was obtained as reported above; however, the difference among groups fell short of significance.

Intercorrelations between articulation and several language measures for each of eight age levels (three through eight years) were made by Templin (1957). The range of obtained correlations for the different language responses was as follows: length of remark, nonsignificant (seven and eight years) to .62 (three years); complexity of remark (a scale similar to Williams'), nonsignificant (seven and eight years) to .66 (three years); number of different words, nonsignificant (eight years) to .65 (three years). Vocabulary was measured by a modification of the Seashore-Eckerson English Recognition Vocabulary Test (a word definition test used to estimate total vocabulary). The results for ages six, seven, and eight were .39, .46, and .38, respectively. The Ammons Vocabulary was used for ages three through five, and the results were previously reported in this chapter as IQ estimates.

Winitz (1959) obtained the following correlations between the Templin 50-item Screening Test and several language measures for five-year-old children: length of response, nonsignificant; number of different words, nonsignificant; structural complexity score (similar to Williams'), .29; Ammons Full-Range Picture Vocabulary Test, .28; Rimes, .16; Child Names, .20; Adult names, .20; and Thing Names, .33. The last four measures were administered by asking the child to rime or name as many words as possible according to the procedures of Gewirtz (1948).

In yet another study, Van Demark and Mann (1965), using seven language measures (mean length of response, standard deviation of mean length, number of one word responses, mean of the five longest responses, number of different words, structural complexity and type-token ratio) found only one difference to be significant, that of structural complexity. They polarized their groups by using the Templin-Darley screening test cut-off score for eight year old subjects. The subjects ($N = 50$ in each group), who ranged in age from about 8 to 13 years, were matched on sex, socioeconomic status and age.

The findings for these several studies (see Table 3.14) on grammatical and lexical measures and articulation are not entirely consistent. For some of the studies a substantial relation between articulation and certain language measures especially at the young age levels was demonstrated, and for other studies no relation or only a low relation was found. These disparities may reflect test differences, test administration differences, or subject population differences. It would seem that before further relationships are sought, hypotheses need to be developed which take into account the fact that language development involves the simultaneous learning of a set of interrelated systems—phonology, morphology, syntactic and semantic (Berko and Brown, 1960; Ervin and Miller, 1963). Within this frame of reference a great many hypotheses no doubt can be generated.

Fluency

One might ask whether children who show repetitions in their speech also have difficulty articulating sounds. In only one study, that of Davis (1939, 1940), have dysfluency and articulation been related. The subjects selected for her study were 62 children enrolled in a preschool. They ranged in age from two years to five years and two months. The speech of each child was recorded in two one-half-hour sessions. Several measures of repetition were extracted from each child's verbal record. These measures and their relation to scores on the Williams revision of the Wellman and others articulation test were: instances of syllable repetition, nonsignificant; instances of word repetition, nonsignificant; instances of phrase repetition, —.47; instances of syllable, word, and phrase repetitions combined, —.37; and composite measure (total number of words involved in a syllable, phrase, or word repetition), —.53. Repetitions were found to decrease with age, and since articulatory scores increase with age, the negative correlations reflect the different directional effects of CA on these two measures. The last three correlations reported above would, no doubt, be considerably attenuated were the influence of CA not permitted.

Educational Achievement

That defective articulation might impair the learning of reading, spelling, and other academic subjects which require the discrimination and use of speech sounds appears tenable. Therefore, a number of investigations comparing defective- and normal-speaking children on several tests of academic achievement have been made. Some investigators have hypothesized that if retardation in academic subjects can be found for articulatory defective children, it would suggest that an articulation defect merely reflects an underlying language and educational disability. Other authors have suggested that an articulatory defect or factors associated with an

[Table 3.14] Articulation and Its Relation to Certain Lexical and Grammatical Measures

Investigation	Test	Age	Results
VOCABULARY			
Wellman and others (1931)	Smith	2 to 6 yrs. (range)	Nonsignificant r
Williams (1937)	Van Alstyne	3 to 4 yrs. (range)	$r = .57$
Yedinak (1949)	Word meaning subtest of Durrell-Sullivan Reading Capacity	7 yrs. 9 mos. (mean)	No significant difference between control and experimental children
Carrell and Pendergast (1954)	Vocabulary subtest of Wechsler Intelligence Scale for children	8 to 13 yrs. (range)	No significant difference between control and experimental children
Schneiderman (1955)	Combined language score—Van Alstyne vocabulary, length of response, and teacher ratings of language ability	6 to 7 yrs 1 mo. (range)	Significant difference in articulation among three language groups
Templin (1957)	Ammons	3 yrs.	$r = .47$
		3.5 yrs.	$r = .48$
		4 yrs.	$r = $ nonsignificant
		4.5 yrs.	$r = .41$
		5 yrs.	$r = .27$
	Seashore-Eckerson	6 yrs.	$r = .39$
		7 yrs.	$r = .46$
		8 yrs.	$r = .38$
Winitz (1959)	Ammons	5 yrs. 3 mos. (mean)	$r = .28$
Van Demark and Mann (1965)	Number of different words and type-token ratio	8 to 13 (range)	No significant difference between normal and articulatorily impaired
SENTENCE LENGTH			
Davis (1937)	50 responses	5.5 yrs. (mean)	Sentence length significantly shorter for children with faulty articulation
		6.5 yrs. (mean) 9.5 yrs. (mean)	Sentence length longer for children with faulty articulation

[Table 3.14 (Continued)]

Investigation	Test	Age	Results
SENTENCE LENGTH (CONT.)			
Williams (1937)	50 responses	3 to 4 yrs. (range)	r = .60
Yedinak (1949)	25 responses	7 yrs. 9 mos. (mean)	No significant difference between control and experimental subjects
Templin (1957)	50 responses	3 yrs.	r = .62
		3.5 yrs.	r = .47
		4 yrs.	r = .27
		4.5 yrs.	r = .26
		5 yrs.	r = .52
		6 yrs.	r = .45
		7 yrs.	r = nonsignificant
		8 yrs.	r = nonsignificant
Winitz (1959)	50 responses	5 yrs. 3 mos. (mean)	r = nonsignificant
Van Demark and Mann (1966)	50 responses, number of one word responses, 5 longest responses and SD of 50 responses	8 to 13 yrs. (range)	No significant difference between normal and articulatorily impaired
SENTENCE STRUCTURE			
Williams (1937)	Correct usage of words	3 to 4 yrs. (range)	r = .64
	Complete sentences	3 to 4 yrs. (range)	r = .61
	Complexity of remark	3 to 4 yrs. (range)	r = .62
Yedinak (1949)	Complexity of remark	7 yrs. 9 mos. (mean)	No significant difference between control and experimental subjects
	Complexity of remark	7 yrs. 9 mos. (mean)	No significant difference between control and experimental subjects
Templin (1957)	Complexity of remark	3 yrs.	r = .66
		3.5 yrs.	r = .57
		4 yrs.	r = .30
		4.5 yrs.	r = .49
		5 yrs.	r = .35
		6 yrs.	r = .46
		7 yrs.	r = nonsignificant
		8 yrs.	r = nonsignificant

[Table 3.14 (Continued)]

Investigation	Test	Age	Results
SENTENCE STRUCTURE (CONT.)			
Winitz (1959)	Complexity of remark	5 yrs. 3 mos. (mean)	r = .29
Van Demark and Mann (1965)	Structural complexity	8 to 13 yrs. (range)	Significant difference favoring normal speaking children.

articulatory defect, such as auditory discrimination, may be variables which impair learning. Within both frames of reference it seems important to determine the relation between articulation defectiveness and certain academic skills.

READING. The first educational measure to be considered is reading. Hall, in 1938, reported a nonsignificant difference between a group of control and experimental children on a test of silent reading. The reading test was appropriate for the child's age level (grade two, Gates Primary Reading Tests; grades three through five, Gates Silent Reading Test; and grade six, the Iowa Silent Reading Test).

Yedinak (1949) reported comparisons between groups of subjects with and without articulatory errors who were originally screened on a test of reading performance. The subjects were second graders who received a grade score of 2.1 or more on the Gray's Standardized Reading Paragraphs Test (an oral test). The subjects were then assigned to either a control group (N = 74) or an experimental group (N = 42). Those assigned to the experimental group had at least one defective phoneme of frequent occurrence, as tested by a modification of the McCarthy Articulation Test (70 items). This group had a mean of 10 sounds in error (there were also two other experimental groups, a reading-disability group and a reading–articulation-disability group; the latter group was discussed in the section on intelligence). The mean age of both groups was about 93 months. Despite the fact that both groups excluded subjects severely retarded in reading, the articulation disability group was significantly lower than the control group in reading performance, as measured by the above reading test. The grade level difference was approximately six months. On a measure of silent reading (Durrell-Sullivan Reading Achievement Test) the difference between the groups fell short of significance.

Everhart (1953) found that normal-speaking elementary school children performed significantly better than articulatory defective children on the Gates Silent Reading Test (Primary, Advanced, and Basic). The children were from grades one through six.

(FitzSimons (1958), testing beginning first graders, found that a significant proportion of articulatory defective children were deficient in reading readiness (Metropolitan Reading Readiness Test) when compared with a comparable group of nonarticulatory defective children. These same nonarticulatory defective children significantly outperformed the articulatory defective children when tested later in the year for reading achievement (Metropolitan Achievement Tests).

Weaver and others (1960) related the articulation and reading performances of 638 first-grade children. Each child was administered an articulation test (98 consonant items, both singles and blends) and the Gates Reading Readiness Test. Of the 638 children, 163 had no articulation errors. The relation between articulation and reading was studied in two ways. First, the subjects were divided into two groups—those with and those without articulation errors. Subjects with articulation errors were found to have significantly more reading scores below the median reading score for the two combined groups than the subjects without articulation errors. Second, a correlation was computed between articulation errors and reading scores. The obtained coefficient was —.20. These two results and inspection of a table presented in the study suggest that the relationship between these two measures is essentially zero for subjects falling in the middle of the range, but that subjects with no or few articulation errors tend to have better reading scores than subjects with many articulation errors.

Only one study relating articulation and reading ability among adults has been found. Kelly (1932) reports a nonsignificant correlation between articulatory ratings, based on a scale ranging from "1" to "10," and the Iowa Silent Reading Comprehension Test. The ratings were made on 250 college freshmen by a committee selected from the staff of a department of speech.

Of the five studies involving chilen (see Table 3.15), eight comparisons were made between control and experimental subjects. Five significant differences were found, and they all favored the control group. In two instances the difference favored the control group but fell short of significance. In a third instance it was found that a greater proportion of articulatorily impaired than nonarticulatorily impaired subjects had low reading skills. For two of the three studies in which forms of the Gates reading tests were used, significant differences favoring the nonarticulatory defective groups were found. Thus it seems reasonable to conclude that the reading skills of articulatory defective children are delayed.

If reading acquisition is impaired or delayed because articulatory skills have not fully developed, one would expect that improvement in articulatory performance would be accompanied by an improvement in reading scores. This relation may be examined by reviewing those studies on

[Table 3.15] Articulation and Its Relation to Reading

Investigation	Test	Results
CHILDREN		
Hall (1938)	Gates Reading Test or Iowa Reading Test	No significant difference between control and experimental subjects for children in grades one through six
Yedinak (1949)	Gray's Standardized Reading Test	Second grade articulatorily impaired subjects found to be six months behind in reading skills.
	Durrell-Sullivan Reading Test	No significant difference for the same subjects
Everhart (1953)	Gates Reading Test	Significant difference favoring the normal speaking subjects in grades one through six
FitzSimons (1958)	Metropolitan Reading Readiness Test	First-grade articulatorily impaired significantly behind normal speaking children in reading readiness
	Metropolitan Reading Achievement Test	First-grade normal speaking children significantly outperformed articulatorily impaired subjects.
Weaver and others (1960)	Gates Reading Readiness Test	Control first-grade subjects achieved significantly better scores than experimental subjects (median test) and also seemed to achieve very high scores more frequently than control subjects.
ADULTS		
Kelly (1932)	Iowa Reading Test	No significant correlation between reading comprehension and articulatory ratings

speech improvement which included a measure designed to assess reading improvement.

The first study which examined reading improvement as a function of articulatory improvement was conducted by Wilson in 1954. She found nonsignificant differences in reading readiness scores (Metropolitan Readiness Test) between a group of kindergarten children who had participated in a 12-week speech improvement program and a group of kindergarten children who had not,[16] despite the fact that the former group had

---

[16] Speech improvement refers to the teaching of sound discrimination and sound production when conducted in the classroom and when no allowance is made for

significantly outperformed the latter group in articulatory improvement.

Sommers and others (1961) examined reading improvement for several groups of first-grade children: (a) those who received nine months of speech improvement, (b) those who received nine months of speech correction, and (c) those who received three months of speech correction. In the one improvement and two correction groups the same ten consonants were stressed. Appropriate control groups were used. All subjects had at least one of the ten sounds in error. Both the speech improvement group and the nine-month-speech-correction group showed significant gains in articulation scores over a nine-month control group. Also, the nine-month-speech-correction group showed greater articulation gain than the nine-month-speech-improvement group. However, only the speech improvement group demonstrated a significant gain in reading over its respective control group, as tested by four subtests (aptitude, auditory association, word recognition, and word attack) of the Primary Reading Profiles, Level One. The comprehension subtest, which was not evaluated as a gain score since no pretest score was available, did not significantly distinguish the groups.

The effect of speech improvement on reading scores for a group of normal-speaking children was also studied by Sommers and others (1961). Speech improvement lasted nine months. Significant differences favoring the speech improvement group were found for the four reading factors just cited but not for comprehension.

Finally, Sommers and others (1961) looked at the effect of articulation training for a group of severe articulatory defectives. The 25 control and the 25 experimental children had at least six of the ten test consonants in error. The experimental group received speech improvement and speech correction for nine months, and the control group received only speech improvement for nine months. The subjects were matched on intelligence, number of misarticulations, and difference scores on the Carter and Buck prognostic articulation test. The latter score was based on the difference between the number of misarticulations in words and the number of misarticulations, usually less, in nonsense syllables. This test is described in detail in Chapter 4. The experimental group (speech improvement and correction) made significantly more articulatory improvement than the control group (speech improvement only). The groups made about the same gain in reading for the four combined reading factors previously described; however, the experimental group received significantly higher scores than the control group on the comprehension test.

the fact that some students may not have speech errors. The speech sounds selected for training vary, but they are usually sounds which are commonly defective or which develop late according to the normative studies. The instruction may be given by the classroom teacher or by a speech correctionist. Speech correction, as usually defined, refers to articulatory correction of sounds found to be defective. The articulatory correction is given by a speech correctionist outside of the classroom.

Jones (1951) found that a semester of speech improvement significantly improved the reading scores (gain measures based on pretest and posttest evaluations) of third-grade pupils. The children who were found to be normal in articulation were randomly assigned to either an experimental or control group. The reading tests were silent reading, paragraph comprehension, and word recognition derived from the Gates Advanced Primary Reading Test.

As can be seen by the results of these three studies, an improvement in articulatory scores is not always accompanied by an improvement in reading scores. However, the fact that in some cases reading was found to improve and the fact that in many instances the reading ability of articulatory defective children is delayed seem to indicate that the development of these two responses is definitely related. Although a number of hypotheses can be advanced, my feeling is that a delay in reading is the result of a delay in articulatory development. A child, for example, who does not hear differences between sounds (has not acquired the phoneme contrasts of the community language) and who is unable to articulate many of the sounds of English or can articulate all of the sounds but has a phoneme system different from ours is ill-equipped to begin reading lessons. It appears obvious, then, that the relation between these two response classes should be explored in depth. This is not only a fascinating area of research but one which could have a tremendous impact on current educational and speech correction practices.

SPELLING. The spelling ability of articulatory defective children has also been investigated. Carrell and Pendergast (1954) studied 33 experimental children, ages 8 to 13, matched with a control group on the basis of sex, age, intelligence and/or teachers' estimates of academic achievement, personality traits, and home background. The written papers from reading, language, spelling, and social studies classes for each child were analyzed for spelling errors over a two-month period. The errors of spelling were classified in three ways: (a) letter errors—letter additions, substitutions, omissions, and transpositions; (b) word substitutions; and (c) categorization of letter errors as phonetic or nonphonetic. The last category referred to "arrangements of letters which would not permit correct pronunciation of the word or pronunciations heard among the speech defective children" (Carrell and Pendergast, 1954, pp. 329–330).

Mendenhall (1930), from whom these classifications were taken, gives the following example of a word substitution error, "man" for "men," but not "mon" for "men." Phonetic and nonphonetic errors were described as follows: " 'phonetic' implies a misspelling that sounds like the correct pronunciation of the word; . . . 'non-phonetic' implies an error which sounds little or not at all like the correct pronunciation" (Mendenhall, 1930, p. 9). Examples of phonetic errors are as follows: "yello" for "yellow," "comeing" for "coming," and "parck" for "park." Examples of nonphonetic errors are "valcation" for "vacation," "cram" for "cream," and "must" for "mast."

The groups were not found to differ significantly on the total number of spelling errors. In addition, no significant differences were found for six of the seven types of spelling classifications which were studied (four letter error classifications, word substitutions, and phonetic errors). Finally an examination of the letter errors for children in the experimental group revealed no relation between the phonetic equivalents of the spelling errors and the speech errors.

The relation between frequency of /r/, /l/, and /s/ misarticulations and the misspellings of words in which these consonants appeared was studied by Ham (1958). Each subject's articulation and spelling were tested for 24 test words; each consonant appeared in the initial, medial, and final position. The subjects were 40 children in the second (N = 25), third (N = 6), fourth (N = 5), and fifth (N = 4) grades. Of those words misarticulated, 53 percent were misspelled, and of those words correctly articulated, 44 percent were misspelled. Although the magnitude of the difference is small—only 9 percent more spelling errors occurring in those words which contain articulation errors—it proved to be significant. In addition, Ham (1958, p. 296) reports that "at no time was any spelling error related to the type of mispronunciation, e.g., the child who said *wabbit* [for] *rabbit* was more likely to misspell the word than a child who said the word correctly, but the misspelling would not contain a w/r substitution."

Procedural differences may have accounted for Ham's positive finding and Carrell and Pendergast's negative finding: Ham examined the spelling and articulatory error for the same words while Carrell and Pendergast did not; and Carrell and Pendergast's subjects were considerably older than Ham's subjects. With regard to the latter point it seems tenable that children who retain articulation errors in some words will, with continued practice, learn to spell these words. We would assume, however, that children who are initially being taught to spell would experience considerable difficulty with misarticulated words.

Finally a study by Zedler (1956) suggests that spelling ability may improve following speech improvement training. In her study second-grade children received speech improvement for 14 weeks. For 40 spelling words taken from the Buckingham Extension of the Ayres Spelling Scale, the experimental group showed a significant gain over the control group in spelling scores. Zedler was interested in the relation between discrimination and spelling and, therefore, did not report changes in speech production. The findings of Zedler and Ham seem to indicate that spelling and articulatory performance are related. Spelling, like reading, deserves considerable investigative attention.

ACADEMIC EVALUATIONS. Other educational measures have also been related to articulatory defectiveness. Everhart (1953) reports no significant difference between control and experimental elementary school children for arithmetic (Iowa Every-Pupil Test of Basic Skills, Test D: Basic Arithmetic Skills). Nelson (1953) found that third-, fifth-, and seventh-grade articulatory defective children averaged one letter grade lower than nonarticulatory defective children. Also, the seventh-grade experimental subjects were 12 months older than the control subjects.

In one study (FitzSimons, 1958) comparisons between articulatory defective first-grade children were made on several report card grades. The children, 70 in each group, were selected from a large number of children from several schools of a single school district. A greater proportion of articulatory defective than nonarticulatory defective children were graded as unsatisfactory in language, reading, and work habits. Conclusions about the effect of articulatory errors on report card grades should be withheld until additional evidence is available. However, these findings as well as those for reading and spelling seem to suggest that the remediation of articulatory defective than nonarticulatory defective children was graded

Many years from now, when the results are tabulated, the evidence may show that articulatory correction should be the first "course" for those children with articulatory errors. Thus, if it can be shown that articulatory errors have a retarding effect on the educational progress of children in the early grades of school, there may be *no* need to develop tests which predict articulatory development (see Chapter 4). It is assumed, of course, that articulatory instruction can be administered to children of five years of age.

Single and Multiple Factors

It is quite possible that substantial relationships between articulation and other independent variables would be forthcoming if the independent variables were examined collectively rather than singularly. For example, one might wish to study the effect on articulation of a large open bite and a short memory span. For this discussion we shall assume that the relationships are cause-and-effect relations.

One may think about multiple factor relations in several ways. For convenience we shall restrict our discussion to two independent variables. First, we might wish to discover if two variables, which independently show a moderate relation with articulation, are themselves highly correlated. Thus, if auditory memory span (AMS) and open bite (OB) are highly correlated, we then know that these two deficiencies occur together. However, this information will still not be very useful. All it means is that OB can be substituted by AMS, and AMS can be substituted by OB. If the measures are combined, the subjects are ranked on the independent variable exactly as they were before, and our measure of predictability is not increased. Second, we might wish to know whether multiple variables actually "combine" and, if they do, what form the equation takes. As examples, we shall select two simple cases, the additive and the multiplicative cases.

In the simple additive and multiplicative cases articulation errors (E) are a function of two independent variables, X and Y. The equations are $E = X + Y$ and $E = X \times Y$. In both cases, if one variable is held constant, either X or Y, E would still vary as a function of the independent variable. Empirical research, as I have indicated, has not resulted in the identification of variables that are highly correlated with E. In those cases where significant differences were obtained, the magnitude of the differences, although not often reported in this chapter, was small. If these small differences were "transformed" into correlations, the relationship would be too low to be useful for predictive purposes. In some cases X, for example, may not effect E unless Y achieves a certain value (interaction)—that is, Y is an initial and boundary condition for the operation of X. This problem will be mentioned again for a single variable when we discuss step functions.

It is possible that some "combination" of variables may be found that would increase the prediction of E; this problem may be studied within the framework of multiple correlation analysis (see McNemar, 1955, pp. 169–190). However, unless the independent variables show at least a moderate relation with the articulation criterion, a multiple correlation analysis will be of little value.

Articulatory Inconsistency and Organicity

In Chapter 2 data were reported in support of the concept of inconsistent misarticulations. Inconsistent misarticulations probably appear when the terminal articulatory response is in the process of being learned. Learning curves may be generally described as a continuous growth function; after many trials a plateau is reached. If we assume for the moment that when subjects reach a plateau they are responding correctly 100 percent of the time, then, prior to this time they have (with the exception of the 0 percent level) been performing inconsistently.[17]

Inconsistent articulatory productions are not necessarily restricted to

[17] In recent learning theory publications the hypothesis has been presented that individual learning curves are discontinuous and that mean growth curves inaccurately represent individual growth curves. That is, the learning curve is not a monotonically continuous growth function but a discontinuous curve that jumps from "unknowing" to "knowing." Within this framework one can also think of early learning as inconsistent, especially if the "unknowing" part of the curve is above 0 percent.

children whose errors are allegedly functional. Inconsistent articulatory responses for children who have an obvious organic involvement have been observed by clinicians for a variety of organic disorders. It has been validated for one disorder, cleft palate (Spriestersbach and others, 1956). Since inconsistent articulatory productions occur in the presence of an organic disorder, it can be suggested that functional articulatory errors are the result of an undetected organic insufficiency. However, one would expect that inconsistent productions would occur when an individual attempts to compensate for an organic insufficiency. Thus, the inference that an organic defect is common to both functional and nonfunctional articulatory disorders, because inconsistent productions are common to both groups, seems to be incorrect. One still needs to show that functional articulatory errors are related to an organic insufficiency.

Physiological Study of Articulatory Errors

As we have seen, the literature is replete with investigations that relate articulatory errors to physiological dimensions. In most instances the findings of these studies do not seem to have satisfactorily identified physiological factors that may be determinants of articulatory errors. (One exception to this statement is the measure of pitch discrimination.) This continuous lack of success may be a function of the research procedures that have been employed in these studies.

In this section experimental procedures that may have value for the identification of physiological determinants of misarticulations will be suggested. I am not, therefore, suggesting that the study of physiological determinants of misarticulations be abandoned, but simply suggesting, as will be seen, that it may be clinically useful to distinguish between those articulatory errors physiologically determined and those that result from phoneme system mislearning.

Articulation Errors as a Unitary Disorder

In most of the studies reviewed in this book an articulatory disorder is generally considered by the investigator to be the lump sum of the total number of phonetic errors—a single disorder which varies in severity. There have been a few attempts to relate phonemes or types of errors with specific physical dimensions (Spriestersbach and Curtis, 1951; Snow, 1961; Bankson and Byrne, 1962; Prins, 1962a; and Aungst and Frick, 1963, for example).

Since phonemes vary with respect to place and manner of articulation (that is, involve different muscular groups, innervations, and skills), it would not seem fruitful to search for functional relationships between a total articulation score and one or two physiological variables (House, 1961). For example, a search for the physiological determinants of /r/ errors would presumably involve examination of those muscles and nerves involved in the production of /r/ by normal subjects. As discussed in Chapter 2, the substitution error is often phonetically similar to the correct sound and is often produced by the same set of muscles. This fact seems to suggest that unless there is absolutely no phonetic correlation between the error and the correct sound, a unitary approach to articulation disorders is of no value.

Peripheral and Cortical Mechanisms

Investigators who have directed their attention to the relation between articulatory performance and certain physiological variables have concentrated on peripheral variables rather than on central variables. The reason is, of course, obvious; peripheral variables are accessible while cortical variables are not. At the present time, procedures are not available to measure cortical variables. Correlating articulation with certain responses or class of responses that presumably measure cortical functioning, such as IQ, does not solve the problem, since the responses selected for study might also have been influenced by noncortical variables. (See the last section in this chapter.)

It is possible to think of cortical variables as effecting individual differences, and that the scores of the subjects, although different, are not in any way defective. Reference to Figures 3.5 and 3.6 may help to make this point clear. In both figures there are four curves which represent (a) the learning curves of three individual subjects, A, B, and C, learning a hypothetical response, and (b) a mean of the three curves ($\overline{X}$). In Figure 3.5 the subjects all differ in asymptotic (plateau) performance, and in addition, subject C differs from subjects A and B in rate of learning. In Figure 3.6 the subjects all differ in rate of learning but not in asymptotic performance.

It is my opinion that articulatory learning is most typified by the learning curves of subjects A, B, and C in Figure 3.6. That is, given enough trials, physically normal children can learn the articulatory responses required by our language. For experimental purposes asymptotic performance could be defined as the production of a sound in all words and contexts or the correct learning of one sound in one context.

No doubt many types of responses cannot be learned by certain individuals regardless of the number of trials they receive. For instance, not all of us could learn an acrobatic act even if we had expert teachers. This is not to say that we are in ill health or in poor physical condition. Let us assume, then, that two different classes of responses can be identified—

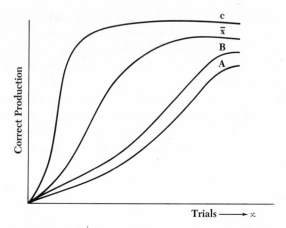

[Figure 3.5] Hypothetical learning curves of three subjects, A, B, and C, and a mean learning curve ($\overline{X}$). These curves indicate that as trials approach infinity, subjects differ in asymptote and that the learning rate of Subject C differs from that of Subjects A and B.

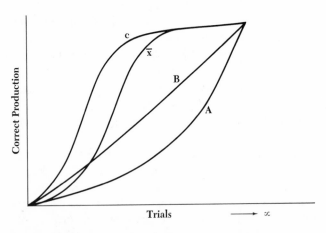

[Figure 3.6] Hypothetical learning curves of three subjects, A, B, and C, and a mean learning curve ($\overline{X}$). These curves indicate that as trials approach infinity, subjects with different learning rates achieve the same asymptote.

those that can be learned by all physically normal individuals and those that cannot be learned by all physically normal individuals. Individuals distinguished with the ability to learn the latter class of responses are probably endowed with certain genetic prerequisites. Perhaps an analogy to walking might prove instructive. Responses like walking are easily learned by physically normal children. Although children differ in their rate of learning this response, they all learn to walk. Similarly, children learn to articulate correctly at different rates, and it is our feeling that if the environmental conditions are conducive to learning, the phoneme system of the speech community can be learned by all children who are physically and mentally normal.

Peripheral Mechanism and Step Functions

One implicit assumption made by investigators interested in the relation between articulation and the peripheral speech mechanism has been that of the "shape" of the relation; it has been assumed that the functional relationship is a monotonic one rather than some sort of step function. In the latter case the slope of the function may be constant (horizontal) after some point. For example, articulation and some physiological variable may be related but the relationship may involve only extreme points —i.e., subjects who fall below a certain cut-off score of some physiological test will have defective articulation. It would seem, then, that research procedures involving articulation and the peripheral speech mechanism might best be directed toward ascertaining the functional relationship between articulation and one or more peripheral speech variables. Research of this kind may reveal that some physiological variables are important, but only within a certain range of scores.

Status Relations[18]

There are essentially four ways in which articulation and other variables may be studied. They are (a) status relations, (b) improvement relations, (c) articulation change as function of a change in one or more other variables, and (d) a change in one or more other variables as a function of a change in articulation. In the majority of studies status relations (either r's or mean differences) have been sought—i.e., a relation between articulation and another variable(s) for a certain cross section in time. These studies have been reviewed in this chapter. There are also a good number of studies on articulatory improvement (see Chapter 5). However, with few exceptions, experimentalists have ignored the procedural approaches

[18] This section first appeared in Winitz (1964, pp. 293–296) and is reproduced with only minor changes.

mentioned in items (c) and (d) above. The exceptions include studies reported in Chapter 5 where articulation change is related to parental counseling, socioeconomic status of the child's family, and speech sound discrimination pretraining, as well as the previously described studies on the effect of articulatory improvement on reading and spelling.

Data from all four types of relations would appear to be important for a complete understanding of articulatory acquisition, defectiveness, and improvement. However, status relationships by themselves are of limited value. That this approach has intrinsic weaknesses is made evident by the fact that many variables used to assess articulatory defectiveness show little or no correlation with articulatory improvement (see Chapter 4). When a significant relationship is obtained from this approach it does not necessarily imply that manipulation of the criterion variable will result in a change in articulation. For example, if articulatory defective children perform below normal children on a rail walking test, this finding does not necessarily imply that training in rail walking is recommended prior to speech correction. It does not even suggest that a different type of speech correction approach (some type of rhythm approach, for example) will be useful. It is true that in some cases variables, such as socioeconomic status, cannot be manipulated directly. However, levels of socioeconomic status can be studied as a function of some other manipulation.

The correlation between IQ and articulation will now be discussed in order to show the limitations of status relationships in research on articulation. The correlations between IQ and articulation as reviewed earlier in this chapter indicate a low positive relationship between intelligence and articulation, suggesting the limited usefulness of the former measure as a predictor of the latter measure, and suggesting the relative unimportance of intelligence as a etiological consideration in articulatory disorders. However, for the purposes of this discussion we shall assume that the relationship is almost perfect.

Typically it has been implied that (a) intelligence may, in part, cause or be a determinant of articulatory behavior, (b) that articulatory retardation may slow intellectual growth, or (c) a combination of (a) and (b) (Powers, 1957, p. 748; Everhart, 1960).

Such statements lose significance when considered from the point of view advanced by Spiker and McCandless (1954). They carefully distinguish between Meaning I (formal, operational meaning) and Meaning II (significance, usefulness and fruitfulness).

For articulation and intelligence, Meaning I implies the "descriptions of the finished tests, and the accompanying instructions for administering and scoring them" (Spiker and McCandless, 1954, p. 261). Thus, when tests are formally defined (Meaning I) this does not necessarily mean that the author of the test has "unambiguously circumscribed the population of 'intellectual [or speech] behavior' or has provided explicit sampling criteria for the selection of items for his tests" (Spiker and McCandless, 1954, p. 261).

Authors of tests generally do not attempt to specify or classify all the items that are included in a test when it is given a name, such as intelligence, articulation, numerical reasoning. Rather, they include those items that their analysis has suggested will perform best the purpose for which the test was designed. Speech and language items are often included in infant intelligence tests. One of the five scales in an infant intelligence test (Griffiths, 1954) is devoted exclusively to hearing and speech items, some of which could be classified as articulation items. Similarly articulation items could be included in intelligence tests; the fact that articulation items have been excluded in children and adult intelligence tests was probably a test construction decision—e.g., poor item discrimination (below eight years) and considerable time needed for scoring. If articulation items were included in intelligence tests, the importance of intelligence in articulation development would probably not be considered. Thus, it would seem that there is no a priori reason to expect that items in articulation tests should be totally independent (or dependent) of items in intelligence tests.

Meaning II refers to the predictive utility of a test. As will be seen in Chapter 4, the correlation between intelligence and articulation is not of sufficient magnitude to warrant its use for predictive purposes. Therefore, the three statements mentioned are poorly phrased if not misleading statements of significance or usefulness.

Possibly the preceding statements imply the notion of response chaining. Response chaining implies that, for a response to be learned, an antecedent response must first be learned and that such responses form a chain of responses eventuating in the final, to-be-learned response—i.e., R_1, R_2, R_3, . . . R_n. Thus, for a certain level of articulation to be acquired, a certain level of responses, classified and sampled by an intelligence test, must first be acquired; and for further intelligence to be acquired, this level of articulation must first have been acquired.

That response chaining may be an accurate description of the development of articulation and intelligence is difficult to deny. However, evidence summarized in Chapter 4 would not appear to support this notion. Templin (1957) found that the relationship between intelligence and articulation was low and similar from ages three ($r = .47$) through eight ($r = .29$), despite the fact that both of these skills increase with age. Reid (1947a, 1947b), Pettit (1957), and Steer and Drexler (1960) found that articulation improvement was essentially unrelated to the initial intelligence score.

It is suggested that intelligence (or articulation) could be viewed as an initial and boundary condition for the learning of articulation (or intelligence), and that below a certain empirically derived score articulation (or intellectual) acquisition could not take place. In this respect both intelligence and articulation are viewed as scores on a test that may be used for predictive purposes (Meaning II); no assumption need be made concerning the mutual development of these skills.

Finally, two additional interpretations of the relationship between articulation and intelligence follow:

(a) A factor is common to both articulation and intelligence. Additional factors may be invoked to explain the relationship between articulation and intelligence. A biological factor may represent a common "neurophysiological" variable, which may account for related growth rates between articulation and intelligence. A psychological factor may indicate a common reinforcement contingency. For example, children may be equally reinforced for linguistic activities that may be tested by both an articulation and an intelligence test.

(b) The choice of sampling procedure may yield a relationship between articulation and intelligence. Festinger comments (1959, p. 363) that "poor sampling procedures might yield data showing a spurious relationship, that is, a relationship showing up in the data when no relationship really exists." Strictly speaking, the relationship is not spurious, since it does exist; it is the interpretation that may be spurious.

He gives the hypothetical example of a research worker who wanted to find out if there was any relationship between school achievement and birth order among sixth-grade children. Using all the available paraphernalia of sampling, the investigator finds that later-born children show poorer performance on school grades and achievement test scores than earlier-born children. Festinger (1959, p. 363) concludes as follows:

> This result would certainly be a spurious one and would have come about because of a poor sampling procedure. . . . In any actual research, of course, the research worker would know that there is a tendency in this country for lower socioeconomic levels to have larger families. As a result of this, the samples of later born children would be more and more weighted with children from low economic level families.

With regard to children of normal intelligence, it is entirely possible that children who are above average in intelligence may, for the most part, come from families of high socioeconomic status, where language stimulation and reinforcement would be expected to be greater than for families of low socioeconomic status. Thus, a positive relationship between intelligence and articulation may be found, when in reality no "functional relationship" exists.

An investigation by Irwin (1960) provides some evidence for this point of view. In this study, systematic langauge stimulation (reading and telling stories) resulted in an increase in "phoneme" frequency scores for young children from low socioeconomic families. If the stimulus conditions in high socioeconomic families are similar to the systematic language stimulation as provided in this study, and since children from high socioeconomic families are more intelligent than children from low socioeconomic families, one would expect a positive relationship to be found between intelligence and "phoneme" frequency.

From the foregoing discussion, then, it would seem that status relationships limit our understanding of the articulatory learning process. Status relationships when high may, to be sure, suggest an area of investigation, but unless the results are followed by longitudinal or laboratory experimentation (stimulus-response manipulations), generalizations about articulatory behavior must be made with extreme caution.

SUMMARY

The relationship between articulation and a number of variables was reviewed. The following variables were discussed: (a) chronological age, (b) intelligence, (c) socioeconomic status, (d) sex, (e) sibling status, (f) general motor skills, (g) oral and facial motor skills, (h) laterality, (i) kinesthetic sensibility, (j) dentition, (k) oral-facial structure, (l) tongue thrust, (m) developmental and health variables, (n) auditory memory span, (o) speech sound discrimination and discrimination of nonspeech sounds, (p) personality, (q) language measures, (r) fluency, and (s) reading, spelling, and academic achievement.

In the concluding pages of the chapter, philosophical approaches and methodological considerations were discussed. Topics included in this section were single versus multiple factors, inconsistency of an articulatory error as evidence of organicity, articulatory errors as a unitary disorder, peripheral and cortical mechanisms, the peripheral speech mechanism and step functions, and status relations.

REFERENCES

Albright, R. W. The motor abilities of speakers with good and poor articulation. *Speech Monographs*, 1948, *15*, 164–172.
Anderson, P. W. The relationship of normal and defec-

tive articulation of the consonant [s] in various phonetic contexts to auditory discrimination between normal and defective [s] productions among children from kindergarten through fourth grade. M.A. Thesis, University of Iowa, 1949.

Aungst, L. F., and Frick, J. V. Auditory discrimination ability and consistency of articulation of /r/. *Journal of Speech and Hearing Disorders*, 1964, *29*, 76–85.

Bangs, J. L. A clinical analysis of the articulatory defects of the feebleminded. *Journal of Speech Disorders*, 1942, *7*, 343–356.

Bankson, N. W., and Byrne, M. C. The relationship between missing teeth and selected consonant sounds. *Journal of Speech and Hearing Disorders*, 1962, *27*, 341–348.

Berko, J., and Brown, R. Psycholinguistic research methods. In P. H. Mussen (Ed.), *Handbook of research methods in child development.* New York: Wiley, 1960.

Bradley, W. H. Some relationships between pitch discrimination and speech development. *The Laryngoscope*, 1959, *69*, 422–437.

Brown, R. W., and Hildum, D. C. Expectancy and the identification of syllables. *Language*, 1956, *32*, 411–419.

Carrell, J., and Pendergast, K. An experimental study of the possible relation between errors of speech and spelling. *Journal of Speech and Hearing Disorders*, 1954, *19*, 327–334.

Clark, R. M. Maturation and speech development, Part I. *Logos*, 1959, *2*, 49–54.

Cohen, J. H., and Diehl, C. F. Relation of speech-sound discrimination ability to articulation-type speech defects. *Journal of Speech and Hearing Disorders*, 1963, *28*, 187–190.

Costello, M. R., and Flowers, A. Responses to distorted speech of children with severe articulation disorders. *Journal of Auditory Research*, 1963, *3*, 133–139.

Cross, D. V., Lane, H., and Sheppard, W. Identification and discrimination functions for a visual continuum and their relation to the motor theory of speech perception. *Journal of Experimental Psychology*, 1965, *70*, 63–74.

Davis, D. M. The relation of repetitions in the speech of young children to certain measures of language maturity and situational factors, Part I. *Journal of Speech Disorders*, 1939, *4*, 303–318.

Davis, D. M. The relation of repetition in the speech of young children to certain measures of language maturity and situational factors, Part II. *Journal of Speech Disorders*, 1940, *5*, 235–241.

Davis, E. A. The development of linguistic skills in twins, singletons with siblings, and only children from age five to ten years. *Institute of Child Welfare, Monograph Series,* No. 14. Minneapolis: University of Minnesota Press, 1937.

Davis, I. P., The speech aspects of reading readiness. In Chapter 2, *New practices in reading in the elementary school, 17th Yearbook, Department of Elementary School Principals,* NEA, 17 (7), 1938.

Denes, P. B. On the statistics of spoken English. *Journal of the Acoustical Society of America,* 1963, 35, 892–904.

Dollard, J., and Miller, N. E. *Personality and psychotherapy, an analysis in terms of learning, thinking, and culture.* New York: McGraw-Hill, 1950.

Eimas, P. D. The relation between identification and discrimination along speech and non-speech continua. *Language and Speech,* 1963, 6, 206–217.

Ervin, S. M., and Miller, W. R. Langauge development. In H. W. Stevenson (Ed.), *Child psychology, The 62nd Yearbook of the National Society for the Study of Education,* Part I. Chicago; The University of Chicago Press, 1963.

Everhart, R. W. The relationship between articulation and other developmental factors in children. *Journal of Speech and Hearing Disorders,* 1953, *18,* 332–338.

Everhart, R. W. Paternal occupational classification and the maturation of articulation. *Speech Monographs,* 1956, *23,* 75–77.

Everhart, R. W. Literature survey of growth and developmental factors in articulatory maturation. *Journal of Speech and Hearing Disorders,* 1960, *25,* 59–69.

Fairbanks, G., and Bebout, B. A. A study of minor organic deviations in "functional" disorders of articulation: 3. The tongue. *Journal of Speech and Hearing Disorders,* 1950, *15,* 348–352.

Fairbanks, G., and Green, E. M. A study of minor organic deviations in "'functional" disorders of articulation: 2. Dimensions and relationships of the lips. *Journal of Speech and Hearing Disorders,* 1950, *15,* 165–168.

Fairbanks, G., and Lintner, M. V. H. A study of minor organic deviations in "functional" disorders of articulation: 4. The teeth and hard palate. *Journal of Speech and Hearing Disorders,* 1951, *16,* 273–279.

Fairbanks, G., and Spriestersbach, D. C. A study of minor organic deviations in "functional" disorders of articulation: 1. Rate of movement of oral structures. *Journal of Speech and Hearing Disorders,* 1950, *15,* 60–69.

Festinger, L. Sampling and related problems in research methodology. *American Journal of Mental Deficiencies,* 1959, *64,* 358–369.

FitzSimons, R. Developmental, psychosocial, and educational factors in children with nonorganic articulation problems. *Child Development,* 1958, *29,* 481–489.

Fletcher, S., Castell, R. L., and Bradley, D. P. Tongue thrust, swallow, speech articulation, and age. *Journal of Speech and Hearing Disorders,* 1961, *26,* 201–208.

Fontaine, V. E. Auditory memory span of children for vowel sounds. M.A. Thesis, University of Wisconsin, 1949.

Francis, T. R. A preliminary note on tongue thrusting and associated speech defects. *Speech Pathology and Therapy,* 1958, *1,* 70–72.

Francis, T. R. The articulation of English speech sounds in anterior open bite accompanied by tongue thrusting. *Speech Pathology and Therapy,* 1960, *3,* 18–26.

Froeschels, E. and Jellinek, A. *Practice of voice and speech therapy.* Boston: Expression Co., 1941.

Fymbo, L. H. The relation of malocclusion of the teeth to defects of speech. *Archives for Speech,* 1936, *1,* 204–216.

Gewirtz, J. L. Studies in word fluency: I. Its relation to vocabulary and mental age in young children. *Journal of Genetic Psychology,* 1948, *72,* 165–176.

Goodenough, F. L., and Smart, R. C. Inter-relationships of motor abilities in young children. *Child Development,* 1935, *6,* 141–153.

Goodstein, L. D. Functional speech disorders and personality: A survey of the research. *Journal of Speech and Hearing Research,* 1958, *1,* 359–376. (a)

Goodstein, L. D. Functional speech disorders and personality: Methodological and theoretical considerations. *Journal of Speech and Hearing Research,* 1958, *1,* 377–382. (b)

Goodwin, F. G. A consideration of etiologies in 454 cases of speech retardation. *Journal of Speech and Hearing Disorders,* 1955, *3,* 300–303.

Goss, A. E. A stimulus-response analysis of the interaction of cue-producing and instrumental responses. *Psychological Review,* 1955, *62,* 20–31.

Goss, A. E. Verbal mediating responses and concept formation. *Psychological Review,* 1961, *68,* 248–274.

Griffiths, R. *The abilities of babies.* New York: McGraw-Hill, 1954.

Hall, M. E. Auditory factors in functional articulatory speech defects. *Journal of Experimental Education,* 1938, *7,* 110–132.

Ham, R. E. Relationship between misspelling and misarticulation. *Journal of Speech and Hearing Disorders,* 1958, *23,* 294–297.

Hanley, C. N., and Supernaw, E. W. A study of the incidence of defective speech in cases of open-bite malocclusion. *Western Speech,* 1956, *20,* 23–28.

Hansen, B. F. The application of sound discrimination

tests to functional articulatory defectives with normal hearing. *Journal of Speech Disorders,* 1944, 9, 347–355.

House, A. Personal communication. 1961.

Irwin, O. C. Infant speech: Effect of systematic reading of stories. *Journal of Speech and Hearing Research,* 1960, 3, 187–190.

Jann, H. W. Tongue-thrusting as a frequent unrecognized cause of malocclusion and speech defects. *New York Dental Journal,* 1960, 26, 72–81.

Jenkins, E., and Lohr, F. E. Severe articulation disorders and motor ability. *Journal of Speech and Hearing Disorders,* 1964, 29, 286–292.

Johnson, W., and House, E. Certain laterality characteristics of children with articulatory disorders. *Elementary School Journal,* 1937, 38, 52–58.

Jones, M. V. The effect of speech training on silent reading achievement. *Journal of Speech and Hearing Disorders,* 1951, 16, 258–263.

Kelly, G. A. Some common factors in reading and speech disabilities. *Psychological Monographs,* 1932, 43, 175–218.

Kendler, H. H., and Kendler, T. S. Vertical and horizontal processes in problem solving. *Psychological Review,* 1962, 69, 1–16.

Koch, H. L. Sibling influence on children's speech. *Journal of Speech and Hearing Disorders,* 1956, 21, 322–328.

Kortsch, W. E. Speech defects in a tongue-thrust group. *Journal of the American Dental Association,* 1963, 67, 698–700.

Kronvall, E. L., and Diehl, C. F. The relationship of auditory discrimination of articulatory defects of children with no known organic impairment. *Journal of Speech and Hearing Disorders,* 1954, 19, 335–338.

Lane, H. The motor theory of speech perception: A critical review. *Psychological Review,* 1965, 72, 275–309.

Liberman, A. M., Harris, K. S., Hoffman, H. S., and Griffith, B. C. The discrimination of speech sounds within and across phoneme boundaries. *Journal of Experimental Psychology,* 1957, 54, 358–368.

Liberman, A. M., Harris, K. S., Eimas, P., Lisker, L., and Bastian, J. An effect of learning on speech perception: The discrimination of durations of silence with and without phonemic significance. *Language and Speech,* 1961, 4, 175–195. (a)

Liberman, A. M., Harris, K. S., Kinney, J. A., and Lane, H. The discrimination of relative onset-time of the components of certain speech and nonspeech patterns. *Journal of Experimental Psychology,* 1961, 61, 379–388. (b)

Lipsitt, L. P. Learning in the first year of life. In L. P. Lipsitt and C. C. Spiker (Eds.), *Advances in Child Development.* New York: Academic Press, 1963.

Lotz, J., Abramson, A. S., Gerstman, L. J., Ingemann, F., and Nemser, W. J. The perception of English stops by speakers of English, Spanish, Hungarian, and Thai: A tape-cutting experiment. *Language and Speech,* 1960, *3,* 71–77.

MacNeilage, P. F., Rootes, T. P., and Chase, R. A. Speech production and perception in a patient with severe impairment of somesthetic perception and motor control. *Journal of Speech and Hearing Research,* 1967, *10,* 449–467.

Mange, C. V. Relationship between selected auditory perceptual factors and articulation ability. *Journal of Speech and Hearing Research,* 1960, *3,* 67–74.

Mase, D. J. Etiology of articulatory speech defects. *Teachers' College contribution to education,* No. 921. New York: Columbia University, 1946.

McCarthy, D. A. Some possible explanations of sex differences in language development and disorders. *Journal of Psychology,* 1953, *35,* 155–160.

McCarthy, D. A. Language development in children. Chapter 9 in L. Carmichael (Ed.), *Manual of Child Psychology,* (2nd ed.) New York: Wiley, 1954.

McNemar, Q. *Psychological statistics,* (2nd ed.) New York: Wiley, 1955.

Mendenhall, J. E. *An analysis of spelling errors.* New York: Teachers' College, Columbia University, 1930.

Meredith, H. V. Methods of studying physical growth. Chapter 5 in P. H. Mussen (Ed.), *Handbook of Research Methods in Child Development.* New York: Wiley, 1960.

Metraux, R. W. Auditory memory span for speech sounds of speech defective children compared with normal children. *Journal of Speech Disorders,* 1942, *7,* 33–36.

Milisen, R. The incidence of speech disorders. Chapter 7 in L. E. Travis (Ed.), *Handbook of Speech Pathology.* New York: Appleton-Century-Crofts, 1957.

Miller, G. A., and Nicely, P. E. An analysis of perceptual confusions among some English consonants. *Journal of the Acoustical Society of America,* 1955, *27,* 338–352.

Mims, H. A., Kolas, C., and Williams, R. Lisping and persistent thumb-sucking among children with open-bite. *Journal of Speech and Hearing Disorders,* 1966, *31,* 176–178.

Moll, K. L., and Darley, F. L. Attitudes of mothers of articulatory-impaired and speech-retarded children. *Journal of Speech and Hearing Disorders,* 1960, *25,* 377–384.

Morgenstern, J. J. Socio-economic factors in stuttering. *Journal of Speech and Hearing Disorders,* 1956, *21,* 25–33.

Nelson, O. W. An investigation of certain factors relating to the nature of children with functional defects of articulation. *Journal of Educational Research,* 1953, *47,* 211–216.

Palmer, J. M. Tongue thrusting: A clinical hypothesis. *Journal of Speech and Hearing Disorders,* 1962, *27,* 323–333.

Palmer, M. F., and Osborn, C. D. A study of tongue pressures of speech defective and normal speaking individuals. *Journal of Speech Disorders,* 1940, *5,* 133–140.

Patton, F. E. A comparison of the kinaesthetic sensibility of speech-defective and normal-speaking children. *Journal of Speech Disorders,* 1942, *7,* 305–310.

Pettit, C. W. The predictive efficiency of a battery of articulatory diagnostic tests. *Speech Monographs,* 1957, *24,* 219–226.

Poole, I. Genetic development of articulation of consonant sounds in speech. *Elementary English Review,* 1934, *11,* 159–161.

Postal, P. M., *Aspects of phonological theory.* New York: Harper & Row, 1968.

Powers, M. H. Functional disorders of articulation symptomatology and etiology. Chapter 23 in L. E. Travis (Ed.), *Handbook of speech pathology.* New York: Appleton-Century-Crofts, 1957.

Prins, T. D. Analysis of correlations among various articulatory deviations. *Journal of Speech and Hearing Research,* 1962, *5,* 152–160. (a)

Prins, T. D. Motor and auditory abilities in different groups of children with articulatory deviations. *Journal of Speech and Hearing Research,* 1962, *5,* 161–168. (b)

Prins, T. D. Relations among specific articulatory deviations and responses to a clinical measure of sound discrimination ability. *Journal of Speech and Hearing Disorders,* 1963, *28,* 382–388.

Reid, G. The etiology and nature of functional articulatory defects in elementary school children. *Journal of Speech Disorders,* 1947, *12,* 143–150. (a)

Reid, G. The efficacy of speech re-education of functional articulatory defectives in the elementary school. *Journal of Speech Disorders,* 1947, *12,* 301–313. (b)

Roe, V., and Milisen, R. The effect of maturation upon defective articulation in elementary grades. *Journal of Speech Disorders,* 1942, *7,* 37–45.

Salzman, J. A. *Orthodontics, principles and prevention.* Philadelphia: Lippincott, 1957.

Sayler, H. K. The effect of maturation upon defective articulation in grades seven through twelve. *Journal* of *Speech and Hearing Disorders,* 1949, *14,* 202–207.

Schiefelbusch, R. L., and Lindsey, M. J. A new test of sound discrimination. *Journal of Speech and Hearing Disorders,* 1958, *23,* 153–159.

Schlanger, B. B. Speech examination of a group of institutionalized mentally handicapped children. *Journal of Speech and Hearing Disorders,* 1953, *18,* 339–364.

Schneiderman, N. A study of the relationship between articulatory ability and language ability. *Journal of Speech and Hearing Disorders,* 1955, *20,* 359–364.

Shelton, R. L., Arndt, W. B., Krueger, A. L., and Huffman, E. Identification of persons with articulation errors from observation of non-speech movements. *American Journal of Physical Medicine,* 1966, *45,* 143–150.

Shelton, R. L., Haskins, R. C., and Bosma, J. P. Tongue thrusting in one of monozygotic twins. *Journal of Speech and Hearing Disorders,* 1959, *24,* 105–117.

Sherman, D., and Geith, A. Speech sound discrimination and articulation skill, *Journal of Speech and Hearing Research,* 1967, *10,* 277–280.

Sirkin, J., and Lyons, W. A study of speech defects in mental deficiency. *American Journal of Mental Deficiencies,* 1941, *46,* 74–80.

Smith, C. R. Articulation problems and ability to store and process stimuli. *Journal of Speech and Hearing Research,* 1967, *10,* 348–353.

Snow, K. Articulation proficiency in relation to certain dental abnormalities. *Journal of Speech and Hearing Disorders,* 1961, *26,* 209–212.

Snow, K. A comparative study of sound substitution used by "normal" first grade children. *Speech Monographs,* 1964, *31,* 135–141.

Solomon, A. L. Personality and behavior patterns of children with functional defects of articulation. *Child Development,* 1961, *32,* 731–737.

Sommers, R. K., Cockerille, C. E., Paul, C. D., Bowser, D. C., Fichter, G. R., Fenton, A. K., and Copetas, F. G. Effects of speech therapy and speech improvement upon articulation and reading. *Journal of Speech and Hearing Disorders,* 1961, *26,* 27–38.

Sommers, R. K., Meyer, W. J., and Fenton, A. K. Pitch discrimination and articulation. *Journal of Speech and Hearing Research,* 1961, *4,* 56–60.

Spiker, C. C., and McCandless, B. R. The concept of intelligence and the philosophy of science. *Psychological Review,* 1954, *61,* 255–266.

Spriestersbach, D. C. Research in articulation disorders and personality. *Journal of Speech and Hearing Disorders,* 1956, *21,* 329–335.

Spriestersbach, D. C., and Curtis, J. F. Misarticulation

and discrimination of speech sounds. *Quarterly Journal of Speech*, 1951, *37*, 483–491.

Spriestersbach, D. C., Darley, F. L., and Rouse, V. Articulation of a group of children with cleft lips and palates. *Journal of Speech and Hearing Disorders*, 1956, *21*, 436–445.

Steer, M. D., and Drexler, H. G. Predicting later articulation ability from kindergarten tests. *Journal of Speech and Hearing Disorders*, 1960, *25*, 391–397.

Straub, W. J. Malfunction of the tongue. Part I, The abnormal swallowing habit: Its cause, effects, and results in relation to orthodontic treatment and speech therapy. *American Journal of Orthodontics*, 1960, *46*, 404–424.

Straub, W. J. Malfunction of the tongue. Part II, The abnormal swallowing habit: Its causes, effects, and results in relation to orthodontic treatment and speech therapy. *American Journal of Orthodontics*, 1961, *47*, 596–617.

Subtelny, J. D., Mestre, J. C., and Subtelny, J. D. Comparative study of normal and defective articulation of /s/ as related to malocclusion and deglutition. *Journal of Speech and Hearing Disorders*, 1964, *29*, 264–285.

Templin, M. C. Certain language skills in children, their development and interrelationships. *Institute of Child Welfare Monograph Series*, No. 26. Minneapolis: University of Minnesota Press, 1957.

Templin, M. C. Development of speech. *Journal of Pediatrics*, 1963, *62*, 11–14.

Trapp, E. P., and Evans, J. Functional articulatory defect and performance on a nonverbal task. *Journal of Speech and Hearing Disorders*, 1960, *25*, 176–180.

Travis, L. E., and Rasmus, B. The speech sound discrimination ability of cases with functional disorders of articulation. *Quarterly Journal of Speech*, 1931, *17*, 217–226.

Tulley, W. J. Adverse muscle forces—their diagnostic significance. *American Journal of Orthodontics*, 1956, *42*, 801–814.

Underwood, B. J., and Schulz, R. W. *Meaningfulness and verbal learning*. New York: Lippincott, 1960.

Van Demark, A. A., and Mann, M. B. Oral language skills of children with defective articulation. *Journal of Speech and Hearing Research*, 1965, 8, 409–414.

Van Riper, C. and Irwin, J. V. *Voice and articulation*. Englewood Cliffs, N.J.: Prentice-Hall, 1958.

Ward, M. M., Malone, H. D., Jann, G. R., and Jann, H. W. Articulation variations associated with visceral swallowing and malocclusion. *Journal of Speech and Hearing Disorders*, 1961, *26*, 334–341.

Weaver, C. H., Furbee, C., and Everhart, R. W.

Paternal occupational class and articulatory defects in children. *Journal of Speech and Hearing Disorders,* 1960, *25,* 171–175.

Wellman, B. L. The development of motor coordination in young children: An experimental study in the control of hand and arm movements. *University of Iowa Studies in Child Welfare,* 3 (4), 1926.

Wellman, B. L., Case, I. M., Mengert, I. G., and Bradbury, D. E. Speech sounds of young children. *University of Iowa Studies in Child Welfare,* 5 (2), 1931.

Wepman, J. M. *Auditory discrimination test: Manual of directions.* Chicago: Language Research Associates, 1958.

White, S. H. Effects of pretraining with varied stimuli in children's discrimination learning. *Child Development,* 1961, *32,* 745–754.

Williams, H. M. An analytical study of language achievement in preschool children, Part I, Development of language vocabulary in young children. *University of Iowa Studies in Child Welfare,* 13 (2), 1937, 9–18. (a)

Williams, H. M. A qualitative analysis of the erroneous speech sound substitutions of preschool children, Part II, Development of language vocabulary in young children. *University of Iowa Studies in Child Welfare,* 13 (2), 1937, 21–32. (b)

Wilson, B. A. The development and evaluation of a speech improvement program for kindergarten children. *Journal of Speech and Hearing Disorders,* 1954, *19,* 4–13.

Winitz, H. Language skills of male and female kindergarten children, *Journal of Speech and Hearing Research,* 1959, *2,* 377–386. (a)

Winitz, H. Relationships between language and non-language measures of kindergarten children. *Journal of Speech and Hearing Research,* 1959, *2,* 387–391. (b)

Winitz, H. Research in articulation and intelligence. *Child Development,* 1964, *35,* 287–297.

Winitz, H., and Bellerose, B. Sound discrimination as a function of pretraining conditions. *Journal of Speech and Hearing Research,* 1962, *5,* 340–348.

Winitz, H., and Bellerose, B. Effects of pretraining on sound discrimination learning. *Journal of Speech and Hearing Research,* 1963, *6,* 171–180.

Winitz, H., and Bellerose, B. Phoneme-cluster learning as a function of instructional method and age. *Journal of Verbal Learning and Verbal Behavior,* 1965, *4,* 99–102.

Winitz, H., and Lawrence, M. Children's articulation and sound learning ability. *Journal of Speech and Hearing Research,* 1961, *4,* 259–268.

Yedinak, J. G. A study of the linguistic functioning of

children with articulation and reading disabilities. *Journal of Genetic Psychology*, 1949, *74*, 23–59.

Zedler, E. Y. Effect of phonic training on speech sound discrimination and spelling performance. *Journal of Speech and Hearing Disorders*, 1956, *21*, 245–250.

4

ARTICULATORY TESTING AND PREDICTION[1]

In this chapter procedures for testing articulatory responses and the use of these procedures to predict articulatory performance will be discussed. Since only current methods will be considered, very little will be said about the use of phonological procedures in articulation testing and prediction.

Sources of Variability in Articulation Testing

Considerable research has been done in the field of speech pathology using the phoneme or a group of phonemes as a response class (criterion measure). Despite the extensive use of articulation test data, test instruments and methods for test administration have varied widely from experiment to experiment. Consequently, data from different investigations have typically been obtained in a variety of circumstances and with variable procedures.

In this section several potential sources of variability in articulation testing are discussed. The potential sources of variation are grouped as follows: variance attributable to the subjects, to the experimenter, to the test instrument, and to the interaction of subject with experimenter.

[1] A substantial part of the first half of this chapter was written in collaboration with Dr. Gerald M. Siegel, Department of Speech and Office of the Dean of Students, University of Minnesota, as part of a series of unpublished papers of the Bureau of Child Research, University of Kansas.

Variance Attributable to the Subjects Tested

A child's score on an articulation test is an estimate of his articulation performance on a given occasion. On a subsequent occasion, this score may be expected to vary. If the interval between tests is small, and systematic training is not introduced, the variation should be minimal. As the intertest interval increases, however, variation in test performance also increases, particularly if the tests are administered during the child's early years, when articulatory skills are developing rapidly.

Temporal reliability, another name for subject variance, has been examined in a number of studies. Templin (1947b, 1953) investigated the consistency of a small number of subjects (ranging in number from 7 to 20) at two, three, four, and five years on a 50-item screening articulation test. The sounds were tested in single words and in sentences, and responses were elicited by either the pictorial or oral imitative methods whichever method was most suitable for the individual child.[2] Subjects were tested within an eight-day interval. The test-retest reliability coefficients ranged from .93 to .99 for the single word test and .95 to .98 for the sentence test.[3]

Siegel (1962) reports correlations and mean differences for 22 institutional mentally retarded children on Templin's (1947b) 50-item screening test. Responses were elicited by oral stimulation. The children ranged in age from 8 to 14 years. They were tested by two experienced and two inexperienced examiners on two occasions, with a week intervening between test occasions. The four correlations for test-retest reliability ranged from .95 to .99; a significant mean difference was obtained for only one examiner, an inexperienced one.

Winitz (1963) investigated temporal reliability for 40 sound elements. The subjects were 100 kindergarten children. Each child was tested on two occasions using the pictorial method; an interval of approximately a week separated test sessions. In order to eliminate visual cues, responses were spoken through a silk screen. The arrangement of test sounds for the two test sessions was independently randomized for each child.

The number of correct responses for each sound did not change significantly from the first to the second test session. However, for some of the sounds considerable intrasubject variability was noticed. For example, the percentage of children who altered their responses from the first to the second test session (correct to incorrect, or incorrect to correct) was 21 percent for /-1-/, 25 percent for /-θ/, 14 percent for /z-/, and 13 percent for /sl-/.

---

[2] The pictorial and oral (spontaneous) methods will be described later.
[3] For each of the several age levels the correlation between the sentence test and the word test was also very high.

The studies reviewed thus far indicate that variations in group articulation scores are minimal over short time intervals. The implications of these findings for intrasubject variability will be discussed shortly.

Additional data for temporal reliability are needed for different age levels and different test-retest intervals. It would be of interest to know, for example, how soon after "introduction" into the child's phonemic repertoire a particular sound is "mastered" and whether this interval varies for children or sounds in any systematic way. In this way we may gain information about the formation of the phonemic systems of children.

Variance Attributable to the Examiner

The usefulness of an articulation test score depends in part upon the accuracy or reliability of the examiner. Both interexaminer and intraexaminer reliability are of concern. Henderson (1937) compared judges' ratings in several test situations. Three judges agreed in their scoring of 80 percent of the responses provided by two third-grade children in a live articulation testing situation when a simple right versus wrong judgment was made for each response. Agreement dropped to 72 percent when judges were required to agree on the type of error they had scored. Agreement among judges was even lower when they scored responses transmitted via free field with visual cues eliminated. The highest examiner agreement occurred when the judge scored recordings of simulated articulation deviations (90 percent for right versus wrong agreement; 85 percent for exact response agreement).

Interexaminer reliability was studied also by Wright (1954). Ten children ranging from approximately five to nine years were administered a pictorial word articulation test. Three judges rated each response on a graduated seven-point scale of articulatory defectiveness. Correlations between pairs of examiners in a live condition ranged from .61 to .75, with an average rank order correlation of .67. The average correlations for judgments made from recordings were .71 and .85.

Curtis and Hardy (1959) made an extensive investigation of the /r/ phoneme. Reliability was estimated by having two judges make independent evaluations of 195 responses, gathered from 30 children, between the ages of five years six months and eight years six months, who were diagnosed as having an /r/ problem. Within a classification system that allowed for seven categories, examiners agreed on 87 percent of the transcribed responses. During the scoring, however, the raters listened to the tapes together, and although the judgments were independently recorded, either judge could request that any portion of the tape be replayed. A request for repetition may have served as an indication that one of the examiners felt the particular response was difficult or questionable, and thus may have reduced the independence of the judgments. In general, where independence of judgment is required, face-to-face assembly of pairs of judges would seem to be a precarious experimental arrangement.

Sommers and others (1959) report percentages of agreement among six clinicians for 30 consonantal elements obtained from two subjects. All responses were judged simultaneously by the clinicians. The percentage of agreement was determined for four categories. The categories and percentages of agreement ranged from 83 percent to 91 percent for omissions, substitutions, distortions, and correct sounds.

The high interexaminer reliability reported above and in many other investigations should be accepted with reservation, as many studies report percentage indices. A percentage agreement index can be spuriously high if many more correct than incorrect responses occur. Examiners may agree on "correct" responses most of the time, but agree on "incorrect" responses part of the time. For example, if 10 of 100 responses are judged as incorrect by one examiner and correct by a second observer, and all of the 90 other responses are judged by both examiners as correct, the percentage agreement for all responses would be 90 percent. This figure is certainly not an accurate description of what is occurring. There are probably a number of ways to handle this problem. One way may be to report the percentages of agreement for incorrect responses if a dichotomous scoring system, such as "correct"-"incorrect," is used. Then, for the preceding example, the percentage of agreement for incorrect responses would be 0 percent. Another way might be to assess reliability for only those subjects whose errors exceed 50 percent for at least one examiner. A high percentage of agreement with these subjects would be a good indication that two examiners show substantial agreement. However, if the score is based on an articulatory test composed of many sounds, a percentage of agreement does not mean high agreement for a particular sound.

Another approach is to compute a correlational coefficient. However, high interexaminer correlations do not necessarily imply examiner equivalence. Siegel (1962) found significant differences among experienced and inexperienced examiners in 16 of 18 comparisons, although correlation coefficients for these comparisons were generally in the .90's.

Intraexaminer reliability (self-agreement) has also been presented in several investigations. Henderson (1937) had two examiners evaluate the same samples of recorded speech on two occasions. The time interval between tests was unspecified, but Henderson reports 98 percent self-agreement for one judge and 90 percent for the second. Wright (1954) evaluated reliability in three testing conditions. The subjects were ten children ranging from approximately five to nine years. In Condition I an examiner administered the tests in the presence of two other examiners who also scored responses. The tests were tape recorded and rescored by the same three examiners 31 days (Condition II) and 47 days later (Condition III). Intraexaminer reliability (rank order correlations using a seven-point scale of articulatory defectiveness) for Conditions I and II ranged from .55 (nonsignificant) to .75. Comparisons of Conditions II and III and of I and III yielded values from .76 to .80 and .55 to .61, respectively. Wright, like Henderson, found self-agreement between live and recorded judgments to be lower than that obtained when all judgments are made from recordings.

Jordan (1960) rescored previously taped responses of five children to the Templin-Darley 176-item diagnostic articulation test several months after the original, live testing. The contingency coefficient for the experimenter's self-agreement was .80 (maximum possible was .87, since responses were evaluated on a four-point scale).

In evaluating the role of the examiner in articulation testing it is important to note that the examiner may introduce certain systematic biases that are not reflected in the reliability measures. Articulation testers typically have had training that creates expectancies concerning the types and distribution of sound errors among subjects. These expectancies may relate to such factors as the age and sex of the subject, the diagnostic or etiological label attached to the subject, the presence of distinguishing physical characteristics, or the transcription methods the examiner employs. To emphasize the last point, consider a child who produces an unvoiced lingual-dental fricative. The [s] may be identified by some examiners as a distortion error and by others as a [θ] substitution error. These possible sources of bias warrant further attention.

Variance Attributable to Test Instrument and Test Administrator

The instruments used to assess articulatory performance have been numerous, varying from the home-made tests frequently employed by practicing clinicians to a variety of commercially prepared tests such as the Templin-Darley (1960). These tests differ in the choice and order of the sounds tested, in the stimulus words used to elicit the sounds, and in the method of stimulus presentation.

Most articulation test procedures used with children are designed to elicit spontaneous verbal responses to pictures. Sometimes, particularly for words that are difficult to depict, the child is asked to imitate a word spoken by the examiner. The effect of these two methods of stimulus presentation, "imitative" versus "spontaneous," on the articulation score has been the source of some controversy in the articulation literature. Templin (1947a) found that total articulation score for 100 children between two and six years of age did not significantly differ when the responses were elicited spontaneously to pictures, imitatively to the examiner's verbal stimulus, or to the examiner's combined oral and pictorial stimulation. The intercorrelations among the three conditions ranged from .95 to .98. Similar results were obtained when the production of individual sounds was evaluated, and Templin concluded that method of stimulus presentation is not an important variable in articulatory measurement.

Snow and Milisen (1954), on the other hand, found that the imitative method of stimulus presentation elicited more correct responses from 164 articulatory defective schoolchildren from grades one, two, seven and eight than did the spontaneous method. A five-point severity scale was applied to each of the 65 items in the test. Subjects produced better responses to imitative stimuli whether the data were analyzed according to total score or to movement along the severity continuum.

A picture test, an imitative word test, and a nonsense syllable test were used by Carter and Buck (1958) to study the articulation of 141 articulatory defective first-grade children. The picture test was administered first and the imitative test followed a week later. When a child did not miss any of the sound items for one of the sounds in the spontaneous test, the sound was not tested in the imitative test. Correlations between the oral and imitative tests ranged from .82 to .97; the children made significantly fewer errors on the imitative tests than on the picture test, thus supporting the Snow and Millisen (1954) findings.

Ham (1958) reports that for the /w/, /r/, and /l/ consonants (tested in all three word positions) no differences were found between the oral and the pictorial method, even though different words were probably used in the two conditions. It is not clear from Ham's description whether the same sounds and word positions were included in both conditions. Siegel and others (1963) tested 100 kindergarten children on a picture and on an imitative test, both administered in the same test session. Test method and the arrangement of items within each method were randomized independently for each child. The examiner's face was not visible to the child during the imitative test. Subjects performed significantly better on the oral test for 8 of the 40 sounds. In many instances in which no group differences were obtained for a single sound element, considerable intra-subject variability was noted. For example, 48 percent of the subjects correctly produced /z-/ in the picture test, and a similar percentage, 52 percent, correctly produced this sound on the imitative test. Though the percentage of correct responses was similar for both conditions, 28 percent of the subjects changed their responses (correct to incorrect, or incorrect to correct) as a function of the two test conditions. Of course, some of this variability could be the result of examiner and subject variability.

Most recently the findings of Smith and Ainsworth (1967) give further evidence which suggests that the presentation method will effect slightly the number of correct articulatory scores. They used three conditions, pictorial, imitative, and pictorial plus imitative. Selecting 40 articulatory defective children enrolled in first-grade classes, and counterbalancing conditions, they found that the total scores for ten test-sounds ordered the errors as follows: pictorial, imitative, and pictorial plus imitative. Although the differences seemed to hold for all three word positions, they were not very large.

Clearly the findings of the three studies (Snow and Milisen, 1954; Carter and Buck, 1958; and Smith and Ainsworth, 1967), which tested articulatory defective children, are in agreement despite the fact that the test units (see discussion below) were not always comparable. The Siegel and others study is also in agreement with the above three studies, although no attempt was made to restrict the sample to children with articulatory errors. The two studies (Templin, 1947a and Ham, 1958) showing no differences were conducted with children not designated as articulatory defective, although in the Ham study the criterion for subject inclusion is not specified.

In general the results indicate that stimulation results in an increase in the number of correct responses. Possibly a pictorial stimulus increases the likelihood of an error sound, since it maximizes verbal context (see section on acquisition interference, pp. 292–295). The increase is often small, however, and does not occur for all sound items. It may also be that effectiveness of oral versus imitative stimulation varies with such factors as age of the children, severity of the problem, or differences in scoring method.

Another source of variance in the test instrument may be the units selected as stimuli. A particular sound may be adequately produced in one word or phonetic context and not in another. Two investigations have been devoted to this topic.

Templin (1947a) presented ten sounds, each in two different words, to 159 preschool children. Three different stimulus procedures were used: a spontaneous condition in which the stimuli consisted only of pictures; a combined imitative-pictorial condition in which the examiner uttered the word for the child and, at the same time, showed him a picture; and an imitative condition in which the only stimulus presented the child was the adult's utterance. Though 5 of the 30 differences were significant, Templin concluded that the particular word used was not a significant determiner of articulatory performance. At the .05 level of confidence, however, only 1.5 of the comparisons should have been significant. The data presented by Templin, therefore, would seem to argue that the stimulus word used may be an important variable. Further, Templin's analysis was based on relatively few test sounds. The effects of stimulus word may not be equal for the various phonemes and phonemic combinations.

This variable was also studied by Siegel and others (1963). Fifty kindergarten children were tested on 40 sound elements in each of two different words. The order of item presentation was randomly determined for each subject. For only three test sounds was a significant difference obtained. However, for some of the sounds considerable variability of responses (correct to incorrect, or incorrect to correct) was noted.

The sources of variability considered above do not appear to be critical when performance is described in terms of the total number of correct or incorrect items, as is typically done in developmental studies (e.g., Poole, 1934, and Templin, 1957). In some instances, however, the focus is on individual sounds rather than total score. In studies of the effects of poor dentition on articulation, for example, there is usually more interest in specific sounds, such as the linguo-dental and labio-dental fricatives, than on overall articulatory performance. When attention is shifted to these more discrete considerations, the variability within individual sounds becomes quite important, and the sources of variability previously discussed should be considered. When such considerations are appropriate, the following suggested procedures may prove useful in research studies: (a) sounds should be elicited by stimulus words that are constant for all subjects, (b) a particular sound should be elicited by several stimulus words, (c) the method of elicitation (oral or pictorial) should be constant for all sounds, (d) if possible, both methods of elicitation should be used, (e) the criterion of correct production should be based on more than a single response, e.g., three of four responses or the sound elements might be combined with regard to position.

Other variables, such as linguistic unit and phonetic context, require study. We have only the skimpy findings of Scott and Milisen (1954) and Carter and Buck (1958) that imitative nonsense syllable tests yield fewer errors than imitative word tests. The following questions are suggestive of additional directions research might take. Does word familiarity affect articulatory performance? Does systematic altering of the final consonant in a word or syllable affect performance on the initial consonant? Is articulatory performance related to the structural units of the language such as the morphemic elements or the parts of speech?

The method of organizing items within articulatory tests may also be an important determiner of the child's performance. Most articulatory tests have a stereotyped format. Sounds are presented in initial, medial, and final positions; vowels are presented before consonants, and consonants before blends; items are grouped so that particular blends are tested together. This arrangement of items may reduce independence of examiner judgment from item to item. Once having scored the /r/ sound incorrect in the initial position of a word, the examiner may be more likely to score the sound incorrect in the medial and final positions. Similarly, if /s/ blends are presented in series, the child's performance on the first items of the series may influence the examiner's evaluations of the remaining items in the series. While it is unlikely that the influence of previous judgments can be entirely eliminated from articulatory test procedures, these effects may be minimized by randomizing the items within the test.

Variance Attributable to Subject-Examiner Interaction

In any situation in which two or more persons are assembled, even where one is "subject" and the other "examiner," the nature of the assembly itself may affect the behavior of each of the individuals. The direction of these effects, moreover, may be complex. In the usual articulatory testing situation we tend to think of the examiner as a "standard measuring instrument" who provides certain stimuli for the child and who evaluates the child's responses. It should be noted, however, that the child in turn presents stimuli which may exert some influence over the examiner's behavior. A child who is unresponsive or taciturn may elicit different responses from an examiner than one who is quite responsive and talkative. Similarly, children with gross physical anomalies may encourage different behavior from the examiner than do more attractive children. A child with an obvious cleft palate (or with the label of having one) may incur more judgments of nasality and difficulty with pressure sounds because examiners are generally taught to expect such deviations among cleft palate children. It would be interesting to determine whether the same speech samples would be scored differently by speech correctionists as a function of diagnostic labels attached to the samples.

The interactions between child and examiner in the test situation may be subtle. The child with relatively good articulation, for example, will have many more opportunities to obtain approval from the examiner than will the child with numerous articulatory errors. To the degree that this kind of social reinforcement affects articulatory test performance, the poor articulator may respond with proportionately more errors toward the end of the test because the situation has been generally nonrewarding for him. Sex of the examiner relative to the sex and age of the subject may also be an important factor (Hartup, 1961; Stevenson, 1961).

Winitz and Siegel (1961) speculated that systematic differences in test performance might occur during the course of the test session as a function of such factors as increased fatigue on the part of the child, progressively increasing rapport between examiner and child, or increased ability of the examiner to decode the child's speech, etc. Each of 7 examiners tested 21 different kindergarten children on a 21-item test. As the examiner went from child to child the items were systematically rotated so that each item appeared an equal number of times in the first, middle, and last third of the test. The hypothesis of systematic changes within sessions was evaluated by comparing the number of errors occurring in the first, middle, and final segments, irrespective of specific sounds tested. The differences among test segments were not significant (Table 4.1). In this experiment the articulation items were initially randomized. It would be of value to determine whether the usual systematic arrangement of items

[Table 4.1] Means and SD's of Correct Responses in Percentages for an Articulation Test of 21 Sounds Divided into One-Third Segments (Sounds 1 to 7, 8 to 14, and 15 to 21) for Seven Examiners, Each Testing 21 Children

		Segments of Articulation Test		
Examiner		FIRST THIRD	SECOND THIRD	FINAL THIRD
1	mean	45.00	57.75	52.71
	SD	29.42	25.89	25.43
2	mean	59.86	63.03	61.49
	SD	27.75	28.89	29.55
3	mean	78.77	76.18	75.50
	SD	22.12	22.65	25.02
4	mean	71.65	75.61	73.69
	SD	20.02	19.39	13.59
5	mean	79.31	79.92	77.27
	SD	29.80	25.24	32.84
6	mean	79.36	73.23	79.58
	SD	25.72	27.69	24.80
7	mean	73.01	74.98	79.13
	SD	27.13	30.93	20.89

in an articulation test influences the responses of examiner and children. Also, it would be useful to know whether examiners change their evaluations when they do repeated testing of different children over some selected interval of time.

Siegel (1962) reports data that suggest examiners may change their testing behavior during the course of an experiment. The procedures involved two experienced and two inexperienced examiners who tested retarded children on three occasions. Before the experiment began, the equivalence of the two experienced examiners was determined by having them simultaneously test 13 children. One examiner stimulated the children, but both scored the responses. The difference in mean scores between the two examiners was negligible, and the correlation between examiners was high. Subsequently, these same examiners independently tested a second group of children on two occasions separated by a week, and two weeks later they independently tested a new group of children. The number of children tested on the first, second, and third occasions was 26, 22, and 21, respectively. Though interexaminer reliability on these three occasions remained high, the mean scores for the two examiners differed significantly in favor of one of the experimenters on each of the three experimental test occasions. Thus, when both examiners were assembled with the child during testing, they achieved equivalent results. When they tested the children independently, however, systematic differences were introduced. The findings suggest that the examiners differed in the responses they evoked from the children, rather than in the way they scored the responses.

In another study Winitz and Bellerose (1963b) assessed reliability by comparing the results of one examiner who had conducted a stimulus generalization study with three additional examiners, only one of whom knew the results of the study. The percentage of agreement for all three examiners exceeded 95 percent. (In light of our preceding discussion it should be mentioned that a little less than half of the subjects generalized.) Apparently the original examiner did not change her criteria of evaluation as a function of repeated test sessions.[4]

Summary

The articulation test has been one of the more widely used and valuable tools of the speech pathologist. Articulation research, however, has not had the benefit of standardized testing procedures. In our discussion a variety of factors which may affect systematically the results of an articulation test have been considered. These sources of variance have been discussed and grouped under four categories: variance attributable to the child; variance attributable to the examiner; variance attributable to the test instrument; and variances attributable to some interaction between subject and examiner. Several of the variables discussed have been treated within an experimental framework; however, other variables remain to be explored more fully.

Purposes of Articulation Tests

Articulation tests can be used in a variety of ways: (a) to determine phonetic proficiency, (b) for purposes of screening, (c) for diagnosis, (d) to assess developmental progress, (e) for prediction, and (f) to test for programming. The first five uses will be discussed in this chapter. Testing for programming will be reserved for Chapter 5 after a discussion of programming principles has been presented.

[4] A technique which may have great potential for increasing reliability among examiners has not yet been mentioned. It involves simply the use of taped stimuli rather than live stimuli. Examiners would match the child's response with the taped utterance and would not have to rely on their own specialized criterion of correctness. My experience with taped stimuli in learning experiments seems to support this premise.

Phonetic Proficiency

The traditional articulatory test has as its primary purpose the assessment of accurate articulatory productions in words. Usually pictures are used to elicit responses, but sometimes words or sentences are used for older-aged subjects. Often the sounds are tested in several word positions and in several phoneme clusters. In order to minimize errors of testing it is important that this type of test, as well as the other types mentioned in this chapter, possesses adequate reliability.

Validity, however defined, has been of little concern to users of phonetic proficiency tests. The test has been designed to simplify testing of articulatory responses and to provide for a standard instrument for measuring articulatory responses. It is generally assumed that tests of this type give reliable descriptions of articulatory responses in other social settings.

Screening

When an articulatory test is used to provide a comparison of a child's articulatory performance with that of his peers, it is referred to as a screening test. The child's total articulation score, irrespective of specific errors, is first determined. This score is then compared with a cut-off score which separates adequate from inadequate performance. The cut-off score is a statistical score which has been determined in advance for all age levels for which the test is designed. A well-known screening test is the Templin-Darley 50-item Screening Test (1960). The authors describe (1960, pp. 13–14) the development and the validity of their test as follows:

> The screening test consists of those 50 items which have been found best to discriminate between good and poor articulation of preschool and kindergarten children. . . .
> The 50 items which constitute the screening device were selected on the basis of a study of the production of 113 speech sound elements by 100 preschool and kindergarten children in which three techniques of testing were used: spontaneous utterance in response to a picture, imitative utterance with the picture, and imitative utterance without the picture. . . . The 27 per cent of children with the highest total articulation scores made up the "good articulation" group and the 27 per cent with the lowest total articulation scores the "poor articulation" group. Through the use of the Lawshe Nomograph technique of item analysis a "Discrimination-value," or D-value, was determined to identify

those sounds which best discriminated between good and poor articulators.

The 50 items correlate with outside criteria about as highly as do the 113 and 176 items [the 176 items form the diagnostic test which is described below]. The correlation of the 113 items and the 50 items with MA are .70 and .71, respectively, and with CA .64 for both measures. The correlations computed at eight age levels between both the total number of words and the number of different words uttered by a child in a controlled situation and the 50-item Screening and 176-item Diagnostic Test were similar in magnitude. At no age is the difference between the correlations greater than .06, and the mean difference for 16 pairs is .02.

The 50 items obtained from this analysis were administered to a new group of 480 subjects (Templin, 1953). A description of the subjects has been previously given in Chapter 2. At each age level a cut-off score, described in full by Templin (1953), was established. Children whose articulation scores fall below the cut-off score are considered to have defective articulation.[5]

Screening tests of this sort have only one function. They are used to compare a child's articulatory score with his peers. In some ways the test is similar to height and weight tests. For these tests a person's score is assessed relative to all other scores; a score is considered "above or below average" with respect to the distribution of all the scores. When an individual's score falls at one or the other end of the distribution it may be considered to be defective.

Often the pronouncement of a child's status is withheld until scores at several age levels are available. A child may not be considered overweight, for example, until he is consistently measured as overweight when compared with his peers. Screening tests, then, have the particular function of sorting out children who are by definition deviant in their (articulatory) behavior or physical makeup.

Screening tests of this type, although useful in assessing some physical or behavioral traits, are of limited value when used with articulatory responses. At least two reasons are clearly evident. First, many children, as we know, have a single "consistent" error (e.g., /w/ for /r/) and require intensive instruction. It seems unreasonable to select a child for articulatory instruction on the basis of his "total" sound errors. Second, it seems unreasonable to select a child for articulatory instruction when he may improve without speech correction.

In summary, a statistical norm such as that provided by Templin and Darley may be only one of several criteria that should be used in a screen-

---

[5] Phonemic frequency is a factor that could be incorporated into a screening test of articulation (see Barker, 1960).

ing test. Some others are (a) level of developmental achievement of phoneme contrasts (discussed later), (b) level of articulatory performance necessary for beginning school, (c) parental concern if displayed, and (d) knowledge as to whether the sound will be corrected by the child. All of these factors and perhaps others need to be incorporated into an "articulatory screening test" before it can become generally applicable.

Diagnosis

Templin and Darley (1960), making use of the findings obtained from a 176-item articulatory test designed by Templin (1957), have developed a diagnostic articulatory test. A complete description of Templin's sampling procedures was given in Chapter 2. The reader may recall that 176 sound elements were administered to 480 children ($N = 30$ males and 30 females at each age level) at half-year age levels from three to five and at full-year age levels from five to eight. According to the authors (Templin and Darley, 1960, p. 1) a diagnostic test has the following purpose: "Such a test may be used in deciding whether a child needs speech correction, but more frequently it is used with children already identified as having articulatory problems to aid in prescribing the nature of speech correction. It provides detailed information about a child's ability to produce a wide range of speech sounds in a variety of positions and phonetic contexts."

Templin and Darley suggest that the diagnostic test protocols may be used in the following ways: (a) to compare the individual's results with the norm, (b) to analyze the error types (omissions, substitutions and distortions), (c) to determine consistency of misarticulations, (d) to determine whether errors are corrected when stimulated with the correct production of the sound, (e) to determine resistance to training as shown by those sounds most consistently erred, (f) to identify those factors related to the misarticulations (such as distinctive features of errors which are common to several phonemes), and (g) to determine the relation between sound errors on the test and sound errors in connected speech.

In terms of present knowledge about articulatory instruction, all of the seven suggested uses of the test appear to have value. However, their importance as diagnostic items needs to be validated experimentally before we can attest to the fact that they are indeed diagnostic. For example, although it seems reasonable that some types of errors would be more easily replaced by the correct sound (the sound to be learned) than would other types of errors, this information is not as yet available. The authors (Templin and Darley, 1960) suggest that distortion errors are less resistant to correction than omission errors. It is possible that "distortion" errors (substitution errors of perceptually similar sounds) are more resistant to correction than omission errors, as it may be more difficult to replace one sound by another than to learn a new sound.

Inconsistency of misarticulation further illustrates this point. Although the Templin-Darley Diagnostic Test provides for the testing of more than one allophone for several phonemes and for the testing of some of the same allophones more than once, there is currently no experimental support for the authors' statement that "consistently misarticulated sounds are probably the most resistant to therapy. It may well be that unless there is a special reason, these will be the last to be included in therapy" (Templin and Darley, 1960, p. 12). Possibly the "consistency of an error" is not related to resistance to training. Sounds may be learned within specific linguistic contexts, as we have mentioned previously; and, therefore, resistance to correction may be unrelated to the occurrence or nonoccurrence of other errors of the sound in question.

Thinking this to be a reasonable assumption, Baer and Winitz (1968) sought to determine whether inconsistency of articulatory productions was an important consideration in articulatory acquisition when clinical training was withheld. A matching-to-sample stimulus task was designed, using the frequently misarticulated /v/ phoneme as the test sound. Three groups of young children were selected: those with few /v/ errors, those with average /v/ errors, and those with high /v/ errors. The subjects did not differ on the production of the /f/ sound, all showing few /f/ errors. On a /v/ articulation test consisting of 36 items—12 word-initial, 12 word-medial and 12 word-final—the low-error group had an average of 1.3 errors, the average-error group an average of 11.0 errors, and the high-error group an average of 22.7 errors (Baer, 1965). For both the average-error and high-error groups a greater number of errors occurred in the initial position than at either the medial or final positions. On the Templin-Darley 50-item Screening Test the scores of the average and high-error groups were similar: 10.2 and 12.1 errors respectively. However, the screening score for the low-error group was 4.1 errors.

All subjects were instructed to learn the training syllables /viʃ/ and /voʊm/, each a referent for an unusual object, and each presented for 21 trials, admistered separately. Correct responses were evaluated by two test examiners who were unaware of the categories into which the subjects had been placed. For both training syllables the average-error and high-error groups, showing no differences between themselves, lagged significantly behind the low-error group (see Figure 4.1 and 4.2). Although all groups improved their scores over the 21 trials of the /viʃ/ syllable, the first syllable of the sound learning task, additional learning was not evident for the /voʊm/ syllable.

Consistency of misarticulation has been cited in the literature as a relevant variable for prediction of sound learning because it has been assumed that if a speech sound is articulated correctly in more contexts than not, correct production will generalize to new contexts and to the relatively infrequent error contexts without training. This assumption was not validated in the above described study nor in a large-scale longitudinal study by Templin (1966), currently in progress. Templin's

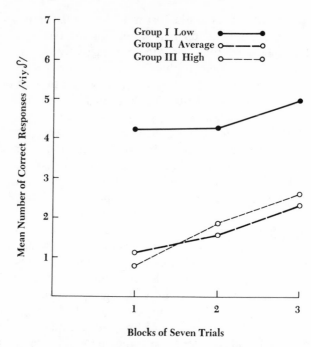

[Figure 4.1] Mean acquisition curves for the test syllable /viyʃ/ (/viʃ/), for the three groups of subjects divided according to frequency of /v/ error. SOURCE: Baer and Winitz, 1968.

(1966, pp. 177–178) preliminary observations caused her to remark as follows:

> . . . that children who could produce adequate phonemes but did not do so consistently would improve more rapidly because . . . they were able to produce the correct phonemes. This prediction has not been borne out. . . . the articulation measure shows that this group of children performed more like . . . the children below the median and have not shown any rapid increments as yet.

Finally, it should be added that none of the seven uses suggested by Templin and Darley is detailed enough to "prescribe the nature of speech correction." In conclusion it would seem that this test approaches but does not realize the goal of a diagnostic instrument. Articulation tests have not yet been developed to the point where specific and detailed teaching instructions may be programmed on the basis of the test protocols.

Validity for this test has also been cited by the authors. They refer to

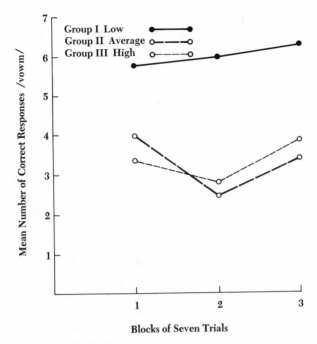

[Figure 4.2] Mean acquisition curves for the test syllable /vowm/ (/voʊm/), for the three groups of subjects divided according to frequency of /v/ error.

SOURCE: Baer and Winitz, 1968.

the findings of Jordan (1960) in which articulation severity ratings derived from responses of listeners to continuous speech were correlated with several variables obtained from the diagnostic test. Jordan extracted 23 different measures from this test, several independent variables were studied, such as the number of defective items, the number of defective sounds (roughly corresponding to the number of phonemes), number of defective single sounds (total errors excluding errors of phoneme clusters), frequency of occurrence of error sounds, consistency of individual errors, types of errors, and position of errors. The variables correlating most highly with judged severity were number of defective single sounds (.78), number of defective sounds (.75), and number of defective items (.72). A multiple R of .86 was obtained for 23 selected variables; the multiple R decreased to .82 when a combination of only three variables was used (number of defective singles, phonetic consistency and omissions).

Validity for this test can, of course, be defined in terms of severity ratings. However, in keeping with the authors' stated purpose of the test, it would seem that the validity measure should be derived from those procedures used to "prescribe the nature of speech correction." Thus, validation for this test would include, among other things, the validity of the seven proposed uses described above. The criterion measure would be, of course, articulatory change or proficiency.

Development

The studies of Wellman and others (1931), Davis (1938), and Templin (1957) on phoneme mastery and age have been discussed in Chapter 2. As a way of review, I mention again that the findings of these studies are often interpreted to be a chronological account of phonetic mastery. It was suggested that they reflect, for the most part, phonemic mastery. In the following discussion no distinction is made between these two points of view.

A frequent procedure used by speech clinicians is to examine a child's articulation of several sounds and then to evaluate the developmental status of each of the individual sounds tested. This procedure is accomplished by noting the age at which the child's defective sounds are mastered by the children of the normative study. Since Templin's data are the most recent, her findings are now commonly used.

When a child has not learned to produce a certain sound that is uttered correctly by most of his peers, the sound is considered to be defective in articulation. When more than one sound is in error, clinicians will often select for initial correction that sound which, according to the developmental norms, is mastered early. The inference is that early mastery means easy learning. Future studies of articulatory learning may reveal the advantages or disadvantages of this practice. It is possible that developmental mastery is uncorrelated with ease of correction.

Prediction

Still another function of an articulation test is prediction. The aim here is to determine those children who will or will not retain their early articulatory errors. The general procedure employed in studies designed to perform this function involves the selection of (a) age levels and the interval over which the prediction is to be made, (b) measures to be used as predictive variables, and (c) articulatory tests which will measure improvement at the end of the test interval. In some studies speech improvement or correction has been administered to the subjects, and in other studies it has not. As we shall see in a moment, a variety of measures has been selected as potentially predictive. Included are such measures as the number of articulatory errors, the ability to correct an articulatory error when stimulated with the correct production of the sound, the ability to learn non-English sounds, performance on intelligence and motor tests, and performance on speech sound discrimination tests.

Reid (1947), in a study previously described, investigated the articulatory improvement of two groups of children with articulatory errors. The experimental group (N = 38) received speech correction while the control group (N = 41) did not. The speech correction for the experimental group was centered upon the child's defective sounds and administered twice a week for periods of 30 to 40 minutes. Articulation improvement was determined for both groups after an interval of six months (testing was done one month after completion of the speech correction program for the experimental group). The relationships between initial and final articulation scores for the control group and the experimental group were .63 and .76, respectively. These are fairly respectable correlations.

Several additional relations were examined for the subjects of the experimental groups. These involved correlations between speech improvement (holding initial scores constant) and the following variables: MA, IQ (California Mental Maturity Test), CA, Fontaine's auditory memory span test (1940), Templin's sound discrimination test (1943), Patton's kinesthetic sensibility test (1940) with three additional but undescribed kinesthetic tests of the speech mechanism, and the California Test of Personality. Only two correlations were significantly different from zero at the 5 percent level: .34 for IQ and .37 for speech sound discrimination.

Snow and Milisen (1954) studied the effectiveness of an articulation difference score, obtained from an imitative test and a picture test, in predicting articulatory improvement. Subjects were 38 first- and 43 second-grade articulatory defective children. These children were not enrolled in speech correction classes. Twenty-five consonants were tested in words in the three word positions in both a picture test (spontaneous utterance) and an oral test (imitative utterance). The children were tested again on the picture test six months later.

Responses were scored with the following weights: (a) omission, 5; (b) substitution, 4; (c) very indistinct, 3; (d) moderately indistinct, 2; and (e) correct, 1. For each subject the mean of these values was his articulation score. Thus the range of possible scores for each subject was 1.00 to 5.00.

For each subject two difference scores were computed, and these scores were used for obtaining the correlations to be described. First, the difference score between the initial oral test and initial picture test was correlated with the difference score between the initial picture test and the final picture test. The correlations were .71 and .53 for grade one and grade two, respectively. Second, difference scores were obtained, as above, for each position separately. For grade one the correlations were .67 (initial position), .44 (medial position), and .52 (final position). All correlations in this study were significantly different from zero at or beyond the 5 percent level.

A similar procedure was employed by Sommers and others (1961). They used the Carter and Buck Test, described below, to obtain correction scores (nonsense syllable test minus picture test). The subjects were 25 first-grade children who had severe articulation problems. All subjects received speech correction and speech improvement lessons during the nine-month period. The correction score correlated .56 (p ≤ .01) with the final picture test.

Pettit (1957), in an attempt to uncover variables that may be important in predicting speech improvement without instruction, administered a consonant articulation test to 60 five-year-old children. Children were excluded who made no articulation errors on a 69-item consonant test scored according to an index devised by Wood (1949). The subjects were retested seven to eight months later on the same articulation test and a gain score was computed. Correlations were computed between the gain score and a handtapping test (the number of simultaneous taps with both hands per second), IQ, as measured by the California Test of Mental Maturity, initial articulatory score, personality score, as measured by the total adjustment score of the California Test of Personality, and an articulatory score. This last test consisted of repeating four nonsense words composed of English phonemes; words were evaluated as correct or incorrect, and each child was given several trials.

The correlations between articulatory improvement (gain score) and the test scores were as follows: tapping, nonsignificant; IQ, nonsignificant; initial articulatory score, —.68; imitation articulatory score, —.39; personality score, —.30. A multiple correlation was computed between articulatory improvement and the last three factors. The obtained coefficient was .70.

The three variables that are significantly related to articulatory improvement are negatively correlated, indicating that the higher the score on the pretest measures, the lower the articulatory gain. The negative correlations probably reflect the fact that children with good articulatory scores need to make only a small improvement before they obtain perfect scores, while children with poor articulatory scores need to made a large improvement before they obtain perfect scores. Thus, the posttest scores of many children who originally had mild articulatory errors probably clustered near the top of the posttest distribution. This situation would account for the fact that a low pretest articulatory score would be negatively correlated with articulatory gain. The multiple correlation coefficient, as is always the case, is positive. The multiple R of .70 indicates that articulatory gain is positively related to the three pretest variables when they are used as weighted independent variables in a multiple correlation analysis. It is obvious, however, that in this case the use of a multiple R did not appreciably change the correlational index. The major finding of this study is that a gain in articulation shows a fairly high correlation with an individual articulatory score. The negative sign, as stated, may be due to a ceiling imposed upon the children with good articulatory scores. The ceiling effect may have acted also to reduce the magnitude of the correlational index.

A different analytical approach was used by Carter and Buck (1958) in their attempt to predict articulatory improvement. The investigators examined the predictive utility of nonsense syllable imitation. They selected 77 first-grade children who had functional articulatory problems. These children received no speech correction during the study. The production of 13 sounds in each of the three positions was tested in words by pictorial elicitation (spontaneous picture test) and in nonsense syllables at the beginning of the school year. The spontaneous test was administered first; one week later the nonsense syllable test was given. Only those sounds incorrectly uttered in the spontaneous (pictorial) test were tested in the nonsense syllable test. In this situation the subject was given both auditory and visual stimulation. Subjects, as indicated earlier, "significantly" improved their scores on the nonsense syllable test. At the close of the school year, about nine months later, the spontaneous test was administered again.

The results of this study are presented in Table 4.2. In the first column of this table a list of percentages is given. These values indicate the percent correction in the nonsense syllable test over the initial spontaneous test. Column two indicates the cumulative number of subjects in each percentage category given in column one. For example, the top line indicates that 23 subjects (column two) corrected all of their errors in the nonsense syllable test. The second line indicates that 25 subjects (column two) corrected 80 percent or more of their errors in the nonsense syllable test; 23 of these 25 subjects were among those subjects that had achieved 100 percent correction. Column three gives the cumulative number of subjects that made no errors on the final spontaneous test for each of the percentage categories given in column one. For example, the first line shows that 22 of the subjects (column three) made no errors on the final spontaneous test. Further, by looking at column two it is clear that only one subject who made 100 percent correction on the nonsense syllable test did not correct all of his errors on the final spontaneous test. Glancing at the next-to-the-bottom line of column three it can be seen that of the 46 subjects that achieved 25 percent or more correction on the nonsense syllable test, 33 achieved 100 percent correction on the final spontaneous test. We can also note from the last line of column three that of the 41 subjects who made perfect scores (100 percent correction) on the final test, 8 subjects made less than 25 percent correction on the nonsense syllable test.

The values in column four are percentage values and are based on

[Table 4.2] The Number of Cases in the Experimental Group with
100 Percent Correction on the Final Spontaneous Test for
Various Percent Corrections on the Nonsense Syllable
Test over the Initial Spontaneous Test

Percent Correction of Initial N.S. Test over Initial Sp. Test	Number of Subjects Who Made Some Degree of Correction During the Nonsense Syllable Test	Number of Children Who Made 100% Correction During the Final Spontaneous Test	Percentages of 100% Correction During the Final Spontaneous Test Based on Columns Two and Three
100	23	22	95.6
80 or more	25	24	96.0
75 or more	26	24	92.3
65 or more	27	24	88.9
60 or more	31	25	80.6
55 or more	31	25	80.6
50 or more	38	30	78.9
40 or more	39	31	79.5
35 or more	40	31	77.5
30 or more	44	33	75.0
25 or more	46	33	71.7
0 or more	77	41	53.3

SOURCE: Carter, E. T. and Buck, M. W. *Journal of Speech and Hearing Disorders,* 1958, 23, 124–133.

columns two and three. For example, the value of 95.6, appearing in the first row of column four, means that 95.6 percent (22 out of 23) of the subjects who made 100 percent correction on the nonsense syllable test made 100 percent correction on the final spontaneous test. One can note from column four that the percentage values decrease from 95.6 to 53.3, indicating that as the criterion of correction on the nonsense syllable test decreases, the percentage of total subjects who achieve 100 percent correction on the final spontaneous test decreases.

The values in column four, according to Carter and Buck, can be used as cut-off values for determining those children who need speech correction. For example, let us assume that we will not give speech correction to a group of children if 90 percent achieve perfect scores on the final test. A value of approximately 90 percent can be found by looking at the fourth line of Table 2. Here we see that 24 of 27 subjects, or 88.9 percent, achieved correct production of all sounds on the final test. Thus the authors might suggest that since 88.9 percent achieved 100 percent production on the final test, these subjects should not be given speech correction, and that the remaining subjects should be given speech correction.

Thus, if this cut-off criterion were selected, only 3 subjects would need speech correction after the final spontaneous test was given. Yet 17 subjects (41 minus 24) who would have received speech correction would not have needed it. That is, if a 65 percent cut-off score is selected, 3 children predicted to achieve perfect performance will not and 17 children not predicted to achieve perfect performance will. We can think of the efficiency of this cut-off score as the ratio of "hits" (77 minus 20 or 57) to "total shots" (77) or 57/77 which equals 74 percent. If no children were given speech correction, 41 of 77 children would not need speech correction, an efficiency rating of 41/77 which equals 53 percent. Although efficiency might be increased 21 percent by using the Carter and Buck test, a great deal of energy is expended to achieve this added efficiency; i.e., therapy would be administered to 50 children during the year and 3 children would still need therapy; a total of 53 children would eventually be given articulatory instruction. On the other hand, only 36 children (77 − 41) would be given speech correction if the test were not used. (It is possible, of course, that the latter 36 children would not correct their errors as easily in the second grade as in the first grade.)

It can be observed, then, that the Carter and Buck test, although stimulating and thought provoking, does not increase greatly the precision of articulatory prediction. However, tests using this general format may eventually prove to be useful.

In one study (Steer and Drexler, 1960) the predictive utility of single sound errors and combinations of single sound errors was tested. The subjects were 93 kindergarten children who demonstrated at least one articulatory error on an 18-item test at the close of 12-week speech improvement study (Wilson, 1954). Of the 93 subjects, 54 children had served as the experimental group (received 12 weeks of speech improvement) and 39 children had served as the control group. The children were tested five years later on the Templin 50-item Screening Test of Articulation. At the time of retesting the subjects were found in grades three through six. The independent variables studied were IQ (Goodenough Draw-a-Man Test), social quotient (SQ), and a variety of articulatory error measurements. All of the foregoing measures were administered in the kindergarten grade.

The findings for this study are summarized in Table 4.3. As can be seen from this table a number of measurements were used, including responses to single sounds.

The last measurement pertains to the 12 consonants, (/p/, /b/, /m/, /n/, /t/, /d/, /k/, /g/, /f/, /l/, /r/, and /s/) used in the speech improvement program. The aim here was to determine whether or not articulatory improvement over a relatively short period of time, in this case 12 weeks, was related to articulatory scores five years later. Subjects who had less than 3 of the 12 consonants in error were excluded from this part of the analysis.

[Table 4.3] Correlation Coefficients Between Errors on the Templin Articulation Test at the Kindergarten plus Five-Year Level and a Variety of Measurements (Predictive Variables) Made at the Kindergarten Level

Predictive Variables	Correlation Coefficients EXPERIMENTAL GROUP	CONTROL GROUP
IQ scores	.068	.094
SQ scores	−.053	−.040
Articulation		
Initial position	.464[a]	.225
Medial position	.585[a]	.286
Final position	.473[a]	.367[b]
Total errors	.546[a]	.327[b]
Omissions in final position	.514[a]	.364[b]
Errors on [p], [b], and [m]	.311[b]	.029
Errors on [t], [d], and [n]	.465[a]	−.075
Errors on [k] and [g]	.322[b]	−.017
Errors on [f] and [l]	.419[a]	.449[a]
Errors on [v]	.355[a]	.107
Errors on [θ]	.253	.420[a]
Errors on [ð]	.222	.174
Errors on [r]	.396[a]	.237
Errors on [s]	.291[b]	.035
Errors on [z]	.337[a]	.183
Errors on [ʃ]	.289	.198
Errors on [tʃ]	.403[a]	.081
Improvement on 12 consonants independent of number of errors	−.379[b]	−.509[a]

[a] Significant at 1% level of confidence.
[b] Significant at 5% level of confidence.

SOURCE: Steer, M. D. and Drexler, H. G. *Journal of Speech and Hearing Disorders,* 1960, *25,* 391–397.

It may be observed from Table 4.3 that the highest coefficient for the experimental group is .59 and for the control group is .45. The former value is for the number of articulatory errors in the medial position, and the latter value is for the total number of errors for the phonemes /f/ and /l/. It may also be observed from Table 4.3 that the predictive utility of the /f/ and /l/ combination is fairly high (.42 experimental group and .45 control group). A multiple correlation, using the /f/ and /l/ score and the /θ/ score as the two independent variables, yielded coefficients of .51 ($p \leqslant .01$) for the control group and .47 ($p \leqslant .01$) for the experimental group. The correlations (last line of Table 3) between the Templin test and improvement on the 12 sounds used in the speech improvement program are moderately high, —.38 (experimental group) and —.51 (control group). These are partial correlations; thus, the influence of the total articulatory error score, errors on these 12 sounds and several others, was held constant. The correlations are negative in sign because error scores rather than correct sounds were used. These correlations suggest that when the number of articulatory errors at the beginning of the speech improvement program is kept constant, posttest articulatory error scores are positively related to articulatory improvement on the 12 sounds used in the speech improvement program; i.e., children who showed the greatest improvement during the speech improvement program tended to have the highest scores on the Templin test when the initial articulatory score was held constant. Finally, we may note from Table 4.3 that IQ and SQ do not relate significantly to articulatory improvement.

The predictive utility of articulatory imitation tests and sound discrimination tests was studied by Farquhar (1961). A picture articulation test was administered to 300 kindergarten children in the second week of school. The articulation test consisted of the "most frequently misarticulated sounds by young children." Each sound was tested in several word positions. The test was then scored according to the 1949 Wood Articulation Index. From the original sample of 300 children, 100 subjects were selected. Each subject was assigned to either a mild group or a severe group on the basis of his score on the articulation test. The mild group consisted of the first 50 children who misarticulated one phoneme in at least two word positions. The severe group was composed of the 50 children with the lowest articulation scores.

The following tests were administered: (a) imitation by the child of the correct production of his error sounds when correctly uttered by the examiner in isolation, nonsense syllables and words, and (b) discrimination of the correct production of the child's misarticulated sounds in a series of vowels, dissimilar consonants, and similar consonants. For the discrimination test the correct production of each child's misarticulated sounds was placed at random among nine sounds. An example of a vowel subtest for a child who misarticulated the /s/ phoneme is as follows: /a/, /i/, /ʊ/, /i/, /s/, /a/, /ʊ/, /a/, /s/,_/s/, /ʊ/, and /i/. The child was instructed to clap when he heard his misarticulated sound. For the acoustically similar or dissimilar sound tests, the vowels were replaced by consonants. Similarity or dissimilarity was defined in terms of phonetic features, such as voicing and frication. An example of an acoustically dissimilar test for the /s/ is as follows: /m/, /d/, /m/, /r/, /s/, /g/, /s/, /l/, /b/, /g/, /n/, and /s/. A maximum of five sounds was tested for each child; when more than five sounds were defective, the sounds most frequently misarticulated in all three word positions were chosen. Children were tested again seven months later, and an articulatory gain score (final performance minus initial performance) was determined for each child.

Both groups were found to have improved significantly their scores during this seven-month interval. Farquhar (1961, p. 345) reports that "the score for each child was computed as the percentage of correct responses in the total possible number of responses. The statistical technique . . . was the chi-square test." Farquhar (1961, pp. 345–346) obtained the following results:

> One testing procedure was found to be prognostically significant for the "mild" group. The ability to imitate the correct form of a misarticulated sound in words was prognostically significant at the .01 level of confidence. Two of the test items were found to have prognostic significance for the "severe" group. The ability to imitate the correct form of a misarticulated sound in nonsense syllables and in words was prognostically significant for both items at the .05 level of confidence. The auditory discrimination tests designed for this study were not found to have predictive value that was statistically significant for either the "mild" or "severe" groups.

In one study (Andersland, 1961) the predictive utility of socioeconomic level was investigated. Socioeconomic status, as measured by a six-point rating scale, was administered when the posttest articulatory evaluations were made. The evaluation included the quality of the home and the manner in which it was furnished, the dwelling area, and the occupation and education of the parents. The subjects were children who were available five years after they had participated in a speech improvement program; 94 of the original 242 children were included. The children served in 1952 as control or experimental subjects for a kindergarten speech improvement program. An articulation test devised by Wilson (1954) was used for the pretest and posttest evaluations. This test was composed of 18 consonants. The mothers were told that the questions were part of an opinion poll. The author (Andersland, 1961, p. 82) states, "There was no evidence that any mother was aware of a relationship between the study and the speech of her children."

At the time of the study the subjects were assigned to one of the following seven groups:

> Group I, children without articulation errors in 1952, no formal speech training (N = 8);
> Group II, children with articulation errors in 1952, no speech lessons, no articulation errors in 1957 (N = 7);

Group III, children without articulation errors in 1952 following . . . speech improvement lessons ($N = 7$);

Group IV, children with articulation errors in 1952 after . . . speech improvement lessons, no additional speech therapy, no articulation errors in 1957 ($N = 17$);

Group V, children with articulation errors in 1952 after . . . speech improvement lessons, no additional speech therapy, articulation errors still present in 1957 ($N = 16$);

Group VI, children with articulation errors in 1952 after . . . speech improvement lessons, additional speech therapy (an average of 23 hours of public school group speech therapy), articulation errors still present in 1957 ($N = 10$);

Group VII, children with articulation errors in 1952, no formal speech training, articulation errors still present in 1957 ($N = 29$) (Andersland, 1961, p. 81)

Andersland found that the socioeconomic level of Groups I and II were significantly higher than Groups IV, V, VI, and VII, and Group III was significantly higher than Groups VI and VII. These findings suggest, for the most part, that children in the early grades who are from higher socioeconomic levels either have no errors, tend to correct their errors when placed in a speech improvement program, or correct their own errors without speech instruction. On the other hand, children who retain articulation errors or who do not entirely profit from a speech improvement program come from families of lower socioeconomic status. Andersland (1961, p. 84) states, "after five years, children of lower socioeconomic groups who had been in the . . . speech improvement program had attained a level of articulation achievement approximating that of middle and upper socioeconomic group members."

In a subsequent analysis of the data the children who received speech improvement lessons and the children who did not receive speech improvement lessons were examined separately. The subjects of each group were classified as belonging to one of three socioeconomic levels (upper, middle, and lower) and one of two speech groups (articulation errors and no articulation errors). Subjects were assigned to one of the two speech groups on the basis of their performance on the Wilson test in 1957. Andersland found that for those children who did not participate in the speech improvement lessons in 1952 (Groups I, II, and VII) the proportion of children with articulation errors decreased as the socioeconomic level increased. This relationship was significant. In addition, for those subjects who had participated in the speech improvement program in 1952 (Groups III, IV, V, and VI) no relationship was found between socioeconomic status and the proportion of children with articulation errors.

The latter finding seems to be in conflict with the preceding finding reported by Andersland—that articulatory improvement from speech correction or speech improvement lessons is related to socioeconomic status. This contradiction probably arises from the fact that the scores of the few subjects in Group III (a group which was included even though they did not possess errors in 1952 following speech improvement lessons) did not influence the results of the subsequent analysis.

It would be interesting to modify Andersland's procedures as follows: (a) select subjects who have articulatory errors, (b) classify the subjects by socioeconomic status and severity of articulatory problem, and (c) assign half of the children in each group to either a control or an experimental group (speech improvement or articulatory instruction). This design would allow us to study the relation between socioeconomic status for children who do and do not receive therapy and for children of different levels of articulatory severity. As of now Andersland's findings suggest that socioeconomic level is unrelated to speech improvement for children with articulation errors; i.e., socioeconomic level is not a useful predictor of articulatory improvement.

In this same investigation Andersland also studied parental personality measures and articulatory improvement. Maternal personality measures were obtained from the Gordon Personal Profile Test, which tests for ascendancy, responsibility, emotional stability, and sociability. The Parental Attitude Research Instrument (PARI) was used to test for maternal attitudes. The factors used in this study were authoritarian-control, hostility-rejection, and democratic attitudes. These measures, like the socioeconomic ratings, were made at the time the posttest articulatory evaluations were made. Although we may assume that socioeconomic ratings will not change appreciably in five years, we cannot assume that this would be true for maternal attitude. However, we will report the findings of this part of the study with the foregoing limitation in mind.

The results for each of the groups were not presented in a table; the author summarized what appeared to be the most important findings. Mothers of group I[6] were found to score higher on emotional stability and total Gordon scale (combination of the four Gordon subtests) than four of the other groups. In contrast with Group I, Group VI was significantly lower than at least four other groups on ascendancy, responsibility, sociability, and total Gordon scale. Group II was significantly lower than Group I in emotional stability, but the two groups did not differ on the three other Gordon scales. Group III was significantly lower than Group I in responsibility, emotional stability, and total Gordon scale and was significantly higher than Group VI on the total Gordon scale. Mothers of Groups IV and V did not differ from each other. Both of these groups

[6] For brevity the phrase "mothers of" will sometimes be omitted.

were significantly higher than Group VI in emotional stability, ascendancy, responsibility, and total Gordon scale. Group VII was significantly higher than Group VI in ascendancy and responsibility but significantly lower than Group I in emotional stability and total Gordon scale. Also it was found that none of the mothers in Group I scored below the median on the total Gordon scale, and none in Group V scored above the median. The author concludes that mothers of children having the best articulation development scored highest in adjustment ratings, while mothers of children with articulation problems which were resistant to therapy scored lowest on the adjustment scale.

For the PARI scales it was found that group I showed significantly less hostility-rejection than Groups III, IV, VI, and VII. Group III showed the greatest hostility, the differences being significant in three cases. The author comments that the speech success of Group III suggests that speech improvement given in kindergarten may be used to overcome the bad effects of maternal hostility and rejection of home and family. Finally it was found that the hostility-rejection ratings of the mothers were not related to whether or not their children had participated in the speech improvement program. For those children who had received speech improvement lessons, hostility-rejection scores were not related to differences in articulation in 1957. However, for those children who had not participated in the speech improvement program, significant differences in articulation in 1957 were related to maternal hostility-rejection.

It would seem that additional research is needed before we can conclude with confidence that parental attitudes are a critical factor in articulation improvement. However, several studies that seem to show that the removal of poor parental attitudes is an important factor in the articulatory improvement of children in articulation correction classes will be reported in Chapter 5, where studies on the counseling and educating of mothers of articulatory defective children will also be discussed.

In the last study to be reviewed in this section, the investigator used a dichotomous measure of speech performance (Dickson, 1962). Children who had eliminated all of their articulatory errors during an interval of one year were compared with children who did not eliminate all of their errors. These children (N = 30 in each group) were originally tested in the kindergarten, first or second grades on the Hejna Developmental Articulation Test (1955). The following year the subjects were again tested on the same articulation test. The subjects were then assigned to one of two groups, those who eliminated their errors and those who reduced their errors but did not eliminate all of them. (It should be noted that the group of subjects who eliminated their errors had less errors than the second group when originally tested.) During this interval the subjects were not enrolled in speech correction classes.

At the time the subjects were assigned to their respective groups they were administered an auditory discrimination test and a motor test, and their parents filled out a personality test. The same reservations with regard to the time the tests were administered apply here as in the Andersland study. No significant differences were obtained between the groups on the auditory discrimination test (Templin Discrimination Test, 1943). However, a significant difference was obtained between the groups on the motor test (Oseretsky Tests of Motor Performance).[7]

Some significant differences were noted between the parents of the two groups on the personality test (Minnesota Multiphasic Personality Inventory). However, Dickson (1962, p. 269) concludes, "From the obtained results regarding the relative differences between the fathers, or mothers and fathers combined, there is no definitive picture relative to the persistence of speech errors of the children studied. Although some differences were noted, they were not supported by other findings on the MMPI."

SUMMARY AND INTERPRETATIONS OF TESTS. The studies reported here indicate that articulatory improvement, whether measured by a gain score or a final absolute score, is most reliably predicted from two indices: response to stimulation and articulatory pretest score. This generalization applies whether or not articulation instruction is provided. Continual refinement of these measures may result in tests that are sufficiently valid for use by the speech correctionist.

The studies showed also that intelligence is not highly correlated with articulatory improvement for children within the normal range of intelligence. For the reader's convenience the results are summarized in Table 4.4. As can be observed from Table 4.4 intelligence cannot be used as a reliable measure of articulatory improvement.

There are a number of points that must be taken into consideration in developing predictive tests of articulatory improvement. Some of these points have already been alluded to. They are discussed briefly below.

Age Level. The first question that needs to be answered concerns the relation between age level and articulatory prediction. Normally, the number of children with articulatory errors decreases as a function of age. Therefore, at what age level should speech correction begin? Only a small percentage, perhaps 1 to 3 percent, of the children in the third grade

---

[7] As indicated in Chapter 3, the Oseretsky test involves six measures of motor capacity. For the four-year age level they are as follows: "(1) general static coordination (remain standing, eyes closed for 15 minutes); (2) dynamic coordination of the hands (touch the point of the nose alternately with the right and left index fingers, eyes closed); (3) general dynamic coordination (jump up and down [hop] in the same place, keeping the feet together, seven or eight times in five seconds); (4) motor speed (put 20 coins in a box, spending no more than 15 seconds at this task); (5) simultaneous voluntary movements (describe circles [in the air] with the index fingers of both hands for 10 seconds, with the arms extended horizontally at the sides); (6) synkinesia (clasp the experimenter's right hand, first with the right hand, then the left, and finally with both hands" Doll, pp. 5, 8–9).

[Table 4.4] Summary of Studies Relating Intelligence and Articulation Improvement

Study	Age of Subjects	N	Sample	Articulation Test (Items)	IQ Test	Results (r)
Reid (1947a, 1947b)	8 yrs. 8 mos. (mean)	38	Judged as articulatory defective in grades 1 to 8	23	School records and California Mental Maturity Test (tested 6 mos. after speech training program and a gain score computed)	IQ = .34[a] MA = .02
Petit (1957)	5 yrs. (mode)	60	Not developed all of their consonant sounds	69	California Mental Maturity Test (tested 6 mos. after IQ and a gain score computed)	IQ = −.05
Steer and Drexler (1960)	Kindergarten (mode)	54	One articulatory error on 18-item test at end of kindergarten improvement program (experimental group)	50	Goodenough Draw-a-Man (articulation tested 5 yrs. after IQ)	IQ = .07
Steer and Drexler (1960)	Kindergarten (mode)	39	Same as above but control group	50	Goodenough Draw-a-Man (articulation tested 5 yrs. after IQ)	IQ = .09

[a] Significant at or beyond the .05 level.

have articulation errors. Accordingly a test designed to predict those kindergarten children who will retain their articulation errors in the third grade or beyond, for example, would need to be highly precise, so as to ferret out a small group of articulatory defective children. This procedure, if highly accurate, would permit the identification of those children who would need articulation correction in kindergarten. It would minimize the clinician's task in that a considerable number of children who now receive articulation correction in the early grades would no longer need this attention. However, other problems may arise. For example, those children unidentified until the third grade may be highly resistant to correction, or their articulation errors may have impaired their educational progress in reading, spelling, or writing. They may even develop behavioral problems. Thus studies devoted to articulatory prediction need to take into account a host of other problems.

Articulation Performance. A second consideration pertains to the level (and kind) of articulation performance we wish to predict. Carter and Buck established perfect performance as their criterion. In other studies no criterion per se was established; articulatory improvement was approximated by a linear function. In addition, most of the studies emphasized prediction of the child's total articulation score, rather than being concerned with those sounds most frequently defective. In summary, then, the design of articulatory predictive tests rests, in part, with the type of performance level to be predicted and the age level to which the prediction is to be made.

Resistance to Correction. A third consideration, also previously mentioned, is resistance to correction. It is generally assumed that a child's ability to correct his own errors decreases with age. We know practically nothing about the relation between articulatory correction and age. We tend to act on the assumption that articulatory errors are more difficult to correct in the later grades. We also tend to think that, with the passing of each grade, the difficulty increases. It may very well be the ability to correct errors increases with grade level up to a point and then begins to decrease; i.e., we do not know the function for articulatory correction or if there are different functions for different sounds.

Some of the studies which have been conducted seem to show that both discrimination learning ability and articulation learning ability increase with age (Winitz and Bellerose, 1963a, 1965); however, these studies are by no means definitive. Thus, it would seem that data on "resistance to correction" should be gathered so that we can more carefully plan our studies on the prediction of articulatory improvement.

Statistical Considerations. Finally, there are some statistical and design problems that need to be handled. The first is that of the improvement score. Should it be a total articulation measure or should it be a gain score? If the former measure is used, the correlation between articulation gain and the initial articulation score needs to be considered. If it is the latter measure, the large number of perfect scores occurring in the final retest prevents the use of linear correlations or related types of tests. These problems may be handled by appropriate statistical procedures and carefully designed research projects. Hopefully, satisfactory predictive articulation tests will be developed within the next decade.

Concluding Remarks on Articulation Tests

Five different types of articulation tests—proficiency, screening, diagnostic, developmental, and predictive—have been reviewed and discussed. Although some of the tests can serve more than one function, it has been convenient to classify a test under only one of the preceding five headings.

In this discussion the deficiencies inherent in some of the tests classified under one of these five headings have often been considered. In considering them there was no wish to imply that these tests are of no value, but simply to point up some of the inadequacies inherent in the design and/or function of these tests.

Proficiency tests, for example, are important although, as we know, speech correction cannot begin without obtaining additional information —e.g., a phonological analysis or detailed testing of one or two error sounds. Screening tests are also important and valuable, but when they are used independently of predictive tests they are of little value. By using a screening test we can, for example, classify a child as articulatory defective and suggest that articulatory training is necessary, but a child so classified will often improve without instruction. The same comments apply to a developmental test which, in most cases, is used as a screening test. That portion of diagnostic tests which pertain to remediation is also useful. Yet there would be no purpose in "prescribing treatment" without knowing the possibilities for spontaneous improvement.

However, if no assistance is given to children with articulatory errors, retardation in academic skills may result. It seems evident, then, that the selection, design, and implementation of articulation tests are complex matters, involving educational, social, and man-power priorities, factors inextricably tied to the identification, description, and treatment of articulatory disorders. At this time there are no simple solutions to these many problems.

SUMMARY

Tests of articulation performance and prediction are important tools of the speech correctionist. When the tests are administered, certain sources of error may contribute to the unreliability of the test. The sources of error were categorized under four general topics: (a) variance attributable to the subjects tested, (b) variance attributable to the examiner, (c) variance attributable to test instrument and test administration, and (d) variance attributable to subject-examiner interaction. Research studies devoted to these four topics were summarized and discussed.

Articulation performance has been assessed in a variety of ways and for a variety of purposes. In this chapter articulation tests were categorized as follows: (a) phonetic proficiency, (b) screening, (c) diagnostic, (d) developmental, and (e) predictive. Considerable time was spent on the distinguishing features of each of these tests. In addition, a detailed summary was made of those studies concerned with articulation prediction. The predictive utility of variables, such as intelligence, motor skills, articulation performance, auditory discrimination, and response to stimulation, was mentioned. Also, problems involved in the design of predictive articulation tests were considered.

REFERENCES

Andersland, P. B. Maternal and environmental factors related to success in speech improvement training. *Journal of Speech and Hearing Research,* 1961, *4,* 79–90.

Barker, J. O. A numerical test of articulation. *Journal of Speech and Hearing Disorders,* 1960, *25,* 79–88.

Baer, W. P. The acquisition of the /v/ sound in new words as a function of the consistency of /v/ sound errors. Ph.D. dissertation, Western Reserve University, 1965.

Baer, W. P., and Winitz, H. Acquisition of /v/ in "words" as a function of the consistency of /v/ errors. *Journal of Speech and Hearing Research,* 1968, *11,* 316–333.

Carter, E. T., and Buck, M. W. Prognostic testing for functional articulation disorders among children in the first grade. *Journal of Speech and Hearing Disorders,* 1958, *23,* 124–133.

Curtis, J. F., and Hardy, J. C. A phonetic study of misarticulation of /r/. *Journal of Speech and Hearing Research*, 1959, 2, 244–257.

Davis, I. P. The speech aspects of reading readiness. *Newer Practices in Reading in the Elementary School, 17th Yearbook of the Department of Elementary School Principals, NEA*, 1938, 17(7), 282–289.

Dickson, S. Differences between children who spontaneously outgrow and children who retain functional articulation errors. *Journal of Speech and Hearing Research*, 1962, 5, 263–271.

Doll, E. A. (ed.). *The Oseretsky tests of motor proficiency*. Minneapolis: American Guidance Service, Educational Test Bureau, 1946.

Farquhar, M. S. Prognostic value of imitative and auditory discrimination tests. *Journal of Speech and Hearing Disorders*, 1961, 26, 342–347.

Fontaine, V. E. *Auditory memory span of children for vowel sounds*. Unpublished M.A. Thesis, University of Wisconsin, 1940.

Ham, R. E. Relationship between misspelling and misarticulation. *Journal of Speech and Hearing Disorders*, 1958, 23, 294–297.

Hartup, W. W. *Sex and social reinforcement effects with children*. Paper presented at the meeting of the American Psychological Association, New York, September, 1961.

Hejna, R. *Hejna developmental articulation test*. Madison: Wisconsin College Typing, 1955.

Henderson, F. M. Accuracy in testing the articulation of speech sounds. *Journal of Educational Research*, 1938, 31, 348–356.

Jordan, E. P. Articulation test measures and listener ratings of articulation defectiveness. *Journal of Speech and Hearing Research*, 1960, 3, 304–319.

Patton, F. E. A comparison of the kinesthetic sensibility of speech defective and normal speaking children. *Journal of Speech Disorders*, 1940, 7, 305–310.

Pettit, C. W. The predictive efficiency of a battery of articulatory diagnostic tests. *Speech Monographs*, 1957, 24, 219–226.

Poole, I. Genetic development of articulation of consonant sounds in speech. *Elementary English Review*, 1934, 11, 159–161.

Reid, G. The etiology and nature of functional articulatory defects in elementary school children. *Journal of Speech Disorders*, 1947, 12, 143–150.

Scott, D. A., and Milisen, R. The effectiveness of combined visual-auditory stimulation in improving articulation. *Journal of Speech and Hearing Disorders*, Monograph Supplement 1954, 4, 51–56.

Siegel, G. M. Experienced and inexperienced articulation examiners. *Journal of Speech and Hearing Disorders*, 1962, *27*, 28–35.

Siegel, G. M., Winitz, H., and Conkey, H. The influence of testing instruments on articulatory responses of children. *Journal of Speech and Hearing Disorders*, 1963, *28*, 67–76.

Smith, M. W., and Ainsworth, S. The effects of three types of stimulation on articulatory responses of speech defective children. *Journal of Speech and Hearing Research*, 1967, *10*, 348–353.

Snow, K., and Milisen, R. The influence of oral versus pictorial presentation upon articulation testing results. *Journal of Speech and Hearing Disorders*, Monograph Supplement, 1954, *4*, 29–36.

Sommers, R. K. Factors in the effectiveness of mothers trained to aid in speech correction. *Journal of Speech and Hearing Disorders*, 1962, *27*, 178–186.

Sommers, R. K., Shilling, S. P., Paul, C. D., Copetas, F., Bowser, D. C., and McClinton, C. J. Training parents of children with functional misarticulation. *Journal of Speech and Hearing Research*, 1959, *2*, 258–265.

Steer, M. D., and Drexler, H. G. Predicting later articulation ability from kindergarten tests. *Journal of Speech and Hearing Disorders*, 1960, *25*, 391–397.

Stevenson, H. W. Social reinforcement with children as a function of CA, sex of E, and sex of S. *Journal of Abnormal Social Psychology*, 1961, *63*, 147–154.

Templin, M. C. A study of sound discrimination ability of elementary school pupils. *Journal of Speech Disorders*, 1943, *8*, 127–132.

Templin, M. C. Spontaneous versus imitated verbalization in testing articulation in preschool children. *Journal of Speech Disorders*, 1947, *12*, 293–300. (a)

Templin, M. C. A non-diagnostic articulation test. *Journal of Speech Disorders*, 1947, *12*, 392–396. (b)

Templin, M. C. Norms on a screening test of articulation for ages three through eight. *Journal of Speech and Hearing Disorders*, 1953, *18*, 323–331.

Templin, M. C. Certain language skills in children. *Institute of Child Welfare, Monograph Series*, No. 26. Minneapolis: University of Minnesota Press, 1957.

Templin, M. C. The study of articulation and language development during the early school years. In G. A. Miller and F. Smith (Eds.), *The Genesis of Language*. Cambridge, Mass.: M.I.T. Press, 1966.

Templin, M. C., and Darley, F. L. *The Templin-Darley tests of articulation*. Iowa City, Iowa: Bureau of Educational Research and Service, Extension Division, State University of Iowa, 1960.

Wellman, B. L. Case, I. M., Mengert, I. G., and Bradbury, D. E. *University of Iowa Studies in Child Welfare*, 5 (2). Iowa City: University of Iowa, 1931.

Wilson, B. A. The development and evaluation of a

speech improvement program for kindergarten children. *Journal of Speech and Hearing Disorders*, 1954, *19*, 4–13.

Winitz, H. Temporal reliability in articulation testing. *Journal of Speech and Hearing Disorders*, 1963, *28*, 247–251.

Winitz, H., and Bellerose, B. Effects of pretraining on sound discrimination learning. *Journal of Speech and Hearing Research*, 1963, *6*, 171–180. (a)

Winitz, H., and Bellerose, B. Phoneme generalization as a function of phoneme similarity and verbal unit of test and training stimuli. *Journal of Speech and Hearing Research*, 1963, *6*, 379–392. (b)

Winitz, H., and Bellerose, B. Phoneme cluster learning as a function of instructional method and age. *Journal of Verbal Learning and Verbal Behavior*, 1965, *4*, 98–102.

Winitz, H., and Siegel, G. M. *Intratest variability in articulation testing.* Unpublished study, 1961.

Wood, K. S. Measurement of progress in the correction of articulatory speech defects. *Journal of Speech and Hearing Disorders*, 1949, *14*, 171–174.

Wright, H. N. Reliability of evaluations during basic articulation and stimulation testing. *Journal of Speech and Hearing Disorders, 1954, Monograph Supplement* 4, 19–27.

5

ARTICULATORY
PROGRAMMING

Programming, in general, refers to "the performance of those activities, and the manipulation of those conditions, that produce learning" (Deterline, 1962, p. 2). The specific aim of a program is to teach a selected response called the *terminal response*. Variables chosen for manipulation are derived from established principles of learning theory. After the variables have been tested and studied for a selected terminal response or set of terminal responses a program is developed. Thus, a program may be defined as a standard sequence of operations or events which has been determined to increase most effectively the acquisition of a desired response, task, or skill. Furthermore, the program will include operations that provide for retention of the terminal response and generalization to other responses similar to the terminal response. At some later time, of course, a new program may be developed, one that is more effective than any previously devised program. It will then supplant the older, less effective program. A teaching machine will often be used to facilitate the programmed instruction.

Programs, once developed, are used in a standard way by clinicians. Clinicians, therefore, are not bound to established methods, schools of thought, or sets of operations. Since programs can be tested, there is no scientific basis for loyalty to any method.

In this chapter those topics considered most applicable to the study of articulatory programming will be discussed in a very preliminary way. In addition, the results of some articulatory programming studies will be reviewed.

Four general areas of articulatory programming will be considered:[1] (a) mechanics of articulatory programming, (b) articulatory testing for programming, (c) child-child interaction, and (d) parent-child interaction.

Articulatory programming refers to the procedures used in teaching speech sounds. *Articulatory testing for programming* concerns the testing of certain articulatory or oral responses for the expressed purpose of selecting an appropriate program of instruction. *Child-child interaction* refers to the grouping of clients in articulation training. Of concern here are the social groupings that enhance articulatory acquisition. *Parent-child interaction* refers to the programmed instruction of the parent(s) assembled with the child. Of interest here is an assessment of the parent's skill in handling the child's speech problem at home as well as the parent's ability to guide the child in his speech assignments.

Mechanics of Articulatory Programming

Principles for teaching the mechanics of speech sounds will be drawn from several areas of learning theory.[2] The order in which these principles are presented parallels to some extent their order of consideration in articulatory training.

Discrimination

In Chapter 3 the relation between articulation and discrimination was discussed. It was noted that the findings from several studies were somewhat equivocal, although the weight of the evidence seemed to suggest that children with articulation problems were less able to discriminate speech sounds than children without articulation errors. Moreover, the findings of some studies seemed to indicate that discrimination was most often impaired for those sounds whose production was in error. Even with this bit of evidence it remains to be determined whether a change in discrimination performance is prerequisite to a change in articulation performance. The author takes the point of view that for some children intensive speech sound discrimination training between the error sound and the correct sound will facilitate the subsequent learning of the correct sound. Discrimination training would be appropriate for only those children who have difficulty in discriminating the correct sound from their error sound.

---

[1] The term *programming* will be used to refer to the general area of articulatory programming and to the specific mechanics of speech sound training.

[2] For an excellent discussion of the application of learning principles to teaching machines and programming see the article by J. G. Holland (1960).

Many articulatory training procedures have been devised so that sound discrimination and sound production are learned simultaneously. This practice would at first appear noteworthy, but the author feels that a considerable amount of sound discrimination learning is essential before a child attempts to learn a new sound. At later stages of sound learning, discrimination and production might be combined. Sound discrimination pretraining, as we will see shortly, may be administered to the child by automatic programming procedures. Not only will automation free the clinician for other tasks, but it will provide for systematic and continuous presentation of the stimuli selected for training.

Very few studies have been conducted which show that speech sound discrimination improves following speech sound discrimination training. Verification would hardly seem necessary to most clinicians. We concur, of course, with this point of view. What is essential, however, are the ways in which speech sound discrimination is most effectively achieved, providing that speech sound discrimination is a necessary condition for subsequent sound production learning.

The importance of speech sound discrimination training as a prerequisite to sound learning was investigated by Winitz and Preisler (1965). The general plan of the study involved (a) selecting a phoneme cluster which occurs infrequently in English, (b) determining the error children make when trying to produce this cluster, (c) training children to discriminate between the error and the correct cluster, and (d) assessing the effectiveness of the discrimination training on learning to say the new phoneme cluster. The /sr/ cluster was selected as the experimental consonantal cluster. Children who attempted to learn the /sr/ cluster would most often say /skr/.

The procedure of the study was as follows: Thirty first-grade children without articulatory errors who uttered /skrɔb/ when they heard /srɔb/ on two separate days, 21 trials a day, were given discrimination training on the second day. Group A received training on /srɔb/-/skrɔb/, and Group B received training on /slip/-/ʃlip/. The procedure was the same as that described in Chapter 3 wherein a two-bar discrimination device was utilized. However, electronic equipment was used so that the apparatus was arranged to function automatically. Discrimination training continued until each subject achieved 10 correct responses in 12 consecutive trials. Following the discrimination training all subjects again heard the stimulus of /srɔb/ for 21 trials. They were told that if they said the "sound" correctly they would receive a peg and that the experimenter would place it in a pegboard. The purpose of the investigation was to assess differences in the acquisition of /sr/ responses as a function of the above types of discrimination training.

The results of the study are shown in Figure 5.1. From this figure it may be observed that none of the subjects in either Group A or Group B

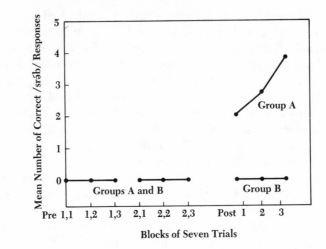

[**Figure 5.1**] Mean acquisition curves for the learning of the production of the syllable /srɔ́b/ for two different discrimination groups: Group A, discrimination of /srɔ́b/ – /ʃrɔ́b/ and Group B, discrimination of /slip/ – /ʃlip/. Pre and Post on the abscissa refer to prediscrimination training and postdiscrimination, respectively. The first number following Pre indicates the day of testing, and the second number indicates the trial block. The number following Post refers to the trial block.

Reprinted with permission of author and publisher: Winitz, H. and Preisler, L. Discrimination pretraining and sound learning. *Percept. mot. Skills*, 1965, *20*, 912–913.

uttered a correct /srɔ́b/ response on the two occasions preceding the discrimination training. Again, referring to Figure 1 we note that /sr/ learning took place for only those subjects in Group A, the group which received the discrimination training between the error sound, /skr/, and the correct sound, /sr/. The results for Group A are somewhat dramatic in that a "limited" amount of discrimination training made learning of /sr/ possible. The individual curves for subjects in Group A are presented in Figure 5.2. From these curves it is apparent that 10 of the 15 subjects were able to produce correctly the /sr/ response on three or more of the stimulus trials.

The general findings of this study indicate that sound discrimination pretraining, which involves the error sound and the correct sound (the sound to be learned), facilitates the learning of the correct sound. Discrimination pretraining on two sounds unrelated to the correct sound or the error sound does not seem to be of any value in facilitating sound learning. However, discrimination pretraining involving the correct sound and the error sound does not seem to assure sound learning, as 5 of the 15 subjects in the experimental group did not evidence learning of the /sr/ cluster. Thus, it would seem that sound discrimination learning is a necessary but not a sufficient condition for sound learning.

The preceding conclusion needs to be accepted with reservation. In two previous studies (Winitz and Lawrence, 1961; Winitz and Bellerose, 1965) the learning of non-English sounds and phoneme clusters was demonstrated for subjects who received no discrimination pretraining. Although some subjects in both studies did not learn the sounds, those subjects who did evidence sound learning acquired the correct responses after several stimulus exposures (trials). In this respect they were like those children who were excluded from the later study because they were able to utter /srɔb/ correctly after a few stimulus trials. Of the children included in the later study, all were unable to produce /sr/ on two separate days after repeated stimulus presentations. For this reason their responses are similar to the articulatory responses of children with articulation errors, in that their errors were demonstrated for a number of "utterances" (trials) over a specified interval of time. It might then seem reasonable to conclude that sound discrimination training of the type administered to Group A in this present study is a necessary but not sufficient condition for sound learning when sound errors can be reliably demonstrated.

The findings and procedures of this study by Winitz and Preisler suggested three "clinical" subgroups: (a) subjects who can learn to discriminate the correct sound from the error sound and who subsequently learn with no additional response training to produce the correct sound, (b) subjects who learn to discriminate the correct sound from the error sound but who fail to produce the correct sound, and (c) subjects who do not learn to discriminate the correct sound from the error sound (this latter subgroup includes subjects similar to those eliminated from this study because they were unable to learn 10 of the 12 correct responses in 208 discrimination trials).

In summary, then, the findings of this study indicate that for some children sound discrimination improves following sound discrimination training and that sound discrimination training effectively facilitates sound production learning. In addition, the use of automatic programming devices appears useful for accomplishing this training.

Automatic programming has only in the last few years been employed as an instrument for teaching sound discrimination. The first attempt to develop sound discrimination programs for children with articulatory errors and to test the difference between several programs was by Holland and Matthews (1963). Their program contained a graded series of

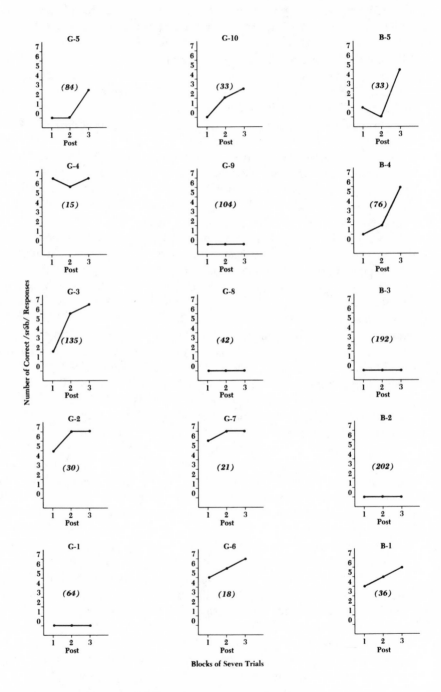

discrimination tasks developed for children with /s/ errors between 8 and 11 years old.

The subjects sat before a panel with three buttons; in some cases only two of the buttons were used. Each subject was instructed how to use the buttons—e.g., he was to press a certain button when he heard a particular stimulus. Correct responses resulted in the presentation of the next trial; incorrect responses resulted in the rewinding of the tape recorder and replaying of the item. The rewinding of the tape recorder produced the usual mechanical noises which signified nonreinforcement.

The subjects were assigned to one of three sound discrimination programs. The first program had four phases: (a) discrimination of /s/ from other sounds, (b) discrimination of /s/ in words, (c) discrimination of /s/ in the initial, medial, and final position in a word, (d) discrimination of /s/ from incorrect /s/ errors (distortions, omissions, or substitutions). Within each of these four phases the difficulty of items, as judged by the experimenters, was graded from "easy" to "hard." The second program was very similar to phase one of the first program, but it consisted of more and varied items. The third program was an extension of the fourth phase of the first program with additional items.

The training period consisted of several sessions averaging 40 minutes and totaled not much more than two hours. Retesting was conducted within three days following completion of the program. Several discrimination tests were employed to assess success. On an /s/ discrimination test, similar to the four phases of the first program, only the group trained on the first program improved significantly. On a discrimination test composed of "sibilant" items and similar in construction to the /s/ discrimination test, subjects in programs I and II improved significantly. This finding is really remarkable when one considers that the training was about two hours in length. On the Templin Discrimination Test (1943) none of the groups improved.

In addition, the authors report that all three groups significantly improved their scores on an /s/ articulation test. This latter finding should be accepted with considerable reservation, since a fourth control group was

---

[Figure 5.2] Individual acquisition curves for the learning of the production of the syllable /srɔb/ for Group A. The number in parentheses refers to the number of trials needed to reach criterion discrimination learning.

Reprinted with permission of author and publisher: Winitz, H. and Preisler, L. Discrimination pretraining and sound learning. *Percept. mot. Skills,* 1965, *20,* 912–913.

not employed—one that was pretested and posttested and trained on a neutral discrimination task—improvement of /s/ articulation cannot be reliably attributed to the program sessions. Variables, such as examiner error (adaptation to /s/ errors, for example) and improved motivation or lessened anxiety on the part of the subjects may have accounted for the improved articulation scores.

The novel features of this study were threefold. First, it included automatic programming equipment; second, several programs were developed; and third, the effects of the various programs were tested, although the programs themselves were not developed on the basis of previous research. Programming research in discrimination training, as well as in other areas of articulatory training, if conducted within the framework of programming principles, will need to be concerned with the experimental development of programs. The Holland and Matthews study was of course, a first attempt to compare the effectiveness and generality of several programs, but the programs they offer come from the traditional operations of the speech clinician rather than being generated by research findings.

One principle of discrimination programming implicit in the Holland and Matthews study involved the concept of *distinctive stimuli training.* This notion will become clear in discussing a study by Spiker (1959). Spiker has conducted a simultaneous visual discrimination study that has important implications for speech sound discrimination learning. He assumed that highly similar stimuli retard the development of appropriate orienting responses. He states (1959, p. 513) as follows:

> If the stimuli differ with respect to brightness, for example, a small difference may result in the S's orienting toward irrelevant features of the stimuli, whereas a large difference may result in a relatively rapid orientation toward the brightness dimension. If this hypothesis is correct, preliminary training with stimuli differing markedly with respect to a given dimension should facilitate subsequent performance with stimuli differing only slightly on this dimension.

Spiker selected preschool children and randomly assigned these children to two groups, E and C. The subjects in Group E were required to discriminate between a bright light and a dim light; the subjects in Group C were required to discriminate between a bright light and a medium-bright light. After 24 trials the subjects in both groups were then required to discriminate between the bright light and the medium-bright light for 24 additional trials; that is, Group C received the same visual stimuli throughout the training period (48 trials), and Group E was changed to C's schedule in the latter half of the training period (the last 24 trials).

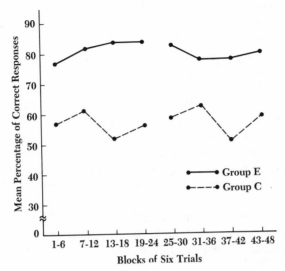

[Figure 5.3] Mean percentage of correct responses
per block of six trials for experimental and control
groups.
SOURCE: Spiker, 1959. By permission of The Society
for Research in Child Development, Inc. Copyright 1959 by the Society for Research in Child
Development, Inc.

The subjects were seated before a boxlike panel which contained two
glass-enclosed apertures. Directly below each of the apertures was a
button. A tube projecting from the front of the box led to a container into
which marbles could be injected. Both pairs of lights (dim and bright or
medium-bright and bright) were shown at the same time. Subjects were
reinforced with a marble when they pressed the button below the positive
stimulus.

The mean percentage of correct responses is presented in Figure 5.3. It
may be observed from this figure that on all 48 trials the performance of
Group E is markedly superior to that of Group C. On the first 24 trials
the difference between stimuli for Group E is more distinctive than for
Group C, resulting in the superior performance of Group E. On the last
24 trials Group E's superiority reflects the advantages obtained from distinctive feature training; that is, the two stimuli used for Group E on
the first 24 trials permitted the sampling of certain distinctive features
(orientation to relevant stimuli) which facilitated transfer on the last 24
trials.

Spiker's study suggests that discrimination training between sounds
should first begin with two sounds whose distinctive features show

minimal overlap. After this discrimination is learned, one of the two original sounds should be replaced by a sound less distinctive. This graded sequence of stimuli would be continued for several trials; finally the subject would be faced with the discrimination he was originally unable to make. At this time he would presumably be able to learn this originally difficult discrimination. This procedure might be especially useful for teaching discrimination between the correct sound and a "distortion" of the correct sound. In one study this method was carried out with a dysphasic patient (Lane and Moore, 1962) and was found to be most effective. In another study (Winitz and Preisler, 1967) Spiker's paradigm proved to be successful when the subjects were first- and second-grade children and the terminal discrimination task was relatively difficult.

In the first of two experiments by Winitz and Preisler (1967) the children of the experimental and control groups were taught to discriminate between /ç/ and /ʃ/ as follows:

Experimental Group	Trials	Control Group	Trials
1. /ʃɝm/-/pɝm/	1–24	/ʃɝm/-/çɝm/	1–72
2. /ʃɝm/-/θɝm/	25–48		
3. /ʃɝm/-/çɝm/	49–72		

Using a two-bar successive discrimination task, as described on p. 277, the subjects in the experimental group learned or were exposed to the contrasts /ʃ/-/p/ and /ʃ/-/θ/ prior to learning the /ʃ/-/ç/ contrast. The first two contrasts were selected so as to share many of the distinctive features of the final contrast (/ʃ/-/ç/), no doubt a necessary condition for discrimination pretraining to be effective.

In the second experiment young children learned the difficult discrimination of /vr/-/br/ with the following pretraining schedule:

Experimental Subjects	Trials	Control Subjects	Trials
/fr/-/br/°	1–48	/vr/-/br/	1–80
/vr/-/br/	49–80		

That is, the experimental subjects were to learn or were to be exposed to the /fr/-/br/ contrast prior to learning of the /vr/-/br/ contrast while the control subjects were to learn only the /vr/-/br/ contrast. Particularly strong in this second study was the effect of distinctive stimulus pretraining, as the experimental subjects found no difficulty learning the /vr/-/br/ contrast while the control group experienced considerable difficulty with this contrast.

Returning to the first of the two experiments by Winitz and Preisler

---

° Syllabic element was /ɛ/ throughout.

(1967) another seemingly important clinical finding was obtained. Consider first the following two discrimination programs:

	A	B
1.	/ʃ/-/p/	/ç/-/p/
2.	/ʃ/-/θ/	/ç/-/θ/
3.	/ʃ/-/ç/	/ç/-/ʃ/

Note that in program A /ʃ/ is a contrasting sound in items 1 and 2 above, while in program B /ç/ is a contrasting sound for the same two items. The sequence given in program A was found to facilitate the discrimination learning of /ʃ/-/ç/ while the sequence given in program B was not. Since young children will often utter /ʃ/ in response to /ç/, possibly the subjects given the sequence of program B regarded [ç] as a variation of /ʃ/ ([ç] was placed in the /ʃ/ phoneme bin), only later to rediscover /ç/ as a contrasting stimulus. This finding suggests that discrimination programs provide, at least in the early stages of training, an invariant relation between error responses and stimuli. For example, when teaching the /w/-/r/ contrast for children who substitute the /w/ for /r/, the above findings would insist that /w/ not /r/ be employed as an early contrasting stimulus.

Discrimination pretraining is a challenging and interesting area, as well as a very basic one. It represents, however, a shift in our approach from that of an attempt to describe "underlying" auditory deficiencies to that of describing auditory training procedures.

Successive Approximation

The principle of successive approximation or shaping allows us to obtain from an organism a response or set of responses that have never been performed. These new responses are obtained by "reinforcing crude approximations of the final topography instead of waiting for the complete response" (Skinner, 1959, p. 134). The organism is, therefore, reinforced for successively approximating responses in a chain of responses.

This process is illustrated in an early experiment by Skinner (1959, p. 132) as follows:

> In 1943 Keller Breland, Norman Guttman, and I were working on a wartime project sponsored by General Mills, Inc. Our laboratory was the top floor of a flour mill in Minneapolis, where we spent a good deal of time waiting for decisions to be made in Washington. All day long, around the mill, wheeled great flocks of pigeons. They were easily snared on the window sills and proved to be an irresistible supply of experimental subjects. We built a magnetic food-magazine, which

dispensed grain on the principle of an automatic peanut vendor, and conditioned pigeons to turn at the sound it made and eat the grain it discharged into a cup. We used the device to condition several kinds of behavior. For example, we built a gauge to measure the force with which a pigeon pecked a horizontal block, and by differentially reinforcing harder pecks we built up such forceful blows that the base of the pigeons' beaks quickly became inflamed. This was serious research, but we had our lighter moments. One day we decided to teach a pigeon to bowl. The pigeon was to send a wooden ball down a miniature alley toward a set of toy pins by swiping the ball with a sharp sideward movement of the beak. To condition the response, we put the ball on the floor of an experimental box and prepared to operate the food-magazine as soon as the first swipe occurred. But nothing happened. Though we had all the time in the world, we grew tired of waiting. We decided to reinforce any response which had the slightest resemblance to a swipe—perhaps, at first, merely the behavior of looking at the ball—and then to select responses which more closely approximated the final form. The result amazed us. In a few minutes, the ball was caroming off the walls of the box as if the pigeon had been a champion squash player.

This principle may be extremely useful in articulatory correction. The general procedure would be to begin with some approximation of the sound to be learned and to reinforce in successive stages "sounds" that eventually lead to the sound to be learned. The first stage of sound learning requires a sound response, not necessarily an English sound, that the subject is able to produce. In some cases this assessment may take intensive testing. We will discuss this problem in the next section. This stage and successive stages should also include some of the distinctive features of the sound to be learned.

In successive approximation learning, then, successive stages of sound learning are ordered into a sequence which will provide rapid acquisition of a desired sound. This type of a program, however, has two additional features: (a) the subject may omit one or several stages, and (b) the subject's responses to the stimuli may also be ordered—that is, in addition to successive approximation learning of the programmed stimuli there is successive response approximation for a particular stimulus.

We shall now illustrate a program we have used with a fair amount of success when teaching the $[\chi]^3$ sound. The "important" (distinctive)

[3] The [χ] is a voiceless, dorso-uvular fricative. The [ʁ] is the voiced, dorso-uvular fricative.

features for this uvular sound are consonantal, compact, tense (voiceless-ness), oral, and continuant (frication).

In this program "←" symbolizes inspiration, "→" symbolizes expiration, and *sn* symbolizes a snore. The program is as follows:

(a) sn	(b) sn	(c) /h/	(d) [χ]
←	←	←	
	sn	sn	
	→	→	

That is, (a) the subject first utters a snorelike inspiration, (b) the snore-like inspirated sound is again uttered, but this time it is followed im-mediately by a snorelike expiration, (c) the subject now replaces the inspirated snore with an inspirated /h/ followed immediately by a snore-like expiration, and (d) the subject inhales in the usual manner and then attempts to utter the [χ] phone.

These four stages were developed so as to provide a sequence of sounds that successively approximated the [χ] sound. Within each stage certain responses may be reinforced successively. For example, for the first stage the inspirated /h/ may be reinforced first. When this inspirated voiceless fricative is learned, it is no longer reinforced until *sn* is uttered. A program ←
for the [χ] sound involving successive response shaping is symbolized as follows:

PROGRAMMED STIMULI

(a) sn	(b) sn	(c) /h/	(d) [χ]
←	←	←	
	→		
		sn	
		→	

INITIALLY ACCEPTABLE RESPONSES

/h/	sn	/k/	[ʁ] (voiced dorso-uvular fricative)
←	←	←	
or	/h/	sn	[x] (voiceless dorso-velar fricative)
	→	→	
/k/	or		[γ] (voiced dorso-velar fricative)
←			
	sn		
	←		
	/k/		
	→		

That is, (a) /h/ and /k/ are initially reinforced. After several consecutive
correct /h/ or /k/ responses only sn responses are reinforced when they
occur. Parts (b), (c), and (d) may be easily interpreted from the program.

No doubt other programs may be suggested by the reader. As a passing
remark, we shall simply state without support from data that we have
employed the [χ] sound to teach the /k/ sound. The [χ] sound, using the
foregoing programs, can be learned fairly easily by young children. The
uvular fricative can then be transmuted into a /k/. We will shortly
describe a teaching machine which facilitates the acquisition of successively programmed stimuli.

Generalization Learning

We have previously defined and described the behavioral process of
stimulus generalization. Stimulus generalization is described schematically
as follows:

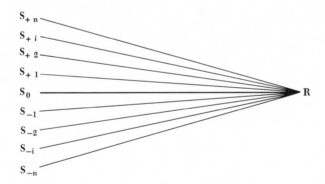

That is, a response conditioned to a single stimulus, denoted S_0, generalizes
to other stimuli, $\pm S_1, \pm S_2, \ldots \pm S_n$. The "+" and "−" signs indicate
that generalization occurs to stimuli which lie either to the right (+) or
to the left (−) of the original stimulus. You may recall from Chapter 1
that generalization gradients are often almost symmetrical.

In *response generalization* the transference is in the reverse; the stimulus
remains the same and the responses are altered. It is schematically represented as follows:

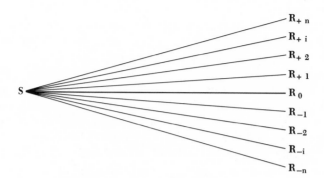

That is, the stimulus which evoked the original response, denoted R_0, soon evokes other responses, $R_{\pm 1}$, $R_{\pm 2}$, ... $R_{\pm n}$.

In stimulus-response generalization, stimuli resembling the training stimulus become associated with responses resembling the training response. This process may be represented as follows:[4]

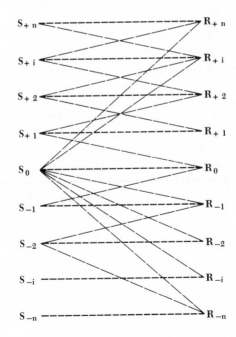

[4] For reasons of clarity, some cross lines have been omitted in the schema.

The latter two generalization processes are described in two experiments by Wickens (1943, 1948). Instrumental aversive conditioning was the experimental paradigm. With the palm down the subjects were conditioned to avoid an electrical shock by removing (extending) their middle finger from an electrode. The CS was a pure tone. After conditioning was completed, the hand was turned over. Subjects could then avoid the shock by again removing (flexing) the finger from the electrode. The flexor movement is an indication of response generalization. Flexing also occurred in response to a tone that differed in frequency from the original tone, an example of stimulus generalization even though the flexor movement had not been conditioned to the original CS. This type of generalization is called stimulus-response generalization; I will use this term rather generally—simply to describe new responses that become associated with new stimuli.

The term *transference* is often used to describe complex generalization tasks. However, for our purposes we will not distinguish between generalization and transference.

The generalization learning process that concerns us most directly in articulatory training is stimulus-response generalization learning. Here responses similar to other responses become conditioned to stimuli similar to other stimuli. For example, this procedure may be used to teach /z/ from /s/, assuming that /z/ is incorrectly spoken and /s/ is correctly spoken. The audible stimulus and motor response of /s/ are very similar to /z/. The essential difference is voicing. The clinician may try to obtain the /z/ response from the syllable /as/ (stimulus generalization), assuming, of course, that the individual can say /as/. The assumption is that the voicing feature of /a/ will continue during the production of the following consonant. The correct /z/ production may then be taught to generalize to a /z/ stimulus (response generalization). This entire process may be called "stimulus-response generalization." The procedure would be as follows: (a) The child is asked to say /as/ to the stimulus /as/ for a number of trials, and each correct response is reinforced; (b) the stimulus /az/ is presented and the subject will probably say /as/ (stimulus generalization); (c) /as/ in response to /az/ is now reinforced for a number of trials; (d) /as/ is no longer reinforced to /az/; (e) the subject may now say /az/ in response to the stimulus /az/ (response generalization). This procedure will probably be most effective if the error for /z/ is some other sound besides /s/. If, however, we tried to obtain the /z/ from /az/, a subject might continue to utter the /z/ error.

The /g/ sound might be taught from the /sk/ blend. The subject is instructed to produce the cluster /zk/. In most cases the /k/ will be voiced following the /z/, producing a fairly good /g/.

More precision might be added to this approach by making use of the distinctive feature matrices presented in Chapter 2. Sounds for a program could be selected that differ on a minimum number of distinctive feature dimensions. If two or more sounds are equally appropriate, then further research is necessary in order to determine which one of the two or more sounds will most often facilitate generalization. For example, for the defective /ʃ/ sounds, either the /s/ sound or the /f/ sound might be used. Both of these sounds, according to Saporta's table (see Chapter 2, p. 85), have a distinctive feature difference of three. Which of the two sounds, assuming both are in the child's repertoire, do we select initially for stimulus-response generalization learning? The allophones of the /r/ phoneme can also be taught in various contexts. Should [r] in *road* be taught from [ɝ] in bird or [r̥] (unvoiced) in *train*? Research is, therefore, needed to determine the generalization procedures that are most effective for teaching sounds from sounds already available in the child's response repertoire.

There is still another variation of this general procedure that may facilitate acquisition. It is possible that a sound learned in nonsense words will transfer most effectively to connected speech by the initial learning of a second sound. We refer to this technique as *generalization by substitution*. For example, transference of the sound [r] in the word *road* may be facilitated by first learning *toad*.

The tongue position for [t] and [r] is similar; they are both alveolar. As we know, many [r] errors are [w] substitutions. Thus subjects who are taught to say [r] for [w] must substitute a newly learned alveolar sound for a highly learned bilabial sound. However, if a highly learned sound, such as [t], is learned for [w], transfer to the alveolar [r] may be facilitated.

That generalization is a valid and useful concept is shown in the studies of Elbert and others (1967) and Shelton et al. (1967). In one study (Elbert and others, 1967) children with /s/, /z/ and /r/ errors were taught to say /s/ correctly. Improvement of /z/, but not of /r/ was noted. In the other study (Shelton and others, 1967) children with /r/ errors and /s/ or /ʃ/ errors were trained to say /r/ correctly but there was no improvement on /s/ or /ʃ/. In both studies generalization learning seems to have been related to the number of distinctive features the test and training sounds have in common.

Another approach, which is only tentatively suggested, may be to ignore initially the teaching of any specific sound. Perhaps we may wish to teach distinctive features (frication, plosion, etc.) and then in some way combine the learned features into the sounds of the language. Haas (1963), as reviewed in Chapter 2, did a phonological analysis of a six-and-a-half-year-old boy with a severe articulatory disorder. He suggested a program of correction based on the relationship between the child's acquired sound contrasts and the contrasts that occur in English. For example, the child he studied had not learned all of the stop contrasts of English, but he did distinguish between [p] and [t]; thus Haas suggested that the related

[b]-[d] contrast be learned. Similarly other distinctions, such as the voice-voiceless distinction, were emphasized.

Finally it should be mentioned that generalization principles are employed in the teaching of successive approximations. The major distinction between successive approximation learning and generalization learning is, for the most part, a classificatory one; they do not represent two entirely different behavioral processes. Successive approximation techniques are, in addition, somewhat more encompassing; that is, the technique makes use of other behavioral principles in addition to generalization principles.

Acquisition Interference

Generally the stress in articulatory correction centers on the teaching of a new response in place of a highly learned incorrect response. Little emphasis, however, has been placed on the competitional nature of the incorrect response. It seems reasonable that if interference from the old articulatory response, the incorrect articulatory response, is held to a minimum, the new response will be more easily acquired. In many cases, as we know, children often possess the phonetic features (or even the sound itself) essential for making the new sound, although it is not produced correctly in several or all of the linguistic environments tested. A major source of difficulty in learning the new sound seems to lie in the fact that the old sound is continually elicited in familiar words. Presumably the error sound has been learned as an integral part of a word, and when the child is asked to say a familiar word, the error sound is evoked and, therefore, uttered. (This might be considered to be a morphemic problem rather than a phonological or articulatory one.) For example, a child who has learned /w/ for /r/ in *road*, when asked to utter *road*, may mediate the external stimulus *road* by the response /woud/. This mediating response would then evoke the /w/ sound, which will compete vigorously with the response to be learned (correct sound). This type of interference may be termed negative transfer. However, the situation is not exactly parallel to that of the typical negative transfer paradigms. To make this point clear let us assume that subjects first learned a list of paired words. They were then asked to learn a second list of paired words, the stimulus word of each pair being identical with that of the first list. Any difficulty encountered in this endeavor would be primarily a function of the interference from the first list. However, the young child who is told that the correct response is an imitation of the stimulus word should be clear as to "the list" he is learning. His difficulty is presumably not a function of the fact that he does not know the response term, but that he has previously learned a different response term. He has learned that the stimulus [r] is said as [w]. All new [r] terms are then mediated by the implicit "word" response of which [w] is the initial sound.

Interference of this sort would seem to be operating when adults are confronted with the learning of a new language. Their old language habits seem to interfere with the acquisition of new language habits. For example, the Korean adult, when asked to pronounce the [r] in the prevocalic position, will say [l]. When asked to say [l] in the postvocalic position, he will say [r]. ". . . the Korean alphabet has only one letter for the two sounds, in [maru] "floor" and [pal] "foot," for instance. The Czech words /karar/, /volal/, /oral/, and /kolar/ are all perceived and reproduced by a Korean as terminating in [-ral]" (Jakobson and others, 1952, p. 22).

No doubt the Korean adult would be able to hear the difference between the [r] and [l] sounds in the prevocal and postvocal positions if he were informed about this phonological rule and then were told to listen to the words again. However, the [r] and [l] sounds in the same vocalic position are not distinguished by the Korean adult because the implicit mediational response is vocalic position or, possibly, word position. When the [r], for example, is spoken in the final word position or postvocalic position, the [r] will be perceived and spoken as an [l] because of the fact that (a) [r] and [l] are perceptually similar and (b) [r] elicits the implicit mediational response of final word or vocalic position, which elicits the external response of [l].

In a study by Winitz and Bellerose (1965) the effect of just this type of interference for first- and second-grade children was investigated. In their investigation the interfering effects of a familiar word on the acquisition of a new consonantal cluster were studied. The experimental cluster was /sr/ appearing in the syllable /srɔb/. Preliminary research had indicated that subjects from a certain school district often uttered /ʃrɔb/ when they heard /srɔb/. It was assumed that /sr/ acquisition would be facilitated if it did not occur in a context which evoked a familar word, in this case *shrub*. Subjects were assigned to one of three instructional groups: (a) Group I—the word *shrub* was pronounced by the examiner, depicted pictorially and subjects were told to pronounce this word differently; (b) Group II—subjects were told to pronounce a word; and (c) Group III —a picture of an unfamiliar object was shown and subjects were told to learn the name of the object. The experimental syllable was played from a tape recorder 28 times. Data were grouped into four seven-trial blocks. The reinforcer was the movement of a mechanical toy car.

The findings are indicated in Figure 5.4. The learning of groups I and II was significantly impaired in comparison to the learning of group III. No significant difference was found between groups I and II, indicating that learning is similarly reduced whether or not the word is identified for the subject. A significant difference favoring the second grade was obtained for all instructional groups. The findings of this study suggest that a sound is more easily learned in an unfamiliar linguistic context and that

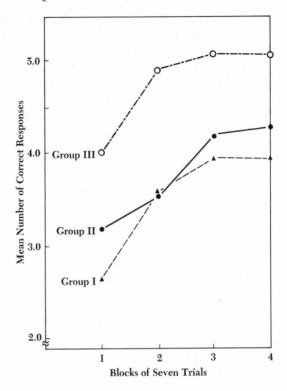

[**Figure 5.4**] Mean number of correct responses per block of seven trials for three groups of subjects learning the response /srɔb/: Group I, the word *shrub* was pronounced by the examiner, depicted pictorially, and subjects were told to say the word differently; Group II, the subjects were told to pronounce a word; and Group III, a picture of an unfamiliar object was shown, and subjects were told to learn the name of the object.
SOURCE: Winitz and Bellerose, 1965.

a sound may be more quickly acquired in the second than in the first grade (see Figure 5.5). It is important to emphasize that interference as discussed here refers to the acquisition stage of sound learning and not to the retention of an acquired sound in a word. Presumably interference factors operate after a sound has been learned in a word as well as when a sound is first acquired. The "word-interference" stage of learning will be discussed later in this chapter.

This study did not provide evidence to show that newly learned sounds in nonsense syllables will transfer to words in isolation and to words in

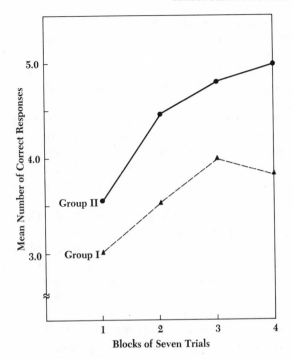

[Figure 5.5] Mean number of correct responses per
block of seven trials for subjects in grade one
(Group I) and grade two (Group II) learning the
response /srɔ́b/.
SOURCE: Winitz and Bellerose, 1965.

connected speech. The transference of sounds learned in nonsense syllable
material or in isolation to words in connected speech has continually
plagued clinicians. However, if nonsense words denoting an "unfamiliar"
object are used, sounds may be learned as part of a "linguistic unit." At
first a few nonsense objects may be learned; gradually others are acquired.
These "words" are then learned as units within sentences. Finally, when
the sounds within the nonsense words are highly learned in connected
speech, a few English words are introduced. Generalization of the newly
learned sounds in English words should then occur more rapidly than if
the nonsense word pretraining had not been done.

Motivation

The concept of motivation has previously been discussed. Drive was
described as a condition imposed on the organism which facilitates
learning. Primary drives, such as hunger and thirst, or secondary drives,

such as social deprivation and sensory deprivation, may be involved. A study that may have important implications for articulatory programming will now be discussed.

Gewirtz and Baer (1958) studied social reinforcement as a function of social deprivation. The subjects were first- and second-grade children. The goal of the study was to determine if social reinforcement would encourage more marble playing for children who were socially deprived as compared with children who were not socially deprived. The apparatus for this game was a boxlike panel with two holes on the top. When marbles were dropped in either of the two holes they fell through a chute to an open tray at the base of the panel. Several marbles were made available to the subjects.

Three groups were employed to test the hypothesis. Group I, the deprivation group, was left alone in a room for 20 minutes prior to playing the marble game; Group II, the nondeprivation group, played the marble game immediately upon their arrival; Group III, the satiation group, played with the experimenter, drew or cut out designs while the experimenter maintained a stream of friendly conversation for 20 minutes, and then played the marble game.

A base line period of marble dropping was established for 4 minutes, and then subjects were given 10 additional minutes during which time marbles dropped in one of the two holes were reinforced with phrases, such as *good, Hm-hmmm,* and *fine.*

The results of this study are shown in Figure 5.6. The "mean reinforcer effectiveness score," the ordinate of Figure 5.6, was calculated using the base line period as a reference for the number of correct responses. It

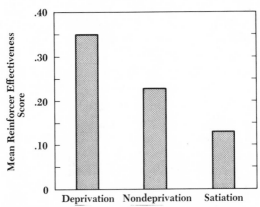

[Figure 5.6] A pictorial representation of the means for the three social groups employed by Gewirtz and Baer.

SOURCE: Gewirtz and Baer, 1958, Figure 2, p. 57.

may be interpreted as the mean gain in relative frequency of marble-dropping responses. It is clear from this graph that the "deprivation" condition enhances most effectively the social reinforcement of correct responses.

Gewirtz and Bear discuss the theoretical implications of their study and in particular point out that there is need for additional study of social reinforcers under a variety of drive and reinforcement conditions. We wish only to point out that articulatory acquisition, which involves considerable social reinforcement, may be increased if the child is placed in a nonsocial environment for about 20 minutes prior to his articulation lesson. A silent reading period or a painting period may serve as a deprivational experience.

Incentive Motivation

An additional variable that may play an important role in articulatory training is the magnitude of the reinforcer. The magnitude of the reinforcer has been discussed previously under incentive motivation and came to our attention when the theory of the r_g-s_g mechanism and its role in babbling behavior were presented. In instrumental reward conditioning, incentive motivation is determined, in part, by the magnitude of the reinforcer and, according to Spence (1960, p. 95), by the number of times a reinforcer follows a response.[5]

Speech clinicians are aware that reinforcement in general and social reinforcement in particular are effective agents in articulatory acquisition. Future research is needed to assess the reinforcing magnitude of social reinforcers in comparison to other reinforcers.

We have not discussed habit strength (H) as a separate programming area. It is obvious though that performance improves with the number of reinforced responses or the number of responses in a reinforcing situation (see Spence, 1960, pp. 95–97). Repetition of a response is a basic, clinical speech technique. However, repetition per se should be evaluated and assessed with regard to the acquisition task and with regard to the learning variables discussed previously and later.

Extinction

Extinction is defined by Kimble (1961, p. 281) as follows: "If the CS is repeatedly presented unaccompanied by the usual reinforcer, the CR undergoes a progressive decrement called extinction, and finally fails to occur." The theoretical nature of extinction and the variables influ-

---

[5] When consummatory time in the goal box was controlled, acquisition varied with time in the goal box rather than the gram weight of the pellet (Spence, 1956, pp. 137–148).

encing extinction have been discussed by Kimble (1961). One variable particularly pertinent to the study of articulatory extinction is *partial reinforcement*.

Partial reinforcement, in contrast to continuous reinforcement, refers to a reinforcement schedule wherein only a portion of all responses are reinforced. Resistance to extinction under partial reinforcement is greater than under continuous reinforcement; the greatest resistance occurs when approximately 50 percent of the correct responses are reinforced. Although the partial reinforcement effect has not been applied to articulatory learning, we can illustrate this effect with results obtained with other responses.

Jensen and Cotton (1960) report the findings of a partial reinforcement study involving one continuous reinforcement group and two different partial reinforcement groups. The subjects were rats which were given 30 trials in a runway for 9 consecutive days. On the first day all groups were continuously reinforced (100 percent schedule). On days 2 through 9 subjects in group "A" were rewarded on every trial (continuous reinforcement); subjects in groups "1E-1A" and "Random" were reinforced on 50 percent of the trials. Group 1E-1A was reinforced on an alternate schedule so arranged that the first trial of each day was not reinforced and the last trial was reinforced. Group Random received 15 rewarded and 15 nonrewarded trials according to a predetermined random schedule. On the tenth day all 30 trials were nonrewarded.

The results of this study are shown in Figure 5.7. It is apparent from this graph that extinction (day 10) occurs most rapidly for Group A (continuous reinforcement). It should also be noted that as training continues beyond the third day, Group A's speed in comparison to the speed of groups Random and 1E-1A becomes progressively worse.

There is practically no information on the long-term effects of partial reinforcement. We have one report from Skinner (1959, pp. 49–50) that a pecking response had not extinguished in one pigeon after four years:

> More than five years ago, twenty pigeons were conditioned to strike a large translucent key upon which a complex visual pattern was projected. Reinforcement was contingent upon the maintenance of a high and steady rate of responding and upon striking a particular feature of the visual pattern. These birds were set aside in order to study retention. They were transferred to the usual living quarters, where they served as breeders. Small groups were tested for extinction at the end of six months, one year, two years, and four years. Before the test each bird was transferred to a separate living cage. A controlled feeding schedule was used to reduce the weight to approximately 80 percent of the *ad lib* weight. The bird was then fed in the dimly lighted experimental apparatus in the absence of the key for sev-

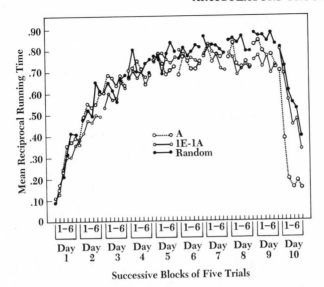

[Figure 5.7] Extinction as a function of three schedules of reinforcement: A, continuous; 1E-1A, alternate fifty percent reinforcement; and Random, random fifty percent reinforcement. The subjects were rats and mean reciprocal running time in seconds was used as the criterion measure. There were five trials per block and six blocks per day. SOURCE: Jensen and Cotton, 1960, Figure 1, p. 43.

eral days, during which emotional responses to the apparatus disappeared. On the day of the test the bird was placed in the darkened box. The translucent key was present but not lighted. No responses were made. When the pattern was projected upon the key, all four birds responded quickly and extensively. . . . [One] bird struck the key within two seconds after presentation of a visual pattern which it had not seen for four years, and at the precise spot upon which differential reinforcement had previously been based. It continued to respond for the next hour, emitting about 700 respones. This is of the order of one-half to one-quarter of the responses it would have emitted if extinction had not been delayed four years, but otherwise the curve is fairly typical.

The specific details for the partial reinforcement training were not given, although it was stated that some type of a partial reinforcement schedule was used.

Partial reinforcement effects have been studied also with verbal

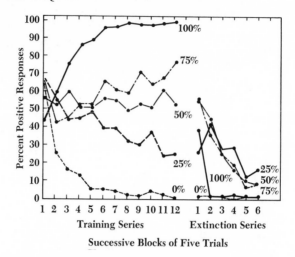

[Figure 5.8] Extinction of a verbal response for human subjects as a function of the schedule of reinforcement used during the training session. There were five trials per block.

SOURCE: Grant and others, 1951, Figure 1, p. 2.

responses. One study will be described. Grant and associates (1951) investigated the effect of 0, 25, 50, 75, and 100 percent reinforcement on guessed verbal responses. The subjects were seated before two lamps; they were instructed to guess on each trial, during the flash of the left lamp, whether the right lamp (positive response) would or would not flash on. The results are presented in Figure 5.8. In this graph acquisition is presented on the left side and extinction on the right side. From the acquisition curves it may be noted that the subjects' rate of positive responses gradually approaches the percentage of positive trials. During extinction the rate of emission of positive responses decreases. As may be noted, the drop is most rapid for the 100 percent group.

The results of the Grant study suggest that partial reinforcement retards extinction of verbal responses. If these findings and those of Jensen and Cotton (1960) are generalizable to articulatory responses, they would seem to suggest that sounds should be taught first on a continuous reinforcement schedule and then on a partial reinforcement schedule. Once a child has acquired a new sound, a partial reinforcement program should be instituted. This means that the child should be reinforced by the speech correctionist for only half of his correct responses. This regimen should be introduced systematically near the end of each clinical session.

One may question the relevance or usefulness of extinction theory for articulatory programming. Articulatory responses appear to be reconditioned continually; that is, once a response is well learned a child will continually use a newly learned response when he is not in the clinical setting. This is not true in the early stages of sound learning; the sound has not yet been incorporated into words and, therefore, it cannot be continually reconditioned. However, in the later stages of sound learning the sound is used in words outside of the clinical session. In many cases the correct utterance of one word may not be reinforced differentially; i.e., parents and peers may respond, for the most part, to correct utterances as they do to incorrect utterances. Thus in this respect the effects of partial reinforcement and distribution of practice may well be used to maintain more readily newly learned sound responses in words from one clinical session to another.

Delay of Reinforcement

In our discussion of the technique of successive approximation learning it was suggested by Skinner that conditioning occurs more rapidly when responses are reinforced immediately after they occur. It has been generally shown that for animals delay of reinforcement impedes the acquisition of a task (Kimble, 1961, pp. 140–155). This is because, as Skinner has suggested, responses which occur during the delay interval, after the correct response has occurred, are often reinforced. According to Spence (1956, pp. 154–164) the subject's attention to the goal box is lessened during the delay interval. When the reinforcement is not immediate, confining of a rat within a small area should theoretically reduce competing responses; that is, within certain time limits the rat's orientation to the goal box should be maintained. Spence reports confirmation of this hypothesis. The findings are presented in Figure 5.9. In this figure acquisition curves for confinement (C) and unconfinement (UC) for zero and ten-second delay intervals are presented. It is clear from the results of Figure 5.9 that there is no difference between the speed of learning for the confined and unconfined groups for zero delay but that the confined and unconfined groups differ for the ten-second delay; the confined group does better than the unconfined group.

Recent research with children and adults has suggested that when the delay interval is less than about 30 seconds it may not always impair learning (see Brackbill, 1964, and Etzel and Wright, 1964, for example). In some instances it has been reported that a delay interval will improve retention (Brackbill, 1964). In summary, then, delay of reward is an interesting variable that deserves attention by those interested in articulatory programming.

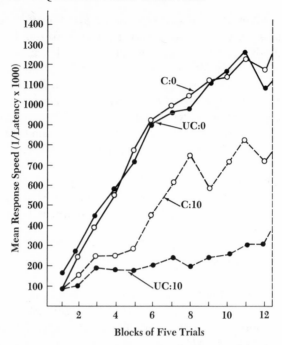

[Figure 5.9] Bar pressing as a joint function of delay of reward and confinement. The subjects were rats and they delayed either 0 or 10 seconds in a confined (C) or in an unconfined area (UC). The data are reported in blocks of five trials and the response criterion is the reciprocal of the time it took for the subject to respond.
SOURCE: Spence, 1956.

Latency of Response

The interval of time from the onset of a stimulus to the occurrence of a conditioned response is defined as *response latency*. This measure is sometimes employed as an index of learning or response strength. In some cases response latency may be manipulated by the experimenter. For example, subjects may be told to respond to a stimulus after a certain time interval has elapsed. This time interval may be systematically varied and its effect on learning can be studied.

Romans and Milisen (1954) have manipulated latency in an experiment with speech sounds. Several non-English sounds were employed. These sounds were described as follows: (1) labial-lingual-plosive, (2) lingual-trill, (3) uvular-fricative, (4) forced-labial-fricative, (5) lingual-alveolar-

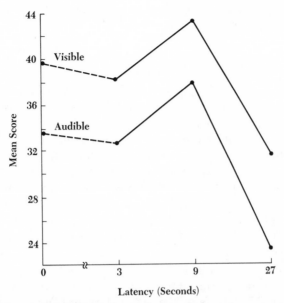

[**Figure 5.10**] Speech and sound learning curves for four latency items and for two types of stimulus procedures.
SOURCE: Romans and Milisen, 1954.

click, and (6) lateral /s/. Sixth-, seventh, and eighth-grade subjects were asked to repeat these sounds as they were produced by the experimenter. The subjects were able to see and hear the experimenter. No reinforcement, however, was given for correct responses. The sounds were presented five consecutive times in the above order; the procedure was repeated, making a total of 60 trials. For each production both visual and auditory responses were evaluated. Latency intervals of 0, 3, 9, and 27 seconds were employed.

The findings are presented in Figure 5.10. As may be observed from this figure a latency interval of 9 seconds produced the greatest number of correct responses for both the visible and audible evaluations. However, the differences between the 0 and 9-second latencies for both visible and audible evaluations were not found to be significant.

In addition Romans and Milisen compared the first 30 trials with the second 30 trials. For all latency periods the number of correct responses increased from the first to the second set of 30 trials. Therefore, learning did occur. The authors, however, conclude that learning occurred without reinforcement of correct responses. It is possible, of course, that subtle social expressions inadvertently made by the experimenter served as reinforcers. On the other hand, older-aged subjects may be able to evaluate their own responses as correct or incorrect; that is, their own evaluations are by definition self-reinforcing.

Retention

It might be useful at this point to make a distinction between two stages of articulatory learning, *response integration* and *response association* (Underwood and Postman, 1960). Response integration refers to the acquisition of articulatory responses; it is the learning period during which articulatory responses become available to the child. In this stage, children with omission or substitution errors are first taught to articulate correctly a sound which they do not currently possess. In some cases, of course, the child may possess the sound but in only a small number of contexts. In this case response-integration learning refers to the voluntary production of a response in "isolation" or in a nonsense syllable or in a nonsense "word."

As mentioned, an available articulatory response needs to be learned as an item in a word and retained in the word when it is used in connected speech. That is, once the articulatory response can be produced voluntarily it must then be "associated" (learned) and retained in words and later in words that occur in continuous discourse. Because different behavioral laws may govern this second phase of learning (Underwood, 1961; Postman, 1961), a phase which is most important for speech sound learning, it is necessary to make this distinction.

Before considering the implications of learning theory for articulatory retention three variables generally conceded to play a role in retention will be mentioned. The first is that of the degree of original learning, the second pertains to the retention interval, and the third involves the spacing of trials during acquisition.

The higher the degree of original learning and the shorter the retention interval, the greater the retention, other things being equal; this is a well-documented fact, and we have one study with articulatory responses that corroborates it. In this study (Rice and Milisen, 1954) degree of learning was defined as the number of reinforced trials. The subjects were high school students and their task was to learn three non-English sounds (voiced bilabial fricative, voiced linguo-alveolar fricative, and unvoiced soft palatal fricative).

Three groups of subjects were employed. The subjects in each group were administered five consecutive trials for each of the three sounds. All correct responses were reinforced. After the five trials were completed for the first sound, the subjects were asked to produce the sound for 15 consecutive times. Stimulation and reinforcement were not provided for these 15 production trials. This same procedure was followed for the second and third sounds. The mean score for these 45 utterances was used as a basal score. The subjects were then assigned to three different groups. Subjects in Group I received no more training, but subjects in Groups II and III received additional training on the sounds. Group II was given five additional trials on each sound, and Group III was given 15 additional trials on each sound. All correct responses were reinforced.

The subjects in each group were then asked to produce each sound, without stimulation for 15 consecutive trials one hour later and 72 hours later. The results indicated that retention was less 72 hours (fewer responses were recalled) after training than one hour after training for all three groups. It is possible that correct responses may have been extinguished during the first test interval (one hour later), since reinforcement was not provided during this test interval, thus reducing the scores for the 72-hour period. For both time intervals the additional training was monotonically related to the number of responses recalled; that is, Group III recalled more responses than Group II, and Group II recalled more responses than Group I.

The implications of this study for articulatory teaching are, of course, obvious. One implication is that retention intervals need to be examined so that, within practical limits, maximum potential is made of a child's ability to recall speech sounds. If, for example, research findings demonstrate that retention deteriorates markedly after three or four days, then the intervals between speech sessions should be reduced.

The recent study by Shelton, Arndt and Elbert (1967) is relevant here. As described on p. 291, the children in this investigation received instruction on the /r/ sound for about eight weeks, two days per week (Tuesday and Thursday). Each session lasted about 20 minutes. Retention was tested by a 30-item imitative articulation test composed of syllables, words, and sentences. Testing was conducted prior to and following each clinic session. The six subjects showed practically no loss of sound responses, as measured by this test, for both the two-day and five-day intervals.

Posttesting was conducted one week, one month, and five months following the close of articulation instruction and, judging from the curves of the individual subjects, forgetting was not as great as one might expect. In fact the five-month posttest showed no significant decline.

Two methodological procedures seem to distinguish this study from the Rise and Milisen study, namely presentation rather than nonpresentation of the stimulus and repeated rather than nonrepeated test material. An imitation task, practically speaking, resembles the assessment procedures of retention from clinic session to clinic session, while a nonimitative task seems to measure retention from clinic session to speaking situation. Possibly retention is not a critical factor (judging from the findings of Shelton, Elbert and Arndt) from clinic session to clinic session for imitative tasks. This remark is made with reservation, since the retention scores were averages, either for the 20 week session or for one-third segments of the 20 weeks, or about 7 weeks. Conceivably, the retention interval may be a critical factor for nonimitative productions of the acquisition phase as well as for imitative and nonimitative productions of the response association phase. See the discussion below for a description of the acquisition and associative phases of articulatory learning.

Another implication of the above studies is that levels of original learning need to be defined for various retention intervals and for various generalization tasks. The intertrial acquisition intervals and their relationship to retention have been investigated in a host of studies (McGeoch and Irion, 1952, and Underwood, 1961). When trials are closely spaced, the condition is referred to as *massed practice*; when trials are not closely spaced, the condition is called *distributed practice*. The effect of distributed practice on retention varies with regard to the task, the acquisition interval, the retention interval, and the degree of response interference. This effect needs to be studied in order to assess its worthwhileness as a variable in retarding the forgetting of articulatory responses.

In the section on extinction we stated that response associations are difficult to retain because newly learned responses either are not used or are continually extinguished outside of the clinical setting. There is another way of looking at this forgetting process. Possibly new articulatory responses are forgotten because the old responses, the incorrect articulatory responses, are relearned outside of the clinical setting. Relearning would seem to involve not only unlearning or extinction of the correct response but also interference or competition from the correct response (Postman, 1961).

Forgetting as a function of intervening activity has been termed retroactive inhibition or retroactive interference. As defined by McGeoch and Irion (1952, p. 404), these terms refer to a "decrement in retention resulting from activity, usually a learning activity, interpolated between an original learning and a later measurement of retention."

Several findings in verbal learning (Underwood, 1957; Underwood and Postman, 1960; Postman, 1961, 1963, and 1964) would seem to suggest an alternative interpretation for understanding why newly learned articulatory responses are quickly forgotten. According to this point of view, new articulatory responses are forgotten because old articulatory responses regain strength during the retention interval. This situation which fosters forgetting is referred to as *proactive inhibition*; that is, interference "may occur as a consequence of learning which had occurred prior to the learning of the task to be recalled" (Underwood and Postman, 1960, p. 73). The study of proactive interference is not new, but Underwood and Postman (1960) suggest an exciting and novel approach to the study of this problem. This area of study is referred to as "extraexperimental sources of interference," and it pertains to the identification of competing verbal habits that the subject may bring to the learning situation.

In the study of articulatory retention, proactive inhibition seems to be a more potent inhibitor than retroactive inhibition. To be sure, both sources of interference presumably operate during a specified retention interval. However, it would seem that the use of old articulatory responses outside of the clinical setting (retroactive inhibition) would seem to account for considerably less of the total amount of attrition, especially when the retention interval is only a few days. That is, recovery of the old response (or forgetting of the new response) would presumably occur if no intervening articulatory behavior (or related behavior) occurred.

Let us schematize the forgetting processes of retroactive and proactive inhibition, and extinction. We will assume that a young child has come to a speech clinic with a /w/ for /r/ substitution and that he has been taught to utter /r/ for /w/ in one or more words. When he returns to the clinic the /w/ error has returned. We will illustrate the three forgetting processes with four response stages—preclinic, clinic, outside clinic, and retention (return to clinic):

	PRECLINIC	CLINIC	OUTSIDE CLINIC	RETENTION (RETURN TO CLINIC)
1. Extinction	/w/ for /r/	/r/ for /w/	/r/ is extinguished	/w/ is uttered for /r/
2. Retroactive Inhibition	/w/ for /r/	/r/ for /w/	/w/ is used	/w/ is uttered for /r/
3. Proactive Inhibition	/w/ for /r/	/r/ for /w/	/w/ is not used	/w/ is uttered for /r/

The first forgetting process is simply extinction. The /r/ sound is extinguished because correct /r/ responses are not reinforced differentially. By differential reinforcement we mean that correct /r/ responses would need to be noticed and, therefore, praised by the child's parents or peers. Presumably correct /r/ responses are simply accepted and, therefore, not differentially reinforced. The /w/ returns because this is the response that was previously used and previously reinforced. Or perhaps the /r/ has not generalized to nonclinical settings; the stimulus conditions of the nonclinical environment do not elicit the /r/ appropriately, and thus /w/ is consistently produced for /r/. Since the stimulus elements of the clinical environment are a proper subset of the general speaking environment, we could conceive of forgetting, in this case, as following some generalization principles. That is to say, the use of /w/ outside of the clinical setting generalizes to other speaking situations, the clinic being one of these.

In the second forgetting process (retroactive inhibition) conflicting associations learned outside the clinic are involved. We will assume for the moment that extinction, the process described above, is not taking place. This forgetting process is initiated by the fact that there is a large physical difference between the stimulus settings of the clinic and the activities outside the clinic. The two environments are so different that stimulus conditions do not promote the correct use of the /r/ response outside of the clinic. Thus the use of the /w/ sound will retroactively interfere with the retention of the /r/ sound. Retroactive interference, as we will see, is probably of minor significance in the retention of newly learned /r/ responses.

The third forgetting process to be illustrated is proactive inhibition—the other forgetting processes will be discounted for the moment. After the /r/ has been highly learned in the clinic, the /w/ is again used outside of the clinic and is not retained when the child returns to the clinic. Why? Because the /w/ interferes proactively with the retention of /r/. This loss of the /r/ response would occur presumably if the child had not talked until he returned to the clinic.

The powerful interference of previously learned responses may be illustrated by the following hypothetical example. Let us say you were told that the pronunciation of the first five digits was incorrect. Instead you were to substitute the following terms:

1. *vap* for *one*
2. *so* for *two*
3. *mep* for *three*
4. *dup* for *four*
5. *zent* for *five*

Let us also assume that you learned these new terms after considerable practice with numerical problems and that your work was so arranged that no use of numbers was made during the next two weeks (a truly impossible situation). You were then asked to use these new names for the first five digits. You would experience considerable difficulty in doing so. This difficulty would, in part, be related to the fact that the degree of original learning was much greater for the first list than for the second one. Now let us assume that the original learning of the two sets of digit numbers was the same. If you were asked to use one list in preference to the other, you would still have difficulty, at least in the early phase of such a task, as the symbols for each of the five digits would tend to be elicited equally. Each member of the five pairs of names would be continually interfering with its partner. You could, of course, learn two names for each of the five numbers if you needed to use the labels interchangeably or under different stimulus settings (see the ensuing discussion of differentiation). This, of course, is not the goal of articulatory training.

Aside from adding a new dimension to the theoretical notions of articulatory forgetting, does this new interpretation suggest approaches that may be effective in improving articulatory retention? It does seem to say that our concern, at least in the early stages of articulatory response association, should not be exclusively centered on the intervening articulatory behavior, but rather, it should be directed toward an attempt to equate the strength of the old and new responses.

One way to accomplish this equalization may be through the use of paired-associate learning. Let us again assume that a subject's substitution error is /w/ for /r/ and also assume that the subject has learned to say /r/ correctly and has mastered this sound in words that occur infrequently in English. The critical task that confronts the subject is that of using the /r/ sound in connected speech in those words in which he has mastered the /r/. Before the subject learns to do this, however, he must be able to distinguish easily (rapidly) the correct and incorrect use of this sound in connected speech. At this time it seems important to introduce the term *differentiation*. Differentiation "refers to the subject's ability to discriminate between correct and incorrect responses and thus to reject errors at the time of recall" (Postman, 1963). Recent evidence seems to suggest that differentiation is "maximal when all the competing responses are high in the subject's response hierarchy" (Postman, 1963, p. 43).

How can maximal differentiation be accomplished to provide for high retention in connected speech of newly learned articulatory responses? One obvious way seems to be through the continued strengthening of new responses by repeated practice in the clinical setting. However, it would seem that maximal discrimination might be accomplished more easily with the introduction of mediating discriminative stimuli. The term *proactive facilitation* might also be appropriate here.

Mediating discriminative stimuli are introduced by teaching a paired-associate learning task which consists of pairs of stimulus words, minimal pairs, that contain the /w/-/r/ contrast—e.g., /roʊd/-/woʊd/; /rɔ́n/-/wɔ́n/; /ræbət/-/wæbət/. This may be done by having the child utter the correct word when he hears the incorrect word. Lists might contain four or five pairs. Gradually other paired lists are also learned. It is assumed, then, that the high association between the paired items will provide discriminative mediating stimuli which will permit differentiation of incorrect responses that are to be uttered (or have been uttered). That is, when the child is about to say /woʊd/ for *road* the /woʊd/ will elicit the mediating stimulus /roʊd/ which will permit "differentiation" between the correct response and the incorrect response. Evidence provided by verbal learning experiments suggests this to be a feasible and pragmatic approach (Bugelski and Scharlock, 1952; Russell and Storms, 1955).

Other variables that may facilitate retention of articulatory responses are suggested by the verbal learning experiments. We suggest that detailed exploration of the following variables be considered: (*a*) retention interval, (b) frequency of occurrence of the words used, (c) degree of original learning of new responses, and (d) distribution of practice.[6]

Teaching Machine

A teaching machine may be defined as a device or instrument which facilitates or makes possible the presentation of a program. When a program is selected the teaching machine permits the subject to learn at his own rate and often without the assistance of a teacher.

We have developed a speech sound teaching machine for both discrimination and sound learning.[7] The front panel of the machine is presented in Figure 5.11.

In the left center position of the front panel is a tape deck with a four-channel magnetic tape head. On the tape deck is a continuously running tape loop. Above the tape deck are four record buttons; with these buttons four previously recorded sounds are recorded onto the tape loop. On the lower right are four buttons, corresponding to each of the four sounds, for sound playout.

The top part of the panel has 64 channels, each channel corresponding to one learning trial. The channels are arranged in two rows of 32 channels. Each channel is composed of four vertical jacks and an indicator light. One of four previously recorded sounds may be played on each of the 64 trials. Illumination of the indicator light denotes the trial on which the sound is being played. On the lower right side of the panel, channels are provided for programming the two bars of the discrimination apparatus. The discrimination device was described in Chapter 3.

A discrimination learning program is made by placing a plug in one of the four jacks of each channel. For example, for the two sounds /s/ and /v/ the procedure would be as follows: (a) record /s/ and /v/ on the tape loop; (b) make up a random sequence of /s/ and /v/ with whatever restrictions are desired, such as three /s/ sounds and three /v/ sounds in a block of six trials; and (c) whenever /v/ is to be played, place a plug in the first row, and whenever /s/ is to be played, place a plug in the second row. The discrimination sequence pictured in Figure 5.11 is for two

---

[6] Retention may also be facilitated by coordinating articulation training with reading. Words that occur frequently in reading lessons may be used to heighten the strength of newly acquired sounds (response integration) and also provide instances for the transference of sounds (response association) into utterances units that are very similar to connected speech.

[7] The electronic teaching machine was designed and built by Mr. Wes Heisey. Funds for the support of this machine were provided by U.S. Public Health Grant M-3987, the University of Kansas, and the Kellogg Foundation. The latter grant was under the auspices of Dr. David S. Ruhe, Department of Medical Communications, University of Kansas Medical Center.

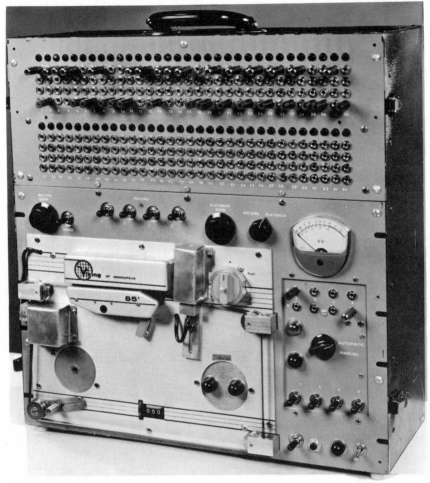

[**Figure 5.11**] Teaching machine.

sounds recorded on the first and fourth rows for the first 32 trials. The tape speed is 7.5 inches per second and the interval between sounds is about five seconds.

Thus for the program shown in Figure 5.11, the two bars of the discrimination apparatus are programmed for rows one and four. Correct discriminatory responses are immediately reinforced by electronic relays, and the number of correct responses can be recorded automatically in blocks of trials.

This instrument may also be used to teach phonetic responses. In so doing it provides the unique feature of having any one of four previously recorded responses immediately available to the clinician. The same four-track tape loop is used, but this time the clinician, rather than the automatic relay system, controls the playout of the sounds. Thus the clinician can press one of four buttons playing out one of four previously recorded sounds in any desired sequence. The sequence is determined, for the most part, by the program itself. This is a feature that cannot be handled with the ordinary tape recorder. However, with this arrangement the clinician can change from one sound to the next as might be appropriate for the individual subject. The reinforcement is administered manually by pressing the button in the lower right panel (see Figure 5.11). Social reinforcers, such as "good" and "ok" may also be used.

Some Programming Studies

We have already discussed several learning studies, by Winitz and Lawrence (1961), Winitz and Bellerose (1962, 1963), and Romans and Milisen (1954), that have contributed to our knowledge and methods of studying articulatory programming. Several additional studies have been completed which compare teaching methods.

The first two studies involved comparisons among several stimulus procedures for teaching speech sounds. Scott and Milisen (1954a) studied the effect of visual, auditory, and combined visual-auditory stimulation. Subjects were children with defective articulation; they ranged in age from 4 to 14 years. The following eight sounds were selected for study: /r/, /l/, /s/, /z/, /k/, /g/, /f/, and /v/. Subjects were first tested for correct production of these sounds in response to pictures. Then each subject was asked to repeat only those sounds found to be defective using the following stimulus methods: combined visual and auditory stimulation, visual stimulation alone, and auditory stimulation alone. Visual cues were concealed from the subject by having the examiner cover his mouth. Auditory cues were controlled by having the examiner produce the sound without vocalization. Sounds were stimulated in isolation.

The authors found that the combined visual and auditory stimulation method was only slightly more effective than the audible stimulation method for all sounds including the sounds /f/ and /v/ which are readily visible. Visual stimulation was about as effective as auditory stimulation for the voiceless sounds, but it was not as effective as auditory stimulation for the voiced sounds. One would expect this finding, since the voiced and voiceless cognates would be similarly imitated when the stimuli were visual models.

Humphrey and Milisen (1954) investigated the effectiveness of the same three methods of stimulation, as well as reconditioning and retention, upon sound production for nine non-English sounds.[8] Visible responses were scored for six of the sounds that were visible, and audible responses were scored for all nine sounds. It should be recognized that a sound perceived by an examiner as auditorily correct, but visually incorrect, is a phonetic contradiction. For example, a voiceless fronto-palatal fricative scored as auditorily correct for the [θ] sound reflects the naïveté of the examiner. The voiceless fronto-palatal fricative [ç] can be distinguished from [θ] by individuals who have had training in the phonetics of foreign sounds.

College freshmen were given thirty stimulations per sound, per stimulus method. They did not respond after each stimulation but after each of three successive stimulations. Thus ten responses for each sound per stimulus method were evaluated. The results indicated that when all nine sounds were evaluated auditorily, the combined visual and auditory stimulation was no more effective than auditory stimulation alone. When the three visible and three partially visible sounds were evaluated visually, the number of correct responses was about the same for the combined effects of visual and auditory stimulation as for visual stimulation alone.

Thus far it seems that the additional stimulation provided by a second sensory modality (in addition to the major sensory modality) does not contribute greatly to increased effectiveness of sound learning for both visible and nonvisible sounds. These findings are essentially in agreement with the study reported immediately above. In addition, the results of

---

[8] The authors described the sounds as follows:

Visible

1. Unvoiced, bilabial, friction sound produced by compressing the lips and forcing air between them.

2. Voiced, upper labial, lower dental sound produced by exploding the air through an opening between the teeth and lip.

3. Voiced, bilabial, friction sound produced by blowing a stream of air between lips which were approximated.

Partially Visible

4. Medial lingual, hard palate, explosive click produced by sucking air into the oral cavity as the tongue is quickly lowered.

5. Voiced, lingual, alveolar, friction sound produced by folding the tip of the tongue under and forcing the top of the tongue against the alveolar ridge and teeth. The air forced between this focal articulation point sounded like a distortion between the [z] and [ʒ].

6. Voiced, lingual, medial hard palate, friction sound produced by flattening the tongue parallel with the hard palate and about a quarter-inch behind the alveolar ridge. The air stream was forced between a loose focal articulation point.

Nonvisible

7. Voiced, posterior lingual, soft palate, explosive sound produced by forcing the back portion of the tongue against the soft palate and quickly lowering it.

8. Unvoiced, soft palate, friction sound produced by forcing air against a relaxed soft palate. The sound, produced by the vibrations of the velum, passes through the nasal and the oral cavities.

9. Posterior lingual, pharyngeal, explosive sound produced by sucking air inward by enlarging the pharynx while the tongue breaks contact with the pharynx (Humphrey and Milisen, 1954, p. 59).

this study showed that visual stimulation is not as effective as auditory stimulation and auditory and visual stimulation combined in eliciting correct audible responses (based on all nine sounds); and auditory stimulation is not as effective as visual stimulation and visual and auditory stimulation combined for eliciting correct visual responses for the visible and partially visible sounds.

It would, of course, have been nice if all sounds were evaluated as correct both visually and auditorily. Since this was not done, let us assume that a sound evaluated as correct auditorily was correctly produced. Then the results of this study as well as the previous one do not clearly indicate that the learning of new sounds or the correction of old sounds is substantially aided by the addition of visual stimulation. This conclusion, if supported by future research, would mean that teaching machines need not include a component which presents sounds visually. It should be mentioned, however, that feedback was not administered, either auditory or visual, in these two studies. Combined auditory and visual feedback may prove to be more effective than auditory feedback alone.

The subjects in this study (Humphrey and Milisen, 1954) were tested for retention fourteen days later. They were asked to say without stimulation all the sounds they could remember. Those visible responses most quickly recalled were produced correctly most often during the learning session for all three stimulation conditions. This relation, however, was not found for auditory responses. After the recall session the sound tasks were administered again. There was general evidence for reconditioning under all three stimulus conditions; that is, subjects responded to stimulation with a greater number of correct responses at this time than when the stimuli were originally presented.

A third study involved comparisons between the "linguistic" units within which the sound was being stimulated. Scott and Milisen (1954b) studied the relative effectiveness of the combined visual and auditory stimulation method when the sounds were uttered in isolation,[9] in nonsense syllables, and in words. The subjects and the test sounds were the same as those used by Scott and Milisen (1954a) in the first study reported in this section. For the nonsense syllables and words each sound was stimulated in the initial, medial, and final positions. A child was given three stimulation opportunities to produce the sound correctly in each sound-test condition. Only those subjects who produced the sound incorrectly in the picture articulation test were stimulated.

The results are summarized as follows:

---

[9] The difference between a sound uttered in isolation and in a nonsense syllable is not always clear, especially when the sounds are stops.

With but one exception, [1], there were greater percentages of correct responses following stimulation of
a sound in isolation than there were at any other level
of the stimulation test. Except for one sound, [r], there
were greater percentages of correct responses in the
initial position of nonsense syllables than there were in
the initial position of words. Except for the [r] sound,
there were greater percentages of correct responses in
the medial position of nonsense syllables than there
were in the medial position of words. Except for three
sounds, [r s z], there were greater percentages of correct responses in the final position of nonsense syllables
than there were in the final position of words. Except
for the [f] and [z] sounds, there were greater percentages of correct responses in the initial position of
words than there were in the medial or final positions of
words. For the [f k s z] sounds, there were greater percentages of correct responses in the final position of
words than there were in the medial position; for the
sounds [v g r l] there were greater percentages of correct responses in the medial position of words than there
were in the final position (Scott and Milisen, 1954b, pp.
54–55).

These findings appear to support the results obtained by Winitz and
Bellerose (1965) in that a greater proportion of the children tested correctly produced, for the most part, sounds in nonsense syllables and in
isolation than sounds which were part of words. It would appear, then,
that there is now substantial evidence to indicate that sounds are more
easily learned (learned with fewer trials) when they are not taught as
part of an English word.

The findings of Scott and Milisen also suggest that new sounds may be
more easily acquired in the initial position than in the medial or final word
positions. However, in this study there is no description of the syllables
or words within which the sounds were tested; thus, we cannot determine
whether the sounds stimulated in the medial position were syllable initial
or syllable final. Further research is needed to determine the relative
importance of syllable versus linguistic position.

A question often raised by speech clinicians is that of the order of the
sounds to be taught. From the results of this study we may have a partial
answer to that question if we assume that those to be taught first are
those most easily learned. Then for the following eight sounds the order
of teaching would be /f/, /k/, /v/, /g/, /l/, /z/, /s/, and /r/, since this
was the relative order of improvement for these sounds.

The effectiveness of several instructional and evaluative methods was
tested in a fourth study (Webb and Siegenthaler, 1957). Three experimental sounds were used. They were described as (a) an umlauted [u],

(b) a lingually trilled [r], and (c) a lateral [ʃ]. The subjects were third-grade children. Six experimental conditions were used. They were as follows:

> A. *Stimulation only.* The subject heard the experimental syllable and said it immediately thereafter for each of 25 trials.
>
> B. *Stimulation and evaluation.* The subject heard the experimental syllable and said it immediately thereafter for each of 25 trials; if he said the new sound correctly, a light in front of him went on, i.e., each attempt was evaluated for him.
>
> C. *Stimulation and hearing of self.* The subject heard the experimental syllable, said it immediately thereafter, and heard his own production played back one second later for each of 25 trials.
>
> D. *Stimulation with spaced practice and evaluation.* The subject heard the experimental syllable five times and said it once; if he made the new sound correctly, a light in front of him went on. The sequence was repeated five times. [Scores for subjects in this group were multiplied by five to facilitate comparisons among groups.]
>
> E. *Stimulation with simultaneous production and evaluation.* The subject heard and simultaneously said the experimental syllable for each of 25 trials; if he made the new sound correctly, a light in front of him went on. (The stimulus intensity was raised to mask the subject's hearing of his own speech. Subjects learned to say the syllable simultaneously with hearing it after several practice trials with another syllable.)
>
> F. *Stimulation and verbal instruction.* The subject heard the experimental syllable and said it immediately thereafter. After eight repetitions, verbal instructions were given regarding how to produce the new sound; if the subject was already correctly performing, he was urged to continue what he had been doing. Care was taken to avoid giving acoustic examples of the sound to be learned during the instructions. Verbal instructions were given again after the sixteenth repetition, and nine additional repetitions were done (Webb and Siegenthaler, 1957, pp. 265-266).

For sounds combined the rank order for mean number of correct responses by methods was:

> 1. F. Stimulation and verbal instruction
> 2. B. Stimulation and evaluation
> 3. D. Stimulation with spaced practice and evaluation
> 4. C. Stimulation and hearing of self
> 5. A. Stimulation only
> 6. E. Stimulation with simultaneous production and evaluation.

However, some methods were more effective for one sound than for another. Method E (stimulation with simultaneous production and evaluation), however, was least effective for all sounds. The fact that method B (stimulation and evaluation) was superior to method C (stimulation and hearing of self) would suggest that (a) the clinician's evaluation is more reliable than the subject's evaluation and/or (b) reinforcement from the clinician provides greater incentive motivation than self-reinforcement for the subjects of this study. The findings also suggest that verbal instruction and clinician evaluation are effective techniques.

The authors did not include a group that received both clinical evaluation and subject's hearing of his own response (methods B and C combined). This method, if studied, could prove to be more effective than all of the methods used in this study.

These several programming studies, as well as the few others mentioned elsewhere in this chapter, are the first attempts by individuals in our field to study some of the important behavioral manipulations that are currently being practiced or can be practiced in the clinical session. Without reviewing the findings of these studies here, the author simply wishes to make two points. First, the programming studies indicate that articulatory responses may be modified and that some methods of modification are more effective than others. Second, they suggest that principles of learning—reinforcement, extinction, etc.—may be applied to articulatory responses. It is hoped that in the next decade articulatory research conducted within this general behavioral framework will be an appealing area for many investigators.

Articulation Testing for Programming

The testing procedures discussed in Chapter 4 were concerned with four kinds of articulatory testing—proficiency, development, diagnosis, and prediction. A fifth testing objective involves program selection. The choice of a suitable program for a particular child is based on the child's responses to a detailed articulation test. We have not designed any of these tests, as yet; therefore, examples of test protocols cannot be given. It will become clear below that a number of test protocols can be developed. The test which is administered to an individual child will, of course, depend upon the child's present response errors and other factors such as age. The program selected for teaching will be determined by the child's performance on the articulatory test for programming.

Let us assume that an articulatory proficiency test was administered to a young child and it was found that the /s/ was defective in both singles and blends. Our first task would be to assess the child's discrimination ability. Our emphasis, derived from the discussion of discrimination in

Chapter 3, would be to examine a child's discrimination of the correct sound and the error sound using minimal pairs and contrasting nonsense syllables. The teaching machine may even be employed in this phase of the testing. If the child has difficulty discriminating the correct sound from the error sound, then a regimen of sound discrimination training would be planned.

Our second task might be to ascertain whether the error is a highly consistent one. One reason for testing error consistency is apparent: stimulus-response generalization procedures might be used to transfer the correct production of the sound to those contexts where it is in error. We would test for the following:

Correct production of /s/ in:

> a. nonsense syllables
> b. infrequent words
> c. pre- and/or postinternal open juncture,
>   as in /base + ball/ and /buzz + saw/[10]
> d. initial, medial, or final word positions

Our third task might be to determine the ease with which the defective /s/ sound may be modified. We would test whether the /s/ sound could be imitated correctly after few stimulus trials.

Fourth, if the sound is not easily modified or is not produced correctly in any contexts, then we might wish to determine if the child produces the distinctive features essential for the production of this sound. In a sense this would be a modified phoneme system analysis. We would determine whether:

> a. The voiced-voiceless contrast is used and whether
>   voicelessness occurs as a phonetic feature.
> b. The stop-fricative contrast is used and whether
>   frication occurs as a phonetic feature.

Other analyses similar to these two can, of course, be made.

The fifth question we might ask concerns the type of error(s). Are the errors substitutions and/or omissions, and if so what are they? This inquiry might lead to a program of successive approximations for teaching the /s/ sound.

No doubt other questions may be asked. The foregoing supply a representative sampling of the general type of questions that may be employed

---

[10] Internal open junctures, phonemically transcribed as "+" marks, are short pauses that occur between syllables. Sometimes words are distinguished by these short pauses—e.g., nitrate versus nit + rate and a + name versus an + aim.

to determine the appropriate articulatory program for this child. It is apparent that considerable work needs to be done in this area of articulatory testing. In most instances, the programmed articulation tests will simply be a by-product of the results obtained from the research on articulatory programming. For example, we might test whether or not an adult can produce an inspirated snore before we would use the first of the two programs for the [χ] sound described above.

Testing for programming seems to be a lengthy and detailed operation. It also seems to increase greatly the complexity of the clinician's testing procedures as well as requiring proficiency in program selection. We think, however, that in this case the end will justify the means.

Another point that needs consideration is the problem of program proliferation. It might seem that eventually many programs could be developed —perhaps as many programs as there are children with articulatory errors. This state of affairs would, of course, lead to the dissolution of standardized programs. Programs need to be developed that are general enough for a good proportion of the children with a particular sound in error and yet specific enough to provide for rapid acquisition by an individual. Articulatory testing for programming will facilitate the selection of one program from a variety of available programs.

Finally, program selection would need to be made in light of several additional clinical factors. The most important of these is initial success for the child. Sounds, which testing reveals may be corrected in the shortest period of time, should be selected first as those to be taught. If parents question the clinician's choice, they should be advised and counseled. The choice of the second sound may be made in terms of the generalization principles we have discussed.

Child-Child Interaction

In articulation teaching sessions children are often assembled into small groups. The reasons are many, ranging from economic expediency to the benefits accrued from group therapeutics. We would assume that there is value in group articulatory therapy if for no other reason than for the child to obtain proficiency of newly learned sounds in conversation with his peers.

Articulatory learning may, in some cases, be facilitated by assigning children to groups on the basis of certain behavioral and physical characteristics. There is general evidence to indicate that, for adults, homogeneity of behavior—such as IQ, age, educational level—plays an important part in interpersonal attraction. Rosenberg, Spradlin, and Mabel (1961) have found that the prior language performance of mentally retarded adolescents affected substantially their interpersonal language behavior when the subjects were assembled in dyads.

In this study subjects from an institute for mental retardates were tested on the Parsons Language Sample (Spradlin, 1963), a test used to assess very primitive kinds of verbal behavior. From the results of this test subjects were designated as high (H) in linguistic skills or low (L) in linguistic skills. H subjects' Wechsler Verbal IQ's ranged from 45 to 82. None of the L subjects could be tested on this IQ test. The subjects in both groups were originally drawn from a large population of mentally retarded children who ranged in age from 12 years 11 months to 15 years.

The children were assembled in pairs forming the following four dyads: H–H, H–L, L–H, and L–L. (The H–L and L–H groups do not constitute different experimental groups; the duplication of the assembly was dictated by the experimental design.) The groups were formed from a row (H and L) by column (H and L) matrix with the restriction that row subjects were never paired with row subjects and column subjects were never paired with column subjects.

The heterogeneous and homogeneous assemblies constituted treatments; response measures were thus available for both row and column subjects in each assembly. Each pair of subjects was placed in a playroom where toys were available. The subjects could be observed through a one-way-vision mirror. Two observers recorded the responses of the subjects, one observer for each subject. The following three response measures were recorded:

> *Vocalization:* All verbalization excluding shrieking, screaming, crying, laughing, and other reflexive noises.
>
> *Gesture:* Commonly learned gestures clearly observed by the other child. Included only:
>> Beckoning with finger or hand
>> Shrugging
>> Pointing
>> Nodding yes or no
>> Waving
>
> *Physical Contact:* Includes actual grasping of part of other child with hand, touching, hitting, pushing, chasing, offering of toys toward other child, throwing ball or object toward other child. Mutual hugging of an object. This *excluded* rocking (Rosenberg, Spradlin, and Mabel, 1961, p. 404).

Each dyad participated in thirteen sessions. The first eight sessions occurred within an interval of two to four days, and the last five sessions within an interval of about a week. The findings are presented in Figure 5.12. For both vocal and gestural responses homogeneous dyads, H–H and L–L, averaged a greater number of responses per session than heterogeneous dyads, H–L and L–H. Interestingly enough, on vocal and gestural responses subjects in the L–L dyads seemed to perform as well as subjects in the H–H dyads. The results for contact responses are shown and are apparent. The findings of this study clearly show that the verbal skills of mentally retarded subjects influence their interpersonal language behavior.

The implications of this study for articulatory correction are evident, although we realize that the vocalizations of mental retardates are "qualitatively" different from the verbal responses of normal children. Pre-

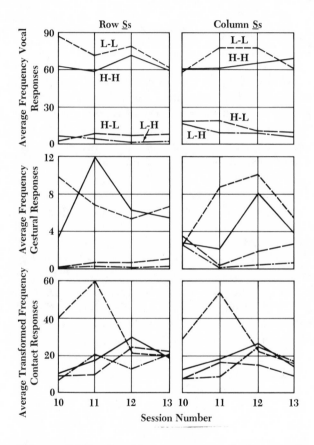

[Figure 5.12] Graphic summary of the results showing each of the three response classes for row and column subjects. The symbols, e.g., H–L, refer to response data of a "high" speaker assembled with a "low" listener; other symbols are similarly interpreted.

SOURCE: Rosenberg and others, 1961, Figure 2, p. 407.

sumably assemblies can be formed that will facilitate verbal exchange and increase the reinforcement value of the training sessions.

In articulation correction the clinician is also a part of this assembly, and presumably some clinicians may be more effective in some types of assemblies than are other clinicians. The behavioral properties of the clinician, such as sex, age, and so forth, also need to be examined and studied. In some public school settings, however, present restrictions on personnel and on classroom schedules may not permit implementation of findings obtained from assembly studies.

Parent-Child Interaction

Because family-child interaction is presumed to play an important role in the onset of the "stuttering," the family background of dysfluent children has received extensive study (Johnson and others, 1942, 1959; Darley, 1955). For this reason clinicians are trained to elicit detailed information about the onset of stuttering from the parents of stuttering children. They question parents about the first occasion of the dysfluency; whether it occurred in some situations and not in others; what they did about it, etc. In general, it has been my experience that clinicians generally do not seek answers to questions of this nature from parents of articulatory defective children. However, questions directed toward the onset of the articulatory errors asked in a parallel fashion to that of the onset of dysfluencies may reveal some of the initiating or aggravating conditions of the disorder. We might ask questions like: Who first discovered that the child had an articulatory problem? What made you aware of the child's problem? What did you do about it? How old was the child? What sounds were defective? Did you eventually seek help? Did your husband (wife) think the child also had an articulatory problem?

Interpersonal variables might also be uncovered by systematic study of children assembled with parents or other adults under highly controlled conditions. Siegel (1963) and Siegel and Harkins (1963), in a series of studies, have investigated the verbal behavior of adults assembled with mentally retarded children. They studied the adults' verbal behavior as a function of the linguistic level of the children and as a function of the interpersonal task. Adaptations of their methods may prove to be useful in articulatory research.

Jensen (1962) studied the verbal behavior of mothers assembled with speech-defective children and normal-speaking children. Parents were instructed to elicit samples of their child's speech from pictures. The study was primarily devoted to the critical task of defining and recording verbal responses and assessing the reliability of these processes. However, Jensen reports that this technique may be used for observing interpersonal communicative behavior. He demonstrated his newly developed techniques for a "normal-speaking mother-child pair" and an "articulatory defective mother-child pair." In contrast to the "normal-speaking pair" it was observed that the child of the "articulatory defective pair" used relatively more of the total speaking time, initiated verbalizations, and responded to verbalizations relatively more.

It is quite possible that mothers of articulatory defective children are more permissive with regard to speech utterances than mothers of normal-speaking children. That is, parents who encourage and reinforce verbal behavior on the part of their child may be disposed to accept (reinforce) articulatory errors when they occur. As indicated in Chapter 3, the articulatory scores of children in lower socioeconomic groups are generally lower than the articulatory scores of children in higher socioeconomic groups. The gap, as indicated, widens between four and seven years of age. This age interval, then, may be the period during which articulatory errors are reinforced, if a parent is so inclined.

Often experienced clinicians will spend a great deal of time obtaining the usual case history information and will spend only a limited amount of time observing the child-parent interaction. In the public schools, of course, the clinician rarely sees the parent. Three situations mentioned by Siegel (1963) and Siegel and Harkins (1963) that may elicit different kinds of information are structured, unstructured, and educational situations. In structured situations the parent might ask the child to give detailed instructions about a task, or the child might direct the parent's behavior in some activity. In unstructured situations the parent might tell the child to tell a story, or the child and the parent might participate in a game. In educational situations the parent would be instructed by a speech correctionist as to the procedures for teaching a sound and would then teach his child the sound.

From such assembly situations the clinician would particularly notice (a) inappropriate and appropriate correction of the error, (b) parental behavior that encourages verbalization and a positive communicative attitude, and (c) the ability of the parent to administer the home speech correction lesson. The assemblies might occur as frequently as the articulation lessons. They would not have to last more than 15 minutes. In these situations the child, and in some cases the parent, should not be aware of the fact that they are being observed. From these sessions the clinician may obtain important information about handling the interaction of the child and parent as the child continues his speech correction lessons.

That counseling and educating parents about articulatory errors and parent-child relationships are an important part of the articulatory instructional program seems to be supported by four studies (Wood, 1946; Sommers and others, 1959; Sommers, 1962; and Sommers and others, 1964). Wood (1946) selected 50 children from a group of public school children who were screened for articulatory defects. The children ranged in age from 5 to 15 years. Each child was assigned to one of two groups (N = 25 in each group), "Child Therapy Group" and "Maternal Therapy Group." Children in each group were matched on the basis of the mother's score on the "Neurotic Tendency Scale" of the Bernreuter Personality Inventory. Children in both groups were given speech instruction for an average of one and a half hours per week for ten months. The parents of the Maternal Therapy Group received additionally a program of parental counseling. This counseling program included (a) discussion of the results of several personality tests, (b) discussion of undesirable tendencies and maladjustments, (c) discussion of each mother's written report of a running account of a complete day at home for each week, (d) suggestions for handling problems in the home, and (e) assignment of two books to be read by each parent; one book was on mental hygiene and the other was on the emotional development of the child.

Wood (1946, p. 270) reports: "None of the clinicians working with the children knew to which group their cases belonged." The articulatory test consisted of an index developed by Wood. It was based on the frequency with which 25 test phonemes occur in English using a count provided by Travis (1931, p. 223). Gain scores on this index showed a significant difference favoring the children of the Maternal Therapy Group.

A similar study was conducted by Sommers and others (1959). Two groups of children who averaged about seven years of age and who had functional articulatory errors were selected. The parents of the experimental group were given information about articulatory errors at the time their children were receiving speech correction. The parents were involved in a 30-minute lecture and discussion period about speech development and disorders and, in addition, observed speech instruction given by trained personnel. Verbal interactions that occurred in the home were discussed. Finally, the parents were given specific instructions about speech assignments that they were to administer in their homes. The control group parents received essentially no instruction about speech disorders, did not observe speech instruction, and were given no advice about home assignments. Children and experimental parents met four days a week for three and a half weeks. Articulation instruction was given to the children in both groups for one hour on one or several of 10 test sounds that were found to be defective. The children were given articulatory correction in groups numbering approximately five to six children to a group. The experimental and control children were enrolled in separate clinics, 20 miles apart. Three weekly meetings of the six clinicians, three at each center, were held to increase homogeneity of teaching procedures. The experimental group in general made greater improvement; however, in most cases the differences between groups were small and nonsignificant.

In a second study Sommers (1962) followed similar procedures. However, in this study three factors were varied, training of the mother, intelligence of the child, and group versus individual articulation instruction. There were eight groups and ten subjects in each group. In four groups the mothers were trained and in four groups the mothers were untrained. In each of the two subgroups (trained and untrained mothers) the type of instruction, group and individual, was paired separately for children of normal intelligence and for children with below normal intelligence. For purposes of clarity the eight experimental groups are listed in Table 5.1.

[Table 5.1] Description of Groups Used
by Sommers (1962)

Experimental Group	Type of Group
A	Normal IQ, individual therapy, mothers trained
B	Normal IQ, individual therapy, mothers not trained
C	Normal IQ, group therapy, mothers trained
D	Normal IQ, group therapy, mothers not trained
E	Slow learning, individual therapy, mothers trained
F	Slow learning, individual therapy, mothers not trained
G	Slow learning, group therapy, mothers trained
H	Slow learning, group therapy, mothers not trained

The group sessions lasted 50 minutes and averaged 4.2 children in each group. The individual sessions lasted 30 minutes. The IQ's of the children with below normal intelligence ranged from 70 to 90, and the IQ's of the children with normal intelligence ranged from 90 to 115. Eleven sounds were selected for instruction. The training of the mothers and children was conducted each weekday for four weeks.

The results indicated that with one exception the children of trained mothers showed greater articulatory improvement than those of the untrained mothers. This exception was for the pair of groups that was below average in intelligence and who received group therapy. In all cases children of normal intelligence made more gains than children of below normal intelligence. Finally, individual instruction seemed to be more effective than group instruction with the exception of the untrained mothers for the children of below normal intelligence.[11]

As discussed in Chapter 3, a substantial relation between IQ and articulatory improvement has not been shown to exist. In the foregoing study, however, the IQ of the children seemed to be significantly related to their articulatory improvement. It is possible, however, that the relation found in this study was a function of the parent's intelligence, which as we know is related to the child's intelligence. Presumably the intelligent parent is more able to carry out the instructions of a counselor than is the less intelligent parent. This matter, of course, could be settled with additional groups of children where the child's IQ is kept constant and the mother's IQ is varied, and the mother's IQ is kept constant and the child's IQ is varied.

In a third study Sommers and others (1964) compared mothers with varying attitudes and backgrounds of training. The children of these mothers were attending an intensive speech correction program. The authors mention that it was a terminal speech program, which presumably means that some children had received speech training prior to this study.

Four groups of mothers were selected: not trained and unhealthy attitude, not trained and healthy attitude, trained and unhealthy attitude, and trained and healthy attitude. In order to determine maternal attitudes the mothers were given the Parental Attitude Research Instrument. This test, as indicated elsewhere, is a paper and pencil inventory of parental attitudes. The children of 40 mothers who scored in the top 35 percent (unhealthy) and the children of 40 mothers who scored in the bottom 35 percent (healthy) were retained as subjects. The mothers in each of these two groups attended the speech center while their children received speech correction lessons. Half of the mothers designated as having healthy attitudes and half of the mothers designated as having unhealthy attitudes attended classes for about 50 minutes. These classes consisted of lectures and discussions on the correction of consonants and observation of speech correction classes.

All 80 of the children in the study received speech correction for 50 minutes, four days a week for four weeks. The children were assembled in groups of about five children. All children were tested (Stage I) prior to training, tested after the four weeks of training (Stage II), and tested again twelve weeks later prior to the beginning of the next school term (Stage III). An articulation test consisting of 200 items was used. Care

---

[11] Further analysis of this variable was made by Martin A. Young. The results indicated that the group versus individual means were not significantly different for the other three pairs of groups.

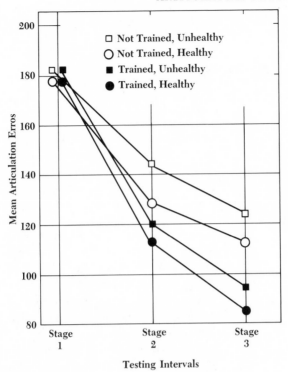

[**Figure 5.13**] Mean articulation error scores for children belonging to one of four maternal groups at three stages of testing: (1) before the children received articulation training; (2) four weeks later when articulation training was completed; and (3) twelve weeks later.

SOURCE: Sommers and others, 1964.

was taken in both the administration of the tests and the speech instruction to insure anonymity of the children for the testers and the clinicians.

The results of this study are shown in Figure 5.13. Note in this graph that the two variables, maternal attitude and training, played a significant role in reducing the articulatory errors of the children from Stage I to Stage II. The relationship seems to be systematic in that the children of "unhealthy, untrained" mothers showed the least improvement while the children of "healthy, trained" mothers showed the greatest improvement. The other two groups, "untrained, healthy," and "trained, unhealthy," as may be observed from Figure 5.13, occupied positions intermediate to the above two groups.

The foregoing group of studies demonstrates rather conclusively that parental counseling, broadly defined, is an important ingredient of articulatory teaching. These studies and those in the preceding section encourage continuation of this kind of research and, in addition, provide information that is useful at this time.

SUMMARY

Several principles of articulation programming were presented in this chapter. The principles were derived from the concepts and procedures of modern learning theory. They include discrimination, successive approximation, generalization, interference, motivation, extinction, delay of reinforcement, latency of response, and retention. A teaching machine, designed to facilitate sound discrimination and sound learning, was presented. The research findings of several investigations on articulation programming were also reviewed. Finally, testing procedures for selecting an articulation program were discussed preliminarily.

The last part of this chapter was concerned with variables other than those involved in the mechanics of teaching sounds. Here the topics discussed were child-child interaction and parent-child interaction.

REFERENCES

Brackbill, Y. The impairment of learning under immediate reinforcement. *Journal of Experimental Child Psychology*, 1964, *1*, 199–207.

Bugelski, B. R., and Scharlock, D. P. An experimental demonstration of unconscious mediated association. *Journal of Experimental Psychology*, 1952, *44*, 334–338.

Darley, F. L. The relationship of parental attitudes and adjustment to the development of stuttering. Chapter 4 in W. Johnson (Ed.), *Stuttering in children and adults.* Minneapolis: University of Minnesota Press, 1955.

Deterline, W. A. *An introduction to programmed instruction.* Englewood Cliffs, N.J.: Prentice-Hall, 1962.

Elbert, M., Shelton, R. L., and Arndt, W. B. A task for evaluation of articulation change: 1. Development of methodology. *Journal of Speech and Hearing Research*, 1967, *10*, 281–288.

Etzel, B. C., and Wright, E. S. Effects of delayed rein-

forcement on response latency and acquisition learning under simultaneous and successive discrimination
learning on the child. *Journal of Experimental Child
Psychology*, 1964, *1*, 281–293.

Gewirtz, J. L., and Baer, D. M. Deprivation and satiation of social reinforcers as drive conditions. *Journal
of Abnormal and Social Psychology*, 1958, 57, 165–
172.

Grant, D. A., Hake, H. W., and Hornseth, J. P. Acquisition and extinction of a verbal conditioned response
with differing percentages of reinforcement. *Journal
of Experimental Psychology*, 1951, 42, 1–5.

Haas, W. Phonological analysis of a case of dyslalia.
Journal of Speech and Hearing Disorders, 1963, 28,
239–246.

Holland, A. L., and Matthews, J. Application of teaching
machine concepts to speech pathology and audiology.
Asha, 1963, 5, 474–482.

Holland, J. G. Teaching machines: An application of
principles from the laboratory. *Journal of Experimental Analysis Behavior*, 1960, 3, 275–287.

Humphrey, W. R., and Milisen, R. A study of the
ability to reproduce unfamiliar sounds which have
been presented orally. *Journal of Speech and Hearing
Disorders*, 1954, (Monogr. Suppl. 4), 57–69.

Jakobson, R., Fant, C. G. M., and Halle, M. *Prelimi-
naries to speech analysis*. Cambridge: Acoustical
Laboratory, Massachusetts Institute of Technology,
Technical Report Number 13, 1952.

Jensen, G. D., and Cotton, J. W. Successive acquisitions
and extinctions as related to differing percentages of
reinforcement. *Journal of Experimental Psychology*,
1960, 60, 41–49.

Jensen, P. J. Mother-child intercommunicative behavior:
A methodological study. Ph.D. Dissertation, University of Iowa, 1962.

Johnson, W., et al. A study of the onset and early
development of stuttering. *Journal of Speech Disorders*, 1942, 7, 251–257.

Johnson, W., et al. *The onset of stuttering*. Minneapolis:
University of Minnesota Press, 1959.

Kimble, G. A. *Hilgard and Marquis' conditioning and
learning* (2nd ed.). New York: Appleton-Century-
Crofts, 1961.

Lane, H. L., and Moore, D. J. Reconditioning a consonant discrimination in an aphasic: An experimental
case history. *Journal of Speech and Hearing Disorders*, 1962, 27, 232–243.

McGeoch, J. A., and Irion, A. L. *The psychology of
human learning* (2nd ed.). New York: Longmans,
1952.

Postman, L. The present status of interference theory.

Chapter 7. In C. N. Cofer (Ed.), *Verbal learning and verbal behavior*. New York: McGraw-Hill, 1961.

Postman, L. Does interference theory predict too much forgetting? *Journal of Verbal Learning and Verbal Behavior*, 1963, *2*, 40–48.

Postman, L. Acquisition and retention of consistent associative responses. *Journal of Experimental Psychology*, 1964, *67*, 183–190.

Rice, D. B., and Milisen, R. The influence of increased stimulation upon the production of unfamiliar sounds as a function of time. *Journal of Speech and Hearing Disorders*, 1954, (Monogr. Suppl. 4), 79–86.

Romans, E. F., and Milisen, R. Effect of latency between stimulation and response on reproduction of sounds. *Journal of Speech and Hearing Disorders*, 1954, (Monogr. Suppl. 4), 71–78.

Rosenberg, S., Spradlin, J., and Mabel, S. Interaction among retarded children as a function of their relative language skills. *Journal of Abnormal and Social Psychology*, 1961, *63*, 402–410.

Russell, W. A., and Storms, L. H. Implicit verbal chaining in paired associate learning. *Journal of Experimental Psychology*, 1955, *49*, 287–293.

Scott, D. A., and Milisen, R. The effect of visual, auditory and combined visual-auditory stimulation upon the speech responses of defective speaking children. *Journal of Speech and Hearing Disorders*, 1954, (Monogr. Suppl. 4), 37–43. (a)

Scott, D. A., and Milisen, R. The effectiveness of combined visual-auditory stimulation in improving articulation. *Journal of Speech and Hearing Disorders*, 1954, (Monogr. Suppl. 4), 51–56. (b)

Shelton, R. L., Elbert, M., and Arndt, W. B. A task for evaluation of articulation change: II. Comparison of task scores during baseline and lesson series testing. *Journal of Speech and Hearing Research*, 1967, *10*, 578–585.

Siegel, G. M., Adult verbal behavior in "play therapy" sessions with retarded children. *Journal of Speech and Hearing Disorders*, 1963, (Monogr. Suppl. 10), 34–38.

Siegel, G. M., and Harkins, J. P. Verbal behavior of adults in two conditions with institutionalized retarded children. *Journal of Speech and Hearing Disorders*, 1963, (Monogr. Suppl. 10), 39–46.

Skinner, B. F. *Cumulative record*. New York: Appleton-Century-Crofts, 1959.

Sommers, R. K. Factors in the effectiveness of mothers trained to aid in speech correction. *Journal of Speech and Hearing Disorders*, 1962, *27*, 178–186.

Sommers, R. K., Furlong, A. K., Rhodes, F. E., Fichter, G. R., Bowser, D. C., Copetas, F. G., and Saunders, Z. G. Effects of maternal attitudes upon improvement in articulation when mothers are trained to assist in speech correction. *Journal of Speech and Hearing Disorders*, 1964, *29*, 126–132.

Sommers, R. K., Shilling, S. P., Paul, C. D., Copetas, F. G., Bowser, D. C., and McClintock, C. J. Training parents of children with functional misarticulation. *Journal of Speech and Hearing Research*, 1959, *2*, 258–265.

Spence, K. W. *Behavior theory and conditioning*. New Haven: Yale University Press, 1956.

Spence, K. W. *Behavior theory and learning, selected papers*. Englewood Cliffs, N.J.: Prentice-Hall, 1960.

Spiker, C. C. Performance on a difficult discrimination following pretraining with distinctive stimuli. *Child Development*, 1959, *30*, 513–521.

Spradlin, J. E. Assessment of speech and language of retarded children: The Parsons language sample. *Journal of Speech and Hearing Disorders*, 1963, (Monogr. Suppl. 10), 8–31.

Templin, M. C. A study of sound discrimination ability in elementary school pupils. *Journal of Speech and Hearing Disorders*, 1943, *8*, 127–132.

Travis, L. E. *Speech pathology*. New York: Appleton-Century-Crofts, 1931.

Underwood, B. J. Interference and forgetting. *Psychological Review*, 1957, *64*, 49–60.

Underwood, B. J., and Postman, L. Extra-experimental sources of interference in forgetting. *Psychological Review*, 1960, *67*, 73–95.

Underwood, B. J. Ten years of massed practice on distributed practice. *Psychological Review*, 1961, *68*, 229–247.

Webb, C. E., and Siegenthaler, B. M. Comparison of aural stimulation methods for teaching speech sounds. *Journal of Speech and Hearing Disorders*, 1957, *22*, 264–270.

Wickens, D. D. Studies of response generalization in conditioning. I: Stimulus generalization during response generalization. *Journal of Experimental Psychology*, 1943, *33*, 221–227.

Wickens, D. D. Stimulus identity as related to response specificity and response generalization. *Journal of Experimental Psychology*, 1948, *38*, 389–394.

Winitz, H., and Bellerose, B. Sound discrimination as a function of pretraining conditions. *Journal of Speech and Hearing Research*, 1962, *5*, 340–348.

Winitz, H., and Bellerose, B. Effects of pretraining on sound discrimination learning. *Journal of Speech and Hearing Research*, 1963, *6*, 171–180.

Winitz, H., and Bellerose, B. Phoneme cluster learning as a function of instructional method and age. *Journal of Verbal Learning and Verbal Behavior*, 1965, *4*, 98–102.

Winitz, H., and Lawrence, M. Children's articulation and sound learning ability. *Journal of Speech and Hearing Research*, 1961, *4*, 259–268.

Winitz, H., and Preisler, L. Discrimination pretraining and sound learning. *Perceptual and Motor Skills*, 1965, *20*, 905–916.

Winitz, H., and Preisler, L. Effect of distinctive feature pretraining in phoneme discrimination learning. *Journal of Speech and Hearing Research*, 1967, *10*, 515–530.

Wood, K. S. Parental maladjustment and functional articulatory defects in children. *Journal of Speech Disorders*, 1946, *11*, 255–275.

Author Index

Subject Index

Academic evaluations, 215–216
Acquired equivalence and distinctiveness of cues, 189–191
Acquisition interference, 292–295
Age, chronological, 141
Allomorph, 71
Anterior teeth. See Dentition.
Articulation tests. See Tests of articulation.
Auditory flutter fusion, 199
Auditory memory span, 178–180

Babbling, definition, 6
Bead pattern, 179–181
Bladder control, 175
Bottle feeding and weaning, 176, 177
Breath groups, 7–8

Carter-Buck Test, 256, 257–259
Child-child interaction, 319–322
Childhood illnesses and problems, 176, 177
Complementary distribution. See Phoneme.
Conditioning. See Learning.
Crawling, 175, 177

Delay of reinforcement. See Reinforcement.
Dentition:
    anterior teeth, 174
    and articulation, 162–169
    eruption of first tooth, 175
    following eruption of permanent teeth, 164, 168
    loss of deciduous teeth, 164, 168
    malocclusion, 162–169, 173–174
    open bite, 162–163, 168, 176–177
    spaces, 166–167, 168
Development, physical, 175–178
Diadochokinesis. See Oral and facial motor skills.
Differentiation, 309

Discrimination, 97–102
    apparatus, 192
    Estes model, 100–102
    as a function of speech sound learning, 185–198
    pitch, intensity, and rhythm, 198–200
    simultaneous, 101
    speech sound, 181–185, 255, 276–285
    Spence model, 98–100
    successive, 101
Distinctive features:
    definition of, 79
    differences between, 85
    Jakobson, Fant and Halle's system, 80–84
    limitations of, 86–87
    Miller and Nicely's system, 85–86
    universal ordering, 61–62

Errors:
    and educational achievement, 207–216
    frequency for German and American children, 126–128
    and inconsistency, 77–78
    Lewis' substitution rule, 125–126
    omissions, 118
    and organicity, 217–218
    and phonetic features, 126
    phonetic or phonemic problem, 126–132
    and prediction, 259–261
    substitutions for German, Danish, and American children, 128
Extinction, 30, 297, 307

Fluency, 207
Fractional anticipatory goal response. See Learning.
Free variation. See Phoneme.